English in Action
Teacher's Guide

Second Edition

Barbara H. Foley

Elizabeth R. Neblett

Amy Lawler

HEINLE
CENGAGE Learning

Australia • Brazil • Japan • Korea • Mexico • Singapore • Spain • United Kingdom • United States

HEINLE
CENGAGE Learning

English in Action 4, Teacher's Guide, Second Edition
Barbara H. Foley, Elizabeth R. Neblett, and Amy Lawler

Publisher: Sherrise Roehr

Acquisitions Editor: Tom Jefferies

Managing Development Editor: Jill Korey O'Sullivan

Associate Development Editors: Marissa Petrarca, Lauren Stephenson

Director of Content and Media Production: Michael Burggren

Director of Marketing, U.S.: Jim McDonough

Sr. Product Marketing Manager: Katie Kelley

Sr. Content Project Manager: Maryellen E. Killeen

Sr. Print Buyer: Susan Spencer

Cover/Text Designer: Muse Group, Inc.

Compositor: PreMediaGlobal

ISBN-13: 978-1-4240-8500-2

ISBN-10: 1-4240-8500-4

Heinle
20 Channel Center Street
Boston, MA 02210
USA

Cengage Learning is a leading provider of customized learning solutions with office locations around the globe, including Singapore, the United Kingdom, Australia, Mexico, Brazil, and Japan. Locate your local office at **www.cengage.com/global**

Cengage Learning products are represented in Canada by Nelson Education, Ltd.

Visit Heinle online at **elt.heinle.com**

Visit our corporate website at **www.cengage.com**

Printed in the United States of America
1 2 3 4 5   17 16 15 14 13

Acknowledgments

The authors and publisher would like to thank the following reviewers and consultants:

Karin Abell
Durham Technical Community College, Durham, NC

Sandra Anderson
El Monte-Rosemead Adult School, El Monte, CA

Sandra Andreessen
Merced Adult School, Merced, CA

Julie Barrett
Madison Area Technical College, Madison, WI

Bea Berretini
Fresno Adult School, Fresno, CA

Mark Brik
College of Mount Saint Vincent, The Institute for Immigrant Concerns, New York, NY

Debra Brooks
BEGIN Managed Programs, Brooklyn, NY

Rocio Castiblanco
Seminole Community College / Orange County Public Schools, Sanford, FL

Sandy Cropper
Fresno Adult School, Fresno, CA

Carol Culver
Central New Mexico Community College, Albuquerque, NM

Shanta David
Union County College – IIE, Elizabeth, NJ

Luciana Diniz
Portland Community College, Portland, OR

Gail Ellsworth
Milwaukee Area Technical College, Oak Creek, WI

Sally Gearhart
Santa Rosa Junior College, Santa Rosa, CA

Jeane Hetland
Merced Adult School, Merced, CA

Laura Horani
Portland Community College, Portland, OR

Bill Hrycyna
Franklin Community Adult School, Los Angeles, CA

Callie Hutchinson
Sunrise Tech Center, Citrus Heights, CA

Mary Jenison
Merced Adult School, Merced, CA

Mark Labinski
Fox Valley Technical College, Appleton, WI

Rhonda Labor
Northside Learning Center, San Antonio, TX

Lisa Lor
Merced Adult School, Merced, CA

Eileen McKee
Westchester Community College, Valhalla, NY

Lynn Meng
Union County College – IIE, Elizabeth, NJ

Jennifer Newman-Cornell
College of Southern Nevada, Las Vegas, NV

Sonja Pantry
Robert Morgan Educational Center, Miami, FL

Eric Rosenbaum
BEGIN Managed Programs, Brooklyn, NY

Jodi Ruback
College of Southern Nevada, Las Vegas, NV

Linda Salem
Northside Learning Center, San Antonio, TX

Evelyn Trottier
Seattle Central Community College, Lynnwood, WA

Maliheh Vafai
Overfelt Adult Center, San Jose, CA

Nancy Williams
Bakersfield Adult School, Bakersfield, CA

Contents

Contents • **v**

Contents

Contents

To the Teacher

In our many years of teaching, we have found that most textbooks progress too quickly. There is a presentation of a new structure and a few exercises to practice it, and then another grammar point is introduced. We discovered that our students needed more time with the grammar—time to practice it, see it in context, use it to talk about a theme, and apply it to themselves. We could not find a series that provided sufficient practice and recycling, so we decided to write our own series—and *English in Action* was born.

English in Action is a four-level core language series for English language learners. Each level provides extensive practice and review with basic structures, as it gradually adds more advanced structures to challenge students. It teaches language through thematic units that are clear, engaging, and interactive.

English in Action, 2nd edition is a comprehensive revision and expansion of the first edition. Content has been added, deleted, and changed based on our experiences teaching with the text and feedback from our students and colleagues. In addition, one of the major goals of the revision was to provide a more explicit focus on language competencies.

Book 4 is designed for students who are familiar with the basic tenses and can apply them in everyday situations. Now they are ready for more difficult structures such as the present perfect tense. The text presents structures in more challenging contexts and encourages students to expand their use of English while discussing topics such as education, driving, travel, job performance, and citizenship. By the end of Book 4, students will feel comfortable talking, reading, and writing about their lives and the world around them.

Each unit will take between five and seven hours of classroom time. In classes with less time, the teacher may need to choose the exercises that are most appropriate for the students. Some of the activities can be assigned for homework. For example, after previewing Writing Our Stories, students can write their own stories at home instead of in class.

Features

- **Unit Opener:** Each unit opens with an illustration or photo and discussion questions to introduce the topic and draw the students into the unit.

- **Active Grammar:** The first half of the unit integrates the context and the new grammar. Users of the first edition will notice that there is enhanced grammar support, with full-color grammar charts and sample sentences. There are many whole-class, teacher-directed activities.

- **Pronunciation:** The pronunciation points, such as verb endings, contractions, question intonation, and syllable stress, complement the grammar or vocabulary of the lesson.

- **The Big Picture:** This is our favorite section. It integrates listening, vocabulary, and structure. A large, engaging picture shows a familiar setting, such as a restaurant, a doctor's office, or an office supply store. Students listen to a short story or conversation and then answer questions, fill in information, review structures, or write conversations.

- **Reading:** A short reading expands the context of the lesson. We did not manipulate reading selections so that every sentence fits into the grammatical structures presented in the unit. The readings include new vocabulary and structures. Teachers can help students learn that understanding the main idea is their primary goal. If students can find the information they need, it isn't necessary to understand every word.

- **Writing Our Stories:** In the writing section, students first read a paragraph written by an English language learner or teacher. Students then brainstorm and organize their ideas using graphic organizers. Next, students write about their experiences, ideas, or their research on a topic.

New to this Edition

The new features in the second edition include:

- The expanded and improved grammar feature presents easy-to-read charts and grammar notes throughout the units. In addition, grammar charts in the appendix provide a valuable student reference of all the grammar points covered in the book. A new exercise, Teacher Dictations, is located in the Active Grammar section.
- **Word Partnerships Boxes** This feature presents high-frequency word collocations that relate to the theme of the unit.
- **Working Together** These partner and group activities are spread throughout the units. They encourage students to work together in active ways. There are pictures to discuss, interview activities, conversations to develop, and discussion questions. Several units also include a **Student to Student** activity in which each student in a pair looks at a different page containing a different set of information. Students exchange information in order to answer questions about a picture, or to complete maps, charts, or menus with missing information.
- **Sharing Our Stories** These activities encourage students to read and talk about each other's writing.
- **Reading and Writing Notes** The notes give students additional support in developing reading and writing skills in English.
- **English in Action** This two-page section provides practice in the everyday skills students need to interact as community members, citizens, students, and workers. Activities such as role plays, presentations, and problem-solving exercises help students become more comfortable in real-life situations.

The second edition includes three new or adapted units. Unit 3 is now Changing Lifestyles. Unit 6, Travel, is a new unit that focuses on modals. Unit 13, Music, formerly Country Music, has been expanded to include more current musicians. All readings have been updated or replaced with a more current topic.

Ancillary Components

- **Student Book Audio CDs:** These include all of the audio in the Student Book: dialogs, descriptions, pronunciation exercises, and The Big Picture.
- **Workbook** and **Workbook Audio CD:** These components include vocabulary, grammar, reading, and writing activities related to key topics in the Student Book. Each unit also includes listening activities related to the audio on the Workbook Audio CD. The new edition of the Workbook includes new material to reflect content changes made to the new edition of *English in Action 4*.
- **Teachers Guide:** The guide includes Student Book pages with embedded answer keys, audio scripts, and a grammar summary designed to give teachers more information about the grammatical structures and points taught in each Student Book unit. It includes new material to reflect content changes made to the new edition of *English in Action 4*. Each unit includes two new features, **More Action!** and **Teaching Tips.** These activities provide teachers with supplemental activities, explanations of difficult concepts, and a variety of classroom management topics.
- **Interactive CD-ROM:** This gives students the opportunity for practice and self-study at their own convenience. It provides interactive practice activities of the grammar, vocabulary, listening, and speaking skills taught in the Student Book.
- **Presentation Tool:** These pre-loaded interactive worksheets for every unit can be used on any IWB or data-projector. It also includes an asset bank with all Student Book 4 art files, grammar charts, audio files, and audio scripts.
- **Assessment CD-ROM with Exam*View*®: A bank of test items** allows teachers to create and customize tests and quizzes quickly and easily.
- **Website:** Teachers can access an *English in Action* website that provides additional practice activities, games, and the answer key to the Workbook.

The complete *English in Action* package includes everything necessary to facilitate learning. Visit **elt.heinle.com** to learn more about available resources.

Fun, engaging, and action-packed!

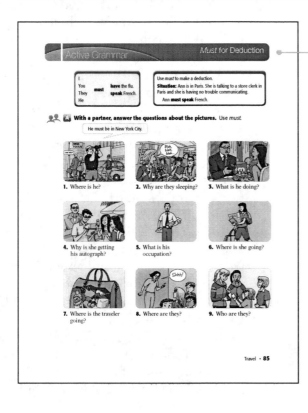

"**Active Grammar**" sections present clear, contextualized grammar explanations along with a rich variety of practice activities.

UPDATED FOR THIS EDITION!

"**Working Together**" activities build learner persistence through cooperative tasks, enhancing the classroom community.

"**Working Together**" activities build workplace skills with teamwork tasks such as labeling and presenting.

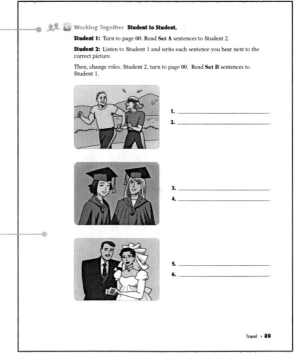

Fun, engaging, and action-packed!

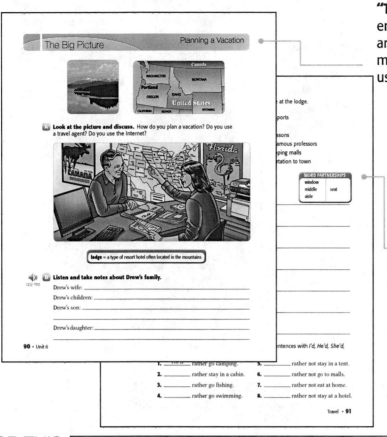

"The Big Picture" sections include engaging integrated skills practice around a story or conversation, motivating students to listen and use new grammar and vocabulary.

NEW TO THIS EDITION!
"Word Partnerships" provide students with common collocations to promote fluency.

UPDATED FOR THIS EDITION!

"Reading" sections provide before-you-read discussion questions, encouraging students to think about the reading topic.

"Word Builder" activities provide additional vocabulary practice, encouraging students to develop a deeper understanding of the target words.

Interesting readings based on the unit theme recycle the vocabulary and grammar presented earlier in the unit.

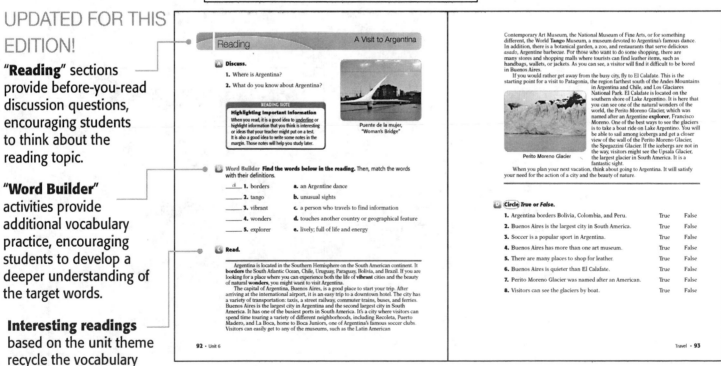

Fun, engaging, and action-packed!

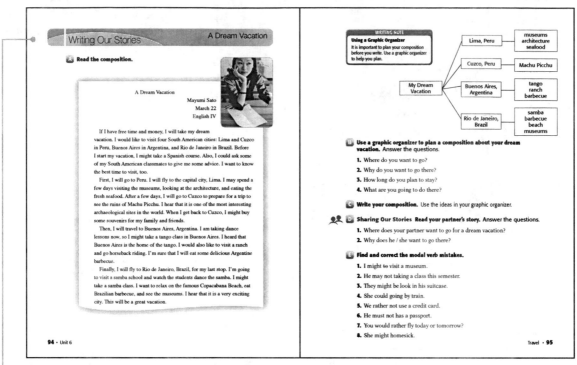

"Writing Our Stories" sections expand students' literacy by giving a closer look at real people in real communities and provide students with guided practice activities.

NEW TO THIS EDITION!

"English in Action" sections practice the everyday skills students need to interact and solve problems in the real world.

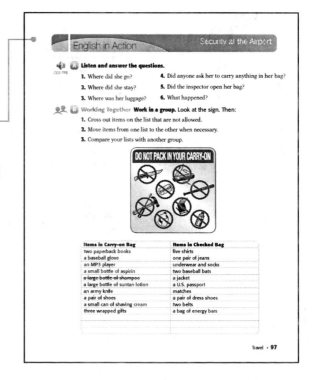

About the Authors

Liz and I work at Union County College in Elizabeth, New Jersey. We teach at the Institute for Intensive English, a large English as a Second Language program. Students from over 80 different countries study in our classes. Between us, Liz and I have been teaching at the college for over 40 years! When Liz isn't writing, she spends her time traveling, taking pictures, and worrying about her favorite baseball team, the New York Mets. I love the outdoors. I can't start my day without a 15- or 20-mile bicycle ride. My idea of a good time always involves being active: hiking, swimming, or simply working in my garden. I also enjoy watching my favorite baseball team, the New York Yankees.

Barbara H. Foley
Elizabeth R. Neblett

Unit

1  Education

 A **Discuss. Look at the pictures and answer the questions.**

• Point to the four photographs and ask students to describe what each room looks like and what activities are taking place. Then, help students identify the country where each photo might have been taken. For example:

T: *What are the students wearing in Picture 1?*
S1: *They are wearing uniforms.*
T: *What are the students doing?*
S2: *They are reading their textbooks.*
T: *What country do you think this is?*
S3: *Is it China?*
S4: *It could be Japan.*

• Discuss the questions as a class. Ask students to choose the classroom that is the most similar to your classroom. Encourage students to point out the similarities between the photograph and your classroom.

 A **Discuss.** Look at the pictures and answer the questions. (Answers will vary.)

1.    2.

3.    4.

1. Which classroom is most similar to a high school classroom in your native country?

2. Which classroom is similar to your English classroom?

3. Which classroom has the most students?

4. Which classroom has the fewest students?

5. Which classroom looks the most casual?

6. Which classroom looks the most formal?

7. Describe a typical classroom in your native country.

2 • Unit 1

More Action!

Expand the discussion of the photographs on this page by asking students to elaborate on their answers to Question 1. Ask students which specific actions and activities in the photographs are the same in their country. Encourage them to explain their answers in more depth.

A **Working Together** **Work with a small group of students.** Talk about your school and complete the chart. Then talk and write about two more places in your school. *(Answers will vary.)*

> Does our school have a principal's office?

> Yes, it does.

> Where is it?

> It's on the first floor, near the entrance.

Place or Person	Does our school have _____?	Where?
1. A principal's or ESL director's office		
2. A teachers' room		
3. A bookstore		
4. A library		
5. A counselor		
6. A learning center or tutoring center		
7. A computer lab		
8. A cafeteria		
9. Restrooms		
10. A gym		
11. A student center		
12. A study room or a study hall		
13. A student activities office		
14. A copy machine for students		
15.		
16.		

Education • **3**

Learning About Your School

 A **Working Together Work with a small group of students. Talk about your school and complete the chart. Then talk and write about two more places in your school.**

• Point out that some of the places and people in the list may be called different things at your school. For example, for Item 4, in some schools a *library* may be called a *learning center*.
• Then, have students complete the activity with a partner or in small groups.
• Review the responses with the class.

Teaching Tip

Some students might need help thinking of two more places for Items 15 and 16. To help them get started, as a class brainstorm a short list of other places and people that can be found in a school. For example: *nurse's office, health clinic, librarian, custodian (janitor),* and so on.

Active Grammar

A **Circle the correct verb to make true statements about high school in your native country.**

- Review the grammar chart at the top of the page. Ask students to describe the formation of simple present tense sentences. Point out the note box next to the grammar chart.
- Read the directions aloud. Answer any questions students may have. Then, have students complete the activity.

B **Complete the sentences about high school in your native country.**

- Review how affirmative and negative statements are formed. For example:

  T: *Which pronouns are followed by a verb with an -s ending?*
  S1: He *and* she.
  T: *Which pronouns use* do not *or* don't?
  S2: I, we, you, *and* they.

 Working Together

- Put students in groups of three or four. Ask students to discuss the answers as a group, comparing and contrasting high schools in various countries.
- Appoint a discussion leader in each group. The discussion leader should keep the discussion on topic and make sure that each group member gets a chance to participate.
- Circulate in the room and check to ensure that all groups understand the task. Answer any questions students may have.

4 · Unit 1

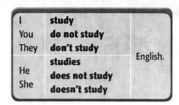

I	study	
You	do not study	
They	don't study	English.
He	studies	
She	does not study	
	doesn't study	

> Use the present tense to describe everyday activities, habits, and repeated actions.

A **Circle the correct verb to make true statements about high school in your native country.** (Answers will vary.)

1. The school year **begins / doesn't begin** in September.
2. The school day **starts / doesn't start** at 8:30 A.M.
3. School **meets / doesn't meet** on Saturdays.
4. High school students **choose / don't choose** some of their own courses.
5. Students **write / don't write** their papers on a computer.
6. Students **study / don't study** with students of the same ability.
7. Most students **work / don't work** after school.
8. Students **wear / don't wear** uniforms.

B **Complete the sentences about high school in your native country.** Use the correct form of the verb. (Answers will vary.)

1. Teachers (move) _____ from classroom to classroom.
2. Students (call) _____ their teachers by their first names.
3. Teachers (wear) _____ jeans in class.
4. Teachers (sit) _____ on their desks during class.
5. There (be) _____ after-school programs for students.
6. Families (pay) _____ for textbooks.
7. The teacher (give) _____ many tests.
8. There (be) _____ homework every night.

C Working Together **Work with a small group of students.** Read the statements in Exercise B about your school. Discuss your answers.

4 · Unit 1

More Action!

- Put students in the same groups that they worked with while completing Exercise C. Have groups review the sentences in Exercise A. Tell groups to rewrite each sentence so that it is true for your school (as opposed to schools in students' native countries).
- As a class, compare and contrast the answers about your school with answers about high schools in your students' native countries.

- On the board, make a chart to show the results. Draw three columns and label them: *Our School, High Schools in Our Native Countries,* and *Both.* Categorize the answers as students provide them.
- If answers about high schools in your students' native countries vary widely, tailor the activity to focus only on the most common answers.

4 · Unit 1

| Do | I you they | work? study in the library? |
| Does | she he | walk to school? |

Yes, you **do**.
Yes, I **do**.
Yes, they **do**.
Yes, she **does**.
Yes, he **does**.

No, you **don't**.
No, I **don't**.
No, they **don't**.
No, she **doesn't**.
No, he **doesn't**.

CD1•TR1

A **Listen to the story about Sophie and Lizzy, two college roommates.** Complete the questions with *Do* or *Does*. Then, answer the questions.

1. _Does_ Sophie take all of her courses in the morning? ___Yes, she does.___
2. _Do_ you take your English class in the morning? (Answers will vary.)
3. _Does_ Sophie keep her side of the room neat? ___Yes, she does.___
4. _Does_ Sophie get up early? ___Yes, she does.___
5. _Do_ you get up early? (Answers will vary.)
6. _Does_ Sophie study in the room? ___Yes, she does.___
7. _Do_ you study in your bedroom? (Answers will vary.)
8. _Do_ Lizzy and Sophie have the same schedule? ___No, they don't.___
9. _Does_ Lizzy keep her side of the room neat? ___No, she doesn't.___
10. _Do_ you keep your home neat? (Answers will vary.)
11. _Does_ Lizzy hand in her papers on time? ___No, she doesn't.___
12. _Do_ you hand in your homework on time? (Answers will vary.)

 B **Are you more like Sophie or Lizzy?** Explain.

More Action!

Invite several students to describe to the class how they are like Sophie or Lizzy. Encourage students to give specific examples from their own lives.
Encourage higher-level students to explain their ideas in more depth to give them more speaking practice.
Lower-level students should be expected to answer, using the target grammar structure. Correct grammar as needed.

Teaching Tip

For pair activities, consider giving lower-level students more exposure to higher language skills by pairing them with higher-level students.
The higher-level students can model the language and help lower-level students with pronunciation and vocabulary.
Make sure students of both abilities are given equal chance to speak when you use this kind of pairing.

Active Grammar: Simple Present Tense– *Yes / No* Questions

 A **Listen to the story about Sophie and Lizzy, two college roommates. Complete the questions with *Do* or *Does*. Then, answer the questions.**
(CD1•TR1)

• Review the *Yes / No* question boxes at the top of the page. Call on a student to ask each question. Call on a second student to give a possible answer. For example:
S1: *Do you work?*
S2: *Yes, I do.*
• Have students listen to the audio. What differences can the students remember?
• Review the twelve questions in Exercise A. Point out the blank at the beginning of each sentence and the short answer blank at the end of each sentence. Have students fill in the helping verbs on their own. Review the completed questions with the class.
• Play the audio again and have students write the appropriate short answer at the end of each sentence. Review the correct answers with the class.

 B **Are you more like Sophie or Lizzy? Explain.**

Put students in pairs to discuss the question. Suggest they refer back to the questions and answers in Exercise A if they need help.

Active Grammar

 A Working Together

• Ask students to use the grammar charts to practice forming present tense *Wh-* questions.

• Have students form groups of three. Each student should ask his or her group members the questions and record their answers in the chart.

• Then, prompt students to write one more question at the bottom of the chart. Ask some students to read their questions to the class. Correct as necessary.

B Pronunciation

(CD1 • TR2)

• Point out that *do* and *you* are linked together and pronounced almost as if they were a single word.

• Then, play the audio and have students repeat each question.

C Answer these questions about students in your class.

Have students read aloud questions one at a time. Choose another student to answer the question. Try to give all students a chance to ask or answer a question.

 D Write three more *Who* questions.

Have students write three questions on their own. Then, have them read one question at a time and choose another student to answer their question.

What		I	
Where	**do**	you	
Why		they	**study**?
How		she	
How often	**does**	he	

	studies	English?
Who	**goes**	to work?
	lives	close to school?

 A Working Together Work with a small group of students. Interview each other about your daily schedules and habits. (Answers will vary.)

Questions	You	Partner 1	Partner 2
1. What time do you get up?			
2. What time do you leave for school?			
3. How do you get to school?			
4. How long does it take?			
5. When do you study?			
6. How often do you study?			
Write one more question to ask your partners.			
7.			

 B Pronunciation: Linking / *do you* / Listen and repeat.

CD1·TR2

1. What do you do?

2. Where do you work?

3. How do you get home?

4. Where do you live?

5. Why do you study here?

6. What do you do on weekends?

C Answer these questions about students in your class.

1. Who always arrives on time?

2. Who wears a baseball cap to class?

3. Who often arrives late?

4. Who goes to work after class?

5. Who usually asks questions in class?

I do.
You do.
They do.

He does.
She does.

 D Write three more *Who* questions. Then, ask a classmate your questions.

6 · Unit 1

More Action!

Have students work with a partner and take turns asking and answering the questions in Exercise B. If time permits, have volunteer pairs do a mock interview by asking and answering the questions for the class. Point out any similarities and differences among the answers.

I	am		
He	is		using a computer.
She		(not)	studying for a test.
We			sitting at a desk.
You	are		
They			

(Answers to Exercise A will vary. Students should use the present continuous in all responses.)

  A **Working Together** **Work with a small group of students.** Write three sentences about each photo. Make one of the sentences negative.

1.

a. *The students are taking an important exam.*

b. _____

c. _____

2.

a. _____

b. _____

c. _____

3.

a. _____

b. _____

c. _____

4.

a. _____

b. _____

c. _____

Education • **7**

Active Grammar: Present Continuous Tense– Statements

  A **Working Together Work with a small group of students. Write three sentences about each photo. Make one of the sentences negative.**

• Review the grammar chart at the top of the page. Ask students to describe the formation of present continuous sentences. For example:

T: *What comes first in a present continuous statement?*

S1: *A pronoun.*

T: *What comes next?*

S1: *The verb* be *in the present tense. You can also have the negative form of* be.

T: *What comes last?*

S1: *The base form of the main verb followed by* -ing.

• Have students read the instructions. Answer any questions they may have.

• Point out the sample answer. Tell groups to work together to write additional sentences for each photograph. Have groups share their sentences with the class.

Active Grammar

A Work with a partner.

- Have students describe the formation of present continuous *Yes / No* questions.
- Review the questions in the exercise. Answer any questions students may have. Then, have them ask and answer the questions in small groups.
- Review the answers with the class.

B Look around your classroom.

- Review the grammar charts by having students make up sentences using the questions from the charts. Call on different students to give a possible answer.
For example:
S1: *What is he studying?*
S2: *He's studying math.*
- Read and discuss the instructions. Then, have students write their answers individually.
- Review the answers with the class. Elicit several true and grammatically correct answers for each question. For example, correct answers to Question 1 might include:
I am. Gina and Carlo are. Kenji is. No one is.

C Dictation

- Dictate the questions as written on page 263. Read each question aloud slowly; then, repeat the question for students. Allow students enough time to record their answers.
- Read each sentence a third and final time so students can check their work.

8 • Unit 1

 Active Grammar

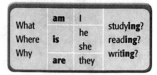 Present Continuous Tense: Questions

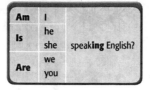

A Work with a partner. Answer the questions about your class.

1. Are the students taking a test?
2. Are they working together?
3. Are they speaking English?
4. Is the teacher helping the students?
5. Is anyone using a dictionary?
6. Are any students writing?
7. Are any students drinking water?
8. Is the teacher writing on the board?

B Look around your classroom. Write your answers to these questions.

1. Who is sitting next to the door? (Answers will vary.)
2. Who is talking to the teacher? (Answers will vary.)
3. Who is speaking another language? (Answers will vary.)
4. What is the teacher doing? (Answers will vary.)
5. Where are you sitting? (Answers will vary.)
6. What are you wearing? (Answers will vary.)

C Dictation Your teacher will dictate the questions on page 263. Listen and write the questions you hear. Then, answer the questions.

1. Are any students eating?
2. Are all the students writing in their notebooks?
3. Does anyone have a pencil sharpener?
4. Do you go to work after class?
5. Who is sitting next to you?
6. How many hours do you study for this class?

8 • Unit 1

Teaching Tip

If appropriate for your class, provide additional oral practice. Have students close their books. Then, ask different students to take turns asking one of the questions from Exercise B from memory. The student who asks a question can call on a classmate to answer. If students are able to do this with a fair degree of accuracy, invite volunteers to make up original present continuous *Wh-* questions to ask each other.

8 • Unit 1

appear	have	miss	smell
believe	hear	need	sound
belong	know	own	taste
feel	like	prefer	understand
hate	look	see	want

Use the *simple present tense* with non-action verbs.

He **knows** my name.
I **miss** my grandparents.

Exceptions:

They **are having** a party.
I'm **having** a cup of tea.

A In your notebook, write sentences about the students in the student center.

1. Students / like / to meet / student center
   Students like to meet at the student center.

2. They / need to relax / between classes
   They need to relax between classes.

3. Two students / play / video games
   Two students are playing video games.

4. Some students / study / together
   Some students are studying together.

5. Some music / play / in the background
   Some music is playing in the background.

6. Students / hope to pass / their exams
   Students hope to pass their exams.

7. They / (not) hear / the noise
   They don't hear the noise.

8. Lana and her boyfriend / watch / TV
   Lana and her boyfriend are watching TV.

9. Bill / look / bored
   Bill looks bored.

10. He / (not) like / daytime dramas
    He doesn't like daytime dramas.

11. Two students / buy / pizza
    Two students are buying pizza.

12. The pizza / smell / good
    The pizza smells good.

Education • 9

More Action!

Have students write a paragraph in their notebook about a student or students from the picture of the Student Center. Encourage students to choose a person who is not labeled in the illustration. Begin by eliciting a few possible statements that use the simple present and the present continuous. Then, have students complete their paragraphs on their own. Collect the paragraphs and mark any errors before returning them. If there are any common errors, point them out to the class at your next meeting.

Active Grammar: Non-action Verbs

A In your notebook, write sentences about the students in the student center.

• Review the non-action verb chart at the top of the page. Give examples of correct and incorrect uses of some of the verbs. For example: *Linda appears tired.* (correct) *Linda is appearing tired.* (incorrect)

• Discuss the picture with the class. Ask students to point out Lana, Bill, Lee, and Jamal (all of whom are labeled) and tell what each one is doing.

• Read the instructions. Remind students that some of the sentences will require the present continuous tense and some the simple present tense. Suggest that they refer back to the box at the top of this page if they aren't sure which tense to use.

• Have students complete the sentences on their own and check their answers with a partner. Then, review all the answers by having different students write one sentence each on the board. Correct errors as you review the sentences with the class.

The Big Picture:
The University of Texas at San Antonio

  A Listen to the description of the University of Texas at San Antonio. Circle or complete the information.

(CD1•TR3)

• Ask students what information they think is important to consider when choosing a college to attend. Tell students that there are thousands of colleges in the United States and that students often have difficulty deciding where to apply.

• Direct students to read numbers 1 to 11 to themselves before they listen. Ask about any new words or information. Explain the terms in the Word Partnerships box.

• Play the audio and ask students just to listen the first time through. Then, play it again and ask them to circle the correct information and fill in the blanks as they listen.

• Play the audio a third time to confirm answers. Review the correct answers with the class.

The Big Picture | The University of Texas at San Antonio

 A Listen to the description of the University of Texas at San Antonio. (Circle) or complete the information.

CD1•TR3

1. Location: urban (suburban) rural
2. Degrees: two-year   four-year   (four-year and graduate)
3. Type of university: (public)   private
4. Number of undergraduate students: *Over 24,000*
5. Percentage of international students: *2 percent*
6. Number of graduate students: *Over 3,000*
7. Number of faculty: *1,224*
8. Application Checklist

   a. Application fee: $ *40*   Online application available: (Yes) No

   b. *high school* transcript

   c. Official ACT or *SAT* scores

9. Minimum SAT score for students in top 25 percent: *No minimum*

10. Two possible majors: *accounting / criminal justice / engineering / international business*

11. Services available for students:

    a. Academic *help*

    b. A health clinic and *personal* counseling

    c. Examples of student activities: *athletic teams / sports / drama*

    d. Orientation for *new* and *transfer students*

WORD PARTNERSHIPS	
undergraduate	student
graduate	
associate's	degree
bachelor's	
master's	
doctoral	

B (Circle) *True* or *False*.

1. The University of Texas at San Antonio is a large university.   (True)   False
2. U.T.S.A. is a private university.   True   (False)
3. The main campus is in downtown San Antonio.   True   (False)
4. The university has two campuses.   True   (False)
5. U.T.S.A. has a graduate school.   (True)   False
6. U.T.S.A. employs about eight hundred faculty.   True   (False)
7. Students pay $35 for the application fee.   True   (False)
8. Transfer students can have an orientation.   (True)   False

🔊 **C** **Listen and write short answers to the questions about the university.**

CD1·TR4

1. No, it isn't.
2. Yes, it does.
3. Yes, there is.
4. Yes, it does.
5. No, it isn't.
6. Yes, there are.
7. Yes, there is.
8. Yes, they are.

D **Complete the sentences with the present tense form of the verb.**

1. The University of Texas at San Antonio (have) ____has____ many campuses.
2. About 24,000 undergraduate students (study) ____study____ at U.T.S.A.
3. Future students (pay) ____pay____ an application fee.
4. A student (take) ____takes____ standardized tests before he or she goes to U.T.S.A.
5. U.T.S.A. (have) ____has____ a learning center with tutors and counselors for the students.
6. The university (give) ____gives____ the students free career counseling.
7. Students (go) ____go____ to the employment service when they (need) ____need____ to find jobs.

Education · **11**

B **Circle *True* or *False*.**

Have students complete the activity. Refer students back to Exercise A and the audio if they need assistance. Then, review the correct answers with the class.

🔊 **C** **Listen and write short answers to the questions about the university.**

(CD1 • TR4)

• Give students examples of short answers. Refer them back to the chart on page 5 if necessary.
• Then, play the audio and have students write their answers. Review the correct answers orally with the class.

D **Complete the sentences with the present tense form of the verb.**

• Go over the example sentence in Item 1 together.
• Have students complete the exercise individually and then check their answers with a partner.
• Review the correct answers with the class.

Teaching Tip

Students may be unsure of some of the answers in Exercise B. If appropriate for your class, you may wish to have students complete only the Exercise B answers they are sure of the first time around. Then, play CD1 Track 3 again and have students listen for the answers they missed.

Reading: New Jersey Institute of Technology (N.J.I.T.)

A **Scan the reading to find the answers to the questions.**

- Go over the information in the Reading Note. Explain that *scanning* means that you don't read every single word of a passage. When scanning, you look over the paragraphs very quickly, trying to find the answer to a specific question.
- Review how to scan for specific information. Read Question 1 and ask students what kinds of words they would look for to find this information. (They might look for the name of a city or state or for the word *located*.)
- Call attention to the other five questions. Ask students to read each question, think about what kinds of words they would look for to find this information, and then scan the article, quickly looking for that information.

> **READING NOTE**
>
> **Scanning**
>
> When you are looking for specific information, it is a good idea to **scan**, or read quickly. Do not read every word. Look only for the answers to your questions. For example, if you are looking for the number of undergraduate students, look for the word "undergraduate."

A **Scan the reading to find the answers to the questions.**

1. Where is the school located? Newark, New Jersey

2. Does N.J.I.T. have graduate programs? Yes, it does.

3. How much is the application fee? $70

4. What is the suggested SAT score? 1000 or higher

5. What is the minimum grade average that N.J.I.T. accepts? a B average

6. Can students get degrees online? Yes, they can.

New Jersey Institute of Technology, or N.J.I.T., is located in Newark, New Jersey, ten miles from New York City. It is a four-year public university and technical college. The college offers bachelor's degrees in engineering, computer science, management, technology, and many other fields. N.J.I.T. also has graduate programs in many subjects. <u>Ninety percent</u> of the students come from New Jersey and <u>70 percent</u> commute between home and school. The average age of entering students is eighteen.

In addition to an application, students who are interested in applying to N.J.I.T. need to prepare the following materials for admission:

- the application fee; in 2010, the fee was $70
- an official high school transcript of grades
- official SAT I (Scholastic Aptitude Test) or ACT (American College Testing) scores; the recommended score is 1000 total or above
- <u>for non-U.S. citizens</u>, students must send a photocopy of visas or permanent resident cards

The college requires interested students to have a strong math and science background. Students must have a B average, four years of high school English, and two years of science, including one of a laboratory science such as chemistry.

12 · Unit 1

N.J.I.T. has a program available for students who prefer <u>distance learning, or learning online.</u> N.J.I.T. offers bachelor's and master's degree programs and graduate certificates online. <u>Online courses are designed for students who need flexibility.</u> Maybe they have demanding jobs that require overtime during the week, so they cannot take classes during the week. Maybe they have an odd work shift. Some students may have disabilities, which do not permit them to go to classes in person. Distance learning courses may be right for students who want to study from home.

In addition, N.J.I.T. offers many evening and early morning classes. It also has a summer session. <u>Students who need extra preparation get special instruction, English as a second language classes, or tutoring.</u> Like many other colleges today, N.J.I.T. requires that each student have a computer. The college offers good deals for students who need to buy computers and necessary software.

There are dormitories for students who prefer to live on campus or who live too far away to commute. Students can participate in many <u>clubs, sports teams, and organizations.</u> For example, there are organizations for groups such as the Korean Student Association and the Caribbean Student Organization. There are also many organizations for students in different majors.

If you think you might be interested in this college, look at its website for more information.

B In the reading, number and <u>underline</u> the answers to the questions.

1. What percentage of the students come from New Jersey?
   90 percent
2. What percentage of the students commute to the campus?
   70 percent
3. Does the college accept foreign students?
   Yes, it does.
4. What is *distance learning*?
   Learning online or by computers
5. Who takes online courses?
   Students with demanding jobs, odd work shifts, or disabilities
6. Why do students like online courses?
   They can study from home.
7. What kinds of services are available for students who need more preparation?
   ESL courses, tutoring
8. What kinds of clubs and organizations can students join?
   Sports teams and cultural organizations

> **CULTURE NOTE**
>
> Most colleges and universities have websites that describe their programs, activities, and admission procedures. Their URLs (Internet addresses) end in **.edu**, which stands for *education.* Here are two examples: New York University's URL is www.nyu.edu. The University of Texas at San Antonio's URL is www.utsa.edu.

 Go online. Research a college or university that interests you.

More Action!

Ask volunteers to present their findings from Exercise C to the class. Encourage other students to ask *Yes / No* and *Wh-* questions about each college or university. For example: *Does the school have a bookstore? Where do students study?* Tell the volunteers to answer the students' questions to the best of their ability.

B **In the reading, number and underline the answers to the questions.**

- Ask students to read the questions to themselves and ask about anything they don't understand.
- Then, have them scan the reading to locate the information and underline and number the answers.
- Review the answers by reading each question aloud and calling on a student to tell which paragraph the answer is located in. Then, have the student read his or her underlined answer to the class.

C **Go online. Research a college or university that interests you.**

- Go over the information in the Culture Note.
- Have students decide on a college or university to research, and then have them use an Internet search engine to locate the website and find the information. Students can look for information on location, admissions procedures, the campus and facilities, and degree programs available.
- If students can't think of a college or university to research, provide them with the names of a few local or well-known universities in your area.

Writing Our Stories: My Schedule

A **Write a composition about your school schedule and your classes. Answer these questions.**

• Ask students to read the text to themselves. When they finish, invite them to ask about anything they don't understand and to make any comments about Amelia's schedule.

• Read the instructions and review the list of questions to ensure that students understand them.

• Tell students they can use the list of questions to organize their composition.

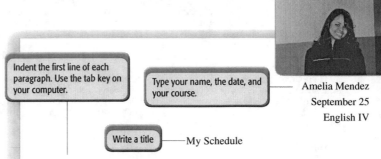

Indent the first line of each paragraph. Use the tab key on your computer.

Type your name, the date, and your course.

Amelia Mendez
September 25
English IV

Write a title —— My Schedule

I am a student at Union County College. The school is in New Jersey. This is my first semester, and my major is education.

I have a busy schedule. On Mondays and Wednesdays, I have an ESL grammar and listening class from 5:00 to 7:30. I have a reading and writing course on Tuesdays and Thursdays from 6:30 to 9:00. On Fridays, I have a math class from 6:00 to 8:30. I belong to a study group, and we study together for three hours on Saturday mornings. I do my homework at home after my classes. I spend about two hours a night on my homework. Math is my hardest subject.

I like my classes and my school. I have a lot of friends. I like spending time at the student center.

A **Write a composition about your school schedule and your classes.** Answer these questions.

1. What school do you attend? Where is it located?

2. What is your weekly school schedule?

3. Are your classes difficult, easy, or just right?

4. How often do you have tests?

5. When and where do you study? How many hours do you study a week?

6. Do you like your school? Why or why not?

14 · Unit 1

Teaching Tip

It may be useful to have students outline the information they are going to use in their descriptions before they start writing. For example, you might have them make brief notes about class times, study times, the kinds of tests they take, and so forth. This way they will have all the necessary facts, vocabulary, and spelling figured out ahead of time and will be better prepared to focus on other aspects of correct language usage as they begin writing.

B **Complete each sentence with appropriate examples.** (Answers will vary.)

1. My classmates come from different countries, such as _____ and _____.

2. In our English class, we are studying many things, such as _____ and _____.

3. Computers are useful for many things, such as _____ and _____.

4. A medical student has to study sciences, such as _____ and _____.

5. Languages, such as _____ and _____, are difficult to learn.

6. Sports, such as _____ and _____, are very popular in the United States.

C **There is one underlined verb mistake in each sentence.** Correct the mistakes.

1. The Division of Physical Education <u>offer</u> many recreational programs. *offers*
2. N.J.I.T. <u>is develop</u> many programs to attract women and minority students to engineering and the sciences. *is developing*
3. U.T.S.A.'s campuses <u>provides</u> opportunities for many students. *provide*
4. Some students <u>are preferring</u> to study from their own homes, using computers. *prefer*
5. What kind of exams <u>students usually take</u>? *do students usually take*
6. The students <u>leave rarely</u> their classes without a homework assignment. *rarely leave*
7. My roommate <u>is belonging</u> to the women's volleyball team. *belongs*
8. This test <u>is looking</u> difficult. *looks*

Education · 15

Teaching Tip

Explain that editing is an important part of writing. Encourage students to always edit their own work. Suggest that they also exchange papers with a classmate when they have time so they can practice editing each other's work.

B **Complete each sentence with appropriate examples.**

• Review the Writing Note.
• Then, ask students to make up example sentences of their own, following the model in the Writing Note. You may need to give them cues to get them started. For example:
T: *Foods you like.*
S1: *I like desserts, such as ice cream, cake, and cookies.*
T: *Things you can buy in a department store.*
S2: *In a department store you can buy many different types of clothing, such as pants, shoes, and hats.*
• Have students complete the sentences and check their answers with a partner. Review the exercise by calling on several different students to read aloud their answers to each question.

C **There is one underlined verb mistake in each sentence. Correct the mistakes.**

Have students complete the activity on their own and then compare answers with a partner. Go over the answers and explain any edits that students are not sure of.

Practicing on Your Own

A **Complete the story. Use the simple present and the present continuous tense.**

Ask students to do the activity individually and then check their answers with a partner.

B **In your notebook, write ten questions about the story. Write five questions using the simple present and five questions using the present continuous.**

Read the instructions. Elicit or provide a sample question and answer. Have students write both *Yes / No* questions and *Wh-* questions. Ask them to try to make some of the *Yes / No* questions with *yes* answers, and some with *no* answers.

A **Complete the story.** Use the simple present and the present continuous tense.

Joe is the manager of the student center, and this is his twentieth year working there. Joe (know) _____knows_____ the names of almost all of the students who (visit) _____visit_____ the center every day. He (like) _____likes_____ to talk to the students, and he (miss) _____misses_____ them during vacations.

Today is the beginning of final exams, so the student center (negative–be) _____isn't_____ as busy as usual. A few students (talk) _____are talking_____ in a corner, soft music (play) _____is playing_____, and a group of students (discuss) _____is discussing_____ a final project. Many students (study) _____are studying_____ in the library this week and (write) _____are writing_____ their papers in the computer center. Today, Joe (prepare) _____is preparing_____ some special treats for the students because he (understand) _____understands_____ that exam time is very stressful. The students (negative–have) _____don't have_____ a lot of free time during exam weeks, and they (miss–often) _____often miss_____ their meals at the dining hall. It's 11:30 P.M., and Joe (make) _____is making_____ some cookies, and pizzas (bake) _____are baking_____ in the ovens. The center (smell) _____smells_____ wonderful. Students (look) _____are looking_____ up from their books and (get) _____are getting_____ ready to take a study break.

B **In your notebook, write ten questions about the story.** Write five questions using the simple present and five questions using the present continuous.

Teaching Tip

You can use the students' questions for oral review in class. Have students read one of their questions aloud and call on another student to answer.

A **Imagine that you are applying to college.** Complete the sample college application. *(Answers will vary.)*

COLLEGE APPLICATION

ACADEMIC INFORMATION

Status: ☐ Full time ☐ Part time   Term: ☐ Fall ☐ Spring

Program / Major: _____   Degree: _____

Do you plan to take online courses? ☐ Yes ☐ No

Previous Education (Write all high schools and colleges attended.)

HIGH SCHOOL

Name of High School	Location	Graduation Date

COLLEGES / UNIVERSITIES

Name	Location	Dates Attended	Degree Received

SAT / ACT   Date of exam: ___ / ___ / ___

TOEFL   Date of exam: ___ / ___ / ___

WORK EXPERIENCE

List current employer first.

Name of Employer	Location	Dates of Employment

I, _____ , certify that the information on this application is true.
Signature

_____
Date

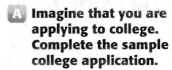

English in Action: Completing a College Application

A **Imagine that you are applying to college. Complete the sample college application.**

• Go over the directions. Review the application as a class and answer any questions about unfamiliar vocabulary.

• Have students complete the application. Tell students if they don't know certain information, they can use their imagination or leave the item blank. Circulate around the room and provide help as needed.

A **Look at the map of the original 13 colonies. Discuss the questions that follow.**

• Discuss the map with the class. Review the four main compass directions: north, south, east, and west.

• Ask questions to orient students to the map and to help them make use of what they already know. For example:

T: *Where is north?*

S1: (pointing) *The top of the map is north.*

T: *Where is the Atlantic Ocean?*

S2: (pointing) *It's here in the east—on the right side of the map.*

• Ask students to read through the questions and ask about anything they don't understand.

• Then, discuss the answers to the questions as a class.

Unit 2 Colonial Times

A **Look at the map of the original 13 colonies.** Discuss the questions that follow.

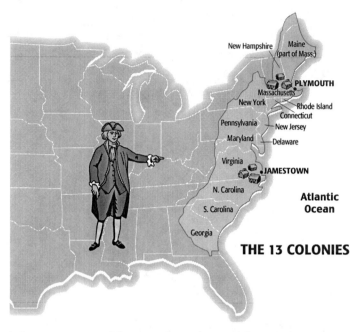

New Hampshire
Maine (part of Mass.)
PLYMOUTH
Massachusetts
New York
Rhode Island
Connecticut
Pennsylvania
New Jersey
Maryland
Delaware
Virginia
JAMESTOWN
N. Carolina
Atlantic Ocean
S. Carolina
Georgia

THE 13 COLONIES

1. Is your state one of the original 13 colonies of the United States?
   (Answers will vary.)
2. Which colony was the farthest south?
   Georgia
3. Which state is Plymouth in?
   Massachusetts
4. Which state is Jamestown in?
   Virginia
5. From 1999–2001, the United States released new quarters representing the 13 colonies. Do you have any of them?
   (Answers will vary.)

18 · Unit 2

More Action!

Ask students to locate the 13 original colonies on the map of the United States on page 289 of their Student Book. Tell students to compare the borders of the 13 original colonies to the borders of these 13 states as they exist today. How have they changed? Students can discuss their answers as a class or in small groups.

Teaching Tip

Define what a *colony* is for students who may not be familiar with the word. Explain that colonies are formed when a group of people live in a new territory but still have ties to their parent country. Explain to students that Jamestown and Plymouth (which are both marked on the map) were two of the earliest settlements in the colonies. Jamestown was settled in 1607 and Plymouth was settled around 1620. Encourage students to research the settlements online for more information about each location.

A Write the past tense forms of the verbs.

Regular verbs

I		
You	**moved**	to the United States.
He	**didn't move**	
They		

1. call ___called___

2. cook ___cooked___

3. milk ___milked___

4. play ___played___

5. talk ___talked___

6. use ___used___

7. travel ___traveled___

8. watch ___watched___

Irregular verbs*

1. buy ___bought___

2. drive ___drove___

3. go ___went___

4. grow ___grew___

5. make ___made___

6. read ___read___

7. sleep ___slept___

8. write ___wrote___

*Note: See the chart of irregular verbs on page 116.

CD1·TR5

B Look at the pictures and listen to the comparison between life in colonial times and life today. Number the pictures in the order you hear them discussed.

 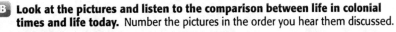 

C Look at each picture. Describe life in Colonial America.

Colonial Times · **19**

Active Grammar: Simple Past Tense

A Write the past tense forms of the verbs.

• Go over the information in the grammar chart. Provide additional examples of the simple past tense.
• Ask students to complete this exercise individually and then check their answers with a partner.

B Look at the pictures and listen to the comparison between life in colonial times and life today.

(CD1 • TR5)

• Invite students to point to different sets of pictures and tell what they see. Explain anything they don't understand about the pictures.
• As you play the audio the first time, ask students to look at the pictures and point to the one that is being talked about.
• Play the audio a second time, pausing after each section that describes a pair of pictures. Ask students to repeat the statement about each pair of pictures using their own words or to make up a new statement about the pair of pictures.

C Look at each picture. Describe life in Colonial America.

• Ask students to work in pairs as they point to the pictures and describe what life was like in Colonial America.
• Review the answers by calling on different students to compare different pairs of pictures. Help them with vocabulary as needed.

Colonial Times · **19**

Active Grammar: Using the Simple Past Tense

 A **Working Together** Complete the sentences about life in Colonial America. Write a verb from the box in the past tense. Some of the verbs are negative. You can use some words more than once. Look at page 19 for help.

• Have students complete the sentences individually. Point out that they can refer to the chart and Exercise A on page 19 if they need help.
• Then, have students check their answers with a partner.

 B **Work with a partner. Ask and answer the questions about your first year in this country.**

Have students take turns asking each other the questions. Move around the room as they work, offering language support as needed.

 A **Working Together** **Complete the sentences about life in Colonial America.** Write a verb from the box in the past tense. Some of the verbs are negative. You can use some words more than once. Look at page 19 for help.

1. People _____didn't go_____ to supermarkets.
2. They ___grew / didn't buy___ their own food.
3. People _____cooked_____ over open fires.
4. They _____didn't have_____ stoves.
5. People _____milked_____ their own cows.
6. They _____didn't buy_____ milk at the supermarket.
7. Families _____used_____ candles for light.
8. People _____didn't sleep_____ on mattresses.
9. At night, families _____didn't watch_____ TV.
10. They _____read_____ books and _____played_____ games.
11. People _____didn't talk_____ to one another on cell phones.
12. They _____wrote_____ letters to one another.
13. People _____traveled_____ by horse and wagon.
14. They __didn't have / didn't use__ cars.

buy	read
cook	sleep
go	talk
grow	travel
have	use
milk	watch
play	write

 B **Work with a partner.** Ask and answer the questions about your first year in this country.

1. When did you arrive in the United States?
2. How did you travel here?
3. Why did you come to this country?
4. What important things did you bring with you?
5. Who did you live with when you arrived?
6. Did you speak any English?
7. Was your first year in this country difficult?

More Action!

If it is appropriate and there is enough class time, invite several students to share their answers to each question in Exercise B with the whole class.

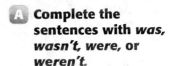
A Complete the sentences with *was, wasn't, were,* or *weren't.*

1. Life ___wasn't___ easy for the first settlers.

2. The first homes ___were___ small buildings made of wood and mud.

3. There ___wasn't___ a kitchen in the house.

4. There ___weren't___ bathrooms, either. There ___was___ a small outhouse in the backyard.

5. Windows ___were___ small because no glass ___was___ available.

6. At first, there ___were___ only a few schools in the colonies.

7. There ___wasn't___ a telephone to communicate.

8. By 1776, the population of the colonies ___was___ over three million.

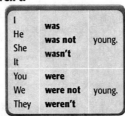

I	was	
He	was not	young.
She	wasn't	
It		
You	were	
We	were not	young.
They	weren't	

	was	a garden.
	was not	
	wasn't	a refrigerator.
There	were	few schools.
	were not	
	weren't	large schools.

B Working Together Use the information below to talk about life today and life in 1790. Use the simple present or simple past tense.

The president is
_____

George Washington was the president.

Today

1. The president is _____.

2. The president earns $400,000.

3. The capital is Washington, D.C.

4. There are 50 states.

5. The largest state is Alaska.

6. The largest city is New York City.

7. The population is about 305 million.

1790

1. George Washington
   George Washington was the president.

2. $25,000
   The president earned $25,000.

3. New York City
   The capital was New York City.

4. 13 states
   There were 13 states.

5. New York
   The largest state was New York.

6. New York City
   The largest city was New York City.

7. four million
   The population was four million.

Colonial Times · 21

More Action!

Discuss the answers to Exercise B as a class. Ask students what information was new to them and what facts they found the most surprising and interesting.

Active Grammar: Past Tense of *Be*

A Complete the sentences with *was, wasn't, were,* or *weren't.*

• Review the grammar charts. Check comprehension by asking:

T: *Which past form of be is used with plural subjects like* we *and* they?

S1: Were.

T: *What form is used with singular subjects like* I, he, *and* she?

S2: Was.

T: *Which subject pronoun is both singular and plural?*

S3: You.

T: *Why?*

S3: *Because sometimes* you *represents one person and sometimes it represents two or more people.*

• Have students complete the sentences individually and compare their answers with a partner.

B Working Together Use the information below to talk about life today and life in 1790. Use the simple present or simple past tense.

• Read and discuss the instructions and sample response.

• Then, have students work in pairs, taking turns reading statements from the first column and responding with past tense statements containing the information from the "1790" column.

Active Grammar: *Used to*

  A **Pronunciation: *Used to* Listen and repeat.**

(CD1 • TR6)

• Play the audio several times as students just listen. Then, have students practice repeating the pronunciation of *used to* in isolation several times.
• Play the audio again and have students repeat the sentences.

  B **Work with a partner. Read about life today. Talk about life in Colonial America. Use the words in the box and *used to*.**

• Review the meaning of the words in the vocabulary box. Use brief explanations, pictures in the book, and simple drawings on the board to clarify the meaning of any items students aren't sure of.
• Go over the first item together. Then, have pairs of students take turns reading the sentences and responses with *used to*. Be sure both students have a chance to practice all the *used to* sentences. Remind them to think about correct pronunciation.

  C **Complete the sentences about life in your native country. Then, read your sentences to a partner.**

Have students complete the sentences on their own. Then, have them read their work to a partner. If time permits, encourage students to read to more than one student.

I You She They	used to	live in Peru. use candles for light. grow all of our vegetables.

> Use *used to* to talk about a habit or a routine that you did in the past but that you don't do now.
> **I used to live** in New York. Now, I live in Sacramento.

 A **Pronunciation: *Used to* Listen and repeat.**

CD1 • TR6

1. In colonial times, people used to drive horses and wagons.
2. People used to cook over open fires.
3. People used to grow their own food.
4. They used to write letters.
5. They used to attend very small schools.

  B **Work with a partner.** Read about life today. Talk about life in Colonial America. Use the words in the box and *used to*.

> In colonial times, girls used to wear long dresses.

1. Today, girls wear jeans, dresses, or skirts.
   Girls used to wear long dresses.
2. Today, people drink from glasses.
   People used to drink from wooden mugs.
3. Today, most children study in large public schools.
   Children used to study in one-room schoolhouses.
4. Today, most children wear sneakers.
   Children used to wear leather boots.
5. Today, people read by electric lights.
   People used to read by candlelight.
6. Today, people eat with forks, knives, and spoons.
   People used to eat with spoons and their fingers.

> wooden mugs
> long dresses
> candlelight
> spoons and their fingers
> one-room schoolhouses
> leather boots

 C **Complete the sentences about life in your native country.** Then, read your sentences to a partner. (Answers will vary.)

1. When I lived in _____, I used to _____.
2. My family and I used to _____ every summer.
3. My friends and I used to _____ on Saturday nights.
4. I used to eat typical foods like _____.
5. I never used to _____.

Teaching Tip

If students have difficulty pronouncing the shortened form of *used to*, spell out the pronunciation on the board. For example: *Used to = you stuh.* Explain that in this case, the letter *o* in the word *to* sounds like the letter *u* in the word *up*. Say the words *used to* in isolation several times, paying careful attention to the sound of the words, and ask students to repeat.

Children **didn't play** with toy trucks.

 Working Together In a small group, try to find the 16 things wrong with this picture. Check your answers below.

• Have students read the instructions. Then, read aloud the sample answer: *Children didn't play with toy trucks.*

• Divide the class into pairs or groups of three and have them see how many wrong things they can find. Tell them to cover the answers at the bottom of the page. Set a time limit of five to ten minutes.

• After the groups have finished discussing the picture, call on different students to point to and describe one of the errors in the picture. Continue this process until all 16 errors are named. If students cannot identify all of the errors, have them check the answers at the bottom of the page.

Answers:

1. Children didn't play with toy trucks.
2. Houses didn't have air conditioners.
3. They didn't have electricity.
4. They didn't have helicopters.
5. Farmers didn't ride tractors.
6. They didn't have grills.
7. They didn't have traffic lights.
8. They didn't drive on paved roads.
9. Houses didn't have doorbells.
10. Cars didn't have rubber tires.
11. Teenagers didn't have music players.
12. Girls didn't wear short skirts.
13. Men didn't smoke cigarettes.
14. Teenagers didn't wear sneakers.
15. They didn't eat hamburgers.
16. They didn't have TVs.

Active Grammar: Simple Past Tense– Questions

  A **Complete the questions. Then, listen to Eric talk about his childhood. Take notes in your notebook. Answer the questions.**

(CD1•TR7)

• Play the audio and ask students to just listen the first time through. Then, read the instructions and go over the questions and cue verbs.
• Play the audio again and ask students to complete the questions. Remind them to use the grammar boxes at the top of the page if they need help with the word order for the questions. Have students check their answers with a partner.
• Play the audio a third time, pausing after each line that contains an answer to one of the questions, and call on a student to respond. Confirm correct answers and correct any wrong answers.

 B **Complete the questions. Use *did, was,* or *were.* Then, ask and answer the questions about your childhood with a partner.**

Have students take turns asking each other the questions. Encourage them to add information after any *yes / no* responses. For example, instead of just saying *Yes, I did* in response to Question 2, suggest that they add a sentence such as: *There were six of us living in our house.*

| Did you **have** any pets? |
| Did she **live** in the country? |
| Did they **play** sports? |

Was	he	in the city?
	it	
Were	you	busy?
	they	

Where		you	go to school?
	did	she	
How		they	get to school?

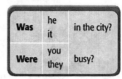 **A** **Complete the questions.** Then, listen to Eric talk about his childhood. Take notes in your notebook. Answer the questions.

CD1•TR7

1. (be) _Was_ he born in the United States?
   No, he wasn't. He was born in Peru.
2. _Did_ he (live) _live_ in a big city?
   No, he didn't.
3. _Did_ he (have) _have_ a big family?
   Yes, he did.
4. (be) _Was_ he the oldest?
   No, he wasn't. He was the youngest.
5. (be) _Were_ his relatives nearby?
   Yes, they were.
6. _Did_ he (live) _live_ in the city or in the country?
   He lived in the country.
7. _Did_ he (walk) _walk_ to school?
   No, he didn't. He rode his bike.
8. (be) _Was_ his grandmother a good cook?
   Yes, she was.

 B **Complete the questions.** Use *did, was,* or *were.* Then, ask and answer the questions about your childhood with a partner.

1. Where _did_ you live?
2. _Did_ you have a big family?
3. _Did_ you spend time with your grandparents?
4. _Was_ your family close?
5. What sports _did_ you play?
6. _Were_ you a good student?
7. How _were_ your grades?
8. When _did_ you begin to study English?

More Action!

If time permits, have students switch partners several times so that they have a chance to practice the questions and answers in Exercise B more. Alternatively, have the pairs report their partners' answers to the class to give them extra oral practice.

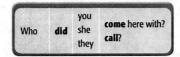

Simple Past Tense: *Who* Questions

Who	did	you she they	come here with? call?

A **Answer the questions.** (Answers will vary.)

1. **Who** did you come to this country with? _I came with my family._

2. Who did you stay with when you came? _____

3. Who did you ask for help to find a place to live? _____

4. Who did you talk to about this school? _____

5. Who did you talk to when you had a problem? _____

6. Who did you call after you arrived here? _____

B **Write two more questions.** Ask a partner your questions. (Answers will vary.)

1. _____

2. _____

C **Work in a small group.** Ask and answer the questions.
Write the name of the student or students on the line. (Answers will vary.)

1. Who came here alone? _____

2. Who brought a pet here? _____

3. Who left family behind? _____

4. Who found a job right away? _____

5. Who studied English before coming to the U.S.? _____

6. Who knew how to drive before coming to this country? _____

Who	came here alone? brought a pet here? left family behind?

D **Write two more questions.** Ask your classmates your questions.

1. _Answers will vary._ _____

2. _____

Active Grammar

A **Answer the questions.**

• Go over the information in the grammar chart at the top of the page. Elicit or provide additional examples.

• Go over the example sentence in Question 1. Point out that the answers in this exercise will always begin with *I*.

• Have students do the exercise on their own. Call on a few volunteers to share their answers for each question with the class.

B **Write two more questions.**

• Have students think of and write two more questions and then ask a partner the questions. Tell them to be sure the questions aren't too personal. Check the accuracy of the spelling of the past tense verbs.

• If time permits, call on volunteers to ask and answer their questions.

C **Work in a small group.**

• Go over the information in the grammar chart. Point out that the answers will not always begin with *I* as they did in Exercise A.

• Circulate around the room while students work. Point out that the answer might sometimes be *No one*.

D **Write two more questions.**

• Have students write two more questions and then ask their group the questions. Have them write down the other group members' answers.

• Check the spelling of the past tense verbs.

The Big Picture: Benjamin Franklin

** A** **Listen. Complete the outline about Benjamin Franklin's life.**

(CD1•TR8)

• Read the information in the box. Explain to students that to complete the outline, they should take notes as they listen. Taking notes involves writing down the most important ideas in a very simple form. People do not usually use complete sentences when they take notes.

• Explain that Benjamin Franklin was an American who lived in Philadelphia, Pennsylvania, during colonial times. Point out Pennsylvania on the map on page 18. Tell students that they are going to hear a story about who Franklin was and some of the things he did.

• Point out the pictures of Franklin's inventions and briefly discuss what each one is used for. If a student wears bifocal glasses, ask him or her to show them to the class.

• Give students time to read and review the outline.

• Play the audio and ask students to just listen the first time through. Then, play the audio again and ask them to complete the outline.

• Go over the completed outline with the class.

** A** **Listen.** Complete the outline about Benjamin Franklin's life.

CD1•TR8

A. Early life

> When you listen to a lecture, take notes. Don't depend on your memory—depend on your notes.

1. Born in ___Boston___ on ___Jan. 17, 1706___
2. Attended school for ___two___ years
3. Trained to become a ___printer___
4. Moved to ___Philadelphia___
5. Opened a ___printing shop___

B. Improvements to Philadelphia

1. Started the first ___public library___
2. Helped to organize the first ___fire department___
3. Served as ___postmaster___ and set up ___routes___
4. Convinced city officials to pave the ___city streets___

C. Four inventions

1. ___odometer___

2. ___lightning rod___

3. ___stove___

4. ___bifocals___

> bifocals
> lightning rod
> odometer
> stove

D. Contributions as a leader

1. Signed the Declaration of ___Independence___
   a. It stated that the 13 colonies were a ___free___ and ___independent___ nation.
2. Served as minister to ___France___

Teaching Tip

While students may be able to identify the four inventions pictured, they may be unsure of the purpose of and use for each invention. Provide simple explanations about each of the items pictured.

An *odometer* measures the distance a person or vehicle travels.

A *lightning rod* protects a building by carrying the electrical charge away from the building and into the earth (ground) where it doesn't cause any damage.

A *Franklin stove* is cleaner and produces more heat than a fireplace.

Bifocals are glasses with two different lenses so that the wearer can see clearly up close and far away.

3. Signed the Constitution

    a. It established a new _____government_____ .

E. Death

  1. Died on _____April 17, 1790_____

 B **Look at your outline.** Ask and answer the questions.

  1. Where was Benjamin Franklin born?
    Boston, Massachusetts
  2. How long did he attend school?
    Two years
  3. What trade did he learn?
    Printing
  4. What city did he move to?
    Philadelphia
  5. What business did he open?
    A printing shop
  6. What services did Franklin help to start?
    The first fire department and public library
  7. How else did he help the city of Philadelphia? *He organized a fire department. / He was postmaster. / He helped pave the streets.*
  8. What did he invent to measure distance?
    An odometer
  9. What important documents did he sign?
    He signed the Declaration of Independence and the Constitution.
  10. What was the Declaration of Independence? *It stated that the 13 colonies were a free and independent nation.*

C **Read the answers.** Then, complete the questions.

  1. When *was Franklin born* ?

    He was born in 1706.

  2. *Did he graduate* from high school?

    No, he didn't graduate from high school.

  3. How many languages ___*did he speak*___ ?

    He spoke five languages.

  4. What ___*did he invent*___ when he was postmaster?

    He invented an odometer.

  5. What *did he experiment* with?

    He experimented with electricity.

B **Look at your outline. Ask and answer the questions.**

• Call on individuals to consult their outline and answer the questions aloud with a partner.
• Rephrase any incorrect responses and ask the student to repeat them.

C **Read the answers. Then, complete the questions.**

• Ask students to answer the questions individually and then check their answers with a partner. Point out that first they will have to read the answers to the questions.
• Then, call on a different student to repeat each question. Write the missing words on the board. Have students correct their work.

More Action!

Benjamin Franklin was famous for his sayings, or proverbs, such as "A penny saved is a penny earned," and "An apple a day keeps the doctor away." Go online and find more of Franklin's proverbs and share them with the class. First, review what a proverb is by asking students to give examples of English language proverbs they already know or by reading one of Franklin's proverbs aloud. Invite students to translate a favorite proverb from their native language into English and explain what it means.

Reading: Plimoth Plantation

A Discuss.

• Go over the Reading Note. Point to the picture, read the caption, and invite students to comment. Ask: *Were the Pilgrims' homes large or small? What did the homes look like?*

• Discuss the prereading question with the class. Ask: *What is one historical place in your country? What is this place famous for? When people visit this place, what do they see?*

B Word Builder Scan the reading to find the words below. Then, match.

• Have students match each word with the correct definition. If necessary, paraphrase the definitions. For example:
a. *An imitation object that looks exactly the same as the real object.*
b. *An object that someone finds in the ground that was left there long ago.*
c. *Someone who looks at very old objects to learn about the period of history they came from.*

• Review the correct answers with the class.

C Read.

Ask students to read the story to themselves. When they finish, invite them to ask about any sentences they don't understand. Try to avoid spending a lot of time defining and discussing individual words. Explain that they only need to understand the main idea of each sentence.

28 · Unit 2

A reproduction of a Pilgrim house from 1627

READING NOTE
Guessing words from context
It is important to guess the meaning of new words from the context. When you see a new word, read the sentence again. Is the new word a verb, an adjective, or a noun? If you can't guess its meaning, read the sentence before the word and read the sentence that follows the word.

A Discuss.

Name one historic place in your country. Why is it famous?

B Word Builder Scan the reading to find the words below. Then, match.

_f_ **1.** colony	**a.**	copies of original items
_d_ **2.** settlers	**b.**	items or pieces of an item from the past
_c_ **3.** archaeologist	**c.**	a person who studies artifacts to learn about the past
_b_ **4.** artifacts	**d.**	people who move to a place to start a new community
_e_ **5.** reconstruction	**e.**	something that is put together again or rebuilt
_a_ **6.** reproductions	**f.**	a group of people who are living in a new place but who are still part of the original country

C Read.

Plymouth, Massachusetts, is a popular tourist attraction. It was the second **colony** in America. On November 11, 1620, a small ship of people from England landed there and started a new colony. These **settlers** were looking for a better life and religious freedom.

One of the most popular attractions in Plymouth is Plimoth Plantation. Plimoth Plantation was the dream of Henry Hornblower II. When he was a boy, Hornblower read stories about the Pilgrims who lived in Plymouth. When he was older, he worked with **archaeologists** in Plymouth. The archaeologists found more than 350,000

28 · Unit 2

artifacts from the original colony. At the same time, historians learned about the lives of the early colonists by reading their journals. In 1945, Henry Hornblower's father gave $20,000 to the Pilgrim Society to begin the **reconstruction** of Plimoth Plantation. The Society made **reproductions** of the clothes, tools, furniture, and houses of the 1620s. The museum opened in 1947, with just one reproduction of a colonial home.

Today, Plimoth Plantation looks like the original settlement of 1627. It is a living museum of more than 20 homes, shops, and gardens. Visitors can walk through the colonial town where each house looks exactly like a house of the 1620s. The museum staff are the "colonists." They wear the same kinds of clothes that the Plymouth colonists used to wear. The women cook on open fireplaces and make colonial recipes. The men grow the same vegetables and raise the same animals as people did in colonial times. Everyone uses the same kinds of tools that the colonists used. When visitors talk to the "colonists," the colonists answer with the same English language and accent that the original colonists had. A trip to Plimoth Plantation is a trip back in history.

D Answer the questions.

1. Why did the colonists leave England?
   They were looking for a better life and religious freedom.
2. Was Plymouth, Massachusetts, the first colony?
   No, it wasn't. It was the second.
3. How did Henry Hornblower find out about the Pilgrims at Plymouth?
   He read about them.
4. What did archaeologists find at the site?
   They found artifacts.
5. How did historians reproduce the plantation?
   They used information from journals.
6. Why is Plimoth Plantation "a living museum"?
   It looks like a town in 1627.
7. What do "colonists" wear?
   They wear the same clothes that the colonists wore.
8. What kind of vegetables do they grow on Plimoth Plantation?
   They raise the same vegetables.
9. What language do the "colonists" speak?
   They speak the English of the original colonies.

E Complete the sentences. Use words from the box.

> archaeologist
> artifact
> ~~colonies~~
> reconstruction
> reproduction
> settlers

1. In the Caribbean, there are many former British ___colonies___ .

2. In my neighborhood, there is a ___reproduction___ of a famous church. It looks almost like the original.

3. The first foreign ___settlers___ in New York were Dutch immigrants.

4. When I was a child, I wanted to become an ___archaeologist___ .

5. After City Hall burned down, the city decided to do a ___reconstruction___ .

6. Some workers found an ___artifact___ from a Native American tribe.

Colonial Times • 29

Ask students to complete the exercise individually and then check their answers with a partner. As you correct the exercise with the class, ask students to read aloud the sentence or sentences from the story that prove the answer is correct.

E Complete the sentences. Use words from the box.

Go over the model, and then have the students complete the exercise. If students are still uncertain of the meaning of some of the vocabulary words, refer them back to the reading. Encourage them to look at the vocabulary word in context to figure out its meaning.

More Action!

For extra practice, have students write additional sentences using the vocabulary words from pages 28 and 29. Have students write sentences leaving a blank for the vocabulary word, as in Exercise E. Then, have them trade papers with a partner who will fill in the appropriate missing word.

Writing Our Stories:
A Historic Place

A **Read the composition.**

• Ask students to read the composition on their own. Clarify any unfamiliar vocabulary.
• Go over the Writing Note to prepare them for the exercises on page 31.

B **Read Laura's brainstorming notes. Circle the ideas she used in her composition.**

• Discuss any questions students might have about the process of brainstorming.
• Do this as a class exercise, especially if students seem to need help identifying the correct answer.
• Have students go back to the composition in Exercise A and circle the ideas Laura used.

A **Read the composition.**

Laura Guigliano
October 18
English IV

The History of Pompeii

I am from Naples, in southern Italy. A popular historic city in southern Italy is Pompeii. Pompeii is an archaeological site by the Bay of Naples. It is at the bottom of Mount Vesuvius, an active volcano. In 79 A.D., the volcano erupted. The hot mud from the volcano poured down into the sea and towns and killed many people. The lava completely covered the city of Pompeii.

In 1738, workers accidentally discovered artifacts from Pompeii. They contacted authorities. Archaeologists and other experts went to the site. Over many years, these experts uncovered the ancient city of Pompeii.

Pompeii used to be an active vacation city for wealthy Romans. There were homes with beautiful gardens, shops, and places for entertainment. Residents used to spend time at the large outdoor theater. Today, visitors can walk around many parts of the city and look at the remains of the homes. Many of the streets are still in good condition. Visitors can see many of the artifacts in the Naples National Archaeological Museum.

WRITING NOTE

Brainstorming
Before writing, it is helpful to think about your topic. Many writers **brainstorm** for five or ten minutes. This means that they write down all their ideas. Then, they use the ideas that they like best for their compositions.

B Read Laura's brainstorming notes. (Circle) the ideas she used in her composition.

Historic Place	Location	What is it?
the Colosseum	Rome	old stadium; place for entertainment for Romans; original seating; lots of tourists; cats
Pompeii	near Naples and Mt. Vesuvius	old city buried by ash from volcano; ruins of homes, gardens; outdoor theater

C Brainstorm about historic places in your native country. Include the names and locations of a few places, what they are, what visitors do there, and other important information. If you need more information, search for it online. Take notes.

D Write a composition about the historic place that you chose. Use your own words to write your composition; do not copy.

E Sharing Our Stories Read your partner's story. What historic place did your partner write about? Where is it? What can tourists see there?

F Find and correct the verb mistakes.
   1. Benjamin Franklin ~~help~~ helped to improve the city of Philadelphia.
   2. ~~Did~~ Was Philadelphia a major city?
   3. When did Washington become the capital?
   4. Boston ~~use~~ used to be one of the major manufacturing centers.
   5. Was Boston Latin School the first public school in America?
   6. Who ~~were~~ was the first vice president of the United States?
   7. The original settlers didn't ~~knew~~ know how to grow their own food.
   8. People used to ~~traveled~~ travel by ship from country to country.

C Brainstorm about historic places in your native country.

• Remind students to write down whatever ideas come to mind when they brainstorm, even if they seem unrelated to the topic. Explain that doing this will help them come up with a greater number of useful ideas.
• Set a time limit of about 10 minutes. Announce how much time remains after five minutes and then when two minutes are left for brainstorming.
• Have them take notes using a graphic organizer like the one in Exercise B.

D Write a composition about the historic place that you chose.

Suggest that students choose two or three key ideas from their brainstorming list as the basis of their composition. The writing can be done as homework or in class.

E Sharing Our Stories Read your partner's story.

Go over the questions in the instructions with the class. Have students look for and write down the answers to these questions as a way of looking for the main ideas and important details of the composition.

F Find and correct the verb mistakes.

• Have students complete the exercise on their own and then compare answers with a partner.
• Go over the answers and explain any edits that may be unclear.

Practicing on Your Own

A **Complete. Write the past tense form of the verbs in parentheses.**

• Have students complete the exercise on their own. Suggest that they use the list of irregular past tense verbs on page 117 or a dictionary if they need help.

• Review the correct answers with the class.

B **Read the answers. Then, complete the questions.**

• Point out the answers to each question. Tell students to use the answers to create the question in the past tense. Do the first item together.

• Have students check their answers with a partner. Correct answers as needed.

A **Complete.** Write the past tense form of the verbs in parentheses.

In January 1607, three small ships (leave) _____left_____₁ England for America. Four months later, they (arrive) _____arrived_____₂ in America. Several of the men (negative—survive) _didn't survive_₃ the long, stormy journey. The men (choose) _____chose_____₄ an area on the James River that is now in the state of Virginia. They (begin) _____began_____₅ to build a fort. The men (be) _____were_____₆ "gentlemen" and (negative—work) _didn't work_₇ with their hands. Their purpose in America (be) _____was_____₈ to hunt for gold and to start a small colony for England. Unfortunately, there (negative—be) _____wasn't_____₉ any gold. Winter (come) _____came_____₁₀ and there (negative—be) _____wasn't_____₁₁ enough food for the colonists. Many men (get) _____got_____₁₂ sick. By the end of the first winter, only 40 men (be) _____were_____₁₃ still alive.

The first few years of the colony (be) _____were_____₁₄ very difficult. Disease, starvation, and Native Americans (kill) _____killed_____₁₅ most of the settlers. Eventually, the colonists (learn) _____learned_____₁₆ more about farming and the weather. They (make) _____made_____₁₇ peace with the Native Americans. Tobacco (be) _____was_____₁₈ the business of the new colony. Gradually more and more settlers (arrive) _____arrived_____₁₉, and many small towns (grow) _____grew_____₂₀ along the river.

B **Read the answers.** Then, complete the questions.

1. When _did the ships leave for America_? In 1607.

2. How long _was the journey_? Four months.

3. _Did the men work with their hands_? No, they didn't. They were gentlemen.

4. Where _did the men choose an area to live_? On the James River.

5. What _did the men want to find / hunt for_? Gold.

6. How many men _survived the first winter_? Only 40.

7. How _were the first years_? Very difficult.

8. Why _did many men die_? Because of disease, starvation, and attacks by the Native Americans.

9. How _did they make money_? They grew and sold tobacco.

More Action!

For further practice, ask students to make up past tense questions similar to those in Exercise B. Students should base their questions on the information about Benjamin Franklin on pages 26 and 27. For example:
1. How long _____?
   Two years.
2. What _____?
   A printing shop.
(1. How long <u>did he attend school</u>?
2. What <u>kind of business did he open</u>?)
Have students exchange papers with a partner and complete the questions. Then, have them return the papers and check each other's work.

A Read. Then, write each sentence under the correct picture.

Making a class presentation takes a lot of practice. Here are some hints for making a good presentation.

- Use note cards or an outline. Don't read your presentation.
- Make eye contact with the audience.
- Smile and greet your audience.
- Practice your presentation.
- Thank your audience.
- Use visuals.

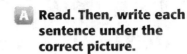

WORD PARTNERSHIPS	
give	
listen to	a presentation
practice	

1.

Smile and greet your audience.

2.

Make eye contact with the audience.

3.

Use visuals.

4.

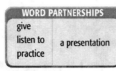

Use note cards or an outline. Don't read your presentation.

5.

Thank your audience.

6.

Practice your presentation.

B Prepare a presentation for your class. Use the information from your composition in Exercise D on page 31. Use visuals and notes or an outline.

English in Action: Making a Class Presentation

A Read. Then, write each sentence under the correct picture.

- Go over the points in the note box. Make sure students understand each one. Ask them why each one is important.
- Have students think about the points they already do well and those that they think they need to work on. Ask for volunteers to share this information.
- After reading the points, do the exercise as a class or have students complete it individually.

B Prepare a presentation for your class. Use the information from your composition in Exercise D on page 31. Use visuals and notes or an outline.

- Allow class time for students to work on their presentations, or allow students to complete their presentations as homework. Provide assistance as needed. If possible, meet for a few minutes with each student to ensure that everyone is on track with his or her presentation.
- Set aside one class for students to do their presentations, or schedule a few presentations every day for a week or two, as time permits.

Changing Lifestyles

Changing Lifestyles

 A **Listen. Write the number of each statement under the correct picture.**

(CD1 • TR9)

• Have students look at the pictures to familiarize themselves with the names they are going to hear. Play the audio for the first and second items and ask for a volunteer to supply the answers. (Students should identify Hugo from Item 3 as the first speaker they hear. They should identify Dan in Item 7 as the second speaker they hear.) Check for understanding.

• Then, play the audio and have the students complete the exercise. Play it again if they need more time to complete it and to check their answers.

 A **Listen.** Write the number of each statement under the correct picture.

CD1•TR9

1.
Kelly ___9___

2.
Sabrina ___6___

3.
Hugo ___1___

4.
James and Carla ___7___

5.
Laura ___5___

6.
Ahmed ___3___

7.
Dan ___2___

8.
Amy and Tom ___4___

9.
Sofia ___8___

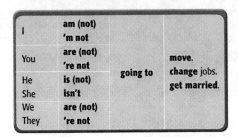

Active Grammar

Future with *Be Going To*: Statements

I	am (not) 'm not			
You	are (not) 're not		move.	
He	is (not)	going to	change jobs.	
She	isn't		get married.	
We	are (not)			
They	're not			

> Use *be going to* to talk about future plans.

 A **Listen.** Complete the sentences. Some of the sentences are negative.

CD1·TR10

1. Julie and Ellie _are not / aren't going to go_ away to college.

2. Julie and Ellie _____are going to go_____ to the community college.

3. Julie _is not / isn't going to study_ education like her mother did.

4. She _____is going to study_____ engineering and architecture.

5. Ellie _____is going to talk to_____ a counselor on Monday.

6. Julie _is not / isn't going to study_ full time.

7. She _____is going to work_____ at a department store, and
   she _____is going to take_____ classes at night.

8. They _are not / aren't going to have_ the same schedules.

9. Ellie _is not / isn't going to take_ classes at night because
   she _____is going to work_____ at her father's restaurant.

 B **Look at the pictures on page 34.** With a partner, discuss how each person's life is going to change.

> Kelly is going to look for an apartment.

> Kelly is going to get a job.

Changing Lifestyles · **35**

Active Grammar: Future with *Be Going To*— Statements

 A **Listen. Complete the sentences. Some of the sentences are negative.**
(CD1 • TR10)

• Go over the information in the grammar chart and the note box at the top of the page.

• Have students answer the questions individually, and then check their answers with a partner. Review the correct answers with the whole class.

• Then, play the audio and have the students complete the exercise. Play it again if they need more time to complete it or to check their answers.

B **Look at the pictures on page 34. With a partner, discuss how each person's life is going to change.**

• In pairs, students discuss the changes that will occur in each person's life. Suggest that students spend no more than one minute on each person. Every minute, announce the time and the illustration that students should be working on.

• Call on several pairs to tell the class their ideas about how life will change for each person shown. When correcting students, focus on the correct use and pronunciation of the future with *be going to*.

Active Grammar: Future with *Be Going To*— Questions

  A **Working Together Find someone who . . . Walk around the classroom and ask your classmates questions about their future plans. Use *be going to*. When someone answers "Yes, I am," write his / her name on the line. If someone answers "No, I'm not," ask another classmate.**

• Go over the directions and check that the students understand the task. Model the first question and call on student volunteers to answer the question.

• Set a time limit (about ten minutes) for students to complete the activity.

• Have students complete the exercise. Invite volunteers to present one or two of their questions and answers to the class. Correct any errors.

B **Talk about your weekend plans. Use the words from the box or your own ideas. Your partner will ask you questions about your plans.**

• Read the instructions and answer any questions about how to do the exercise. Brainstorm additional ideas.

• Ask a pair of students to model the conversation in the speech bubbles aloud for the class.

• Have students complete the exercise with their partner. Consider pairing higher-level students with lower-level ones.

36 · Unit 3

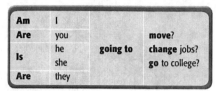 Active Grammar

Am	I		
Are	you		move?
Is	he	going to	change jobs?
	she		go to college?
Are	they		

What **are** you **going to** do?
Where **are** you **going to** move?
How **are** they **going to** get there?
Who **are** you **going to** visit?
Who **is going to** help?

 A **Working Together** **Find someone who . . .** Walk around the classroom and ask your classmates questions about their future plans. Use *be going to*. When someone answers "Yes, I am," write his / her name on the line. If someone answers "No, I'm not," ask another classmate.

1. get married? _____ Are you going to get married?

2. move? _____ Are you going to move?

3. visit your native country? _____ Are you going to visit your native country?

4. buy a house? _____ Are you going to buy a house?

5. attend a wedding? _____ Are you going to attend a wedding?

6. have a party? _____ Are you going to have a party?

7. look for a new job? _____ Are you going to look for a new job?

8. eat out? _____ Are you going to eat out?

 B **Talk about your weekend plans.** Use the words from the box or your own ideas. Your partner will ask you questions about your plans.

see a movie	visit a friend	clean
go to a party	work	go shopping
go dancing	play (a sport)	go to (a place)

My family and I are going to go to a wedding.

Who's going to get married?
Where's the wedding going to be?
What are you going to wear?

36 · Unit 3

More Action!

For additional oral practice, ask students to tell the rest of the class some of the things they learned about their classmates. For example: *Ali is going to get married next month.* Then, encourage students to tell other things they are going to do in the near future.

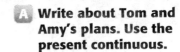

If a specific time in the future is stated or clear, the present continuous can express future time.

I'm working tomorrow.
He **is leaving** at 4:00.

Tom and Amy are getting a divorce.

A Write about Tom and Amy's plans. Use the present continuous.

1. Tom / pack / tonight _Tom is packing tonight._

2. He / hire / not / movers _He is not / isn't hiring movers._

3. Tom's friend / help / him / this weekend _Tom's friend is helping him this weekend._

4. Amy and the children / remain / in the house _Amy and the children are remaining in the house._

5. Tom / buy / not / a new place _Tom is not / isn't buying a new place._

6. He / rent / a two-bedroom condo _He is / 's renting a two-bedroom condo._

7. Amy / meet with / a job counselor / Monday _Amy is meeting with a job counselor on Monday._

8. They / meet with / their lawyers / next week _They are / 're meeting with their lawyers next week._

 B Listen and (circle) the meaning.

CD1·TR11

1. (Now)	Future	4. (Now)	Future	7. Now	(Future)
2. Now	(Future)	5. Now	(Future)	8. Now	(Future)
3. Now	(Future)	6. (Now)	Future	9. (Now)	Future

Changing Lifestyles · **37**

Active Grammar: Present Continuous with Future Meaning

A **Write about Tom and Amy's plans. Use the present continuous.**

• Review the explanation of the present continuous with future meaning in the box. Then, give several examples of pairs of sentences that mean the same thing even though one uses *is going to* and the other uses the present continuous. For example: *I am going to have lunch at 12:00 today. / I'm having lunch at 12:00 today.* Ask students to make up similar pairs of sentences.

• Have students do the exercise. Point out that the negative sentences can be written with and without contractions.

• Call on different students to say one of the exercise sentences. Invite the class to listen for and correct any errors.

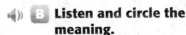 **B** **Listen and circle the meaning.**
(CD1 •TR11)

• Go over the instructions. Play the audio for the first item and complete it with the class.

• Play the audio again and have students complete the exercise.

• Play it again, so students can complete the exercise or check their answers.

Changing Lifestyles · **37**

Active Grammar: *Will* for Promises and Offers

  A Pronunciation: '*ll* Listen and repeat.

(CD1 • TR12)

• Go over the information in the boxes. Provide or elicit additional examples, focusing on offers to help or a promise.

• Go over the exercise instructions. Play the audio and have students repeat.

  B Offer to help your classmate. Use the expressions in the box.

• Have students read the instructions. Review the expressions in the box at the right to make sure students know what all of them mean. Then, have two students role-play the problem and offer of help in the sample answer.

• Call on different students to read each problem aloud. Have the reader choose another student to make the offer of help. After the offer is made, invite other students to confirm if the answer is right, or to offer a different answer.

I		
You		
He	**will**	do it.
She	**'ll**	
We		
They		

Use *will* to make an offer to help or a promise. It is common to use the contraction *'ll*.

I'll help you.

 A Pronunciation: '*ll* Listen and repeat.

CD1 • TR12

1. I'll do it.   **4.** I'll help him.   **7.** She'll do it.

2. I'll get it.   **5.** I'll be there.   **8.** He'll answer it.

3. I'll call you.   **6.** They'll paint it.   **9.** We'll help you.

 B Offer to help your classmate. Use the expressions in the box.

I don't understand this homework.   I'll help you.

1. My car broke down and I don't have a ride to school.
I'll *give you a ride.*

2. I can't find my keys.
I'll *help you look for them.*

3. I don't know how to use my new DVD player.
I'll *show you how.*

4. I just moved in, and I don't know anyone around here.
I'll *introduce you.*

5. I don't know how to get to the mall.
I'll *give you directions.*

6. I wrote this report, but I need someone to read it over for me.
I'll *read it.*

7. I received a letter in English, but I don't understand it.
I'll *translate it.*

8. My car has a flat tire.
I'll *change it.*

9. My income taxes are due next week, but I don't know how to fill out the form.
I'll *explain it.*

explain it
introduce you
give you a ride
help you look
read it
show you how
give you directions
change it
translate it

38 • Unit 3

Teaching Tip

Have students rewrite each sentence in Exercise A. Students should replace the contraction and write out the full form of the word. For example, for Item 1: *I will do it.*

Use *will* to make a prediction about the future.
The United States **will make** new immigration laws.
There **will be** more electric cars.

 A **Working Together** Make predictions about the United States and your native country. Use *will*. Then, read your predictions to the class. *(Answers will vary.)*

1. The economy in the U.S. _____ .

2. The economy in _____ .
native country

3. The population in the U.S. _____ .

4. The population in _____ .
native country

5. There will be more _____ in ten years.

6. There will be less _____ in ten years.

7. _____ .

B Write three predictions about your future. *(Answers will vary.)*

1. I will _____ .

2. I will _____ .

3. I will not _____ .

C **Dictation** Your teacher will dictate the sentences on page 263. Listen and write the sentences you hear.

1. We'll have better jobs after we learn English.

2. She'll help you with the party.

3. He won't need to work next semester.

4. The environment will be cleaner.

5. You'll need to prepare for the final exam.

6. Cars will be more efficient.

7. I'll help you after class.

Changing Lifestyles · **39**

Active Grammar: *Will* for Predictions

 A **Working Together Make predictions about the United States and your native country. Use *will*. Then, read your predictions to the class.**

• Go over the information in the grammar box. Provide or elicit more examples.

• Have students complete the exercise individually. Then, have them share their responses with a small group and practice giving a reason for each choice. Provide an example for the first item to get things started.

B **Write three predictions about your future.**

Ask students to complete the exercise. To help them, first make a list of the changes that will take place in their own lives and the verbs they will use to describe them.

C **Dictation Your teacher will dictate the sentences on page 263. Listen and write the sentences you hear.**

• Turn to page 263 and dictate the sentences one at a time, allowing enough time for students to write.

• Dictate the sentences a second time, so students can complete any sentences they didn't finish and check their work.

• Dictate the sentences a third time. Have them focus on spelling, capitalization, and punctuation.

More Action!

Go over the answers to Exercise A as a class and have students debate their choices. Call on different students to read their predictions and give their reasons. After each prediction, invite a student who feels the opposite (or differently) to give his or her reasons for feeling differently.

More Action!

Have students rehearse their statements from Exercise B with a partner. Then, call on different students to read their predictions.

Teaching Tip

For more oral practice, call on students to read the sentences from Exercise C aloud. Be sure to call on students that need the most practice or who are shy and don't tend to speak much in class.

Changing Lifestyles · **39**

Active Grammar: Future Time Clauses

A Match the two parts of each sentence about a college student's plans.

• Go over the grammar box at the top of the page. Have a student read aloud the four sentences from the box.

• Point out that there are two pairs of sentences in this box (Pair 1: first and third sentence; Pair 2: second and fourth sentence). Ask: *What is the difference in meaning between the sentences in Pair 1? In Pair 2?* (There is no difference in meaning.) *How is the comma used in future time clauses?* (When the *if, when,* or *after* clause comes at the beginning of the sentence, it is followed by a comma. If the main clause comes first, no comma is used.)

• Have students do this exercise in pairs or in small groups. Check the answers with the whole class.

B Complete the sentences about Sonia's future. Use your imagination.

• Tell students to use their own ideas and continue to write about Sonia's future.

• Encourage students to come up with unusual predictions. For example: *Before Sonia gets married, she will sail around the world.*

• Have students take turns reading their answers to the class.

40 · Unit 3

| If I **study** hard, I'll graduate in two years. |
| (time clause)   (main clause) |
| When I **have** time, I'm going to finish my degree. |
| (time clause)   (main clause) |
| I'll graduate in two years <u>if I study hard.</u> |
| (main clause)   (time clause) |
| I'm going to finish my degree <u>when I have time</u>. |
| (main clause)   (time clause) |

1. A time clause begins with time words such as *after, before, when,* and *if.*
2. Use a comma when the time clause is at the beginning of a sentence. Do **not** use a comma when the time clause is at the end of a sentence.

A Match the two parts of each sentence about a college student's plans.

<u>b</u> **1.** If Sonia works hard,   **a.** she'll buy a new car.

<u>d</u> **2.** When Sonia takes a vacation,   **b.** she'll get a promotion.

<u>a</u> **3.** After Sonia saves some money,   **c.** she'll accept the best offer.

<u>e</u> **4.** If Sonia meets the right person,   **d.** she'll travel around Europe.

<u>c</u> **5.** After Sonia interviews for several jobs,   **e.** she'll get married.

B Complete the sentences about Sonia's future. Use your imagination.

(Answers will vary.)

1. Before Sonia gets married, _____.

2. _____ when she has children.

3. If she decides to become a stay-at-home mom, _____.

4. _____ after her children are grown.

5. If Sonia decides to change careers, _____.

6. When Sonia has enough money, _____.

7. _____ when she retires.

8. _____.

9. _____.

40 · Unit 3

C Ask and answer the questions. Use a future time clause with *before, after, if,* or *when*.

> When are you going to get married?

> I'm going to get married after I graduate from college.

1. When are you going to travel out of the country?

2. When are you going to buy a new car?

3. When are you going to move into a bigger place?

4. When are you going to pay your utility bills?

5. When are you going to take a day off?

6. When are you going to become a U.S. citizen?

7. When are you going to leave this classroom?

D Working Together **Number the events in George's life in order from 1 to 8.** Then, make sentences about his life. Use *before, after,* and *when*. (Answers will vary.)

> Before George finds a job, he's going to graduate from college.

> He's going to get married when he meets the right woman.

find a job

buy a house

get married

graduate from college

have a daughter

have a son

meet a wonderful woman

save a lot of money

Changing Lifestyles · 41

C **Ask and answer the questions. Use a future time clause with *before, after, if,* or *when*.**

• Have students take turns asking and answering the questions in pairs. Encourage them to use each of the words (*before, after, if, when*) to form their time clauses.

• When they finish, invite several pairs to present one or two of their questions and answers to the class.

D **Working Together Number the events in George's life in order from 1 to 8. Then, make sentences about his life. Use *before, after,* and *when*.**

• Review the instructions and sample dialogue. Then, have students sit in pairs and number the pictures in the order they think the events happen. (Students may come up with several different sequences of events that are reasonable.)

• Students work in pairs and describe the events in George's life. Encourage students to speak about the sequence using *before, after,* and *when*.

More Action!

Play a game in which students make up events about a fictitious student at their school. You might choose a name, such as Nilda. One student makes a future tense statement about something Nilda is going to do. For example: *Nilda is going to get a new job next year.* The next student makes a related statement containing a future time clause. For example: *After Nilda gets a new job, she is going to move to a bigger apartment.* Play continues until students run out of ideas.

The Big Picture: After the Baby Comes

A Discuss. Laura and her husband are expecting their first child. How do you think their lives are going to change?

• Go over the information in the Word Partnerships box. Provide sentences showing these words in context.

• Point out the illustration of Laura and her friend. As a class, discuss changes that Laura and her husband will have to make after the baby is born. Encourage students to use their imagination and to make sentences with future time clauses. For example: *When the baby is born, Laura is going to be a stay-at-home mom. Laura's husband is going to take paternity leave after the baby is born.*

 B Listen. Circle the changes that Laura and Brady are going to make.

(CD1 • TR13)

• Play the audio and have students circle the changes they hear.
• Play the audio a second time, so students can check their answers.
• Go over the answers orally and clear up any misunderstandings.

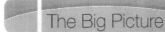

A Discuss. Laura and her husband are expecting their first child. How do you think their lives are going to change?

WORD PARTNERSHIPS	
maternity	
paternity	leave
family	
stay-at-home	dad
	mom

 B Listen. Circle the changes that Laura and Brady are going to make.

CD1·TR13

buy a house	change a schedule	get a cat
find a bigger apartment	go out three nights a week	give away their cats
move	stay home	take some time off
change jobs	take a class	

More Action!

Lead a class discussion on the changes that Laura and Brady are going to make. What other changes should Laura and Brady make? Do students agree or disagree that all of the changes are necessary?

C Listen again and (circle) *True* or *False*.

1. They're still looking for a house.	True	(False)
2. They like their building.	(True)	False
3. They're going to move soon.	(True)	False
4. All of the houses that they looked at needed work.	(True)	False
5. Their building is far from Laura's work.	True	(False)
6. She's going to take off two weeks from work.	True	(False)
7. Laura and Brady are going to go out less often.	(True)	False

D Match.

_d_ **1.** If they like the bigger apartment,

_b_ **2.** When the baby arrives,

_a_ **3.** They're going to do a lot of shopping

_f_ **4.** When Laura's maternity leave begins,

_e_ **5.** They're going to move

_c_ **6.** Laura will call Melissa

a. before the baby comes.

b. Laura's mother is going to help.

c. if she needs help.

d. they'll move next week.

e. after they find a bigger apartment.

f. she'll stay at home.

E Complete the sentences. Use the future, simple past, simple present, or present continuous. Some of the verbs are negative.

1. Laura (tell) _____told_____ her boss about her pregnancy.

2. Her company (give) _is going to give / will give / is giving_ her two months off.

3. When Laura's mother (find) _____found_____ out about the baby, she (decide) _____decided_____ to retire early.

4. Her mother (help) _is going to help / will help_ for a while.

5. They (want / not) _____don't want_____ to move out of their building.

6. They (get / not) _are not going to get / will not get / are not getting_ rid of their cats.

7. Laura and Brady (take) _____are taking_____ a class.

8. Brady (take / not) _is not going to take_ a lot of time off from work.

Changing Lifestyles · **43**

C Listen again and circle *True* or *False*.
(CD1 • TR13)

• Play the audio. Have students read the statements and decide if they are true or false.
• Play the audio again and have students check their answers.
• Go over the answers as a class. Correct any misunderstandings, playing the audio again if necessary.

D Match.

Have students complete the matching exercise on their own and review the answers with a partner. Circulate around the room verifying the correct answers as needed.

E Complete the sentences. Use the future, simple past, simple present, or present continuous. Some of the verbs are negative.

• Have students complete the exercise on their own. Point out that some of the items (Items 2, 4, and 6) could have more than one correct answer.
• Go over the answers as a class and provide all correct answers for Items 2, 4, and 6.

Reading: Empty Nesters

A Discuss.

• Go over the Reading Note. Point out that Exercise B will practice this skill.

• Read and discuss the questions with the whole class.

B Word Builder
Find the words in the reading. Then, write the definitions.

• Have students scan the reading looking for the six words in this exercise. Point out that the words are set in bold, so they will be easy to find. Remind them to use the tips in the Reading Note to find the definitions. Have them circle the definition in the reading first, and then write the definitions on the line.

• Circulate around the room and provide help as needed. Ask for volunteers to provide the answers.

C Read.

Ask students to read the text on their own either in class or for homework.

READING NOTE

Finding Vocabulary Definitions
Sometimes you can find the definitions of new vocabulary words in the reading. Look for a comma after the word and a different word or short phrase that gives the definition. You can also read the sentence before or after the new vocabulary word(s) to find a clue to the meaning.

This a big adjustment, or **change**, for the parents.

A Discuss.

1. Do you have any children? If so, how old are they?

2. At what age do you think children are ready to live on their own?

3. How do you think parents feel when their children move away from home?

B Word Builder Find the words in the reading. Then, write the definitions.

1. adjustment   _change_

2. syndrome   _lonely, depressed feeling_

3. trigger   _suddenly start_

4. majority   _most_

5. cope   _handle_

6. seek   _look for_

C Read.

    Parents whose children have recently left home are called "empty nesters." Their little birds, or children, have flown away to start independent lives. This is a big **adjustment**, or change, for the parents. The lonely, depressed feeling that parents have after a child becomes more independent is called "empty-nest **syndrome**."
    Different sights and sounds can **trigger** the condition. A parent may suddenly start to feel sad. One empty-nester mother said, "I drove past my son's soccer field the other day, and suddenly I started crying. Another time, I heard my son's cell phone ring tone at the mall, and I became very emotional."

Teaching Tip

To further clarify the meaning of the vocabulary items from Exercise B and to provide practice using them in everyday situations, ask volunteers to make up original sentences with each vocabulary word. Correct errors and awkward usages by rewording student sentences. Have students write particularly useful sentences in their notebooks.

Although mothers still take care of the **majority** of childcare responsibilities, fathers also feel unexpected sadness. In general, fathers do not spend most of their time taking care of their children, so fathers do not expect to experience this feeling of loss. One father reported that he had to pull over to the side of the road after he heard his daughter's favorite song on the radio. "I never thought I would miss her so much," he said.

Children do not have to move out of the house for parents to experience empty-nest feelings. When children enter high school, they start going out on weekends, playing sports, and doing other activities with friends. Some parents report that they only see their children at breakfast or on their way out of the house. Parents miss the closeness that they used to have with their children when they were younger. They find it difficult to **cope** with the independence of their children. Parents must learn how to handle their feelings.

When parents do not recover from their sad feelings after a few months, they may want to **seek** professional help. In addition, they may look for assistance online, such as support groups, to help them through this difficult time.

There are many suggestions on how to recover from empty-nest syndrome. This is a good time for parents to remember the things that they wanted to do after the children grew up. Maybe they would like to travel or take some courses. Maybe they wanted to start a business; now they have the time. Cell phones and online chats also help parents to keep in touch with their children. Fortunately, empty-nest syndrome passes with time. Empty nesters should keep busy, renew old friendships, and take time for themselves.

D (Circle) *True* or *False*.

1. Empty-nest syndrome is a problem for college students.   True   (False)

2. Only sights can trigger a parent to feel sad.   True   (False)

3. Both mothers and fathers can experience this syndrome.   (True)   False

4. One parent became upset after she heard her son's voice.   True   (False)

5. Parents with high school age children can also be empty nesters.   (True)   False

6. High school children always spend a lot of time with their parents.   True   (False)

7. There is professional help for empty nesters.   (True)   False

8. One way to recover from empty-nest syndrome is to keep busy.   (True)   False

 E In your own words, write a definition of empty-nest syndrome.
(Answers will vary.)

_____

_____

_____

D **Circle *True* or *False*.**

Have students complete the exercise individually, and then check their answers with a partner. Circulate around the room to verify that students know the correct answer, or check answers as a class.

 E **In your own words, write a definition of empty-nest syndrome.**

Have students complete the exercise on their own. Elicit definitions and write them on the board. Encourage students to add to the definition or revise it.

More Action!

Invite students to make up questions about the reading as a way to summarize the main points of the reading. Choose a few volunteers to answer the questions for the class.

More Action!

Elicit ideas for the best title for this story. Discuss the pros and cons of the title ideas. Decide on a title as a class.

Writing Our Stories: My Goals for English

 Read.

- Ask students to read the text on their own. Then, have them ask a partner for help if there is anything they don't understand or isn't clear.

- Ask the pairs to tell you which words or phrases caused problems. Write them on the board and discuss with the class.

 Underline the transitions in the composition above.

- Go over the information in the Writing Note on transition words.

- Find the first transition word in the reading together. Then, have students complete the exercise on their own. Correct the answers with the whole class.

 Read.

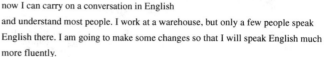

Carlos Garcia

English IV

My Goals for English

I am an ESL student at Union County College. I came from Cuba three years ago. When I first came here, I did not speak any English, but now I can carry on a conversation in English and understand most people. I work at a warehouse, but only a few people speak English there. I am going to make some changes so that I will speak English much more fluently.

First of all, I'm going to continue my English classes. I think I will be able to speak English much better in about two years. After this semester ends, I am going to look for a job where I can use more English. When I find one, I am going to ask my co-workers to correct my English. Next, I think I will register for a pronunciation class because many people do not understand me the first time I say something. Then, I am going to try to find a study partner who speaks a different language. Finally, I am going to start shopping at stores where I will have to speak English. If I do these things, I think my English will improve.

WRITING NOTE

Transition Words

Use **transition** words to explain how to do something or to show what comes first, second, and so on. Use a comma after a transition when it begins a sentence. Here are some transition words and phrases:

First,   First of all,   Second,   Third,   Fourth,   Next,
Then,   After that,   After I . . . ,   Finally,   Last,

Underline the transitions in the composition above.

C Number the sentences in the correct order.

   _2_ I'm going to look at the schedule of classes.

   _1_ I'm going to look for a good nursing program.

   _6_ I'm going to do the homework.

   _3_ I'm going to register for classes.

   _4_ I'm going to buy the books.

   _5_ I'm going to go to my first class.

D In your notebook, write the sentences from Exercise C in order in a paragraph. Use transitions.

E Write a composition about your goals for improving your English. Answer these questions in your composition. Use transitions.

   1. Where do you study English?

   2. What country are you from, and when did you come to the United States?

   3. Which skills do you need to improve: reading, writing, grammar, listening, or speaking?

   4. How are you going to improve your English?

F Sharing Our Stories Read your partner's composition. What are your partner's goals for learning English? Underline the transitions.

G Find and correct the verb mistakes.
   1. In ten years, there ~~are~~ *will be* many more hybrid cars.
   2. Before I quit this job, I *am* ‸going to find a new one.
   3. He's going to stay home with his children if he ~~will lose~~ *loses* his job.
   4. Is she going to go to college when she ~~leave~~ *leaves* the military?
   5. I ~~take~~ *am going to take / 'm going to take / 'm taking* the citizenship test tomorrow at 4:00.
   6. ~~I~~ *I'll* pick it up for you.
   7. Where ‸*are* they ~~are~~ going to live?
   8. They need a bigger apartment if they *'re going to / 'll / will* ‸have another child.

Changing Lifestyles • **47**

Teaching Tip

In Exercise F, consider pairing lower-level students with higher-level ones. Lower-level students can benefit from the language skills of the higher-level students, while the higher-level students can provide additional vocabulary and correct word usage.

C Number the sentences in the correct order.

Have students complete the exercise. Correct answers as a class.

D In your notebook, write the sentences from Exercise C in order in a paragraph.

Point out the list of transitions on page 46 that students can use to complete this exercise. Encourage them to use a variety of transitions.

E Write a composition about your goals for improving your English. Answer these questions in your composition.

• Suggest that students use the story on page 46 as a model for this assignment. Remind them to use transitions, pointing out the list on page 46.
• Have them write the composition as homework or during class.

F Sharing Our Stories Read your partner's composition. Underline the transitions.

Divide the class into pairs.

G Find and correct the verb mistakes.

• Go over the first item.
• Tell students to review the grammar points in the unit.
• Go over the answers as a class. Call on volunteers to supply the corrections.

Practicing on Your Own

A **Complete the conversations with an offer to help or a promise. Use *will*.**

• Point out that this is a review exercise to practice *will*, and that answers will vary.
• Have students do the exercise on their own, and then elicit answers. Accept any answers that use *will* correctly. Encourage students to use contractions.

B **Combine the sentences. Use the word in parentheses and a future time clause.**

• Explain how sentence combining works. Complete Item 1 as a model with the class.
• Point out that usually only one of the verbs in a sentence with a future time clause is in the future tense.
• Have students complete the exercise individually. Call on different volunteers to write one corrected sentence on the board. Review these sentences as a class, and decide if they are correctly rewritten.

A **Complete the conversations with an offer to help or a promise.** Use *will*.

1. Child: Dad, I'm sorry. I broke the window when I was playing baseball.
   Father: _Don't worry. I'll fix it. (Answers will vary.)_

2. Wife: I'm tired tonight. I don't feel like making dinner.
   Husband: _Don't worry. I'll make it. (Answers will vary.)_

3. Father: You can use the car, but make sure you fill up the gas tank.
   Son: _I'll fill it up. (Answers will vary.)_

4. Daughter: I have to be at school tomorrow morning at 7:00.
   Mother: _I'll drive you. / I'll give you a ride. (Answers will vary.)_

5. Son: Mom, my uniform is dirty, and we have a baseball game tomorrow.
   Mother: _I'll wash it. (Answers will vary.)_

6. Son: Dad, my driving test is next week. Can you take me out to practice?
   Father: _I'll take you. (Answers will vary.)_

B **Combine the sentences.** Use the word in parentheses and a future time clause.

1. I'm going to get married. I'm going to meet the right person. (when)
   I'm going to get married when I meet the right person.
2. They're going to get married. They are going to have separate bank accounts. (after)
   After they get married, they're going to have separate bank accounts.
3. The husband is going to cook dinner. His wife is going to feel tired. (when)
   The husband is going to cook dinner when his wife feels tired.
4. His wife is going to cut the lawn. He is going to be busy. (if)
   His wife is going to cut the lawn if he is busy.
5. They are going to have an argument. Their whole family isn't going to know about it. (when)
   When they have an argument, their whole family isn't going to know about it.
6. My mother will only stay for a week. My mother will come for a visit. (when)
   My mother will only stay for a week when she comes for a visit.
7. She is still going to laugh. Her husband is going to tell the same joke twice. (if)
   She is still going to laugh if her husband tells the same joke twice.
8. They are going to have a son. They are going to name him after his father. (if)
   If they have a son, they're going to name him after his father.

 A **Match each person or couple with the home you think is best for them.**
More than one answer is possible. Compare your answers with a partner.

(Answers will vary.)

1.

We have a one-bedroom apartment. We are expecting another child soon, so we need a bigger place. We would like to buy a house with a yard and a garage.
Home _____

2.

Our children are grown, and our house is too big. We don't need four bedrooms, and we definitely don't need such a big yard. We want something smaller.
Home _____

3.

I have a full-time job, and I'm ready to buy a home. I'm excited about getting my own place, but I don't need a big place. I'd like a one-bedroom apartment with parking.
Home _____

a.

$239,000, 3 BDRM, 2½ baths; gas heat; frpl.; attached garage; built 1950s; nr parks, schools

b.

$249,000, 2 BDRM, 2 full baths, central A/C, gas heat, pool, prkg, tennis, nr schools/shops/trans

c.

$199,999, 1 BDRM, 1 bath, central A/C, gas heat, exercise room, pool, 24 hr doorman, nr shops/trans; built 70s

d.

$229,000, 2 BDRM, 2 baths, wall A/C; oil heat; nr shopping; built 80s

 B **Go online.** Search for houses and apartments in your area. Multiple Listing Service (mls.com) lists many homes for sale and rent. Choose a home that you think would be good for you. Discuss your choice with your classmates.

More Action!

Make a class chart that shows the results of the home choices students made. Have a volunteer record the information on the board. Poll students to see how many students chose houses, apartments, condominiums, and so on. Also, poll students on the number of bedrooms in their house. Call on students to make statements about the class's choices, using the information from the board. Remind students to use the future tense where possible. For example: *Five people are going to live in a two-bedroom house.*

Teaching Tip

If Internet access is not easily accessible for all students for Exercise B, print out a small assortment of house and apartment listings from an online source and bring them to class. Then, pass them out to students and have them complete the exercise in class.

English in Action: Finding a New Home

 A **Match each person or couple with the home you think is best for them. More than one answer is possible. Compare your answers with a partner.**

• Go over the instructions. Have students write the letter of the home in the right column on the appropriate line in the left column.
• Circulate around the room while pairs complete the exercise. Help with any unfamiliar abbreviations as needed, such as "Nr" (= "near").

B **Go online. Search for houses and apartments in your area. Multiple Listing Service (mls.com) lists many homes for sale and rent. Choose a home that you think would be good for you. Discuss your choice with your classmates.**

• If you have a computer lab with Internet access in your school, bring students to it, so they can complete this exercise.
• Have students work in small groups and discuss their choices. Go around the room and make sure everyone participates. Ask groups to point out any similarities or differences between their housing choices.

Driving

A Match each traffic rule with the correct sign.

• Point out the twelve lettered descriptions at the top of the page. Read each one aloud, and call on different students to restate the descriptions in their own words. For example:

T: *a. You must not ride bikes here.*

S1: *People aren't allowed to ride a bicycle in this place.*

T: *b. Trucks must not use this road.*

S2: *You can drive a car on this road, but not a truck.*

• Ask students to match the signs and rules individually and then check their answers with a partner. Then, check the answers with the whole class, and explain any signs that students still don't understand.

A Match each traffic rule with the correct sign.

a. You must not ride bikes here.

b. Trucks must not use this road.

c. You must not turn left.

d. You must stop for pedestrians.

e. You must not park here or you will be towed.

f. You must stay to the right.

g. You must look out for deer.

h. You must slow down. This is a school zone.

i. You must not park here.

j. You must slow down. The road is slippery when wet.

k. You must slow down and be prepared to stop. Construction ahead.

l. You must turn right. One-way street.

1. _f_

2. _i_

3. _a_

4. _l_

5. _g_

6. _d_

7. _e_

8. _c_

9. _k_

10. _h_

11. _b_

12. _j_

Modals: *Must / Must not*

I You	**must**	**stop** at a red light. **drive** at the speed limit.
He Drivers	**must not**	**drive** without a license.

Must shows rules, obligation, or necessity.
You **must stop** at a stop sign.
Must not shows that an action is not permitted.
Drivers **must** *not* **drive** through a red light.

A **Use each sentence to state a traffic law.** Use *must* or *must not*.

1. Stop at a stop sign.
   You must stop at a stop sign.
2. Don't pass cars on the right.
   You must not pass cars on the right.
3. Pay traffic fines.
   You must pay traffic fines.
4. Don't drink alcohol and drive.
   You must not drink alcohol and drive.
5. Register your car.
   You must register your car.
6. Don't drive over the speed limit.
   You must not drive over the speed limit.
7. Wear your seat belt.
   You must wear your seat belt.
8. Stop for a school bus with flashing lights.
   You must stop for a school bus with flashing lights.
9. Don't drive without a license.
   You must not drive without a license.

> You must stop at a stop sign.

> You must not pass cars on the right.

B **Read each school rule.** Check (✓) *Yes* or *No* about your school. *(Answers will vary.)*

School Rules	Yes	No
1. We must arrive on time.		
2. We must call or e-mail our teacher if we are absent.		
3. We must wear uniforms.		
4. We must speak English all the time.		
5. We must not copy from other students.		
6. We must not eat in class.		

C **In your notebook, write three more rules about your school or class.**

(Answers will vary.)

Driving · **51**

Active Grammar: Modals— *Must / Must not*

A **Use each sentence to state a traffic law. Use *must* or *must not*.**

• Review the grammar box and the sample sentences with the class. Ask students to give examples of the correct use of *must* and *must not*.
• Do the exercise with the whole class. Answer any questions.

B **Read each school rule. Check *Yes* or *No* about your school.**

Have students complete the exercise, and then check their answers with a partner. Review the answers with the whole class.

C **In your notebook, write three more rules about your school or class.**

Have students write three more rules about their school on their own. Review their responses orally with the whole class.

Teaching Tip

To provide further practice for *must* and *must not*, give students a quick oral review. Have them close their books. In random order, read aloud the sentences in Exercise A and call on different students to state the traffic law using *must* or *must not*.

More Action!

Have several volunteers write one of their sentences from Exercise C on the board. Ask other students to practice reading the rules on the board to a partner.

Active Grammar: *Have to / Doesn't have to / Don't have to*

A **Complete the sentences. Use *have to* or *has to* and an appropriate verb.**

• Review the grammar box and the sample sentences with the class. Ask students to give examples of the correct use of *have to* and *has to*.
• Do the exercise with the whole class. Point out the use of *has to* with *he* and *she*. Answer any questions.

B **Restate each sentence. Use *doesn't have to* or *don't have to*.**

• Go over the model / sample answer for Item 1 in the speech bubble.
• Have students take turns restating the sentences to a partner. Then, call on different students to restate one sentence each. Correct as needed.

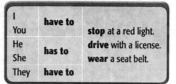

I	have to	
You	have to	stop at a red light.
He	has to	drive with a license.
She	has to	wear a seat belt.
They	have to	

> *Have to* shows necessity or obligation.
> **I have to get** car insurance.
> She **has to babysit** her niece.

A **Complete the sentences.** Use *have to* or *has to* and an appropriate verb.

1. She ___has to move___ her car.
2. She ___has to pay___ for the ticket.
3. He ___has to change___ the tires.
4. He ___has to buy / get___ new tires.
5. They ___have to sell___ their sports car.
6. They ___have to buy / get___ a car seat for their baby.

I	do not have to	
You	don't have to	buy a new car.
She	does not have to	work today.
She	doesn't have to	go to school today.
They	do not have to	
They	don't have to	

> *Doesn't have to / Don't have to* show that something is not necessary.
> You **don't have to own** a car.

B **Restate each sentence.** Use *doesn't have to* or *don't have to*.

1. It's not necessary for a new driver to buy a new car.
   A new driver doesn't have to buy a new car.
2. It's not necessary for you to have a radio in your car.
   You don't have to have a radio in your car.
3. It's not necessary for new drivers to have jobs.
   New drivers don't have to have jobs.
4. It's not necessary for a new learner to go to a driving school.
   A new learner doesn't have to go to a driving school.
5. It's not necessary for drivers to have cell phones.
   Drivers don't have to have cell phones.
6. It's not necessary for you to wash your car every day.
   You don't have to wash your car every day.

> A new driver doesn't have to buy a new car.

52 • Unit 4

C Complete the sentences. Use *must not* (prohibited) or *doesn't have to / don't have to* (not necessary).

1. Students ___don't have to___ buy food in the cafeteria because there are many restaurants nearby.

2. I ___must not___ copy from a classmate during a test.

3. I ___don't have to___ wear a suit or a dress to English class.

4. The instructor ___doesn't have to___ sell the books in class because there is a bookstore at the school.

5. A teacher ___doesn't have to___ wear a uniform at this school.

6. Students ___don't have to___ buy new computers for classes.

7. We ___must not___ use cell phones in the classroom.

8. Students ___must not___ copy essays from the Internet.

9. We ___must not___ bring drinks into the computer lab.

D Listen. Rebecca is talking about her schedule. Check (✓) the tasks that she has completed.

CD1·TR14

Tasks	Completed
1. buy stamps	✓
2. mail her bills	
3. do the laundry	
4. go to the supermarket	
5. make a deposit at the bank	✓
6. confirm an appointment	
7. put gas in her car	

E Ask and answer questions about Rebecca's to-do list. Use the information in Exercise D.

Do	I you		do laundry?
Does	he she	**have to**	**buy** stamps?
Do	they		**see** the dentist?

Does Rebecca have to buy stamps?

No, she doesn't. She bought some yesterday.

Driving · **53**

C Complete the sentences. Use *must not* (prohibited) or *doesn't have to / don't have to* (not necessary).

Have students complete the sentences individually. Then, go over the answers with the class. Explain or elicit the reason for each correct answer.

D Listen. Rebecca is talking about her schedule. Check the tasks that she has completed.
(CD1 • TR14)

• Play the audio the first time while students just listen. The second time, they can check the tasks Rebecca has completed. The third time through, have them check their answers.
• Review the correct answers orally with the class.

E Ask and answer questions about Rebecca's to-do list.

• Explain that the answers in this part of the activity are based on the audio students have just listened to. Play the audio again if students want an additional review before doing this part of the activity. Answer any questions about the audio they may have.
• Point out the grammar box and the sample question and answer in the speech bubbles. Then, have pairs practice asking and answering the questions about the tasks on Rebecca's to-do list.
• Review the answers with the class by having different pairs present one question and answer each.

Driving · **53**

Active Grammar: *Can / Can't*

  A Pronunciation: *Can* and *can't*
Listen. Marcus is talking about his driving experience. Complete the sentences with *can* or *can't*.
(CD1 • TR15)

• Review the explanation in the grammar note box and the sample sentences with the class. Ask students to give original examples of the correct use of *can* and *can't*.

• Play the audio once as students just listen. Answer any questions they may have. Then, play the audio once or twice more and have students complete the sentences. Then, have them check their answers with a partner. Review the correct answers with the whole class.

 B Working Together
Find someone who . . .
Walk around the room. Ask your classmates what they can do. If someone answers, "Yes, I can," write his / her name in the chart. If someone answers, "No, I can't," ask another person.

• Point out the grammar box showing how to form a question using *can*.

• Read the instructions and answer any questions about how to do the activity. Remind students to write only the student's name after each question, not a full-sentence answer.

• Set a time limit (eight to ten minutes) for students to complete the activity.

54 · Unit 4

 Active Grammar — *Can / Can't*

| I You She He They | can / can't | drive. park in this area. |

Can shows ability. *Can't* shows inability.
 I can drive a car.
 I can't drive a truck.
Can also shows that an action is permitted. *Can't / Cannot* shows that an action is *not* permitted.
 I can drive at night by myself.
 You can't drive through red lights.

 A Pronunciation: *Can* and *Can't* Listen. Marcus is talking about his driving experience. Complete the sentences with *can* or *can't*.

1. He ___can't___ drive very well.
2. He ___can___ drive only with a licensed driver in the car.
3. He ___can___ back up.
4. He ___can't___ parallel park.
5. He ___can___ drive on a busy highway.
6. He ___can't___ drive at night alone.
7. He ___can't___ drive with the radio playing.

 B Working Together Find someone who . . . Walk around the room. Ask your classmates what they can do. If someone answers, "Yes, I can," write his / her name in the chart. If someone answers, "No, I can't," ask another person. (Answers will vary.)

Question	Name
1. speak another language	
2. dance	
3. cook well	
4. bake a cake	
5. type fast	
6. swim	
7. play a musical instrument	

| Can | I you she they | drive a truck? swim? speak French? |

54 · Unit 4

Teaching Tip

Explain the differences in the pronunciation of *can* and *can't*. *The word* can *is usually shortened so that it sounds almost like* k ə n. *The word* can't *ends in the letter* t, *but you often cannot hear that* t *pronounced. When you hear the word* can't, *it may just sound like the letter* a *is held longer.* Demonstrate by repeating pairs of *can / can't* phrases several times, emphasizing the differences: *can go* (k ə n go), *can't go* (kaah go).

More Action!

Make a class chart showing the results of Exercise B. Appoint a scribe to write the results on the board or on a piece of poster paper. The scribe can mark down the students that speak another language, dance, and so on. Point out and elicit interesting things students in the class have and don't have in common.

I You	could	**speak** English. **find** a job.
He They	couldn't	**register** for classes.

Could shows past ability.
I **could drive** when I came to this country.
I **couldn't speak** English when I came here.

A **Complete the sentences.** Use *could* or *couldn't* and the verb. (Answers will vary.)

1. When I came to this country, I (speak) _____ English.

2. When I came to this country, I (read) _____ a book without a dictionary.

3. When I came to this country, I (find) _____ a job.

4. When I came here, I (drive) _____ a car.

5. When I came here, I (use) _____ a computer.

B **Complete the sentences.** (Answers will vary.)

1. When my family came here, _____

2. When I came to this English program, _____

3. When I started this class, I _____

C **Ask and answer questions about your first day in English class.**

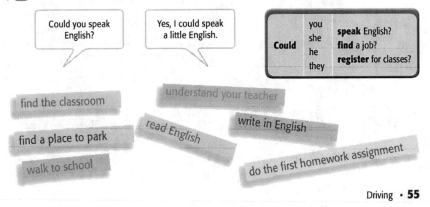

Could you speak English?

Yes, I could speak a little English.

Could	you she he they	**speak** English? **find** a job? **register** for classes?

find the classroom

understand your teacher

find a place to park

read English

write in English

walk to school

do the first homework assignment

Driving · 55

Active Grammar: *Could / Couldn't*

A **Complete the sentences. Use *could* or *couldn't* and the verb.**

• Review the grammar explanation and the sample sentences with the class. Ask students to provide original examples of the correct use of *could* and *couldn't*.

• Have students complete the exercise with answers that are true for them.

• Call on different volunteers to provide one answer each. After each one, ask students to raise their hands if their answer was the same.

• Discuss the similarities and differences.

B **Complete the sentences.**

Have students complete the sentences with information that is true for them. Circulate around the room and provide spelling or vocabulary help as needed.

C **Ask and answer questions about your first day in English class.**

• Have students complete the activity with a partner. Tell students that they can take brief notes of their partners' answers.

• Review the answers as a class. Call on one student in each pair, ask a question from the exercise, and ask them to share their partner's answer.

Active Grammar:
Should / Shouldn't

 A **Working Together**
Read each statement.
Check your opinion.
Then, discuss your
reason with a small
group of classmates.

• Review the grammar
explanation and the
sample sentences with
the class. Ask students to
give original examples of
the correct use of *should*
and *shouldn't*.

• Have students complete
the exercise on their own,
and then discuss their
answers in small groups.
Set a time limit, perhaps
ten minutes, for this
exercise. Tell students
that, for each item in the
exercise, students should
tell whether they agree or
disagree.

 B **Give advice. Use *should***
or *shouldn't*. Discuss
your answers with a
partner.

• Ask students to work
in pairs and discuss each
situation. Move around
the room, offering
language support as
needed.

• Review the answers
by asking two or three
students to explain
their response to each
question. Write any
new words on the
board. Suggest that
students copy into their
notebooks any new
vocabulary that they
think will be useful to
them.

> ***Should*** expresses an opinion or advice.
> I **should buy** a smaller car. Small cars get good gas mileage.
> ***Shouldn't / Should not*** shows that something is *not* a good idea.
> You **shouldn't put** your packages in the back seat. Someone might see them.
> You **should put** them in your trunk.

I You He They	should shouldn't	drive at night. buy that car.

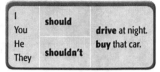
I agree that drivers should drive more carefully near elementary schools. Young children might run into the street.

 A **Working Together** **Read each statement.** Check (✓) your opinion. Then, discuss your reason with a small group of classmates. *(Answers will vary.)*

Opinion	Agree	Disagree
1. Drivers should drive more carefully near elementary schools.		
2. Teenagers are too young to drive cars.		
3. Small children should always ride in the back seat of a car.		
4. People over 80 years old should not drive.		
5. Drivers should not eat and drive at the same time.		
6. The highway speed limit is too low.		
7. All drivers should have car insurance.		

B **Give advice.** Use *should* or *shouldn't*. Discuss your answers with a partner.

1. A family with five children is shopping for a new car. What kind of car should the family buy?

2. Chen wants to learn how to drive. Who should teach him—his grandfather, his mother, or a private teacher?

3. Valeria is 16 years old. In her state, teenagers can drive at 16 years of age. Should she try to get her driver's license now, or should she wait until she graduates from high school?

4. Pierre is a new immigrant to the United States. Everyone at his job speaks his native language. He doesn't speak any English. What should he do?

56 · Unit 4

More Action!

After groups have discussed their
answers to Exercise A, follow up
with the entire class. For each item,
ask students if they agree or disagree
with the opinions. Ask students to
provide a more in-depth explanation
for their choice. Encourage a
discussion of both sides of each
issue when possible.

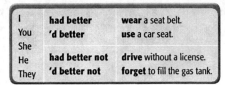

I	had better	**wear** a seat belt.
You	**'d better**	**use** a car seat.
She		
He	had better not	**drive** without a license.
They	**'d better not**	**forget** to fill the gas tank.

Had better expresses a strong warning.
Had better is stronger than **should**.

You'd better check your tire.
(Or you'll get a flat tire.)

I'**d better not miss** another class.
(Or I'll fail the class.)

CD1·TR16

A **Pronunciation:** *'d better / 'd better not* **Listen and complete the sentences.** Then, listen again and repeat.

1. I'd better stay _____ home. I don't feel well.
2. You'd better put _____ the baby in the car seat.
3. She'd better call _____ the police and report the accident.
4. We'd better take _____ the party inside. It's beginning to rain.
5. He'd better not have _____ another piece of cake. He'll get sick.
6. You'd better not get _____ a dog. Your landlord won't allow it.
7. She'd better slow _____ down. The roads are icy.
8. I'd better not buy _____ that. I can't afford it.

B **Give warnings.** Use *'d better* or *'d better not*. (Answers will vary.)

1.

He'd better wear a helmet.

2.

They'd better put the baby in the back seat / in a car seat.

3.

She'd better put her makeup away.

4.

They'd better call the police.

5.

He'd better turn on his lights / drive carefully.

6.

They'd better turn the music down.

Driving · **57**

Active Grammar: *Had better / Had better not*

 A **Pronunciation: *'d better / 'd better not.* Listen and complete the sentences. Then, listen again and repeat.**
(CD1•TR16)

• Read and discuss the grammar explanation. Point out that *had better* is stronger than *should*. Review the sample sentences and elicit new ones. Answer any questions.
• Have students just listen the first time you play the audio. Then, tell them they must listen carefully and fill in their answers as you play the audio the second time.
• Review the answers by playing the audio. As they check their answers, students should repeat each sentence after the speaker. Play the audio one more time (if necessary). Then, have students take turns repeating the sentences to each other in pairs.

B **Give warnings. Use *'d better* or *'d better not*.**

Do the exercise with the whole class. Repeat each warning given by a student, confirming or correcting the response. Then, call on another student to repeat the warning.

Teaching Tip

Extend the pronunciation practice with *'d better* and *'d better not*. Some of the items in Exercise A include a second sentence (Items 1, 4, 5, 6, 7, 8). Read aloud the second sentences and have students come up with a warning using *had better* or *had better not*.
For example:
(Item 1)
T: *I don't feel well.*
S1: *Yes, you'd better not go to work.*
(Item 7)
T: *The roads are icy.*
S2: *We'd better not drive tonight.*

The Big Picture: Getting a Driver's License

 A **Jennifer is talking about how to get her driver's license. Listen and complete the chart.**

(CD1 • TR17)

• Ask students to read the chart before you play the audio. Answer any questions about vocabulary.

• Have students just listen the first time you play the audio. Then, play it again and ask them to fill in the missing information. Play the audio a third time, so they can check their answers.

• Review the correct answers with the whole class.

 A **Jennifer is talking about how to get her driver's license.** Listen and complete the chart.

CD1•TR17

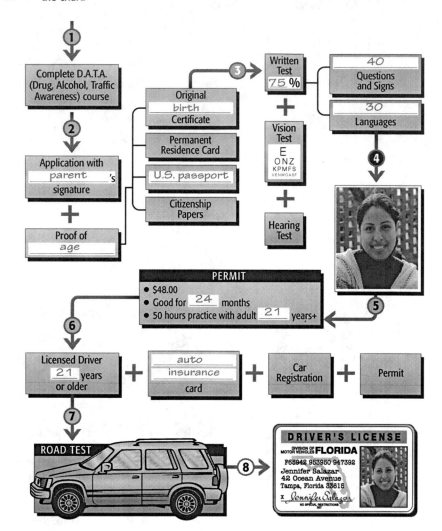

58 · Unit 4

More Action!

Using the information in the chart, call on several students and ask them each to sequentially describe one thing Jennifer has to do in order to get her license.

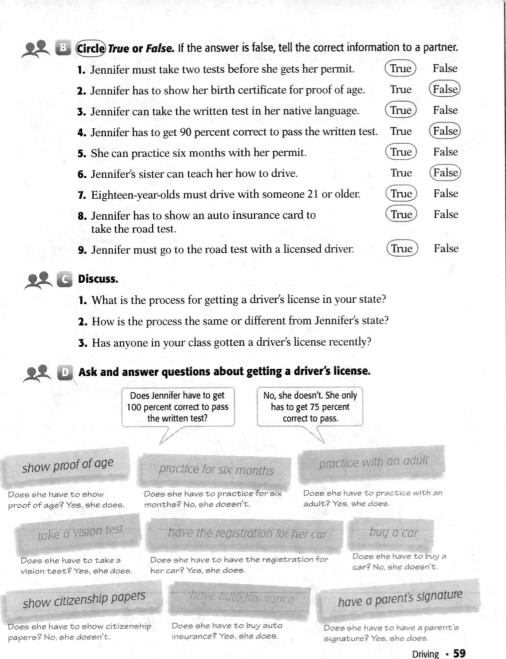

B (Circle) *True* or *False.* If the answer is false, tell the correct information to a partner.

1. Jennifer must take two tests before she gets her permit.   (True)   False

2. Jennifer has to show her birth certificate for proof of age.   True   (False)

3. Jennifer can take the written test in her native language.   (True)   False

4. Jennifer has to get 90 percent correct to pass the written test.   True   (False)

5. She can practice six months with her permit.   (True)   False

6. Jennifer's sister can teach her how to drive.   True   (False)

7. Eighteen-year-olds must drive with someone 21 or older.   (True)   False

8. Jennifer has to show an auto insurance card to take the road test.   (True)   False

9. Jennifer must go to the road test with a licensed driver.   (True)   False

C Discuss.

1. What is the process for getting a driver's license in your state?

2. How is the process the same or different from Jennifer's state?

3. Has anyone in your class gotten a driver's license recently?

D Ask and answer questions about getting a driver's license.

> Does Jennifer have to get 100 percent correct to pass the written test?

> No, she doesn't. She only has to get 75 percent correct to pass.

show proof of age
Does she have to show proof of age? Yes, she does.

practice for six months
Does she have to practice for six months? No, she doesn't.

practice with an adult
Does she have to practice with an adult? Yes, she does.

take a vision test
Does she have to take a vision test? Yes, she does.

have the registration for her car
Does she have to have the registration for her car? Yes, she does.

buy a car
Does she have to buy a car? No, she doesn't.

show citizenship papers
Does she have to show citizenship papers? No, she doesn't.

have auto insurance
Does she have to buy auto insurance? Yes, she does.

have a parent's signature
Does she have to have a parent's signature? Yes, she does.

Driving · 59

B Circle *True* or *False.* If the answer is false, tell the correct information to a partner.

- Have students complete the exercise with a partner.
- Review the answers with the class, having students give the correct information for each answer that they marked *false* (Item 2: Jennifer can show her U.S. passport, original birth certificate, a permanent resident card, or citizenship papers for proof of age. Item 4: Jennifer has to get 75 percent correct to pass the written test. Item 6: Jennifer's sister can't teach her how to drive.

C Discuss.

- Talk as a class about getting a driver's license in your state. If students are not familiar with the process, ask them to research the process online at the state's Department of Motor Vehicles website.
- Help students pool their information to uncover as many facts as possible about the process.

D Ask and answer questions about getting a driver's license.

- Ask two students to read the sample dialogue in the speech bubbles. Then, have students use the information provided in the exercise to form questions. Finally, have them ask and answer the questions in pairs.
- Review the answers with the class by calling on different pairs to say one question and answer each.

More Action!

While discussing the questions in Exercise C, have a volunteer write the driver's license information neatly on a piece of paper or on the board. If students feel this would be helpful information for them to have, encourage them to record the information and share it with their friends or family members who may find it useful.

Reading: The Written Test

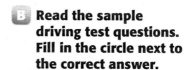

A Discuss.

• Ask the students to look at the license. Ask: *What state is this license from?* (Florida) *Where does the driver live?* (42 Ocean Avenue in Tampa)

• Then, answer the discussion questions as a class, or have students discuss the answers in small groups.

B Read the sample driving test questions. Fill in the circle next to the correct answer.

• Read the Reading Note together. Do the first item together to practice how to answer multiple-choice questions. Ask students which items they would eliminate first.

• Ask students to read through the test questions and answers and raise their hands if there is anything they don't understand. Answer questions as necessary. Have students complete the test on their own.

60 · Unit 4

A Discuss.

1. Do you have a driver's license?

2. If you have a driver's license, did you take the written test in English?

3. What was the minimum passing score on the written test?

B Read the sample driving test questions. Fill in the circle next to the correct answer.

●   ⊗   ☑   ◌
Yes   No   No   No

> **READING NOTE**
> **Multiple-choice Questions**
> When you take a multiple-choice test, read each choice carefully. Then, try to eliminate one or two of the choices.

1. A driver approaching a flashing red traffic signal must . . .

   ○ **a.** drive carefully without stopping.

   ● **b.** stop first, and then pass through the intersection.

   ○ **c.** go through the light slowly.

   ○ **d.** slow down at the intersection.

2. You must stop your vehicle . . .

   ○ **a.** at an intersection with a stop sign.
   ○ **c.** when a traffic officer orders you to stop.

   ○ **b.** where there is a red light.
   ● **d.** All of the above.

3. You must turn on your headlights . . .

   ○ **a.** when you turn on your wipers.
   ○ **c.** one half hour before sunset.

   ○ **b.** in the evening.
   ● **d.** All of the above.

4. If you are driving behind a school bus and it shows a flashing red light, you must . . .

   ○ **a.** slow down.
   ● **c.** stop at least 25 feet away.

   ○ **b.** slow down and pass on the left.
   ○ **d.** All of the above.

5. You are driving on a highway with a 65 mph speed limit. Most of the other vehicles are driving 70 mph or faster. You may legally drive . . .

   ○ **a.** 70 mph or faster.
   ○ **c.** between 65 and 70.

   ● **b.** no faster than 65 mph.
   ○ **d.** as fast as you'd like.

60 · Unit 4

6. You have a green light, but the traffic is blocking the intersection. You must . . .

   ○ **a.** pass the traffic on the left.   ● **c.** wait until the traffic clears. Then, go.

   ○ **b.** honk your horn.   ○ **d.** pass the traffic on the right.

7. You must obey instructions of school crossing guards . . .

   ● **a.** at all times.

   ○ **b.** when school is closed.

   ○ **c.** in the morning.

   ○ **d.** when it is raining.

8. If you pass your exit on a highway, you should . . .

   ● **a.** go to the next exit.

   ○ **b.** turn around on the highway and return to your exit.

   ○ **c.** cross to the other side of the highway and make a U-turn.

   ○ **d.** back up slowly to the exit that you want.

9. What does this sign mean?

   ○ **a.** Three-way intersection.   ● **c.** Railroad crossing ahead.

   ○ **b.** Stop.   ○ **d.** No turns.

10. What does this sign mean?

   ○ **a.** One-way street ahead.   ○ **c.** Left turn only.

   ○ **b.** Pass other cars on the right.   ● **d.** You cannot go straight ahead.

Check your answers below.

1.b 2.d 3.d 4.c 5.b 6.c 7.a 8.a 9.c 10.d

8 or more correct	*Congratulations!* You pass! Get your driver's license.
Below 8	*Sorry.* You're not ready to drive. Study for two more weeks. Then, come back and retake the test.

B **Read the sample driving test questions. (Continued)**

• Tell students to use the answer key on page 61 to check their work. They may need a partner to help them.

• Point out the note in the box at the bottom of the page. Elicit from students how important it is to study since students must answer eight out of ten correctly in order to pass the test.

• Discuss any answers that several students got wrong.

More Action!

If possible, obtain copies of your state's manual that tells how to go about getting a driver's license. Photocopy a sample test from the manual (or from the state's website, if possible) and have students take the test in class. Correct it together orally and discuss any new vocabulary as well as the different rules and regulations that appear on the test.

Writing Our Stories: Giving Directions

A **Look at the street map. Then, read the directions from the starting point.**

• Ask students to work alone as they read both sets of directions. Then, have them read the directions in *Conversation 1* a second time, marking it on the map with a pencil as they read.

• Next, have students read and mark with a pen the directions in *Conversation 2*. Ask them to share their maps with a partner and help each other correct any mistakes in the routes they drew.

• Review the completed routes with the class.

A **Look at the street map.** Then, read the directions from the starting point.

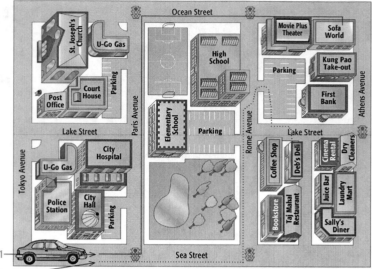

Conversation 1
Conversation 2

Conversation 1

A: My sofa is getting old. I need to buy a new sofa. How do I get to Sofa World? I heard that there's a great selection of sofas there.

B: That's right. Sofa World has a large selection of sofas. You're on Sea Street. Go to the first traffic light and turn left. That's Paris Avenue. Traffic is usually light. Take Paris straight to Ocean Street. There's a gas station on your left and a soccer field on your right. Turn right. Go through one traffic light. Sofa World is the second building on the right. It's on the corner of Ocean Street and Athens Avenue.

Conversation 2

A: I have to pick up sandwiches for a meeting at my office. How do I get to Deb's Deli? I heard that I can get a great sandwich there.

B: That's right. The sandwiches are delicious. It's easy. This is Sea Street. Go to the second light, turn left. That's Rome Avenue. Go to the next corner. That's Lake Street. It's difficult to park around there, so you should park in the public parking lot on the corner. Deb's Deli is across the street from the parking lot.

62 • Unit 4

B In your notebook, write directions from your school to your home or workplace. Include the names of important streets and places such as gas stations, banks, and stores.

C Sharing Our Stories Read your partner's directions. Are the directions clear?

> fender bender = small accident

D Read the paragraph. ~~Cross out~~ the unnecessary sentences.

> I think it should be legal to talk on a cell phone while driving. My parents gave me a cell phone when I got my driver's license. I have a part-time job, and I have to work in the evenings. ~~It was very difficult for me to find a job, so I want to keep this job until I finish high school.~~ I always call my mother from my car to tell her that I'm on my way home. ~~My cell phone is very cute. It's red, and it plays my favorite song when it rings.~~ A few months ago, I had a flat tire on the way home. I used my cell phone to call my father. He called our auto association to come and help me. Then, my father called me back and kept talking to me as he drove to my location to wait with me. I was very nervous and scared. I was very happy to have my cell phone.

E Find and correct the mistakes.

1. She must ~~puts~~ money in the parking meter. *(put)*
2. Can you ~~driving~~ a stick shift? *(drive)*
3. Drivers ~~has~~ to follow the traffic rules. *(have)*
4. I didn't have to ~~took~~ the test in English. *(take)*
5. ~~He~~ better not take another day off, or he'll lose his job. *(He'd)*
6. We didn't have buy a new car. *(to)*

Driving · **63**

Teaching Tip

Review the correct answers for Exercise D by reading the story aloud one sentence at a time and having students raise their hands when you read a sentence that can be deleted. Invite students to tell why the sentence should be eliminated.

B In your notebook, write directions from school to your home or workplace.

• Before they begin the writing part of this assignment, suggest that students draw a simple map that includes the streets and landmarks they pass on their way from school to their home or workplace.
• Go over the Writing Note and the instructions for the exercise. Have students work in pairs, describing the route and tracing it on the map with a finger. Then, have them write out the directions and reread them to be sure they haven't made any mistakes.

C Sharing Our Stories Read your partner's directions. Are the directions clear?

Have students share their directions with a partner. Remind students to look out for unnecessary information, per the Writing Note, as they review their partner's directions.

D Read the paragraph. Cross out the unnecessary sentences.

The first time through, have students read the story without crossing out anything. The second time through, have them cross out the unnecessary sentences.

E Find and correct the mistakes.

Have students correct the sentences on their own. Review the correct answers with the class.

Driving · **63**

Practicing on Your Own

A **Complete the sentences with the correct modal. There is more than one correct answer for each sentence.**

- Ask students to complete the sentences on their own, and then check their answers with a partner.
- If needed, review the modals in the boxes, eliciting or providing examples of each set.

B **Compare the driving rules in your state to the driving rules in your native country. Add an appropriate verb. Use negative forms when necessary.**

- Students complete the sentences individually. Point out the list of helping verbs to the right of the items. They should be using these to complete the sentences.
- Then, review the completed sentences with the class.
- Tell students to write in their notebooks two more rules about driving in their country.
- When students have finished writing their rules, invite volunteers to read their work aloud to the class. If a rule doesn't make sense to another student, ask the person who wrote the statement to explain why the rule is necessary.

Practicing on Your Own

A **Complete the sentences with the correct modal.** There is more than one correct answer for each sentence. (Answers will vary.)

must must not	has to doesn't have to	have to don't have to	should shouldn't	had better had better not

1. You _____don't have to_____ take the written test in English.
2. You _____must not_____ drive over the speed limit.
3. You _____shouldn't_____ drive immediately after you have an argument. Calm down first.
4. Children under seven _____must / have to_____ ride in car seats.
5. You _____must not_____ drive and talk on a cell phone.
6. Drivers _____must / should_____ use a hands-free cell phone.
7. Drivers _____must not_____ drink and drive, or they will lose their licenses.
8. You _____don't have to_____ wash your car every day.
9. I _____should_____ change the oil in my car a few times a year.
10. Bicycle riders _____have to / must_____ ride in the same direction as cars.

B **Compare the driving rules in your state to the driving rules in your native country.** Add an appropriate verb. Use negative forms when necessary. (Answers will vary.)

1. In this state, I _____ a seat belt.
2. In my country, I _____ a seat belt.
3. In this state, children _____ in car seats.
4. In my country, children _____ in car seats.
5. In this state, drivers _____ auto insurance.
6. In my country, I _____ auto insurance.
7. In this state, you _____ a license when you are _____ years old.

> can
> could
> must
> have to
> had to

64 • Unit 4

More Action!

As a change of pace, ask students to make a list of actions called "Recipe for a Car Accident." In it, they can describe all the things a driver *can, must,* and *had better do* to cause a big accident. For example:
You must talk on a cell phone and drive at the same time. You had better not drive slowly in the rain.

Students can take turns reading their recipes to the class. Then, have students practice using negative modals by making a list called "How to Avoid a Car Accident." They can take the sentences from their lists and rewrite them using negative modals. For example: *You must not talk on a cell phone and drive at the same time.*

English in Action — Car Maintenance

 A **Listen and repeat.** Then, match. Write the letter(s) of the car part next to the word.
CD1·TR18

N 1. accelerator	L 4. clutch	G 7. signal	O 9. gear shift	K 12. windshield
M 2. brake	A 5. hood	F 8. steering wheel	C, D 10. tires	I, J 13. windshield wipers
B 3. bumper	H 6. horn		E 11. trunk	

WORD PARTNERSHIPS

check	the oil
	the tire pressure
replace	the filters
	the wiper blades

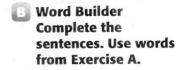

B **Word Builder** **Complete the sentences.** Use words from Exercise A.

1. _Windshield wipers_ clean your windshield.
2. A _bumper_ protects your car from minor accidents.
3. When you want to go forward or faster, press the _accelerator_.
4. Turn on the _signal_ before you make a turn.
5. Open the _hood_ to check the oil.
6. In the United States, many people prefer an automatic car to a car with a _clutch_.
7. Put your packages in the _trunk_ of your car.
8. Step on the _brake_ to stop your car.
9. Press the _horn_ to warn someone that you're coming.
10. In a manual car, the _clutch_ pedal is to the left of the brake.

Driving · **65**

English in Action: Car Maintenance

A **Listen and repeat. Then, match. Write the letter(s) of the car part next to the word.**
(CD1 • TR18)

• Play the audio. Have students listen to the words and repeat them. Play the audio again. Then, have students pronounce each word after you.
• As a class, label the parts of the car. Point out that automatic cars do not have clutches (Letter L), and that they do have gear shifts, but they are simpler.

B **Word Builder Complete the sentences. Use words from Exercise A.**

• Point out the phrases in the Word Partnerships box.
• Have students complete the exercise on their own. Go over the answers as a class. Clarify any incorrect answers.

More Action!

Have students write additional sentences using the vocabulary words from Exercise A. Alternatively, write sentences on the board, and have students fill in the missing words.
For example:
When you are driving, you must always keep your hands on the _____. (steering wheel)
This can be completed either as a written activity or as an oral activity.

Leisure Activities

A Label the leisure activities.

• Explain that *leisure activities* are things that people do when they aren't working, things they enjoy, and things they find relaxing. Another term is *hobbies*.

• Have students label pictures individually. Help with unfamiliar vocabulary. Then, ask students to compare answers with a partner and fill in any missing labels.

• Review the answers with the whole class. Encourage students to add comments about each hobby. Model an example for students: *I think fishing is dull, but many people find it relaxing.* Encourage students to comment on other leisure activities. For example: *My brother plays baseball every Saturday.*

B Which activities in Exercise A do you like to do?

• Invite students to identify any other leisure activities they like to do.

• Go over the information in the Word Partnerships box. Tell students to use the Word Partnerships to create sentences about other leisure activities they like to do. For example: *I know how to knit. I know how to salsa dance.*

66 • Unit 5

Unit 5

Leisure Activities

A Label the leisure activities.

cards	dancing	gardening	scrapbooking
cooking	~~dominoes~~	mah-jongg	sewing
cricket	fishing	photography	traveling

WORD PARTNERSHIPS	
know how to	cook
	garden
	play cards

1. dominoes   2. cricket   3. mah-jongg   4. sewing

5. dancing   6. fishing   7. cards   8. cooking

9. gardening   10. photography   11. traveling   12. scrapbooking

 B Which activities in Exercise A do you like to do? What other activities do you enjoy? Discuss your choices with a partner.

More Action!

Write any new leisure activities on the board and encourage students to tell why they enjoy each activity and who, if anyone, they do the activity with. Tell students to list any new vocabulary words in their notebooks.

Present Tense		
Do	I	
	you	**play**
	they	soccer?
Does	she	
	he	

Past Tense		
	I	
	you	
Did	they	**play**
	she	soccer?
	he	

Future with *Be Going to*			
Am	I		
Are	you		
	they	**going to**	**play**
			soccer?
Is	she		
	he		

Present Continuous		
Am	I	
Are	you	
	they	**playing**
		soccer?
Is	she	
	he	

Past Tense of *Be*		
Was	I	
	she	
	he	athletic?
Were	you	
	they	

Can; Future with *Will*		
	I	
Can	you	
Will	they	**play**
	she	soccer?
	he	

A **Complete the questions.** Use the activities from page 66. (Answers will vary.)

1. Are you going to _____ go fishing _____ this weekend?

2. Are you going to _____ sew _____ next month?

3. Were you _____ playing cricket _____ last weekend?

4. Were you _____ traveling _____ last month?

5. Do you like to _____ take pictures _____ ?

6. Do you _____ cook _____ every day?

7. Did you _____ do scrapbooking today _____ ?

8. Did you _____ play mah-jongg _____ yesterday?

9. Are you _____ playing cards _____ now?

10. Are you _____ gardening _____ right now?

 B **Ask and answer the questions in Exercise A.**

Yes, I am. No, I'm not.	Yes, I was. No, I wasn't.	Yes, I do. No, I don't.	Yes, I did. No, I didn't.

Active Grammar: *Yes / No* Questions Review

A **Complete the questions. Use the activities from page 66.**

• Review the information in the grammar boxes at the top of the page. Elicit or provide additional questions as needed.

• Read the instructions and have students complete the exercise in class.

• Elicit the answers, accepting several possible ones for each sentence. Call on students to write one of their completed sentences on the board.

B **Ask and answer the questions in Exercise A.**

• Review the short answers in the grammar boxes. Ask students to identify the verb tense associated with each short answer. For example:

Yes, I am. = present tense *be.*
Yes, I will. = future tense.
Yes, I was. = past tense *be.*
Yes, I do. = present tense of most verbs.
Yes, I did. = past tense of most verbs.

• Have students take turns asking and answering the questions in pairs. One student reads all the questions he or she wrote and his or her partner gives the answers. Then, they switch roles.

Active Grammar: Questions with *Who* and *Whose*

 A **People are talking about activities they enjoy. Circle the question word. Then, listen and answer the questions.** (CD1 • TR19)

• Present the information in the grammar chart and grammar note; check for understanding. Make sure students can hear the difference between *who* and *whose*. Provide or elicit additional examples.

• Read the instructions and point out the three pictures.

• Play the audio and have students just listen the first time. Then, play it one or two more times as students complete the activity.

 B **Work in a small group. Write the correct question word. Then, ask and answer the questions.**

Have students fill in the question words individually, and then check their answers with the group. Then, have students take turns asking and answering the questions with other group members.

Whose umbrella is that?	It's mine.
Who likes sports?	I do.
Who do you play cards with?	With my cousins.

Whose asks questions about possession.
Who asks questions about the subject or object.

 A **People are talking about activities they enjoy. Circle the question word. Then, listen and answer the questions.**
CD1•TR19

Gina   Roberto   Yelena

1. (Who) / Whose likes to go dancing?   _Gina_ does.
2. Who / (Whose) father taught her chess?   _Yelena_ 's did.
3. (Who) / Whose has many books about his hobby?   _Roberto_ does.
4. (Who) / Whose does Gina go dancing with?   _Her friends_
5. Who / (Whose) friends often meet at dance clubs?   _Gina_ 's do.
6. (Who) / Whose does Roberto meet once a week?   _His friends_
7. (Who) / Whose gets information online?   _Roberto_ does.
8. (Who) / Whose has more free time now?   _Yelena_ does.

 B **Work in a small group. Write the correct question word. Then, ask and answer the questions.**

1. _Who_ has a hobby?   4. _Who_ plays a sport regularly?
2. _Whose_ family has a garden?   5. _Who_ has a pet?
3. _Whose_ family is planning a trip?   6. _Whose_ mother or father likes to cook?

68 • Unit 5

More Action!

Review Exercise B with the whole class by calling on pairs of students from different groups to ask and answer their questions.

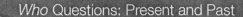
Present	Subject	**Who** goes	to the gym every day?	<u>Beth</u> does.
	Object	**Who** does Beth go	to the gym with?	She goes <u>with her sister</u>.
Past	Subject	**Who** went	to the gym?	<u>Jim</u> did.
	Object	**Who** did Jim go	to the gym with?	He went <u>with his wife</u>.

A Complete the questions about the women's weekend activities.

Rosa

Melba

Paula

1. Who (take) _____took_____ a cooking class?   Rosa did.

2. Who (take) _did Rosa take_ a class with?   With a few other students.

3. Who (plant) _____planted_____ some flowers?   Paula did.

4. Who (play) _____played_____ cards?   Melba did.

5. Who (Melba / play) _did Melba play_ with?   With her friends.

6. Who (Rosa / give) _did Rosa give_ the food to?   To her grandson.

7. Who (help) _____helped_____ Paula with the flowers?   No one did.

8. Who (Paula / buy) _did Paula buy_ flower seeds from?   From an online store.

B Complete the questions about your classmates. Write the answers. Ask and answer the questions with a partner.

1. Who usually (arrive) _____arrives_____ late to class?   (Answers will vary.)

2. Who (sit) ___sits / is sitting___ next to you?   (Answers will vary.)

3. Who (work) _____works_____ full time?   (Answers will vary.)

4. Who (your teacher / give) _does your teacher give_ tests to?   (Answers will vary.)

5. Who (wear) _____wears_____ glasses?   (Answers will vary.)

6. Who (you / come) _do you come_ to school with?   (Answers will vary.)

Active Grammar: *Who* Questions— Present and Past

A Complete the questions about the women's weekend activities.

• Present the information in the chart and check for understanding. Provide or elicit more questions and answers.

• Have students complete the activity on their own. Check the answers orally with the class.

B Complete the questions about your classmates. Write the answers. Ask and answer the questions with a partner.

• Have students complete the questions on their own, and then complete the answers with a partner.

• Elicit answers to items as a class. Try to call on someone who hasn't participated in class recently.

More Action!

Have students find a partner. Designate one member of each pair as Student A and the other as Student B. Have Student A look at the pictures on page 69 for one minute. Then, ask Student A to close his or her book. Student B will ask the questions in Exercise A. Student A must provide the correct answer without looking back at the illustrations.

Teaching Tip

Practice past tense questions by asking the questions in Exercise B, and having students provide the past tense verbs. For example:
T: *Who _____ late to class yesterday?*
S1: *arrived*
Elicit other questions and answers as time permits.

Active Grammar: *How* Questions

- Ask students to close their books. Ask each question in the first column of the chart. Have different students give answers. For example:

T: *How often do you come to school?*
S1: *Three days a week.*
T: *How much money do you have?*
S2: *Two dollars.*

- Have students open their books and study the chart. Answer any questions.

 A Complete the questions with the correct *How* expression.

- Have students complete the activity on their own.
- Review the answers with the class.

B Take turns asking your teacher these questions.

- Ask the class to repeat one or two of the questions in the list in unison.
- Call on individuals to ask each question. Call on lower-level students to give them pronunciation practice.

C Write three more questions to ask your teacher.

- Have students write questions individually. Then, check them with a partner. Encourage groups to correct any grammar errors.
- Then, have students ask you the questions. Correct question formation as necessary.

70 · Unit 5

How do you get to work?	By bus.
How far do you live from school?	About three miles.
How long did you wait?	Thirty minutes.
How much money do you have?	$4.39.
How many tickets do you have?	Just two.
How often do you come to school?	Three days a week.

A Complete the questions with the correct *How* expression. Then, ask and answer the questions with a partner.

1. _How often_ do you visit your native country?
2. _How many_ siblings do you have?
3. _How much_ do you spend on transportation to school?
4. _How long_ are you going to live in this country?
5. _How many_ hours do you sleep a night?
6. _How far_ do you live from your job?
7. _How_ did you find out about this school?
8. _How often_ do you go to the movies?
9. _How long_ did it take you to get to class today?
10. _How far_ is it from your home to school?

B Take turns asking your teacher these questions.

1. How did you find this teaching job?
2. How do you get to school?
3. How many students do you have?
4. How often do you give tests?
5. How difficult are your tests?
6. How far do you live from here?

C Write three more questions to ask your teacher. (Answers will vary.)

1. _____
2. _____
3. _____

70 · Unit 5

More Action!

Have students work in pairs. Tell students to write out two questions they would like to ask their partner. Call on different groups and have each member ask and answer one of their partner's questions. Encourage students to answer any questions they are comfortable with and to answer the questions as truthfully as they can.

Present with *be*	You **are** from Thailand,	**aren't** you?
	It **isn't** cold today,	**is** it?
Present continuous	They **are having** a nice time,	**aren't** they?
	They **aren't having** a bad time,	**are** they?
Simple present	He **plays** soccer every day,	**doesn't** he?
	He **doesn't play** tennis,	**does** he?
Past with *be*	They **were** at the park,	**weren't** they?
	They **weren't** at home,	**were** they?
Simple past	You **took** some pictures,	**didn't** you?
	You **didn't take** these pictures,	**did** you?
Future with *will*	She **will plant** more roses,	**won't** she?
	She **won't plant** any vegetables,	**will** she?

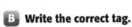 CD1·TR20 **A** **Pronunciation: Tag Questions Listen and repeat.** Pay attention to the arrows.

1. They like to fish, don't they?↘

2. Fishing isn't expensive, is it?↗

3. They will cook their fish, won't they?↘

4. They don't fish every day, do they?↗

5. They're fishing in a lake, aren't they?↗

6. It isn't a hot day, is it?↘

7. Fishing isn't tiring, is it?↗

8. They hope to catch a lot, don't they?↘

B **Write the correct tag.**

1. You are studying English, _____ aren't you ?

2. You will be in class tomorrow, _____ won't you ?

3. You were here yesterday, _____ weren't you ?

4. We won't have a test tomorrow, _____ will we ?

5. You have a car, _____ don't you ?

6. It wasn't raining yesterday morning, _____ was it ?

7. You didn't come to class late today, _____ did you ?

Leisure Activities · **71**

Teaching Tip

Using meaningless sounds instead of words may make it easier for students to identify the intonation patterns of tag questions. You might try "singing" several different sentences with tag questions using syllables like "la, la, la" in place of the actual words. Ask students to say whether the tag has *rising* or *falling* intonation.

More Action!

Have students work in pairs and take turns asking and answering the questions in Exercise B. Remind students that it is important to listen to the intonation of each question, and to respond with the expected affirmative or negative answer.

Active Grammar: Tag Questions

• Read the explanations and examples in the chart aloud, emphasizing the rising and falling intonation.

• Read the examples again and ask students to repeat.

• Explain the difference between rising and falling intonation to students. Write two example sentences on the board:
1. *They like to fish, <u>don't they</u>?*
2. *Fishing isn't expensive, <u>is it</u>?*
Ask students to identify the correct intonation: rising or falling (1. falling; 2. rising). In Example 1, the speaker expects a "yes" answer, so the intonation is falling intonation. In Example 2, the speaker isn't sure of the answer, so the question ends in rising intonation.

 A **Pronunciation: Tag Questions Listen and repeat.**
(CD1 • TR20)

• Play the audio and ask students to follow along in their books, listening and repeating.

• Review the correct answers by writing the item numbers on the board and having a student add the rising or falling arrows as you play the audio once more.

B **Write the correct tag.**

Have students fill in the answers individually. Check the answers orally with the whole class.

More Question Practice

 A **Working Together**
Student to Student

• Read and discuss the instructions for both parts of the activity and be sure students understand how to proceed. Point out that students will switch roles for items 6-10. Help Student 1 locate the sentences on page 263.

• Circulate around the room providing help as needed. Check the answers with the whole class.

 A **Working Together** **Student to Student.**

Student 1: Turn to page 263. Read **Set A** questions to Student 2.

Student 2: Listen to Student 1 and write the questions.

1. Who cooked when you were growing up _____?

   My father did.

2. Who taught you how to cook _____?

   My father did, and I also taught myself from cookbooks.

3. Do you watch cooking programs on TV _____?

   Yes, I regularly watch cooking shows on television.

4. Is your kitchen big enough for you _____?

   Not at first, but we remodeled it a few years ago.

5. What kind of cooking classes did you take before now _____?

   I took Indian cooking, candy-making, and afternoon tea, to name a few.

Student 2: Turn to page 263. Read **Set B** questions to Student 1.

Student 1: Listen to Student 2 and write the questions.

6. Does your husband like to cook _____?

   Yes, sometimes. He took a couple of classes with me.

7. What classes did you take together _____?

   We took a Valentine's Day class and a Mexican cooking class.

8. What was the first dish that you cooked _____?

   I cooked oatmeal, but it was terrible!

9. How does your husband like the food you cook _____?

   He likes everything that I cook.

10. Why did you decide to go to cooking school _____?

    Because my job wasn't fun anymore, and I love to cook.

More Action!

Have students practice asking and answering the questions on this page. Students can take turns asking and answering the questions they have just completed, replacing the listed answers with answers that are true for them.

B **Read.** Then, complete the questions.

There are six people in the Yang family household. They live in San Francisco, but they are originally from Hong Kong. They moved to San Francisco three years ago and lived with relatives until they found jobs. The parents, William and Patricia, spoke English fluently when they arrived, so they found work quickly. William and Patricia work at the same hospital. William is an accountant in the billing department, and Patricia is a pediatric nurse. Their two oldest children, Charles and Margaret, are now college students. Charles is a medical student, and Margaret is studying architecture. Their youngest, Harry, is a high school student. The children are doing well in school. Grandmother Yang speaks English, too, and she volunteers in a library in Chinatown.

The Yangs love to travel. This summer they are going to Vancouver, Canada, to visit William's brother, Victor.

1. How many *people are in the Yang family*?

Six.

2. When *did they move to San Francisco*?

Three years ago.

3. Who *did they live with*?

With relatives.

4. Why *did they find work quickly*?

Because they spoke English.

5. How many *children do they have*?

Three.

6. How *are they doing in school*?

They're doing well.

7. Do *they like to travel*?

Yes, they do.

8. Whose *brother are they going to visit*?

William's brother.

C **Write two *Who* questions about the Yang family.** *(Answers will vary.)*

1. Who _____?

2. Who did _____?

Leisure Activities · **73**

B **Read. Then, complete the questions.**

• Have students read the passage silently, and then answer the questions. Do the first item together, so students understand the writing part of the exercise.

• Remind students to check their work and their spelling; then check the answers as a class. Check for understanding.

C **Write two *Who* questions about the Yang family.**

• If students finish with Exercise B early, have them complete this activity. Remind students that they should ask questions with answers that can be found in the reading.

• Ask volunteers to provide their questions and elicit the answers from others in the class.

The Big Picture: A Trip to Vancouver, British Columbia

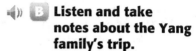 **Discuss. Look at the pictures. What places do the Yangs plan to visit in Vancouver?**

Do this activity together as a class. Find out if students have ever been to Vancouver or to any of the places pictured. Ask: *What kind of leisure activities do the Yang family plan to do in Vancouver? At the Vancouver Harbor? At the Park?*

 Listen and take notes about the Yang family's trip.

(CD1 • TR21)

• Go over good note-taking. Remind students that they do not need to write complete sentences, just the main points that they hear.
• Play the audio once and have students listen without writing.
• Play the audio again and have students take notes.
• Play the audio a third time and have students complete and check their notes. Provide spelling help as needed.

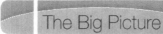
 Discuss. Look at the pictures. What places do the Yangs plan to visit in Vancouver?

The Yang Family

Vancouver Harbor

Granville Island

Queen Elizabeth Park

Chinatown

Listen and take notes about the Yang family's trip.

CD1•TR21

Victor	Lin	This morning	Later
• visited Vancouver on business • liked the city, liked the clean streets, nature, economic opportunities	• didn't want to move • met other immigrants from Hong Kong • likes Vancouver • works three mornings/wk at elem. school • speaks English / Cantonese / Mandarin	• visited Granville Island • Public Market • had tea • watched boats	• trolley tour • Queen Elizabeth Park • Rose Garden • zoo • dinner in Chinatown

74 • Unit 5

Teaching Tip

Point out Vancouver on a map. Explain that Vancouver is located in British Columbia, a province of Canada. If possible, bring in additional pictures of this city.

C Listen again. Circle *True* or *False*.

CD1 • TR21

1. The Yangs are staying in a hotel. True (False)
2. Victor and his family moved to Vancouver five years ago. True (False)
3. Lin likes Vancouver now. (True) False
4. Lin works part time. (True) False
5. Lin can speak both Cantonese and Mandarin. (True) False
6. They had tea at a hotel restaurant. True (False)
7. They are going to see some animals this afternoon. (True) False

D Match.

d	1. What did Victor like about Vancouver?	a. No, she didn't.
a	2. Did Lin want to come to Vancouver at first?	b. In Queen Elizabeth Park.
f	3. How often does Lin work a week?	c. Next year.
e	4. Where did they go this morning?	d. The economic opportunities.
g	5. Where are they going to have dinner?	e. To Granville Island.
b	6. Where can they see a rose garden?	f. Three times.
c	7. When will Victor go to San Francisco?	g. In Chinatown.

E Go online. Search for information on another Canadian province or territory. Find three activities to do there. Report to your classmates. (Answers will vary.)

Activities

1. ______
2. ______
3. ______

C Listen again. Circle *True* or *False*.
(CD1 • TR21)

- Have students listen to the audio again and circle the correct answers.
- Correct answers as a class. Play the audio again as needed to verify answers.

D Match.

- Do the first item together. Then, have students complete the activity on their own.
- Check correct answers by having one student read a question from Column 1, and another student give the correct answer from Column 2.

E Go online. Search for information on another Canadian province or territory. Find three activities to do there. Report to your classmates.

- Tell students to use an Internet search engine to find this information. Brainstorm the search words they might use.
- Create a class list of places to go and things to do in Canada. Plot the places on a map, if possible.

Reading: Community Gardening

Discuss.

Discuss the questions with the class. Appoint a reporter to list the answers given for Item 2. What are the most popular items that people grow or would grow, or have grown in the past? Discuss your findings.

Read.

• Have students read the passage silently to themselves. Point out that the bolded words may be unfamiliar vocabulary and will be covered in Exercise D on the next page.

• Alternatively, have students take turns reading paragraphs of the text. Correct pronunciation as needed.

Discuss.

1. Do you have a garden?

2. If you have a garden, what do you grow?

3. Did you have a garden in your native country?

Read.

In January, the seed catalogues begin to arrive at homes all across the United States. Gardening has become one of the most popular hobbies in this country. For some people, it is not just a relaxing hobby, but it is also an economic bonus. For those who live in apartments and do not have yards where they can start gardens, there may be a community garden in the area.

In many cities throughout the United States, there are community garden programs. According to the American Community Gardening Association (www.communitygarden.org), a community garden is "any piece of land gardened by a group of people." Among the benefits of community gardening are the economic **benefits** for families, the **beautification** of neighborhoods, and the social **interaction** that people experience. You can find community gardens in every state, especially on the east and west coasts and in Midwestern cities.

In cities around the country, **residents** grow gardens on **vacant** city lots, or empty spaces. The gardens are usually organized by community members, and they help other residents select tools, seed, plants, and other materials. Sometimes there is a children's program, which teaches elementary children science and math using the gardens. The program can offer both online learning and class visits. Gardening can also teach residents about healthy, **nutritious** food.

Youth can participate in the gardens, too. Teenagers can do gardening, help people who visit the gardens, or do other activities in the gardens.

As you can see, the community garden does more than just grow fruit, flowers, and vegetables.

More Action!

Compare and contrast the kinds of things that are grown in gardens in this country with the things grown in gardens in the native countries of your students.

C Circle *True* or *False*.

1. Some people start gardens in order to save money. (True) False

2. According to the article, you need more than one person (True) False
   to make a community garden.

3. There are no community gardens in the Midwest. True (False)

4. All gardeners put their gardens on private property. True (False)

5. Members of the garden program always bring their True (False)
   own tools.

6. There are gardening programs for children online. (True) False

7. Gardening can help children learn science and math. (True) False

8. Community garden programs have many purposes. (True) False

D Word Builder **Complete the sentences with the correct word form.**

Noun	Verb	Adjective
benefit(s)	benefit	beneficial
beautification	beautify	beautiful
interaction(s)	interact	interactive
nutrition	_____	nutritious
resident(s)	reside	residential
vacancy(ies)	vacate	vacancy

> **READING NOTE**
> **Word Forms**
> It is important to learn how to use different forms of words. Most words have a verb form, an adjective form, and / or other forms. For example, *benefit* is the noun and verb form, and *beneficial* is the adjective form.

1. In my city, there is a ___beautiful___ community garden on my block.

2. There was a ___vacancy___ in my building, so I told one of my friends who
   was looking for an apartment.

3. The people who work in the garden enjoy the social ___interaction___.

4. Only people who ___reside___ in my neighborhood can use our garden.

5. There are many ___benefits___ to gardening.

6. Many people garden because they want more ___nutritious___ food.

Leisure Activities • 77

C Circle *True* or *False*.

• Do the first item together and check for understanding.
• Have students complete the activity, referring back to the reading as needed to find the correct answers.
• Go around the room eliciting answers. Ask students to point out where in the text they found the answers.

D Word Builder Complete the sentences with the correct word form.

• Go over the Reading Note. Provide or elicit additional examples of word forms; for example, *help / helpful*, *inform / information*, and so on.
• Have students complete the activity on their own and elicit answers.

More Action!

For extra practice, have students write sentences using words from the chart in Exercise D. Encourage students to write sentences for the words not used in the sentences in Exercise D.

Writing Our Stories:
How to Start a Garden

A **Read.**

- Read the Writing Note together. Remind students to keep the information in mind as they read.
- Have them underline any unfamiliar vocabulary, and elicit or provide definitions as needed after they read.

B **Underline the transition words in the reading in Exercise A.**

Discuss the reading and the importance of transition words when describing a process. How did the inclusion of transition words contribute to the understanding of the reading in Exercise A? Ask students to point out specific examples.

A **Read.**

Linda Torres
October 25, 2010
English IV

How to Start a Garden

My husband and I enjoy gardening. We both had gardens in our old village, and now we have a garden in our new home. It is not difficult to start a garden, but it takes regular care and patience.

First, find a sunny spot in your yard. Try to find a place that gets sun all day long. Second, clear out the grass and large rocks in the space. Third, turn over the dirt, and add some compost to make the dirt better for growing vegetables. You can buy compost in a gardening store. After that, plan your garden. Decide what you want to grow. Next, buy the seeds and / or small plants. Plant your seeds and plants according to the instructions on the packets or boxes. Then, cover the ground with mulch to keep down the weeds. We use old newspaper and leaves, but some people use straw and bags of mulch from a store. Finally, water your seeds and plants regularly, and don't forget to weed your garden. After some time, you'll have delicious, healthy vegetables for your family.

> ### WRITING NOTE
> **Transition Words Review**
> In Unit 3, you learned how to use transition words to improve your English. You can use the same words to describe a process.

B **Underline the transition words in the reading in Exercise A.**

| First, | Second, | Third, | After that, | Next, | Then, | Finally, |

C **Read about how to cut a pineapple.** Work with a partner. Number the sentences in the correct order. Then, rewrite the sentences in paragraph form in your notebook. Use the transition words from Exercise B.

   _4_ Cut the halves in half.

   _7_ Slice the pineapple off the tough outer skin, and slice the fruit into smaller pieces.

   _3_ With a sharp knife, cut the pineapple in half lengthwise.

   _1_ Pineapple is a popular fruit in my country, but some people do not know how to cut one properly.

   _2_ Twist off the green top.

   _8_ It's ready to serve.

   _5_ Take one quarter of the pineapple, and slice off the tough inner core.

   _6_ Don't throw away the core. Some people like this part.

D **In your notebook, write about how to do something related to one of your hobbies or interests.** Use transition words in your paragraph. Here are a few examples of topics: how to play dominoes, how to take care of a pet, or how to buy a bicycle.

E **Sharing Our Stories** **Read a classmate's composition.** How many steps are there? <u>Underline</u> each step.

F **Find and correct the mistakes.**

   1. What ^are^ you doing?
   2. Why does she ~~has~~ ^have^ so many pets?
   3. Where did you ~~found~~ ^find^ those stamps?
   4. How long will they ~~plays~~ ^play^ this game?
   5. ~~You~~ ^Are you^ going to work in your garden?
   6. Who ~~did play~~ ^played^ a sport last weekend?
   7. Who you go dancing with?
      (Answers will vary.)

More Action!

If possible, bring in a pineapple and cut it according to the directions listed in Exercise C. Have students take turns reading the steps aloud as you demonstrate the steps. Share the cut pineapple with the class.

Teaching Tip

If appropriate for your class, have students do Exercise D in class. Have students write paragraphs in their entirety. Assign students a partner as they work and encourage partners to help one another by checking grammar and spelling. Remind students to use transition words from Exercise B on page 78. Move around the room offering help as needed.

C **Read about how to cut a pineapple.**

• Read through the list. Ask students to read aloud any words or phrases they don't know. Explain new vocabulary.
• Have students complete the activity individually, and then check their answers with a partner. Have a student write the correct answers on the board. Ask the rest of the class to check their work against it.

D **In your notebook, write about how to do something related to one of your hobbies or interests.**

• Brainstorm a list of possible topics. Help students choose topics.
• Encourage students to make a brief outline of the steps required to complete their hobby or interest.
• As students outline their paragraph, go around the classroom and provide help with language and organization as needed.
• Have students complete the writing as homework.

E **Sharing Our Stories Read a classmate's composition.**

Pair students with a similar language level. Call on students to read their paragraphs aloud.

F **Find and correct the mistakes.**

Have students correct the sentences on their own. Review the correct answers with the class.

Practicing on Your Own

A. Write questions and answers.

• Ask students to write out the questions and answers on their own. Point out that the answers will vary.

• After reviewing how to correctly form questions, ask different students to read aloud their answers to each question.

• Alternatively, put students in pairs to read their answers to their partner.

A **Write questions and answers.** (Answers will vary.)

1. who / your teacher?

   Who is your teacher _____ ?

   _____ .

2. who / immigrate / to this country with you?

   Who immigrated to this country with you _____ ?

   _____ .

3. when / you / come / to this country?

   When did you come to this country _____ ?

   _____ .

4. how / you / get / to school / every day?

   How do you get to school every day _____ ?

   _____ .

5. who / write / on the board / right now?

   Who is writing on the board right now _____ ?

   _____ .

6. what kind of leisure activities / you / like to do?

   What kind of leisure activities do you like to do ____ ?

   _____ .

7. who / you / usually / speak English with?

   Who do you usually speak English with _____ ?

   _____ .

8. who / tell / you / about this English program?

   Who told you about this English program _____ ?

   _____ .

9. when / your class / have / a test?

   When is your class going to have a test / When will your class have a test ?

   _____ .

 A **Look at the graph.** Work with a partner. (Circle) *True* or *False*.

ACTIVITY

1. Fishing is the most popular activity. (True) False

2. Biking is more popular than walking. True (False)

3. Walking is as popular as playing sports. (True) False

4. Working out at a gym is more popular than running. (True) False

5. Running is the least popular activity. (True) False

6. Dancing is more popular than biking. True (False)

 B **Working Together** **Make a survey.** (Answers will vary.)

1. One student asks the questions below to the whole class.

2. Two students count the responses from the class.

3. Complete the chart below.

Questions

1. Who plays a sport?

2. Who watches sports on TV?

3. Who socializes with friends and family?

4. Who rents movies?

5. Who goes to the movies?

6. Who uses the Internet?

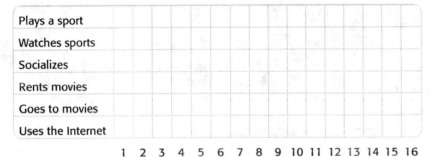

	1 2 3 4 5 6 7 8 9 10 11 12 13 14 15 16
Plays a sport	
Watches sports	
Socializes	
Rents movies	
Goes to movies	
Uses the Internet	

Leisure Activities • **81**

English in Action: Reading Bar Graphs

 A **Look at the graph. Work with a partner. Circle *True* or *False*.**

• Go over the graph of activities, and do the first item together to ensure understanding.

• Have students complete the activity in pairs. Then call on volunteers to give their answers. They should be prepared to explain why their answers are correct.

 B **Working Together Make a survey.**

• Choose three student volunteers and assign them the listed roles. One student should read the questions aloud to the class. The other two students should be note-takers and should record the results on the board. (The note-takers do not have to re-create the chart; they only need to list the final number in each category.)

• Have students use the results listed on the board to complete the chart individually.

• Discuss the results as a class. Ask: *What is the most common way that the class spends their free time? What is the least common way?*

• Ask students if there is another way that they spend their free time that is not asked about here. For example: *Who likes to go shopping? Who likes to do outdoor activities?* Encourage students to come up with additional questions to pose to the class.

Travel

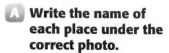

A Write the name of each place under the correct photo.

- Read aloud the nine place names. Complete the first item together.
- Ask students to match the place names and photos individually, and then check their answers with a partner. Have pairs locate each city on the World Map on page 290.
- Check the answers with the whole class and point out each city and country on a large world map, or ask volunteers to do so.

B Discuss. Which places would you like to visit? Why?

- Make this a pair or class discussion. Encourage students to elaborate on their answers and ask follow-up questions. Find out which, if any, of the places people in the class have already visited. Ask for volunteers to talk briefly about their experiences in these locations.
- Take a class vote and find out the top three places that the class would most like to visit. Include your own choices in the voting.

Unit 6 Travel

A Write the name of each place under the correct photo.

Boston, Massachusetts, U.S.A. Shanghai, China Paris, France
Cancun, Mexico Los Angeles, California, U.S.A. Rio de Janeiro, Brazil
Giza, Egypt New York, New York, U.S.A. Rome, Italy

1. Cancun, Mexico

2. Rome, Italy

3. Los Angeles, CA

4. Paris, France

5. Rio de Janeiro, Brazil

6. New York, New York

7. Giza, Egypt

8. Boston, Massachusetts

9. Shanghai, China

B Discuss. Which places would you like to visit? Why?

More Action!

- Share additional information about the places in the photos. For example, for Item 8, elicit or provide background about Boston, Massachusetts. For example: *Boston is one of the oldest cities in the United States. The first subway system in the U.S. was built in Boston in 1897.*

- Alternatively, ask individuals or pairs to choose one of the pictured cities and research information about the city. They can look for information on population, major attractions or landmarks, and interesting facts. Have individuals or pairs present their findings to the class.

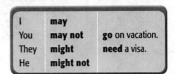

May and *Might* for Possibility

I	may	
You	may not	**go** on vacation.
They	might	**need** a visa.
He	might not	

Use *may* or *might* to express possibility.
I might go on vacation. = Maybe I will go on vacation.
He may not need a visa. = Maybe he will not need a visa.

A **Complete the conversation.** Use *may, might,* or *will.*

A: Where will you go for vacation?

B: We __may / might__ go to San Diego.
          1

A: Are you going to fly?

B: It's not too far. Maybe I __will__ drive.
               2

A: How long are you going to stay?

B: I don't have a lot of vacation time. I __may / might__ only stay a few days.
                                              3

A: Who is going to go with you?

B: Maybe my sister __will__ go if she has time. Our cousin
                    4
__may / might__ go, too.
      5

A: That sounds like fun. Where will you stay?

B: We __may / might__ stay with my brother. Or, we __may / might__ stay
           6   7
with my aunt.

A: Are you going to go to Mexico, too? It's a short trip.

B: That __might__ be a good idea. We can go for the day.
            8

A: Will you send me a postcard?

B: Sure. I __will__ definitely send you a postcard.
             9

B **Practice the conversation in Exercise A with a partner.**

Active Grammar: *May* and *Might* for Possibility

A **Complete the conversation. Use *may, might,* or *will.***

- Go over the grammar explanations and sample sentences with the class. Ask students to give original examples of the correct use of *may* and *might* for possibility.
- Do the exercise with the whole class. Answer any questions students may have. Point out that both *may* and *might* are correct answers for Items 1, 3, 5, 6 and 7.

B **Practice the conversation in Exercise A with a partner.**

- Model the conversation aloud with a student volunteer.
- Put students in pairs and have them practice the conversation with their partner. Have students switch roles several times, so they get a chance to practice the entire conversation.
- Once students have gone through the conversation a few times, ask them to close their books and try to practice the conversation from memory. As students get more comfortable with the conversation, tell them to substitute information that makes the conversation true for them. For example:
S1: *Where will you go for vacation?*
S2: *We might go to Italy.*

Teaching Tip

Provide more example sentences using *might* and *may* if you feel your class needs a review.

C Answer each question with a possible answer. Use *may* or *might*.

C Answer each question with a possible answer. Use *may* or *might*.

(Answers will vary.)

1. Why isn't Anna in school?

She might be sick.

2. Why is the flight late?

_____

3. Why does Pedro always go to the beach for vacation?

_____

4. Why do they have to go to the consulate?

_____

5. Why are you packing a bottle of aspirin in your suitcase?

_____

6. Why is Beth packing heavy sweaters for her beach vacation?

_____

7. Why are they driving to Florida instead of flying?

_____

8. Why are so many people in the train station?

_____

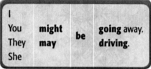

I You They She	might may	be	going away. driving.

Use the continuous modal form to discuss possibilities about something that is happening now.

A: Where are they going?
B: They **might be going** to Europe.

D Change each sentence. Use the continuous modal form.

1. I might study tonight.

> I might be studying tonight.

2. We might go to Beijing.
We might be going to Beijing.

3. They may get a visa.
They may be getting a visa.

4. She might buy some new clothes.
She might be buying some new clothes.

5. The students might prepare for their trip.
The students might be preparing for their trip.

6. He may buy a ticket.
He may be buying a ticket.

7. She might call her mother.
She might be calling her mother.

8. They may take a tour.
They may be taking a tour.

84 · Unit 6

C **Answer each question with a possible answer. Use *may* or *might*.**

• Have students complete the exercise individually in class or as homework.
• Call on several students and elicit their responses to a question. Point out that *might* and *may* are often used interchangeably.

D **Change each sentence. Use the continuous modal form.**

• Go over the information in the boxes. Point out the use of *be*. Elicit and provide more examples as time permits, and as needed.
• Go over the model sentence in the speech bubble. Then, have students do the exercise on their own.
• Check answers as a class. Have students write their sentences on the board. Correct errors as a class.

Must for Deduction

I You They He	**must**	**have** the flu. **speak** French.

Use *must* to make a deduction.

Situation: Ann is in Paris. She is talking to a store clerk in Paris and she is having no trouble communicating.

Ann **must speak** French.

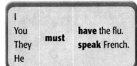

A With a partner, answer the questions about the pictures. Use *must*.

(Answers may vary.)

He must be in New York City.

1. Where is he?

2. Why are they sleeping?
They must be bored.

3. What is he doing?
He must be proposing.

4. Why is she getting his autograph?
He must be famous.

5. What is his occupation?
He must be an engineer.

6. Where is she going?
She must be going to Madrid, Spain.

7. Where is the traveler going?
She must be going to a beach.

8. Where are they?
They must be in a library.

9. Who are they?
They must be athletes.

Travel • 85

More Action!

Bring in magazine or newspaper photos showing people doing things or bring in some magazine advertisements for products. In pairs, have students come up and write down questions about these visuals. Then, have each pair exchange their questions with another pair, who will answer the questions using *must*. For example, a magazine advertisement for cold medication might show a woman who clearly is sick.

Question: *Why is she sneezing?*
Answer: *She must have a cold.*

Active Grammar: *Must* for Deduction

A With a partner, answer the questions about the pictures. Use *must*.

• Go over the information in the grammar boxes at the top of the page. Make sure students understand the term *deduction*. Explain: *A deduction is a conclusion you have reached about something because of other things that you know to be true.* Check for understanding. Elicit and provide additional situations for more practice with deduction.

• As a class, look at the first picture and the sample answer in the speech bubble. Ask students to identify parts of the picture that helped make this deduction. For example: *You can see taxicabs and a sign for Times Square in the background. So, he must be in New York City.*

• Then, have students work in pairs to complete the rest of the exercise. Point out that answers for several items will vary.

• Elicit answers and provide correction as needed.

Active Grammar: *Must* for Empathy and *Could* for Suggestions

  A **Listen. Write the number next to the correct response.**

(CD1 • TR22)

• Go over the information in the presentation box and the examples. Elicit or provide additional examples.

• Play the audio once and have students complete the exercise. Play the audio a second time so students can check their answers.

• Go over the answers and check for understanding.

  B **Work with a partner. Talk about your life. Express empathy, using *must*.**

• Go over the directions and example.

• Try pairing students of mixed ability. Have the higher-level students talk about their lives first and the lower-level students respond, using *must*. Then, have them switch roles.

  C **Listen and complete each suggestion.**

(CD1 • TR23)

• Go over the information and model in the presentation box.

• Play the audio once and have students complete the exercise. Play it a second time so students can check their answers.

Active Grammar — *Must* for Empathy and *Could* for Suggestions

> Use *must* to express empathy (show that you understand another person's feelings).

> I spent ten hours on the plane.

> You **must be** tired.

A **Listen.** Write the number next to the correct response.

CD1 • TR22

   3 **a.** You must be tired.   1 **e.** You must be relieved.

   8 **b.** You must be excited.   6 **f.** You must be bored.

   2 **c.** He must be homesick.   5 **g.** She must be cold.

   4 **d.** She must be nervous.   7 **h.** You must be nervous.

  B **Work with a partner.** Talk about your life. Express empathy, using *must.*

> I'm going to a party this weekend.

> You must be excited.

> Use *could* to make a suggestion.
> **A:** How should I go to the airport?
> **B:** You *could take* the shuttle.

 C **Listen and complete each suggestion.**

CD1 • TR23

1. A: My car broke down. I need to get to work.

   B: You could *take the bus.*

2. A: We want to take a vacation, but we can't afford to spend a lot of money.

   B: You *could go to the beach.*

3. A: My sister's going to Rome, but the hotels are expensive.

   B: *She could exchange apartments.*

4. A: My family wants to stay at my house, but I don't have enough beds.

   B: *They could bring sleeping bags.*

5. A: My children are coming home from college, but flights are too expensive.

   B: *They could take an overnight train.*

6. A: My brother wants to study Spanish in another country.

   B: *He could go to Mexico.*

86 • Unit 6

More Action!

In pairs, have students take turns thinking of additional scenarios and instances that would generate a response using *could*. One partner creates a scenario and makes a statement. The other partner answers using *could*. Provide students with an example (or refer them to the examples in Exercise C) before they begin:

S1: *My computer crashed. I need to finish my paper.*

S2: *You* could *use the computer lab in the library.*

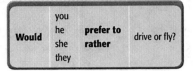

Would	you he she they	**prefer to rather**	drive or fly?

I You They He	**would** **'d**	**prefer to rather**	fly. drive.

> To express a preference, use *would rather* and *would prefer to.*
> The contractions are *'d rather* and *'d prefer to.*
> **I would rather go** to New York than Miami.
> **I would prefer to go** to Chicago than Dallas.

 A **Ask and answer the questions with a partner.** Give reasons for your answers.

1. Would you rather fly or drive?

2. Would you rather travel by bus or by train?

3. Would you prefer to check a bag or take a carry-on?

4. Would you rather go to the beach or to the mountains?

5. Would you prefer to go to a large city or to a small town?

6. Would you rather visit an art museum or a historical site?

7. Would you prefer to visit Tokyo, Japan, or Barcelona, Spain?

> Would you rather
> fly or drive?

> I'd rather fly.
> It's much faster.

B **Working Together** **In your notebook, write five questions about your classmates' preferences.**
Walk around the class and ask five students your questions.
Then, report the results of one of your questions to the class.

> Would you rather
> study in the morning
> or in the evening?

C **Write five sentences about your survey.** *(Answers will vary.)*

Three students would rather study in the evening than in the morning.

1. _____

2. _____

3. _____

4. _____

5. _____

Active Grammar: *Would rather* and *Would prefer to*

 A **Ask and answer the questions with a partner. Give reasons for your answers.**

- Go over the information in the presentation boxes. Check for understanding. Elicit and provide additional examples for more practice.
- Go over the answer to the first item.
- Have students work in pairs to complete the exercise. Check answers with the whole class.

B **Working Together In your notebook, write five questions about your classmates' preferences.**

- Tell students they are writing a survey. They should write different questions from the ones in Exercise A.
- Tell them also to leave enough room after each question for writing five responses.
- Have students interview their classmates and write down the answers to each question.
- Go around the room and have each student report the results.

C **Write five sentences about your survey.**

- Remind students to use both target structures—*would rather* and *would prefer to*—in their sentences.
- Have volunteers share their sentences with the class.

Teaching Tip

For additional practice, have students write each of their sentences from Exercise C twice. They should write one sentence using *would rather,* and the other sentence using *would prefer to.*

Active Grammar: Modals Review

A Match. Write the letter of the correct response.

- Point out that this page reviews all the modals learned in this unit. Go over the possible responses in the right column. Have students name the modals in each sentence.
- Have students complete the exercise individually. Then, check the answers as a class.

B Write three sentences about each picture. Use *may, might, must, would rather,* or *would prefer to.* Then, write one sentence from each picture on the board.

- As a class, come up with sentences to describe one of the pictures. In Picture 1, for example:
  1. *The mother may punish her son for not eating his dinner.*
  2. *The son would rather eat cookies and milk for dinner.*
  3. *He must eat his dinner before he leaves the table.*
- Have students complete their sentences individually.
- Call on a few students to read their sentences aloud. Then, ask for other volunteers to write a sentence of their choice on the board. Correct errors as a class.

A Match. Write the letter of the correct response.

___d___ **1.** I don't feel well, and I have a big test tomorrow.

___e___ **2.** Why isn't Patrick here?

___f___ **3.** The airline lost both of my suitcases!

___h___ **4.** My son has just won a scholarship!

___b___ **5.** It's boring to exercise at the gym.

___c___ **6.** Who's that man with Ellen? Her husband's at work.

___g___ **7.** Where's our teacher? She's never late.

___a___ **8.** I babysat for twins last night.

a. You must be exhausted.

b. Would you rather go running with me?

c. He might be her brother.

d. You could call your professor.

e. He may not be coming.

f. You must be angry.

g. She might be stuck in traffic.

h. You must be so proud.

B Write three sentences about each picture. Use *may, might, must, would rather,* or *would prefer to.* Then, write one sentence from each picture on the board.

(Answers will vary.)

1. The mother _____.
2. The son _____.
3. _____.

4. He _____.
5. The shoes _____.
6. _____.

88 · Unit 6

More Action!

Have students write a short story using the modals they learned in this unit. Find and bring in cartoons or pictures from magazines and newspapers that lend themselves to this exercise. Write three prompts similar to the ones in Exercise B for the cartoons and pictures. If possible, display the prompts on the board. Show students one picture or cartoon and hang it so that everyone can see it during the task. Have students complete the prompts. Call on students to read their completed sentences to the class.

Working Together Student to Student.

Student 1: Turn to page 264. Read **Set A** sentences to Student 2.

Student 2: Listen to Student 1 and write each sentence you hear next to the correct picture.

Then, change roles. Student 2, turn to page 264. Read **Set B** sentences to Student 1. *(Set A answers shown below. See below for Set B.)*

1. They might move to a warmer climate.
2. They would prefer to be closer to their grandchildren.

3. They may not go to college right away.
4. They may get full-time jobs.

5. They could take their honeymoon later.
6. They would rather rent an apartment first.

Answers for Set B
1. They may volunteer at the library.
2. They could move in with their children.
3. They may not work at the same place.
4. They would rather study part time.
5. They'd prefer to buy a house in a couple of years.
6. They might wait to have children.

Travel · 89

**Working Together
Student to Student.**

• Pair up students of mixed ability. Give lower-level students the Student 1 role, so they can have additional speaking practice.
• Make sure Student 1 reads over the sentences to himself or herself before saying them aloud. Remind students to practice good pronunciation, and if needed, repeat the sentences to give Student 2 a chance to write them completely.

The Big Picture: Planning a Vacation

A Look at the picture and discuss. How do you plan a vacation? Do you use a travel agent? Do you use the Internet?

- Discuss the picture and the definition of *lodge*. Ask if any students have stayed in a lodge during a vacation. If so, ask them to describe the lodge.
- Ask students to respond to the questions in the direction line. Be sensitive to the fact that some students may not have taken a vacation recently or planned one.
- Discuss travel agents in your area. Discuss reputable travel websites.

 B Listen and take notes about Drew's family.

(CD1 • TR24)

- Review good note-taking skills. Remind students not to write everything down; they only need to write the most important information.
- Play the audio several times so students can take complete notes.

A Look at the picture and discuss. How do you plan a vacation? Do you use a travel agent? Do you use the Internet?

lodge = a type of resort hotel often located in the mountains

  B Listen and take notes about Drew's family. (Answers will vary.)

CD1 • TR24

Drew's wife: _Maryann is 40. She'll like the pool._

Drew's children: _Gabby is 12 and Leo is 8._

Drew's son: _Leo is 8. He likes almost anything. He loves the outdoors._

Drew's daughter: _Gabby is almost a teenager and a little harder to please._

90 • Unit 6

 ## More Action!

Plan an imaginary trip with the class. Decide on a location that the class would like to travel to. Divide the class in half and ask each group to plan the trip. One group will plan the transportation, and the other group will plan the hotel accommodations. Encourage students to use the Internet to find information on the trip. After they have done the research, discuss the results. Was the Internet easy to use for planning the vacation? What sites were most user friendly? The least user friendly? Do students think that it would be easier to use a travel agent or the Internet to plan a trip? Why?

C Listen again. (Circle) the activities that are available at the lodge.

(sailing)	(waterskiing)	(lessons for sports)
camping	volleyball	(movies)
(basketball)	(baseball)	computer lessons
(swimming)	football	lectures by famous professors
snow skiing	(tennis)	trips to shopping malls
skateboarding	singing contests	(free transportation to town)

D Answer the questions. (Answers may vary.)

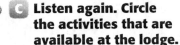

WORD PARTNERSHIPS

window	
middle	seat
aisle	

1. What else can visitors do in the area?
   They can visit the national park; they can go to town.

2. How far away is a major town?
   10 minutes.

3. How often do shuttles leave the lodge?
   They leave every hour.

4. What can tourists do at the national park?
   They can tour the park. They can see wild animals.

5. What is Drew going to do now?
   He's going to take brochures home and talk to his children.

6. Where would Drew prefer to sit on the plane?
   He'd prefer to sit in an aisle seat.

7. What is Gina going to do now?
   She's going to start checking flights.

  E Pronunciation: *'d rather* Listen. Complete the sentences with *I'd, He'd, She'd, We'd,* or *They'd.*

1. __We'd__ rather go camping.
2. __They'd__ rather stay in a cabin.
3. __He'd__ rather go fishing.
4. __She'd__ rather go swimming.

5. __She'd__ rather not stay in a tent.
6. __He'd__ rather not go to malls.
7. __They'd__ rather not eat at home.
8. __I'd__ rather not stay at a hotel.

C Listen again. Circle the activities that are available at the lodge.
(CD1 • TR24)

• Play the audio several times so students can complete the exercise.
• Go over the answers as a class.

Word Partnerships

Go over the information in the box. Draw a rough diagram of the inside of a plane to clearly show the kinds of seats one can sit in. Have students point out where window, middle, and aisle seats are located.

D Answer the questions.

• Have students complete the exercise. If students need help, play the audio again.
• Circulate around the room providing help as needed.

E Pronunciation: *'d rather*. Listen. Complete the sentences with *I'd, He'd, She'd, We'd,* or *They'd.*
(CD1 • TR25)

• Refer students back to the *would rather / 'd rather* chart on the top of page 87 to remind them of this grammar point and prepare them for this exercise.
• Play the audio several times so students can complete the exercise.
• Elicit answers from the class.

Reading:
A Visit to Argentina

A Discuss.

• Ask a student to point out Argentina on a map.
• Discuss the answers to the questions.
• Go over the Reading Note together. Tell students that it is helpful to use a highlighter or a pen in a color other than black so the notes show up.
• Read the first paragraph of the text together and decide what should be highlighted. (The topic sentence is often a good start!)

B Word Builder
Find the words below in the reading.

• Point out that the words the students need to find are in boldface type. If students have trouble identifying the definition of the word, tell them to read the sentence that contains the vocabulary word.
• Have students complete the exercise individually and check answers with the class.

C Read.

• Have students read the passage on their own.
• Remind them of the Reading Note. Have them practice highlighting important information by reading the text a second time and underlining the important ideas.
• Ask volunteers to say what they have highlighted. Accept or correct these ideas.

A Discuss.

1. Where is Argentina?
2. What do you know about Argentina?

> **READING NOTE**
> **Highlighting Important Information**
> When you read, it is a good idea to underline or highlight information that you think is interesting or ideas that your teacher might put on a test. It is also a good idea to write some notes in the margin. Those notes will help you study later.

Puente de la mujer,
"Woman's Bridge"

B Word Builder Find the words below in the reading. Then, match the words with their definitions.

<u>d</u> **1.** borders   **a.** an Argentine dance

<u>a</u> **2.** tango   **b.** unusual sights

<u>e</u> **3.** vibrant   **c.** a person who travels to find information

<u>b</u> **4.** wonders   **d.** touches another country or geographical feature

<u>c</u> **5.** explorer   **e.** lively; full of life and energy

C Read.

Argentina is located in the Southern Hemisphere on the South American continent. It **borders** the South Atlantic Ocean, Chile, Uruguay, Paraguay, Bolivia, and Brazil. If you are looking for a place where you can experience both the life of **vibrant** cities and the beauty of natural **wonders**, you might want to visit Argentina.

The capital of Argentina, Buenos Aires, is a good place to start your trip. After arriving at the international airport, it is an easy trip to a downtown hotel. The city has a variety of transportation: taxis, a street railway, commuter trains, buses, and ferries. Buenos Aires is the largest city in Argentina and the second largest city in South America. It has one of the busiest ports in South America. It's a city where visitors can spend time touring a variety of different neighborhoods, including Recoleta, Puerto Madero, and La Boca, home to Boca Juniors, one of Argentina's famous soccer clubs. Visitors can easily get to any of the museums, such as the Latin American

92 • Unit 6

Teaching Tip

Check comprehension by reviewing the whole story and asking comprehension questions about each paragraph. Ask about certain vocabulary words, too. Possible questions for the first paragraph include: *Where is Argentina located? What body of water does it border? What countries border it?*

Contemporary Art Museum, the National Museum of Fine Arts, or for something different, the World **Tango** Museum, a museum devoted to Argentina's famous dance. In addition, there is a botanical garden, a zoo, and restaurants that serve delicious *asado*, Argentine barbecue. For those who want to do some shopping, there are many stores and shopping malls where tourists can find leather items, such as handbags, wallets, or jackets. As you can see, a visitor will find it difficult to be bored in Buenos Aires.

If you would rather get away from the busy city, fly to El Calafate. This is the starting point for a visit to Patagonia, the region farthest south of the Andes Mountains in Argentina and Chile, and Los Glaciares National Park. El Calafate is located on the southern shore of Lake Argentino. It is here that you can see one of the natural wonders of the world, the Perito Moreno Glacier, which was named after an Argentine **explorer**, Francisco Moreno. One of the best ways to see the glaciers is to take a boat ride on Lake Argentino. You will be able to sail among icebergs and get a closer view of the wall of the Perito Moreno Glacier, the Spegazzini Glacier. If the icebergs are not in the way, visitors might see the Upsala Glacier, the largest glacier in South America. It is a fantastic sight.

Perito Moreno Glacier

When you plan your next vacation, think about going to Argentina. It will satisfy your need for the action of a city and the beauty of nature.

D **Circle** *True* **or** *False*.

1. Argentina borders Bolivia, Colombia, and Peru.   True   (False)

2. Buenos Aires is the largest city in South America.   True   (False)

3. Soccer is a popular sport in Argentina.   (True)   False

4. Buenos Aires has more than one art museum.   (True)   False

5. There are many places to shop for leather.   (True)   False

6. Buenos Aires is quieter than El Calafate.   True   (False)

7. Perito Moreno Glacier was named after an American.   True   (False)

8. Visitors can see the glaciers by boat.   (True)   False

D **Circle** *True* **or** *False*.

Have students complete the exercise individually and check their answers with a partner. Review the answers with the whole class. If students have circled an incorrect answer, ask them to look at the reading again and find the information that pertains to the question.

Writing Our Stories:
A Dream Vacation

 Read the composition.

• Ask students to do the reading on their own.

• When they finish, invite four students to each pick a different paragraph and tell the things that the person *might do* on her vacation in that place. In the first paragraph, for example: *She might visit four cities in South America. She might take a Spanish course.*

• Encourage students to use the modals learned in this unit to summarize the reading.

 Read the composition.

A Dream Vacation

Mayumi Sato
March 22
English IV

If I have free time and money, I will take my dream vacation. I would like to visit four South American cities: Lima and Cuzco in Peru, Buenos Aires in Argentina, and Rio de Janeiro in Brazil. Before I start my vacation, I might take a Spanish course. Also, I could ask some of my South American classmates to give me some advice. I want to know the best time to visit, too.

First, I will go to Peru. I will fly to the capital city, Lima. I may spend a few days visiting the museums, looking at the architecture, and eating the fresh seafood. After a few days, I will go to Cuzco to prepare for a trip to see the ruins of Machu Picchu. I hear that it is one of the most interesting archaeological sites in the world. When I get back to Cuzco, I might buy some souvenirs for my family and friends.

Then, I will travel to Buenos Aires, Argentina. I am taking dance lessons now, so I might take a tango class in Buenos Aires. I heard that Buenos Aires is the home of the tango. I would also like to visit a ranch and go horseback riding. I'm sure that I will eat some delicious Argentine barbecue.

Finally, I will fly to Rio de Janeiro, Brazil, for my last stop. I'm going to visit a samba school and watch the students dance the samba. I might take a samba class. I want to relax on the famous Copacabana Beach, eat Brazilian barbecue, and see the museums. I hear that it is a very exciting city. This will be a great vacation.

94 · Unit 6

More Action!

Ask students to tell which of the vacation spots from the reading they would like to visit most and why.

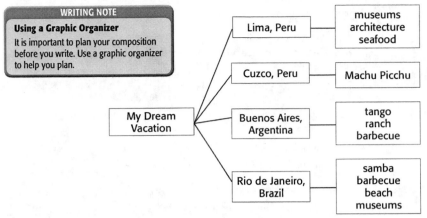

```
                                    ┌──────────────┐      ┌──────────────────┐
                                    │ Lima, Peru   │──────│ museums          │
                                    └──────────────┘      │ architecture     │
                                   /                       │ seafood          │
                                  /                        └──────────────────┘
                                 /   ┌──────────────┐      ┌──────────────────┐
                                /    │ Cuzco, Peru  │──────│ Machu Picchu     │
            ┌──────────────┐   /     └──────────────┘      └──────────────────┘
            │ My Dream     │──┤
            │ Vacation     │   \     ┌──────────────┐      ┌──────────────────┐
            └──────────────┘    \    │ Buenos Aires,│──────│ tango            │
                                 \   │ Argentina    │      │ ranch            │
                                  \  └──────────────┘      │ barbecue         │
                                   \                        └──────────────────┘
                                    \ ┌──────────────┐      ┌──────────────────┐
                                      │ Rio de Janeiro,│────│ samba            │
                                      │ Brazil       │      │ barbecue         │
                                      └──────────────┘      │ beach            │
                                                            │ museums          │
                                                            └──────────────────┘
```

B Use a graphic organizer to plan a composition about your dream vacation. **Answer the questions.**

1. Where do you want to go?
2. Why do you want to go there?
3. How long do you plan to stay?
4. What are you going to do there?

C Write your composition. Use the ideas in your graphic organizer.

 D Sharing Our Stories Read your partner's story. **Answer the questions.**

1. Where does your partner want to go for a dream vacation?
2. Why does he / she want to go there?

E Find and correct the modal verb mistakes.

1. I might ~~to~~ visit a museum.
2. He may not ^be^ taking a class this semester.
3. They might be look^ing^ in his suitcase.
4. She could ^be^ going by train.
5. We ^'d^ rather not use a credit card.
6. He must not ~~has~~ ^have^ a passport.
7. ~~You would~~ ^Would you^ rather fly today or tomorrow?
8. She might ^be^ homesick.

Travel · **95**

Travel · **95**

Practicing on Your Own

A Rewrite each sentence with the correct modal. Some of the sentences are negative.

- Point out to students that they should replace the bolded words in each sentence with an appropriate modal from the box. Ask students to complete the sentences on their own.
- Have students check their answers with a partner and correct any mistakes in their sentences.
- Call on pairs of students for the answers. One student should say the original sentence. The second student should give the rewritten sentence.

A **Rewrite each sentence with the correct modal.** Some of the sentences are negative.

could	may	must	would rather
have to	might	should	would prefer to

1. **I think it's a good idea for you** to apply for your passport early.
   You _should apply for your passport early_ .

2. She **is required** to get a visa.
   She _has to / must get a visa_ .

3. **Maybe** the flight is late because of the weather.
   The flight _might be late because of the weather_ .

4. **Maybe** the students are not listening to the guide.
   The students _may / might not be listening to the guide_ .

5. We **would prefer to take** the shuttle to the airport.
   We _would rather take the shuttle to the airport_ .

6. My **suggestion** is for you to travel during spring break.
   You _could travel during spring break_ .

7. **It is necessary for him to pack** large bottles in his checked bag.
   He _has to / must pack large bottles in his checked bag_ .

8. **Maybe** they are bringing your luggage right now.
   They _may / might be bringing your luggage right now_ .

9. They **would rather not** travel far from home.
   They _would prefer not to travel far from home_ .

10. He thinks that **it isn't a good idea** for his sister to travel alone.
    He thinks that _his sister shouldn't travel alone_ .

More Action!

- For more practice with modals, have students in pairs come up with sentences about what to do when preparing for a trip (what they will need to bring, etc.). They will need to decide what they *must* do, what they *might / may* want to do, what they *could* do, and so forth. For example: *You must bring your passport with you if you are traveling to a different country. You may need to bring an extra toothbrush in case your luggage gets misplaced.*

  You could ask a travel agent to book your hotel.
- Alternatively, you may wish to pivot from the topic of travel and assign a different topic for this activity, such as how to prepare for class or the new school year. Model a few sentences about the new topic before having pairs work. Be sure to use modals. For example: *You have to buy your textbooks for class. You should introduce yourself to the professor.*

Security at the Airport

 A **Listen and answer the questions.** (See answers below.)

CD1·TR26

1. Where did she go?
2. Where did she stay?
3. Where was her luggage?
4. Did anyone ask her to carry anything in her bag?
5. Did the inspector open her bag?
6. What happened?

B **Working Together** **Work in a group.** Look at the sign. Then:

1. Cross out items on the list that are not allowed.
2. Move items from one list to the other when necessary.
3. Compare your lists with another group.

DO NOT PACK IN YOUR CARRY-ON

Items in Carry-on Bag	Items in Checked Bag
two paperback books	five shirts
a baseball glove	one pair of jeans
an MP3 player	underwear and socks
a small bottle of aspirin	two baseball bats
a large bottle of shampoo	a jacket
a large bottle of suntan lotion	a U.S. passport
an army knife	matches
a pair of shoes	a pair of dress shoes
a small can of shaving cream	two belts
three wrapped gifts	a bag of energy bars
a U.S. passport	a large bottle of shampoo
	a large bottle of suntan lotion
	an army knife

Answers for Exercise A:
1. To Barcelona and Madrid.
2. At a hotel and at her sister's apartment.
3. In the hotel and in her sister's apartment
4. No, just presents.
5. Yes, he did.
6. She had to unwrap the presents or put them in her checked bag.

Teaching Tip

For more oral practice, have students discuss the conversation in Exercise A with a partner. If students have traveled by air, ask them to talk about their own experience at airports.

English in Action: Security at the Airport

 A **Listen and answer the questions.**

(CD1 • TR26)

• Play the audio once and have students answer the questions.
• Play it again so they can complete the exercise and check their answers. Play it a third time if needed.

B **Working Together Work in a group. Look at the sign.**

• Have students work in pairs to complete the exercise.
• Have the pairs compare their lists with another group and discuss their choices.
• Check answers with the class. Have volunteers say why the items they moved had to be moved to the other column.
• If time allows, add to the list of items in the book. Ask students to predict whether the items you name are allowed in the carry-on bags or in the checked bags. Tell them to write the name of the item in the correct list.
For example:
a laptop computer (carry-on bag)
golf clubs (checked bags)

Sports

Word Partnerships

Introduce the vocabulary in the Word Partnerships box. Ask if students know the difference between an amateur and professional athlete. Explain that an amateur athlete does not usually get paid for their work, but a professional athlete does.

A Write the letter of each sentence next to the correct name.

- Ask students to read the statements and underline any words they don't understand. Clarify the meaning of any unfamiliar vocabulary.
- Do the first item together. Ask a volunteer to explain the meaning of *doubles* in Letter a. Tell students to use the pictures to help them figure out the rest of the answers on their own.
- Circulate around the room and provide help as needed.
- Go over the completed exercise as a class.

Unit 7 Sports

A Write the letter of each sentence next to the correct name.

a. She has been playing doubles for many years.
b. He has been trying to win the Super Bowl for a long time.
c. She has been racing cars since she was a teenager.
d. He has been talking to his fans for 20 minutes.
e. He has been playing soccer for a Brazilian team for two years.
f. She has been neglecting her schoolwork to play golf.

WORD PARTNERSHIPS

female	
male	
high school	
college	athlete
amateur	
professional	

1.
   a Angelica Jones

2.
   e Marco Ronaldo

3.
   b Dave Meese

4.
   c Melinda Gomez

5.
   f Kristine Park

6.
   d Alfredo Perez

98 · Unit 7

More Action!

- After completing the Active Grammar sections of this unit, ask students to turn back to this page (page 98). Invite each student to cut out three newspaper or magazine pictures of famous athletes and sporting events and bring them to class.
- Have students work in pairs. Each pair should have six pictures.

Pairs should write statements about each picture using the target grammar structures from this unit. Refer students to Exercise A on page 98 for examples.
- Then, have pairs switch pictures and statements with another pair. The other pair of students should match each sentence with the correct picture.

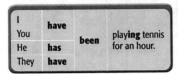
I	have		playing tennis
You	have	been	for an hour.
He	has		
They	have		

Contractions
I have – I've
you have – you've
he has – he's
they have – they've

The *present continuous* describes an action that is happening now.
I am playing tennis.
The *present perfect continuous* describes an action that began in the past and is continuing now.
I have been playing tennis for an hour.

A **Complete the sentences.** Use the correct tense.

1. It's 5:00.

   Carl _____is playing_____ basketball.

   Carl _____began_____ to play basketball at 4:00.

   He _has been playing_ basketball for an hour.

   He _has been playing_ basketball since 4:00.

2. It's 3:00.

   The men _____are playing_____ soccer.

   They _____began_____ to play soccer at 1:00.

   They _have been playing_ soccer for two hours.

   They _____have been playing_____ since 1:00.

3. It's 12:00.

   The women _____are playing_____ tennis.

   They _____began_____ to play tennis at 10:00.

   They _have been playing_ tennis for two hours.

   They _____have been playing_____ tennis since 10:00.

4. I _____am studying_____ English.

   I _____began_____ to study English in ___[year]___.

   I _have been studying_ English for (Answers will vary.)

   I _have been studying_ English since (Answers will vary.)

Sports • **99**

Active Grammar: Present Perfect Continuous

A **Complete the sentences. Use the correct tense.**

• Go over the information in the grammar boxes. Explain that continuous activities began at a specific time in the past and are still taking place now.
For example: *I have been teaching this class for twenty minutes.*

• Read the list of contractions and have students repeat after you.

• Ask a different student to read each of the sentences formed using the words in the chart. Discuss the meaning of each sentence.

• Point to the first picture in Exercise A and have a student read the sentences that go with it. Explain the time period of the action. For example:

S1: *Carl is playing basketball.*

T: Is playing *means that Carl is taking part in a basketball game right now.*

• Continue going over the sentences in Item 1, this time calling on students to explain the time period of the action. For example:

S1: *Carl began to play basketball at 4:00.*

S2: Began to play *means that Carl started a game of basketball.*

• Repeat this activity for the sentences in Item 2. Have students complete the activity on their own.

B **Pronunciation: 've been / 's been Listen and repeat.**

(CD2•TR1)

• Review the contractions in the box on page 99.
• Play the audio and have students listen and repeat. Have them pay close attention to the formation and pronunciation of the contractions.

 C **Listen again. Circle the sentence you hear. Then, practice the sentences with a partner.**

(CD2•TR2)

• Have students look at the pairs of sentences in Exercise B. Explain that they should circle the sentence they hear.
• Play the audio once and have students circle the sentences they hear. Review the correct answers with the whole class.

 D **Listen to the conversation.**

(CD2•TR3)

Ask students to follow along in their books as you play the audio. Answer any questions students may have. Then, have them listen again.

 E **Practice the conversation in Exercise D with a partner. Then, write a new conversation in your notebook. Practice the conversation.**

• Have students practice the conversation in pairs.
• Have students write a new conversation on a piece of paper. Ask them to use the present perfect continuous at least three times in their conversation.

 B **Pronunciation: 've been / 's been Listen and repeat.**

CD2•TR1

1. **a.** She's taking dancing lessons. **b.** She's been taking dancing lessons.
2. **a.** She's learning how to drive. **b.** She's been learning how to drive.
3. **a.** He's playing baseball. **b.** He's been playing baseball.
4. **a.** I'm looking for a new apartment. **b.** I've been looking for a new apartment.
5. **a.** She's recovering from her accident. **b.** She's been recovering from her accident.
6. **a.** He's studying Chinese. **b.** He's been studying Chinese.
7. **a.** He's working hard. **b.** He's been working hard.
8. **a.** I'm training for a new job. **b.** I've been training for a new job.

 C **Listen again.** (Circle) the sentence you hear. Then, practice the sentences with a partner.

CD2•TR2

 1. b 2. b 3. a 4. b 5. a 6. a 7. b 8. a

 **D** **Listen to the conversation.**

CD2•TR3

A: Hi, Juan. What've you been up to?

B: I've been painting the house.

A: And how's your family?

B: We're all fine. Maribel is 16 now, so I've been teaching her how to drive.

A: Good luck with that! And your parents? How are they?

B: They've been enjoying their retirement. They've been visiting their grandchildren a lot.

A: Oh, that's nice. Tell them I asked about them.

B: I sure will.

 E **Practice the conversation in Exercise D with a partner.** Then, write a new conversation in your notebook. Practice the conversation.

More Action!

Have students practice the sentences in Exercise B with a partner. Students take turns saying the sentences to each other. Circulate around the room providing feedback on pronunciation as needed.

Teaching Tip

To help students get started with writing a new conversation, suggest that they start it with the same question that starts the conversation in Exercise C (*What've you been up to?*). When they have practiced their conversation with a partner, call on pairs to role-play their conversations for the class.

For and *Since*

For	Since
For shows an amount of time. **for** a few minutes **for** three days	*Since* shows when an action started. **since** 2009 **since** Monday **since** she moved to the city

A Write each word or phrase under *for* or *since*.

several days	he joined the team	she began to play tennis
three hours	I was a child	a long time
about two weeks	a few minutes	many years
Saturday	he broke his arm	2:00

For	Since
three hours	she began to play tennis
several days	Saturday
about two weeks	he joined the team
a few minutes	I was a child
a long time	he broke his arm
many years	2:00

B **Complete the sentences.** Use *for* or *since*.

1. She's been playing professionally __for__ five years.

2. He's been working out __since__ 8:00 this morning.

3. The team has been practicing __for__ about three hours.

4. She's been riding her bicycle __for__ two hours.

5. The girls have been practicing their routine __since__ 3:00.

6. The players have been listening to the coach __for__ 30 minutes.

7. He hasn't been running well __since__ he hurt his leg.

8. The fans have been buying snacks __since__ they arrived at the stadium.

Sports · **101**

Active Grammar: *For* and *Since*

A **Write each word or phrase under *for* or *since*.**

• Read and discuss with students the descriptions of the use of *for* and *since*. Give a few example sentences using these words. For example: *It has been raining for three days. Pablo has been playing soccer since he was a child.* Ask students to come up with additional sentences using *for* or *since*.

• Have students write the phrases in the correct columns. Review the answers with the class and provide explanations as needed.

B **Complete the sentences. Use *for* or *since*.**

Ask students to complete the sentences and check their answers with a partner. Review the correct answers orally with the class.

More Action!

Divide the class into two teams. (If you have a large class, you may wish to have several sets of teams.) Have a competition in which a member of one team makes a statement using *since* or *for*, and a member of the other team responds using the other word. The second team's response must communicate exactly the same fact. For example:

Team 1: *We have been in class since 9:00.*
Team 2: *We have been in class for two hours.*
Each team gets one point for each correct response it gives.

Active Grammar: Present Perfect Continuous— *Yes / No* Questions

 A **Ask and answer questions. Use the present perfect continuous.**

- Review the questions and answers in the grammar charts at the top of the page. Answer any questions students might have.
- Point out the sample question and answer in the speech bubbles. Then, do the second item as a class. Call on a student to form the question and call on a different student to provide the answer. Encourage usage of contractions in the answers.
- Pair students of varying skill levels. Have pairs take turns asking and answering the questions.
- To check answers, call on pairs and have pairs take turns asking and answering each question. Make corrections as needed.

 B **Read the paragraph. Then, complete the questions. Use the past tense or the present perfect continuous.**

- Have students read the paragraph to themselves and complete the exercise.
- Point out that the short answer for each item provides a clue as to which tense to use. For example, the helping verb *did* in the responses for Items 4 and 5 indicates that the past tense should be used.

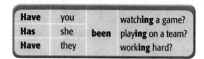

Have	you		watch**ing** a game?
Has	she	been	play**ing** on a team?
Have	they		work**ing** hard?

Yes, I **have**.	No, I **haven't**.
Yes, she **has**.	No, she **hasn't**.
Yes, they **have**.	No, they **haven't**.

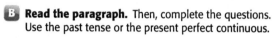 **A** **Ask and answer questions.** Use the present perfect continuous.

> Have you been studying hard?

> Yes, I have.

1. you / study / hard
   Have you been studying hard?
2. you / work / overtime
   Have you been working overtime?
3. you / look for / a new job
   Have you been looking for a new job?
4. you / get / enough sleep
   Have you been getting enough sleep?
5. you / exercise
   Have you been exercising?
6. your classmates / speak / English in class *Have your classmates been speaking English in class?*

7. the teacher / give / a lot of homework *Has the teacher been giving a lot of homework?*
8. the teacher / give / quizzes *Has the teacher been giving quizzes?*
9. you / listen to / music in English *Have you been listening to music in English?*
10. you / watch / TV in English *Have you been watching TV in English?*

B **Read the paragraph.** Then, complete the questions. Use the past tense or the present perfect continuous.

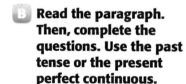

Daniel and Monica are skiers. Daniel has been skiing since he was a young child. Monica has been skiing since she was 14 years old. Now they're training for the Olympics. They have been training for a long time. Daniel won three competitions last year. Monica won the national competition and earned a second-place finish last month. They have been training together for only a short time. They both plan to become professionals after the Olympics.

1. *Has Daniel been skiing since he was a child* ? Yes, he has.
2. *Has Monica been skiing* since she was a child? No, she hasn't.
3. *Have they been training for the Olympics* ? Yes, they have.
4. *Did Daniel win three competitions* last year? Yes, he did.
5. *Did Monica earn second place* last month? Yes, she did.
6. *Have they been training together* for a long time? No, they haven't.

Teaching Tip

For additional oral practice, call on individual students to read one sentence of the paragraph aloud instead of having them read the paragraph to themselves.

Student 1: Turn to page 264. Read **Set A** sentences to Student 2.

Student 2: Listen to Student 1 and write each sentence next to the correct picture.

Then, change roles. Student 2, turn to page 264. Read **Set B** sentences. Student 1, listen and write each sentence next to the correct picture.

"Roger is in the lead!"

1. They've been running for two hours.
   They've been drinking a lot of water.
2. They've been getting lots of support.
   Roger has been leading for 30 minutes.

"I'm not sure what's wrong."

3. I've been feeling tired.
   My stomach has been bothering me.
4. I've been having trouble sleeping.
   I haven't been eating well.

"You haven't been finishing your work on time. Is anything wrong?"

5. You haven't been coming to work on time.
   We've been receiving a lot of complaints.
6. You've been making mistakes in your work.
   You've been arguing with your co-workers.

"Could you take a look at it?"

7. It's been making a strange noise.
   It's been leaking oil.
8. It's been overheating in traffic.
   It hasn't been running smoothly.

 Working Together Student to Student.

• Read and discuss the instructions and be sure students understand how to proceed. Ask different students to describe the situation shown in each picture. Then, help students locate the sentences on page 264.

• Students work in pairs. First, Student 1 reads the Set A statements on page 264 and Student B writes each statement next to the correct picture on page 103. Then, they reverse roles and Student 2 reads the Set B statements on page 264 and Student 1 writes each one in the correct place on page 103.

• Check the correct answers with the whole class.

Teaching Tip

Provide oral practice of this structure by inviting students to make up additional questions to ask about the people in the pictures. Have a student make up a sentence using the present perfect continuous, and call on another student to tell which picture it applies to. For example:

S1: *It hasn't been starting on cold mornings.*

S2: *That sentence goes with Picture 4.*

Active Grammar: Present Perfect Continuous— *How long* Questions

A **Working Together** Work in a group of four or five students. Write each person's name in the chart. Ask the questions and write the answers in the chart.

- Go over the information in the grammar box. Have students practice forming *how long* questions. Provide responses to their questions using *since* or *for*. For example:

S1: *How long has he been studying English?*

S2: *He's been studying English for two months. He's been studying English since last fall.*

- Read the instructions and explain how to use the chart to record answers. Then, help students form groups of five and have them complete the activity. Set a time limit of about ten minutes to help keep groups on task.
- When the time is up, review a few of the questions and answers with the whole class.

B **Complete the sentences. Use the information from your chart.**

- Have each group work together to complete the sentences based on the information in the chart.
- Have a volunteer from each group read two or three sentences aloud to the class.

104 · Unit 7

How long	have	I	been	studying English?
	has	you		living here?
	have	he		
		they		

He**'s been studying** English for two months.

I**'ve been living** here for three years.

A **Working Together** Work in a group of four or five students. Write each person's name in the chart. Ask the questions and write the answers in the chart. (Answers will vary.)

1. How long have you been living in the United States?
2. How long have you been studying English?
3. How long have you been attending this school?
4. How long have you been working?
5. How long have you been working in the United States?

Names	Question 1	Question 2	Question 3	Question 4	Question 5
1.					
2.					
3.					
4.					
5.					

B **Complete the sentences.** Use the information from your chart. (Answers will vary.)

1. _____ has been living in the United States the longest.
2. _____ has been studying English the shortest time.
3. _____ has been attending this school for _____.
4. _____ has been working the longest.
5. _____ doesn't work.
6. _____ has been working in the United States the longest.

104 · Unit 7

More Action!

For additional practice, play *Ask Your Teacher*. Invite students to ask you appropriate questions using *How long?* Give truthful answers whenever possible. Try to incorporate the present perfect continuous into your answers as often as possible. Sample questions include: *Do you play a musical instrument? How long have you played it? Do you live in this city? How long have you been a teacher? Do you have a hobby?*

If students have trouble thinking of appropriate questions, provide these questions to them or have them work with a partner to come up with appropriate questions.

C **Listen.** Then, complete the questions.
CD2·TR4

| Does | How long | How often | How old | What | Who |

1. _How old_ is Robert? *Seven*

2. _What_ did he win? *The state championship*

3. _How long_ has he been playing tennis? *Since he was three.*

4. _Who_ taught him how to play? *His father and a private instructor.*

5. _Does_ he take private lessons? *Yes, he does.*

6. _How long_ has he been taking private lessons? *For two years.*

7. _How often_ do his parents want him to practice? *Three or four days a week.*

8. _What_ is his dream? *To be a professional tennis player.*

D **Ask and answer the questions in Exercise C.**

E **Read the timeline.** Complete the questions. *(Answers may vary.)*

1.	1982	born March 4
2.	1990	started playing soccer
3.	1999	became a professional; signed with a German team
4.	2001	won MLS (Major League Soccer) championship with San José Earthquakes
5.	2003	won MLS championship with San José; named U.S. Soccer Athlete of the Year
6.	2005	won MLS championship with L.A. Galaxy
7.	2009	played in MLS finals; lost game; became captain of team; signed four-year contract extension

1. When _was he born_ ?

2. How long _has he been playing soccer_ ?

3. Who _did he sign with_ ?

4. What _did he win in 2001_ ?

5. How many times _has he won the MLS championship_ ?

6. How long _did he play with the San José Earthquakes_ ?

7. How long _has he been playing with the L.A. Galaxy_ ?

C **Listen. Then, complete the questions.**
(CD2 • TR4)

• Review the directions and answer choices. Answer any questions.
• Point out the picture and ask a student to tell what has happened to the boy. They can respond with a sentence using a modal: *He may have won a contest.* Read through the items and explain what *private lessons* are, if necessary.
• Play the audio and have students fill in the missing words.
• Play the audio a second time and have students answer the questions out loud.

D **Ask and answer the questions in Exercise C.**

• As a way of checking the answers in Exercise C, have students complete this exercise.
• Pair students of varying levels together if possible.

E **Read the timeline. Complete the questions.**

• Go over the information in the timeline. Point out that in many countries, *soccer* is known as *football*.
• Go over the model sentence in Item 1. Have students complete the exercise individually, and then check the answers as a class. Ask: *Are all the questions in the present perfect continuous? If not, what other tenses are used?*

The Big Picture: A Soccer Game

 A **In each circle, write the number of the correct person from the box below.**

• Do this activity as a class. Go over the six words in the box below the picture before you begin.

• Point out figures in the illustration and ask students to choose a word from the box. As students suggest labels for each person, discuss that person's contribution to the game. For example:

T: *What is a fan?*
S1: *Somebody who likes a team.*
T: *That's right. It's a person who likes a team or a player a lot. A fan goes to a lot of games to see the team or the player.*

 B **Listen to the story.**
(CD2 • TR5)

• Read the instructions. Discuss the meaning of each question. Be sure students understand the meaning of the term *minutes left in the game* (number of minutes before the end of the game).

• Play the audio twice as students just listen. Then, read the questions aloud and call on different students to answer each one. Alternatively, have students write the answers in their book. If students are unsure of an answer, replay the audio once more and give them another chance to answer.

106 · Unit 7

A **In each circle, write the number of the correct person from the box below.**

 B **Listen to the story.** Then, answer the questions.
CD2·TR5

1. Is it the first half or the second half?
   Second half
2. How many minutes are left in the game?
   10 minutes
3. What's the score?
   2 to 1
4. How many fans are at the game?
   More than 35,000
5. What have the concession workers been doing?
   They've been working hard.
6. What have people been buying?
   They've been buying water, soda, drinks, and food.
7. How long is the wait at the concession stand?
   15 minutes or more
8. Has there been any fighting on the field?
   No, there hasn't.
9. Which players has the Stars' coach been putting in?
   His best defensive players.
10. Which players has the Kings' coach been substituting?
    His fastest and best players.

1. players
2. fans
3. announcer
4. coach
5. official
6. concession workers

106 · Unit 7

C **Complete the sentences.** Use the correct verb from the box in the present perfect continuous tense.

1. The fans _____ have been making _____ a lot of noise.

2. The fans _____ have been buying _____ a lot of soda and water.

3. People _____ have been waiting _____ in line to buy food.

4. An announcer _____ has been calling _____ the game.

5. The players _____ have been running _____ up and down the field.

6. A few of the players _____ have been pulling _____ each other's shirts.

7. The coaches _____ have been substituting _____ players.

8. Everyone _____ has been watching _____ player number 7.

9. The fans _____ have been supporting _____ their favorite players.

buy
call
~~make~~
pull
run
substitute
support
wait
watch

D **Match the questions with the answers.**

_d_ **1.** Is the stadium full?

_e_ **2.** Did the game start at 2:00?

_a_ **3.** Are there more than 20,000 fans?

_i_ **4.** Have the fans been cheering for their favorites?

_f_ **5.** Are the fans hot?

_b_ **6.** Has the Stars' coach been giving instructions?

_j_ **7.** Do the Stars have four goals?

_c_ **8.** Does player number 7 have the ball?

_g_ **9.** Is the score 4–1?

_h_ **10.** Have the officials been giving any red cards?

a. Yes, there are.

b. Yes, he has.

c. Yes, he does.

d. Yes, it is.

e. Yes, it did.

f. Yes, they are.

g. No, it isn't.

h. No, they haven't.

i. Yes, they have.

j. No, they don't.

C **Complete the sentences. Use the correct verb from the box in the present perfect continuous tense.**

• Have students write their answers individually and check them with a partner. Check the correct answers by having different students write one complete sentence on the board.
• Review the answers with the whole class, correcting them as necessary.

D **Match the questions with the answers.**

• Ask students to complete the matching exercise individually, and then check their answers with a partner.
• Review the correct answers orally with the whole class. Ask which questions contain the past continuous tense (Items 4, 6, and 10).

Sports · **107**

Reading: The History of the World Cup

A Discuss.

Read and discuss the pre-reading questions and **Culture Note**. Ask students to elaborate on their answers or ask additional questions: *What team is your favorite? Who is your favorite player on the team?*

B Word Builder Match the words with the definitions.

• Point out that the words the students need to match are in boldface type in the reading, so they are easy to find. If students have trouble identifying the definition of the word, tell them to read the sentence that contains the vocabulary word. Reading the sentence may help them put the vocabulary word in context and identify the definition more easily.
• Have students complete the exercise on their own. Check answers as a class.

C Read.

Ask students to read the entire story without stopping. Explain that they might not understand everything. Suggest that they just try to understand the main ideas the first time through.

A Discuss.

1. Where is the next World Cup going to be?
2. Which countries do you think are the strongest competition?

B Word Builder Match the words with the definitions.

_d_ **1.** still	**a.** a person or organization that holds an event
_c_ **2.** amateur	**b.** all over
_e_ **3.** exhibition	**c.** not professional
_a_ **4.** host	**d.** continues; remains
_f_ **5.** sparked	**e.** show
_b_ **6.** throughout	**f.** created

> **CULTURE NOTE**
> The word "soccer" is an abbreviation of "association football." The word first appeared in 1889.

C Read.

By January 27, 2010, two-thirds of the available tickets for the 2010 World Cup had already been sold. Even though soccer is not the top sport in the United States, there is **still** interest in the World Cup. The United States was the leader in sales for the 2010 World Cup, with over 50,000 applications for tickets.

In the United States, people call the sport "soccer," but in all other countries, people call it "football." FIFA (Fédération Internationale de Football Association) was founded in Paris, France, in 1904. At that time, seven countries, including France, Spain, and Switzerland, were part of FIFA. At the 1908 Summer Olympics, soccer became an official Olympic sport, organized by FIFA. At that time, only **amateur** athletes were allowed to participate in the Olympics. Because the best soccer players couldn't participate, the Olympic soccer tournament was considered an **exhibition** rather than a real match.

In 1914, FIFA recognized the Olympic soccer tournament as an amateur event. Belgium won the 1920 Summer Olympics, and Uruguay won the next two Olympics.

Soccer wasn't included in the 1932 Olympics. There were two reasons for this. One reason was that the games were in Los Angeles, and soccer was not popular in the United States. Second, the International Olympic Committee and FIFA could not agree about what an "amateur" was.

Uruguay was the **host** of the first World Cup in 1930. Thirteen countries participated: seven from South America, four from Europe, and two from North America. Uruguay was the winner again.

108 · Unit 7

When the World Cup came to the United States in 1994, it **sparked** interest in soccer. Today, in school yards and on fields **throughout** the United States, many young people play soccer. With both men's and women's professional leagues, FIFA can expect to continue to have more and more fans in the U.S.

World Cup Winners 1930–2010	
Country	**Number of wins**
Brazil	5
Italy	4
West Germany	3
Uruguay	2
Argentina	2
Spain	1

World Cup Attendance		
Year	**Location**	**Attendance**
1990	Italy	2,516,354
1994	U.S.A.	3,587,088
1998	France	2,775,400
2002	Korea / Japan	2,705,566
2006	Germany	3,367,000
2010	South Africa	3,180,000

D (Circle) **the sentence that has a similar meaning.**

> **READING NOTE**
> **Sentence Sense**
> It is possible to understand the meaning of a sentence even when you do not understand every word.

1. Even though soccer is not the top sport in the United States, there is interest in the World Cup.

   a. Americans are interested in the World Cup, but soccer is not a very popular sport.

   b. Americans are very interested in soccer, but not in the World Cup.

2. The game was considered an exhibition rather than a real match.

   a. The teams preferred to see an exhibit.

   b. No one thought the game was a serious competition.

3. When the World Cup came to the U.S. in 1994, it sparked interest in soccer.

   a. The 1994 World Cup caused more Americans to think about soccer.

   b. Many Americans attended the fireworks at the World Cup in 1994.

E (Circle) *True* or *False*.

1. Soccer is becoming more popular in the U.S. — (True) False
2. Many people in the U.S. are interested in the World Cup. — (True) False
3. The U.S. organized the first Olympic soccer game. — True (False)
4. Uruguay had a good soccer team in 1924 and 1928. — (True) False
5. In the thirties, soccer was not popular in the U.S. — (True) False
6. The first World Cup was held in Europe. — True (False)
7. Since 1990, Europe has hosted five World Cups. — True (False)

Sports · **109**

Writing Our Stories: A Famous Athlete

A Discuss.

Discuss what students may know about Lance Armstrong. What can they say about him based on the photo?

B Read.

Ask students to read the text on their own. When they finish, answer any questions they have. If they couldn't answer the questions in Exercise A, have them answer them now.

Writing Note

• Read and discuss the Writing Note. Point out the use of the comma before the words *and, but, so,* and *or.*

• Ask students to go back to the reading and locate sentences with *and, but, so,* and *or.* Have a student read each of these sentences aloud and discuss the function of these connecting words. Explain: And *adds information.* But *provides contradictory information.* So *shows that the second statement is the result of the first statement.* Or *indicates that two choices are involved.*

A Discuss.

1. Who is Lance Armstrong?

2. Is he still riding professionally?

B Read.

Lance Armstrong

Lance Armstrong was born on September 18, 1971, in Plano, Texas. His mother raised him alone. He began riding a bike at an early age, and he started entering triathlons (running, swimming, and cycling competitions) before he was a teenager. By the age of 20, Armstrong was the U.S. National Amateur Cycling Champion.

From 1991 to 1996, Armstrong won important races. In 1993, he became the U.S. Pro Champion, and he won one million dollars in the Thrift Drug Triple Crown. In 1995, he was the first American to win the Classico San Sebastian in Italy. In 1996, he was the number one cyclist in the world.

However, in October of 1996, Armstrong began to feel sick. He found out that he had cancer in his lungs, brain, and abdomen. This was the most difficult time in his life. Armstrong had three major operations and months of chemotherapy. In 1997, the doctors declared him cancer free.

After his health returned, Armstrong was very grateful, so he founded the *Lance Armstrong Foundation* to raise money for cancer research, awareness, and early detection.

Armstrong continued to enter competitions, and in 1999, he won the Tour de France, a three-week racing event through the valleys and mountains of France. He won the event again every year from 2000 to 2005. After the 2005 race, Armstrong retired, but he returned to the Tour de France in 2009, earning third place, but in 2010, he was twenty-third.

Armstrong considered a future career in politics, but he decided to spend more time supporting cancer research instead.

WRITING NOTE

Combining Sentences with *and, but,* and *so*

Combine two short sentences with words like *and, but,* and *so.* Each part of the sentence has a subject and a verb.

He began riding a bike at an early age, **and** he started entering triathlons.

Armstrong was very grateful, **so** he founded the *Lance Armstrong Foundation.*

Newspapers have been writing about his possible future in politics, **but** Armstrong has been spending more time talking about cancer research.

C In your notebook, combine the sentences with *and*, *so*, or *but*.

1. My sisters are going to arrive tomorrow. They are going to stay for a week.
   My sisters are going to arrive tomorrow, and they are going to stay for a week.
2. I've been calling Jack for a week. He hasn't returned my calls.
   I've been calling Jack for a week, but he hasn't returned my calls.
3. Bill hasn't been attending soccer practice. The coach is going to suspend him from the team. *Bill hasn't been attending soccer practice, so the coach is going to suspend him from the team.*
4. Julie hasn't been feeling well. She made a doctor's appointment.
   Julie hasn't been feeling well, so she made a doctor's appointment.
5. Ben wanted to attend a private college. He couldn't afford the tuition.
   Ben wanted to attend a private college, but he couldn't afford the tuition.
6. Karin goes to a gym three times a week. She walks in the park every morning.
   Karin goes to a gym three times a week, and she walks in the park every morning.

D In your notebook, write a composition about a famous athlete. Use information from the Internet or from library books. Do not copy sentences.

 E Sharing Our Stories Read your partner's composition. Answer the questions. *(Answers will vary.)*

1. Which athlete did your partner write about? _____

2. Why is the athlete famous? _____

F Find and correct the mistakes.

1. I ^have been playing a lot of soccer this year.
2. He has been ~~show~~ showing me how to play tennis.
3. She hasn't been ~~go~~ going to the gym recently.
4. We have been playing well ~~for~~ since September.
5. They have been ~~live~~ living in Tampa for six months.
6. She ^has been training for the Olympics.
7. ~~You have~~ Have you been working out every day?
8. How long ^have you been watching the game?

Sports · 111

More Action!

Ask some students to read their compositions aloud as an oral report. Invite other students to give positive feedback and ask questions.

C In your notebook, combine the sentences with *and*, *so*, or *but*.

Ask students to complete the assignment individually. Review the correct sentences with the class, writing on the board any that students had difficulty with.

D In your notebook, write a composition about a famous athlete. Use information from the Internet or from library books.

• Students can use Exercise C as a model to complete this exercise. Encourage them to use the present perfect continuous, *for* and *since*, and other grammar structures they learned in this unit.
• If time permits, meet with students individually to help them with their compositions.

E Sharing Our Stories Read your partner's composition. Answers the questions.

Have students of mixed language ability read each other's compositions. Provide additional questions that students can answer about the compositions. For example: *Where is the athlete from? How long has he or she been involved in the sport?*

F Find and correct the mistakes.

Have students correct the sentences on their own. Review the correct answers and elicit explanations of why the original sentences were incorrect.

Sports · **111**

Practicing on Your Own

A Circle the sentence that has the same meaning.

• Have students complete the exercise individually, and then check their answers with a partner.
• Discuss with the class any answers that several students had trouble with.

B Complete. Use the present perfect continuous or the simple past.

• Have students complete the exercise individually.
• Have different students write one question and answer each on the board. Review the correct answers with the class.

A Circle the sentence that has the same meaning.

1. Tara began to play volleyball at 1:00. It's 3:00, and she is still playing.
   a. Tara has been playing volleyball for two hours.
   b. Tara played volleyball for two hours.

2. Tom played tennis in the park from 4:00 to 5:00. Then, he went home.
   a. Tom has been playing tennis for an hour.
   b. Tom played tennis for an hour.

3. Yesterday, Martin rode his bicycle from 8 A.M. to 1 P.M.
   a. Martin has been riding his bicycle for five hours.
   b. Martin rode his bicycle for five hours.

4. The soccer fans sat down an hour ago, and they are watching the game.
   a. The fans have been watching the game for an hour.
   b. The fans watched the game for an hour.

5. Juan lifts weights at the gym every day from 7:00 to 8:00. It's 7:30 now.
   a. Juan has been lifting weights for 30 minutes.
   b. Juan lifted weights for 30 minutes.

B Complete. Use the present perfect continuous or the simple past.

1. **A:** How long (you / play) ___have you been playing___ baseball?
   B: I ___have been playing___ since I was a child.

2. **A:** How long (you / live) ___did you live___ in Chicago?
   B: I ___lived___ there from 2007 to 2009.

3. **A:** How long (she / exercise) ___has she been exercising___ at the gym?
   B: She ___has been exercising___ since January.

4. **A:** How long (you / wait) ___have you been waiting___ in line for tickets?
   B: We ___have been waiting___ since 4:00 this morning!

5. **A:** How long (you / study) ___did you study___ for the test?
   B: I ___studied___ for three hours, and then I went to bed.

More Action!

For additional practice, have students write additional questions using the present perfect continuous tense. Then, have students switch questions with a partner. Each student should write questions that have the same meaning as their partner's original questions. Give cues to help students get started. For example:
1. *you—live—your present apartment*
2. *Carl—work—the cafeteria*

English in Action: Common Sports Injuries

  **A Listen and repeat.**
CD2·TR6

1. I have a bruise.

2. She has a sprained ankle.

3. She has tendonitis.

4. He has a concussion.

5. He has a pulled hamstring.

6. He has a torn rotator cuff.

 B Listen. Take notes about each injury and its treatment. Then, compare your answers with a partner.
CD2·TR7

Conversation 1: Injury: <u>torn rotator cuff</u>

Treatment: <u>Surgery. Two to three months of recovery.</u>

Conversation 2: Injury: <u>a sprained ankle</u>

Treatment: <u>Elevate ankle. Ice every 15 to 20 minutes all day.</u>

Conversation 3: Injury: <u>concussion</u>

Treatment: <u>Quiet and rest. Needs to take an x-ray.</u>

Conversation 4: Injury: <u>pulled hamstring</u>

Treatment: <u>Surgery. A couple months of therapy.</u>

Conversation 5: Injury: <u>tendonitis</u>

Treatment: <u>No tennis or heavy lifting for three weeks. Take over-the-counter medications for pain.</u>

Conversation 6: Injury: <u>a bruise</u>

Treatment: <u>Ice for 15 minutes, let leg warm up, then ice again. Doctor will prescribe pain medication.</u>

Sports · **113**

English in Action: Common Sports Injuries

 A Listen and repeat.
(CD2 • TR6)

• Play the audio several times and have students listen and repeat.
• Provide (or ask students to provide), as needed, the definitions of the injury in each item. Students should have a good idea from looking at the pictures, but may need some additional assistance. Explain: Tendonitis *is a condition where tendons (tissue that connect muscle to the bone) are inflamed. A concussion is also known as a mild traumatic brain injury (MTBI). A* rotator cuff *is part of a shoulder.*

B Listen. Take notes about each injury and its treatment. Then, compare your answers with a partner.
(CD2 • TR7)

• Play the audio and have students take notes. Remind them not to write full sentences.
• Play the audio a second and third time if needed, so students can complete their notes and check them over for completeness.
• Go over the answers as a class and answer any questions about the injuries and their treatment.

Sports · **113**

Unit 8

Changes

 A **Discuss.**

- Review the vocabulary in the Word Partnerships box. Ask students to provide simple definitions of each term. If students are not able to do so, explain: *Your immediate family consists of the people you live with, such as your spouse and your children or your parents and siblings. Your extended family includes your parents, siblings, grandparents, aunts, uncles, and cousins. A nuclear family consists of two parents and their children.*
- Point out the photo of a family reunion and ask students to describe what they see. Then, ask different students to answer the discussion questions. Call on more than one student to answer each question. Point out different ways that families can stay in touch.

 B **Listen. Kathy and Gloria are talking about plans for a family reunion. Circle *True* or *False*.**

(CD2 • TR8)

- Have students just listen the first time as you play the audio. Then, read the statements and answer any questions students have.
- Play the audio once or twice more as students circle their answers. Review the correct answers with the class.

 A **Discuss.**

1. How many people are in your family?

2. How do you keep up-to-date on what is happening in your extended family?

3. What is a family reunion? Have you ever had a family reunion? If so, give some details.

WORD PARTNERSHIPS	
immediate	
extended	family
nuclear	

 CD2 • TR8 **B** **Listen.** Kathy and Gloria are talking about plans for a family reunion. Circle *True* or *False*.

1. Kathy and Gloria haven't spoken for a long time. (True) False
2. There's a date for the reunion. (True) False
3. The family has just had a reunion. True (False)
4. It's June now. (True) False
5. The reunion is going to be very expensive. True (False)
6. The invitations are in the mail. True (False)
7. Everyone's going to help with the food. (True) False
8. Michael has opened a small business. (True) False

I	have		
You	haven't		
He	has	taken a vacation	**for** two years.
	hasn't	worked there	**since** January.
They	have		**since** the company opened.
	haven't		

To form the present perfect, use *have / has* and the past participle.

Use the *present perfect tense*

- to describe an action that began in the past and is still <u>true in the present</u>.

    They **have been** in the city **for** many years.

    She **hasn't seen** him **since** they broke up.

- to describe changes.

    He **has lost** over 50 pounds **since** he started exercising.

    In the past year, Lily **has grown** three inches.

A <u>Underline</u> the present perfect tense. (Circle) *for* or *since.*

1. Kathy and Gloria <u>haven't spoken</u> (for) / since several months.

2. Tuan and Lana <u>have been married</u> **for** / (since) 1999.

3. Henry <u>has belonged</u> to the volunteer fire department **for** / (since) 2005.

4. Joanna <u>has sold</u> life insurance (for) / since six months.

5. Rita <u>has been divorced</u> (for) / since six months.

6. Richard <u>has owned</u> his own business **for** / (since) he moved to Ohio.

7. Tom <u>has been</u> in college (for) / since six years.

8. Anna <u>has walked</u> two miles a day **for** / (since) she had her heart attack.

9. Brian <u>hasn't found</u> a job **for** / (since) he graduated from college.

10. We <u>haven't seen</u> our cat (for) / since a few days.

Active Grammar: Present Perfect Tense—Statements

A 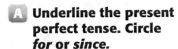 **Underline the present perfect tense. Circle** *for* **or** *since.*

- Review with students the information in the grammar box about the uses and forms of the present perfect tense. Have students use the words in the columns to make up a variety of different sentences.

- Students complete the activity individually and check their answers with a partner. Review the correct answers orally and answer any questions students may have.

More Action!

Play a game with two teams, Team A and Team B. A student on Team A makes a true present perfect statement using *for* or *since.* A student on Team B should respond by restating the sentence using whichever word the Team A student didn't use. For example:

Team A: *We've been in the library for two hours.*

Team B: *We've been in the library since 3:00.*

The team with the most grammatically correct responses wins.

B Make sentences with the information on the left and the *since* clauses on the right. Many combinations are possible.

Review the sentences and clauses to be sure students understand what each one means. Then, call on different students to orally match up a sentence and a clause that make sense together. There are many acceptable combinations.

C Listen and repeat.

(CD2 • TR9)

Play the audio. There is time after each verb to allow students a chance to repeat. Give extra practice on any set of verb forms that students have difficulty pronouncing. Point out the difficulty, and model the correct pronunciation. For example:

T: *Listen to the word* gone. Gone. Gone. *The* o *in* gone *is not pronounced like the* o *in the word* go. *The* o *in* gone *is pronounced* /aw/, *like the words* saw *or* thought. Gone. *Repeat.* Gone.

B Make sentences with the information on the left and the *since* clauses on the right. Many combinations are possible. (Answers will vary.)

1. I haven't had a good night's sleep.
2. I have had several complaints from my neighbors.
3. I have lost 10 pounds.
4. I've made several new friends.
5. I haven't been able to concentrate on my job.

| since I fell in love |
| since I had the baby |
| since I joined a gym |
| since I bought a dog |

C Listen and repeat.

CD2·TR9

Base Form	Simple Past	Past Participle	Base Form	Simple Past	Past Participle
be	was / were	been	leave	left	left
bear	bore	born	lose	lost	lost
become	became	become	make	made	made
begin	began	begun	meet	met	met
break	broke	broken	pay	paid	paid
bring	brought	brought	put	put	put
buy	bought	bought	quit	quit	quit
catch	caught	caught	read	read	read
come	came	come	ride	rode	ridden
do	did	done	say	said	said
drink	drank	drunk	see	saw	seen
drive	drove	driven	sell	sold	sold
eat	ate	eaten	send	sent	sent
fall	fell	fallen	sit	sat	sat
feel	felt	felt	sleep	slept	slept
find	found	found	speak	spoke	spoken
forget	forgot	forgotten	spend	spent	spent
freeze	froze	frozen	steal	stole	stolen
get	got	got / gotten	take	took	taken
give	gave	given	teach	taught	taught
go	went	gone	tell	told	told
grow	grew	grown	think	thought	thought
have	had	had	throw	threw	thrown
hear	heard	heard	win	won	won
know	knew	known	write	wrote	written

Use the *present perfect* with words such as *just, lately,* and *recently* to describe an action in the recent past.

Put *just* between *have / has* and the main verb.

  I **have just quit** my job.

Put *lately* at the end of a sentence.

  He **hasn't been** in class **lately**.

Put *recently* between *have / has* and the main verb or at the end of the sentence.

  They **have recently become** grandparents.
  They **have become** grandparents **recently**.

A **Complete the sentences.** Use the present perfect.

1. I (just / meet) _____have just met_____ Juan.

2. She (recently / fall) _____has recently fallen_____ in love.

3. He (just / make) _____has just made_____ the high school soccer team.

4. Stanley (recently / get) _____has recently gotten_____ his driver's license.

5. Silvia (see / not) _____hasn't seen_____ any new movies lately.

6. Ted and his family (just / move) _____have just moved_____ into a new home.

7. My sister (just / come) _____has just come_____ from Japan.

8. I (recently / find) _____have recently found_____ a new job.

9. My uncle (visited / not) _____hasn't visited_____ us lately.

10. My aunt (bring / not) _____has not brought_____ us any cakes lately.

B **In your notebook, write two sentences about each picture.** Use *just* in one sentence and *recently* in the other sentence.

Carlos and Eva

Changes • 117

Active Grammar: Present Perfect Tense for the Recent Past

A **Complete the sentences. Use the present perfect.**

• Go over the information in the grammar box. Provide additional examples and check for understanding. Answer any questions.
• Students complete the sentences on their own, and then check their answers with a partner. Point out that they should use the list on page 116 if they need help thinking of the correct form of the past participles.
• List the item numbers on the board and have different students write the correct past perfect form after each.
• Review the correct answers with the class.

B **In your notebook, write two sentences about each picture. Use *just* in one sentence and *recently* in the other sentence.**

• Have students complete the exercise on their own. Remind them to watch the placement of the words. Tell them to refer back to the box at the top of the page if needed.
• Call on volunteers to read their sentences. Elicit or provide correction as needed.

Active Grammar: Using the Present Perfect Tense

  A Pronunciation: Stress Listen to the stress as each speaker clarifies the information.

(CD2•TR10)

• Demonstrate the stress pattern in Item 1 by reading it aloud. Then, play the audio. Play it a second time and have students underline the stressed words.

• Review the answers by playing the audio again. Pause after each pair of sentences and ask students which word received the stress.

  B Practice the sentences above with a partner.

• Pair students of mixed language abilities. Have them practice reading the sentences in Exercise A.

• Then, have them work together to fill in the blanks in Items 1 and 2 and practice role-playing the dialogues.

  C Look at the pictures.

• Conduct a brief discussion about each picture. Ask questions to help students discover the differences between the "before" and "after" pictures. For example: *What is Allen wearing?*

• Ask students to work with a partner to identify and discuss the changes. Ask a few groups to tell the class the changes. Remind students to stress the key words that describe the change.

  A Pronunciation: Stress Listen to the stress as each speaker clarifies the information. Underline the stressed word.

CD2•TR10

1. **A:** I hear that David has bought a sailboat.

   B: Not exactly. He's bought a <u>motorboat</u>.

2. **A:** I hear that Amy has moved to North Carolina.

   B: Close. She's moved to <u>South</u> Carolina.

3. **A:** I hear that Nora has gotten her driver's license.

   B: No, just the opposite. She's <u>lost</u> her driver's license!

4. **A:** I hear that Joe and Tom have just opened an Italian restaurant.

   B: Not Italian. They've opened a <u>Mexican</u> restaurant.

 B Practice the sentences above with a partner. Then, complete the conversations below and practice them with your partner. *(Answers will vary.)*

1. **A:** I hear that Paul has just made the baseball team.

   B: No, he's made the _____ team.

2. **A:** I hear that Alex and Kathy have just gotten a cat.

   B: Not exactly. They've just gotten a _____.

  C Look at the pictures. Describe five changes in these people's lives.

1.

Allen ten years ago   Allen today

2.

Mary and Tom five years ago   Mary and Tom today

118 · Unit 8

More Action!

Hand out newspapers or magazines and have students look through articles and circle examples of the present perfect tense. (You can also do the activity using an intermediate reader textbook.) Set a time limit of five minutes. Have students write different present perfect sentences they find on the board. Discuss each one, explaining (or asking a student to explain) why the writer chose to use the present perfect tense.

Already shows that an action is completed. Use *already* in affirmative sentences. You can use the present perfect tense or the past tense with *already*. *Already* with the past tense is more often used in spoken English.

> She **has already bought** the invitations.   She **already bought** the invitations.

Put *already* between *have / has* and the main verb or at the end of the sentence.

> She **has already bought** the invitations.   She **has bought** the invitations **already**.

Yet shows the action has *not* been completed. Use *yet* in questions and negative sentences. Use the present perfect tense or the past tense with *yet*. Put *yet* at the end of the sentence.

> **Has** she **sent** the invitations **yet**?   **Did** she **send** the invitations **yet**?
> She **hasn't sent** the invitations **yet**.

 A **Angela is planning a family reunion.** Listen and check (✓) the things that have already been completed.

CD2·TR11

Completed	Not completed	Things to do for the reunion
✓		form a committee to help plan the reunion
✓		set a date
✓		make the invitations on the computer
	✓	send the invitations
✓		find the addresses of relatives who have moved
	✓	plan the activities and games
✓		plan the menu
	✓	order the cake
✓		buy the decorations
✓		hire staff to help cook, serve, and clean up
	✓	gather photos for the party

 B **Discuss each item on Angela's list.** Use *already* or *yet*.

> She has already formed a committee to help plan the reunion.

> They haven't sent the invitations yet.

Active Grammar: *Already* and *Yet*

  A **Angela is planning a family reunion. Listen and check the things that have already been completed.**

(CD2 • TR11)

• Go over the information in the grammar box. Read aloud the sample sentences showing how to use *already* and *yet*. Provide or elicit additional examples. Check for understanding.
• Review Angela's list of things to do for her reunion.
• Play the audio and have students mark their answers. Play it a second time so they can check their answers.
• Review the correct answers with the whole class.

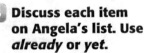 **B** **Discuss each item on Angela's list. Use *already* or *yet*.**

Go over the example sentences in the speech bubbles. Have students work in pairs and discuss each of the items on Angela's list. Monitor the groups to be sure that they are using *already* and *yet* properly.

👥 **C** George and Monica have just had a party. With a partner, talk about what they have and haven't done. Use the cues in the box and *already* or *yet*.

• Read and discuss the directions. Then, have students cover the list of cues below the picture. Ask them to comment on what they see in the picture. Accept any reasonable comment, repeating correct comments and phrasing any incomplete or incorrect statements using *already* and *yet*. For example:

S: *One guest didn't leave.*
T: *That's right. Not everyone has left yet. Monica's brother is asleep.*

• Then, have students look at the list of cues and the word box. Have them work with a partner and talk about the progress George and Monica have made. *What have they* already *done? What haven't they done* yet? Walk around the classroom, listening and assisting students.

👥 **D** Ask a partner about what she or he has done today. Use *yet*.

• Read the instructions and review the sample dialogue. Then, working in pairs, have students take turns using the cues to ask and answers questions about their own lives.
• Call on several different pairs to present their interactions to the class.

👥 **C** George and Monica have just had a party. With a partner, talk about what they have and haven't done. Use the cues in the box and *already* or *yet*.

put away the food	collect the cans and bottles
clear off the table	blow out the candles
take down the decorations	eat the last piece of cake
sweep the floor	close the windows
wash the dishes	get Monica's brother to leave
empty the garbage can	

sweep – swept – swept
blow – blew – blown

👥 **D** Ask a partner about what she or he has done today. Use *yet*.

Have you gotten your mail yet?

Yes, I have. I got it at 10:00.

go to work
Have you gone to work yet?

buy anything
Have you bought anything yet?

make a phone call
Have you made a phone call yet?

make your bed
Have you made your bed yet?

do the dishes
Have you done the dishes yet?

speak in class
Have you spoken in class yet?

get your mail
Have you gotten your mail yet?

do your homework
Have you done your homework yet?

take a shower
Have you taken a shower yet?

watch TV
Have you watched TV yet?

eat a piece of fruit
Have you eaten a piece of fruit yet?

exercise
Have you exercised yet?

read the newspaper
Have you read the newspaper yet?

120 · Unit 8

More Action!

Have students form a single line and play the game "What have you done?" You might start them off with cues, such as *pay my electric bill, have a medical checkup,* and *go to the dentist.* The first student makes a statement, for example: *I haven't paid my electric bill yet.* The second student tells whether or not he or she completed the activity and adds a second item: *I have already paid my electric bill. I haven't had a medical checkup yet.* Each new student reports on whether or not he or she has done each of the previous activities mentioned, and adds a new one to the list.

Use the *present perfect tense* to describe actions that began in the past and are true in the present. The present perfect also describes events in the recent past.

I **have been** in this country for three years.
They **have just won** the lottery.

Use the *present perfect continuous tense* to describe actions that began in the past and are continuing now.

We **have been living** in this country for three years.

Use the *past tense* to show an action <u>completed</u> in the past.

She **graduated** from college in 2009.
They **moved** to New Mexico two years ago.

A **Complete the sentences.** Use the correct form of the verb in parentheses.

1. Dave (move) __moved__ into his apartment one year ago. He (live) __has been living__ in his apartment for a year. The landlord (just / increase) __has just increased__ his rent by $200!

2. My mother and father (be married) __have been married__ for a long time. They (get) __got__ married in 1950.

3. I (begin) __began__ working here in 2000. I (work) __have been working__ here for more than ten years.

4. I (take) __took__ my examination two weeks ago. I (just / receive) __have just received__ my grade.

5. Rachel (look) __has been looking__ for a new job for several months. She (quit) __quit__ her job four months ago.

6. Nick (lose) __has lost__ 15 pounds since he started his diet. He (start) __started__ his diet two months ago.

7. George (buy) __bought__ his car in 1985. George (drive) __has been driving__ his convertible for over 25 years!

8. I (take) __took__ my first art class five years ago. Since that time, I (paint) __have painted__ over 100 pictures.

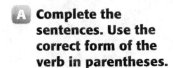

Active Grammar
Contrast: Present Perfect, Present Perfect Continuous, and Simple Past

A **Complete the sentences. Use the correct form of the verb in parentheses.**

• Review the differences between the use of the present perfect, present perfect continuous, and the simple past in the grammar box.

• Ask students to make up pairs of original sentences that demonstrate this difference. Before you call on students for their sentences, model an example: *My cousin, Anna, has just had her third baby. She had two other children before she came to this country. She has been living in the United States for six years.*

• Have students complete the sentences in Exercise A individually, and then check their answers with a partner. Review the correct answers with the whole class.

The Big Picture: Gossip

A. Discuss these words.

Ask students to provide simple definitions of the new words in the list. To help with the meaning of some of the words, refer students to the pictures in Exercise B. For example: *The teenage girl is grounded. When a child is grounded, the parents won't let the child leave the house except to go to school.*

B. Listen. Write each person's name under the correct picture.

(CD2 • TR12)

Play the audio and ask students to label the pictures with the correct names. Play it a second time, pausing after each conversation. Do not check answers to Exercise B at this time; instead have students answer the questions in Exercise C first.

C. Answer the questions.

• Have students answer each question by writing the correct name based on their answers in Exercise B.
• Then, ask one student to read aloud each question and choose a second student to answer each question.
• If students have answered a question incorrectly, it may mean that they misidentified the figures in Exercise B. Replay the audio as necessary and have students correct their answers if needed.

122 · Unit 8

A. Discuss these words.

gossip	grounded	face-lift
clinic	broken off	date / go out with

B. Listen. Write each person's name under the correct picture.

CD2·TR12

Amy   Diana   Grandpa   Mary   Paul   Rosa

1. _____Rosa_____

2. _____Paul_____

3. _____Grandpa_____

4. _____Diana_____

5. _____Mary_____

6. _____Amy_____

C. Answer the questions.

1. Who has had a face-lift?
   Rosa
2. Who has just been promoted?
   Paul
3. Who has recently begun to date a much older man?
   Mary
4. Who has just broken off her engagement?
   Diana
5. Who has bought a convertible?
   Grandpa

122 · Unit 8

6. Who has just been in an accident?
Amy
7. Who has just been at a clinic?
Rosa
8. Who has been grounded?
Amy
9. Who has fallen in love with a neighbor?
Diana
10. Who has left to travel across the country?
Grandpa
11. Who has taken away their daughter's cell phone?
Amy's parents

D **Circle** *True* or *False*.

1.	Diana still has Chris's ring.	True	(False)
2.	Rosa looks wonderful.	(True)	False
3.	Rosa told all her friends that she had a face-lift.	True	(False)
4.	Amy's parents have taken away her cell phone.	(True)	False
5.	This is the first time that Amy has gotten in trouble.	True	(False)
6.	Paul has been promoted.	(True)	False
7.	Paul has the best sales record in the company.	True	(False)
8.	Mary is dating a man who is much older than she is.	(True)	False
9.	Grandpa has bought a new car.	(True)	False
10.	Grandpa now has gray hair.	True	(False)

🔊 **E** **Pronunciation: Surprise Intonation** **Listen and repeat.**
CD2·TR13

1. A: He bought a new convertible.   **B:** A new convertible?

2. A: He left yesterday.   **B:** He left?

3. A: He's just been promoted.   **B:** Promoted?

4. A: She's run off with a man twice her age.   **B:** Twice her age?

👥 **F** **Write three statements with surprising news.** Tell your partner the news. **Your partner will show surprise.** (Answers will vary.)

1. _____

2. _____

3. _____

D **Circle** *True* or *False*.

Ask students to answer the questions individually. Then, ask students to read each statement and tell if it is true. If the statement is false, the student should correct the sentence so that it is true. In Item 1 for example:

S: *Diana still has Chris's ring. False. Diana has given back the ring.*

🔊 **E** **Pronunciation: Surprise Intonation Listen and repeat.**

(CD2 • TR13)

• Point out that to show surprise, a listener often repeats a few words of a speaker's conversation with question intonation.

• Play the audio. Ask students to listen carefully for the surprise intonation. Then, play the audio again and have students repeat with surprise intonation.

• Ask pairs of students to role-play the dialogues. Encourage students to emphasize or exaggerate the surprise intonation.

👥 **F** **Write three statements with surprising news.**

• Ask students to think of ideas for their news. They can write statements about their own lives or come up with original ideas. Encourage them to be a little outlandish. For example:

S1: *I want eleven cars.*
S2: *Eleven cars?*

• Students practice their dialogues. Invite several pairs to present their dialogues.

Reading: A Family Newsletter

A Discuss.

Discuss the questions. Mention that some families like to send out a newsletter once a year. Ask: *What kind of information do people put in family newsletters?*

B Read the first three sections of the newsletter on page 125. What is each section about?

• Introduce the Reading Note on skimming, and then have students do the exercise on their own. Point out that skimming includes looking at visuals, such as photographs, too.
• Review the answers with the whole class. Check for understanding and provide explanations as needed.

C Read the questions. Then, skim the newsletter for the answers.

Have students locate the details individually, and then check their answers with a partner. Discuss with the whole class any items that students had trouble with.

D Word Builder Match the words with their meanings.

Have students match the words with their meanings and fill in the sentences on their own. Have them check their answers with a partner.

Reading   A Family Newsletter

A Discuss.

1. Do you have a family newsletter?

2. Why do some families have newsletters?

B Read the first three sections of the newsletter on page 125. What is each section about?

Section 1: <u>Plans for the family reunion</u>

Section 2: <u>News about Alison Nelson</u>

Section 3: <u>Grandma Mayra Nelson</u>

C Read the questions. Then, skim the newsletter for the answers.

1. What are the dates of the family reunion?
<u>August 14 and August 15</u>
2. Where is the barbecue on Saturday?
<u>Park Resort Hotel</u>
3. What was Alison's college major?
<u>social work</u>
4. What is Alison going to do next?
<u>work with troubled teens</u>
5. How old is Grandma going to be on her next birthday?
<u>100</u>
6. What does Fred do a few mornings a week?
<u>fish</u>
7. What does Fred do for volunteer work?
<u>read with children and deliver meals to the elderly</u>
8. What happened to Laura?
<u>She had a knee replacement.</u>
9. Why does Karen need a new job?
<u>Her company closed.</u>

> **READING NOTE**
>
> **Skimming for the Main Idea**
> Each paragraph has a main idea or topic. Before reading, it is helpful to skim each paragraph to find out what the topic is.

D Word Builder Match the words with their meanings.

<u>d</u> **1.** adjust to	**a.** contribute money or time
<u>f</u> **2.** hassle-free	**b.** became
<u>g</u> **3.** elderly	**c.** job possibilities
<u>b</u> **4.** turned	**d.** handle changes
<u>a</u> **5.** chip in	**e.** in the future
<u>e</u> **6.** ahead	**f.** easy
<u>c</u> **7.** leads	**g.** people who are very old

124 • Unit 8

More Action!

For more practice with the new vocabulary, provide incomplete sentences and have students fill in the correct vocabulary words. For example:
Sunday is the only _____ day of the week. (hassle-free)
All of the children _____ to buy their parents a Bermuda vacation. (chipped in)

Teaching Tip

If you feel your class would benefit from it, conduct a short lesson in how to skim a reading passage. You can suggest the following:

1. Move your eyes quickly through the reading. Don't try to read every word.
2. Try running your finger down the middle of the page following it with your eye to help you remember to continue reading without stopping at individual words or sentences.
3. Pause after each paragraph and summarize in your own words what you just read.

The Nelsons in the News

June

Circle August 14th and 15th on your calendars! This year's reunion committee includes Doris, Frank, Lynn, and Gloria. For Saturday, we've already reserved a space at the Park Resort Hotel. The barbecue is going to be on the lawn by the pool. We'll all **chip in** for the food. We've also reserved a block of rooms for Friday and Saturday nights for anyone who wants to stay overnight. Contact Luisa at 888-555-2422 to reserve a room. People have requested a relaxing, **hassle-free** day on Sunday. We're talking to the resort caterer about a picnic lunch. Look at next month's issue for more details! Send your suggestions and comments to the committee members, or call Angela at 555-6739.

Congratulations to Alison Nelson. After eight years of college, sometimes full-time, sometimes part-time, Alison has just completed her course work in social work. She will graduate this month. Alison has accepted a position at Atlantic Community Services, where she will be working with troubled teens.

Grandma Mayra Nelson **turned** 99 on May 2nd. She lives with her daughter, Eva, and son-in-law, Brad. Mayra enjoys TV, her flower garden, and visits from her four children, twelve grandchildren, and thirty great-grandchildren. She will become a great-great-grandmother in September! Mayra says that she is looking forward to her 100th birthday. She tells her children, "I expect you to give me a big party!"

Hi Everyone!

Our new home in Florida is only five blocks from the beach. Ann and I were wondering how we would **adjust to** retirement. It wasn't hard! Ann has joined a tennis club, and she plays three mornings a week. I've bought a fishing boat, and you'll see me on the water two or three mornings a week. I haven't caught "the big one" yet, but I'm trying! Ann and I also have been volunteering at the local community center. We deliver meals to the **elderly** one day a week. Two days a week, we read with children in an after-school program. Don't worry—we haven't forgotten about all of you. We'll see you at the reunion. If you are planning a trip to Florida, we'd love to see you. Call us at 813-555-3494, or e-mail us.

Fred

Send your get-well cards to Laura. Her knee replacement went well, but she has several weeks of physical therapy **ahead**. Her address is on page 3 of the newsletter.

Karen is looking for job **leads**. Her company closed, leaving 75 accountants looking for work. If you have any suggestions, please e-mail her.

Changes · **125**

Reading: A Family Newsletter

• Students should have already skimmed the reading to answer the questions in Exercise C on the previous page. Now, ask students to read the newsletter in its entirety. Call on several students to each read aloud a paragraph of the newsletter. Help students with any vocabulary or pronunciation issues that come up.

• Ask students to write a class newsletter modeled after the Nelson newsletter. Give the students a few minutes of class time to meet to plan the topics each will write about as homework. If you have a large class, split the class into two or more groups and have each group write their own newsletter to save time.

• Ask students to bring their work to the next class. In their groups, students can exchange their paragraphs and correct each other's work. Ask a volunteer to combine the stories into a final completed newsletter. If possible, photocopy and distribute the completed newsletter(s) to the class.

Writing Our Stories: A Newsletter

A · Has anyone in your extended family recently...?

Tell students that family newsletters include information about family events, both large and small. Ask students to check off all the events from this list that have occurred in their families recently. Encourage them to add other events not mentioned in the blank after the word *other*. Other events could include: *got a promotion, bought a house, opened a business*, and so on.

B · Read the paragraph from a family newsletter.

Ask students to read the letter on their own. Call on one or two students to orally summarize the reading.

C · Write details about each statement. Use your imagination.

• Go over the Writing Note. Tell students this information will help them complete this exercise, and it will also help them write better paragraphs.
• Read and discuss the example sentence in Item 1. Ask: *What is better about the more detailed statement?* Then, have students expand each simple statement by adding details. Remind students that there are many possible answers. Invite several students to read their expanded statements to the class.

A · Has anyone in your extended family recently . . . ? (Answers will vary.)

- ☐ graduated
- ☐ celebrated a birthday
- ☐ lost a job
- ☐ gotten married
- ☐ celebrated an anniversary
- ☐ accepted a new job
- ☐ gotten engaged
- ☐ taken a vacation
- ☐ had an accident
- ☐ gotten divorced
- ☐ moved
- ☐ had an operation
- ☐ had a baby
- ☐ retired
- ☐ passed away (died)
- ☐ other _____

B · Read the paragraph from a family newsletter.

> The Thompson Family Newsletter
> Lena Thompson
> June 4
> English IV
>
> Henry has just accepted a position as distribution manager at Davis and Bates. Davis and Bates is a growing furniture manufacturer in the West. Henry will coordinate all the company's deliveries. Currently, the company employs 25 people in its distribution center. They are planning to expand this to 50 employees. Henry is selling his house, and he will leave for California next month. His wife, Paula, and their two children will move to California after they sell their house.

C · Write details about each statement. Use your imagination. (Answers will vary.)

1. Thomas graduated from college.

   Thomas graduated from the University of Maryland in May with a degree in biology.

2. Randy and Lana had a baby.

   _____

   _____

> **WRITING NOTE**
> **Reporting the Facts**
> When reporting facts, it is important to include details. Specific facts provide interesting and clear information.

More Action!

If time permits, have two or three students tell the class more information about one of the events they checked in Exercise A. Give students a few minutes to write down three sentences before they begin. Students may wish to make a few notes on a piece of paper to help them remember what they want to say. Model your own example for students: *My parents have just celebrated their fiftieth wedding anniversary. We had a big party at my parents' favorite restaurant. My entire extended family came to eat, dance, and celebrate.*

3. Linda celebrated her birthday.

_____

_____

4. Tom was in a car accident.

_____

_____

5. Ken and Susan celebrated their wedding anniversary.

_____

_____

6. Karin and Juan have just returned from a wonderful vacation.

_____

_____

D Write a factual article about an event in your family, your class, or your school.

E **Sharing Our Stories** **Read your partner's article.** What did your partner write about?

F **Find and correct the mistakes.**

1. She ~~have~~ *has* just found a new job.
2. They haven't gotten married ~~already~~ *yet*.
3. They ~~have gotten married~~ *got married* on October 10.
4. They ~~has~~ *have* just celebrated their tenth wedding anniversary.
5. Jason ~~has come already~~ *has already come* home from the hospital.
6. They ~~have live~~ *have lived / have been living* in the same house since 1990.
7. Olga ~~has graduated~~ *graduated* from Duke University last month.
8. Ron ~~has take~~ *has taken* a job in Arizona.
9. Grandma Barnes ~~pass~~ *passed* away on June 15.
10. The whole family ~~just has enjoyed~~ *has just enjoyed* a wonderful family reunion.

D **Write a factual article about an event in your family, your class, or your school.**

• Suggest that students outline what they are going to write about using single words or partial sentences to record each idea. Then, have them look at their outlines and think of ways to add specific details. They can jot down these additional ideas on their original lists. Remind them to use the grammar structures from this unit.

• Collect the articles. As you correct each article, focus mainly on the use of details. Point out what additional information would be interesting. Ask students to correct their articles. Have students share their corrected articles with a partner, or display them on the classroom wall for others to read.

E **Sharing Our Stories Read your partner's article. What did your partner write about?**

Pair students of mixed language ability. Have students read their partner's article and answer the question. Have them ask more about the topic. Lesser ability students will benefit from the higher level of writing, and higher-level students will have a chance to offer suggestions for change to the lower-level student.

F **Find and correct the mistakes.**

Have students correct the mistakes, and check with a partner.

Practicing On Your Own

A Complete the sentences about changes in one town. Use the present perfect tense.

Students complete the sentences on their own, and then check their answers with a partner.

B In your notebook, write eight sentences about how your life has changed since you came to this country.

• Point out that answers will vary. Remind students to use the grammar structures that they learned in this unit.
• If time permits, call on a few students to read their sentences. However, be sensitive to the fact that some of the writing may be personal, so students might not wish to share it.

C Tim had a difficult first semester at college. Now it is the second semester, and Tim has become a serious student. Compare his first and second semesters. Use the present perfect tense.

Remind students to use the present perfect tense to describe what Tim has accomplished so far in his second semester. (They should use their imagination for the answers.) Have them check their answers with a partner.

A Complete the sentences about changes in one town. Use the present perfect tense.

1. Ten years ago, there were two doctors. Now there is a small clinic with six doctors. The health-care system (improve) _has improved_.

2. The population (increase) _has increased_ from 25,000 to 50,000.

3. Many new restaurants (open) _have opened_.

4. The unemployment rate (decrease) _has decreased_ from 15 percent to 9 percent.

5. Tourism (become) _has become_ a major industry.

6. The city (hire) _has hired_ 15 new police officers.

7. The crime rate (drop) _has dropped_ substantially.

8. Many new businesses (move) _have moved_ into the area because of the strong economy.

9. The quiet village (change) _has changed_ into a busy, noisy town.

B In your notebook, write eight sentences about how your life has changed since you came to this country.

C Tim had a difficult first semester at college. Now it is the second semester, and Tim has become a serious student. Compare his first and second semesters. Use the present perfect tense. (Answers will vary.)

First semester: The "old" Tim	Second semester: The "new" Tim
1. He missed ten days of school.	1. He has missed only one day of school.
2. He was late for his classes.	2. He has not been late.
3. He failed every test.	3. He hasn't failed any tests.
4. He didn't ask for extra help.	4. He has asked for extra help.
5. He didn't do his homework.	5. He has done his homework.
6. He failed two courses.	6. He hasn't failed any courses.
7. He didn't study for tests.	7. He has studied for tests.
8. He didn't write any papers.	8. He has written his papers.

More Action!

Invite some or all students to write stories called "A Changed Friend" or "A Changed Relative." Have them describe a personal transformation using the present perfect tense. They should describe changes that have begun to take place in the person's life. The story can be real or imagined.

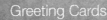

A Match each card message to the appropriate occasion.

_c_ **1.** A new baby

_e_ **2.** A retirement

_d_ **3.** A wedding

_b_ **4.** A gift

_a_ **5.** An illness

_f_ **6.** A death in the family

a. Get well soon! Hope you have a speedy recovery!

b. With appreciation for the beautiful gift.

c. Welcome to parenthood! Diapers, diapers, and more diapers!

d. We wish you joy in your new life together!

e. Good luck! We envy you!

f. We express our deepest sympathy in your time of loss.

 B **Working Together** In a group of three or four students, create a greeting card for a classmate who is moving away. Then, everyone should sign the card.

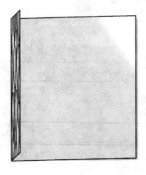

Changes • **129**

English in Action: Greeting Cards

Culture Note

Read the Culture Note aloud or ask a volunteer to do so. Ask if this practice of sending greeting cards is similar to one that students have in their own country. Keep in mind that they may not know the answer to this question.

A Match each card message to the appropriate occasion.

• Go over the directions, and then the words in each column. Provide definitions for any unfamiliar vocabulary.
• Have students complete the exercise on their own, and then check answers with a partner.

B Working Together In a group of three or four students, create a greeting card for a classmate who is moving away. Then, everyone should sign the card.

• Pair students of mixed language ability for this exercise.
• Circulate around the room making sure everyone is participating.
• Ask for volunteers to read the card from their group.

More Action!

For additional oral practice, have a class discussion on greeting cards, asking questions, for example:

1. *Do you send greeting cards? If so, for what occasions?*
2. *Have you ever sent an e-card (an electronic card)?*
3. *Have you ever sent or received an e-invitation (an e-mail invitation)?*

A **Under each picture, write the person's job. Then, discuss the questions.**

- Identify the job shown in Item 1. Say: *This woman is a graphic artist. A graphic artist designs images and prints. Many companies ask graphic artists to design their brochures and advertisements to make them more appealing.* Call on students to name the other jobs pictured on the page. If students have difficulty identifying a particular job, tell them to look carefully at the details in the photograph to help them.
- Read the list of discussion questions aloud. Explain any words that students don't understand. For example: *Production work involves making something. Service work involves doing something for people. Service jobs are found in stores, banks, and other offices.*
- Point to the pictures one by one and ask the questions again. Accept all reasonable answers. Encourage several students to contribute answers to each question.

Unit

9 Job Performance

A **Under each picture, write the person's job.** Then, discuss the questions.

1. Does this person work in production or service?
2. What skills does this person need for the job?
3. Would you like this kind of work? Why or why not?

1. _a graphic artist_

2. _a researcher / a scientist_

3. _an architect_

4. _a telephone repairman_

5. _a firefighter_

6. _a recycling plant worker_

Teaching Tip

If appropriate, have students sit in a group of two or three and talk about their jobs. Tell students that they can discuss the questions from Exercise A in the context of their own jobs. Set a time limit for the discussion. Move from group to group, answering questions and offering language support as needed.

Invite a pair of students to present their partner's answers to the class. Encourage other students to ask for additional information if they wish. For example:

S1: *Louisa works in service as a hotel clerk. She needs to be organized and needs to know how to use the computer.*

S2: *Han works in production at a factory. He needs to be a fast worker. He likes his job very much.*

How long asks about an amount of time. Use *how long* with the present perfect continuous.

> **How long has** she **been repairing** TVs?
> She **has been repairing** TVs <u>for two hours</u>.

How many asks about a specific number. Use *how many* with the present perfect.

> **How many** TVs **has** she **repaired**?
> She **has repaired** <u>three TVs</u>.

 A **Read the conversation.** Then, practice it with a partner.

A: What <u>is Harry doing</u>?

B: He's registering students for classes.

A: How long <u>has he been sitting</u> at the registration counter?

B: He's been sitting there for two hours.

A: How many students <u>has he registered</u> **so far**?

B: He's registered 18 students so far today.

> **VOCABULARY NOTE**
> **so far** – until now

B **Ask and answer questions about each picture.** Use your imagination. Use Exercise A as an example.

1.

2.

3.

4.

5.

6.

Job Performance · **131**

More Action!

Ask students to take turns making quick sketches on the board showing themselves at work. Have other students guess what the person's job is and ask the questions in Exercise A on page 130 as well as any other questions that come to mind. Help students with responses as necessary.

Active Grammar

A **Read the conversation.**

• Review the *How long* questions and answers in the chart.

• Ask students to provide examples. Answer any questions students have about using *how long* and the present perfect continuous.

• Have pairs of students practice the conversation. Point out the underlined verbs, and ask students to identify the tense of each underlined phrase (present perfect, present perfect continuous). Go over the Vocabulary Note on *so far*.

• After pairs have practiced for several minutes, ask a pair of students to read the conversation to the class.

B **Ask and answer questions about each picture.**

• Have partners take turns asking and answering questions about the pictures, using the conversation in Exercise A as a model. Point out that students will have to make up some of the information for the answers. Provide students with a model for Item 1:

S1: *What is she doing?*
S2: *She's making pizzas.*
S1: *How long has she been making pizzas?*
S2: *She has been making pizzas for five hours.*

• Review the exercise by having different pairs present one of their dialogues to the class. Have other students suggest corrections.

Active Grammar

 A **Ask and answer the questions about work.**

- Review the information in the grammar chart. Read the explanations aloud and ask students to restate them in their own words. For example:
  T: *These actions have occurred several times and may occur again. What does this mean?*
  S: *These actions didn't happen just one time. They happened more than once. They also may happen again in the future.*
- Provide additional example sentences. Answer any questions students may have.
- Go over the sample answers in the speech bubbles.
- Have students work with a partner and take turns asking and answering questions about actual work experiences. Remind them to use the present perfect.
- Invite several pairs to ask and answer a few questions in front of the class.

 B **Ask your partner two more questions about work.**

Tell students to write original questions asking about their partner's job. For example: *Have you ever worked in a store?*

(Notes for Exercises C and D are on the following page.)

Active Grammar
Present Perfect for Repeated Actions

Use the present perfect tense for repeated past actions. The following time expressions show a repeated action.

from time to time	I have been late **from time to time**.
a few times	She has worked overtime **a few times**.

Ever and *never* are often used with the present perfect. *Ever* means "in your lifetime" or "in your experience."

 A **Ask and answer the questions about work.**

> A: Have you **ever** called in sick?

> B: No, I haven't. / I've **never** called in sick.

> C: Yes, I've called in sick **a few times**.

1. Have you ever called in sick?
2. Have you ever had an accident at work?
3. Have you ever quit a job?
4. Have you ever received a raise?
5. Have you ever gotten a promotion?
6. Have you ever received a performance evaluation?
7. Have you ever complained to your boss?
8. Have you ever complained about your boss?
9. Have you ever worked a double shift?
10. Have you ever had a problem with a co-worker?

 B **Ask your partner two more questions about work.**

C **Ask your teacher about his or her job and interests.**

1. How long / you / teach / at this school?
2. you / ever / teach / another subject?
3. you / ever / study / another language?
   Have you ever studied another language?
4. you / ever / have / a different kind of job?
   Have you ever had a different kind of job?
5. you / ever / visit _____?
   Have you ever visited …?
6. you / ever / eat / _____ food?
   Have you ever eaten … food?
7. you / ever / play on a sports team?
   Have you ever played on a sports team?

> How long have you been teaching at this school?

> Have you ever taught another subject?

D **Write two more questions to ask your teacher.**

132 · Unit 9

Teaching Tip

Be sure that students understand and can identify the difference between the verbs in Exercise A, Items 7 and 8: *complained to* and *complained about*. If necessary, provide an example that demonstrates the difference between the words. For example: *My neighbors have been playing loud music. I complained to my landlord about the music. I complained about my neighbors.*

Teaching Tip

Make Exercise D into a short game. Have students write each question on a separate strip of paper. Place all the strips in a box or hat and pick several randomly to answer.

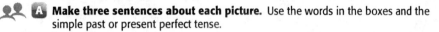

1. Place definite and indefinite time expressions at the end of the sentence.

   I began to work here **in 2005**.
   I have changed jobs **twice**.

   I have been working here **for two years**.
   She's taken four breaks today **so far**!
   (Meaning: up until now)

2. Place adverbs of frequency before the main verb.

   Laura has **never** received a warning at work.
   She has **always** been an excellent employee.

3. Place *just* and *finally* before the main verb.

   Henry has **just** gotten a raise.
   Andrea has **finally** finished her project.

4. Place *already* before the main verb or at the end of the sentence.

   They have **already** repaired three computers.
   They have repaired three computers **already**.

5. Place *yet* and *recently* at the end of the sentence.

   I've spoken to him **recently**.
   Bill hasn't finished the project **yet**.

 A Make three sentences about each picture. Use the words in the boxes and the simple past or present perfect tense.

1. go on a job interview

| twice | just | yesterday |

2. take a vacation

| last summer | recently | three times |

3. get a promotion

| yet | twice | in 2008 |

4. complete the order

| finally | an hour ago | already |

Job Performance · **133**

C Ask your teacher about his or her job and interests. (continued from page 132)

• Read the directions and go over the answers provided to the first two questions.

• Invite students to ask you the questions. Use the present perfect or present perfect continuous in your answers. Answer as truthfully as possible.

D Write two more questions to ask your teacher. (continued from page 132)

Tell students to write additional questions to ask you. Call on students to ask you one of the questions they wrote. Make sure the question is formulated correctly. Correct questions as needed.

Active Grammar

 A Make three sentences about each picture.

• Go over the information in the grammar box at the top of page 133. Point out the placement of time expressions in the simple past and in the present perfect.

• Have students practice making sentences about the pictures in Exercise A. Call on different students to say one sentence each. Give students an example: *Josie has just gone on a job interview. Josie went on a job interview yesterday.* If a student makes an error, ask the student to correct the sentence and read aloud the related rule from the grammar box at the top of the page.

More Action!

Bring in appropriate pictures or cartoons from newspapers or magazines. Have students make sentences about the pictures, using time expressions presented on this page. Remind students to use the present perfect where possible.

Teaching Tip

On the board, write some of the time expressions from the grammar box. Add a few similar ones, for example, *a week ago, yet, finally, last year,* and so on. Then, point to an expression and ask students to make up true sentences about themselves, using that expression. Model an example for students before you begin: *I began to work here last year.*

Job Performance · **133**

Active Grammar: Contrast— Present Perfect and Present Perfect Continuous

A Complete the sentences. Use the present perfect or the present perfect continuous tense. Some of the sentences can use either tense.

- Review the information in the grammar chart at the top of the page.
- Provide additional example sentences. Answer any questions students may have.
- Have students complete the sentences on their own.
- Review the answers with the class. Call on different students to give the reason for their choice of verb.

Some verbs can be used in either the present perfect tense or the present perfect continuous tense.

I **have lived** in this town for six years.
I **have been living** in this town for six years.

They **have worked** on this project since last month.
They **have been working** on this project since last month.

Other verbs, especially non-action verbs, can be used with the present perfect tense but not the present perfect continuous tense.

Non-action: hear see need think (to express an opinion)

Maria **hasn't heard** about the promotion yet.

Refer to page 243 for a list of non-action verbs.

A **Complete the sentences.** Use the present perfect or the present perfect continuous tense. Some of the sentences can use either tense. *(Answers may vary.)*

1. I (live) __'ve been living__ here for six months.

2. They (just / finish) __have just finished__ cleaning the trucks.

3. We (see / not) __haven't seen__ the new schedules yet.

4. The manager (interview) __has been interviewing__ new job applicants this week.

5. My supervisor (ask) __has been asking__ for help with the new project every day this week.

6. I (know) __have known__ her since we first came to this company.

7. That company (have) __has been having__ a lot of problems lately.

8. I (work) __have been working__ on this program all day.

9. Adam (wear / not) __hasn't worn__ the same tie twice!

10. They (already / complete) __have already completed__ four repairs.

11. We (watch) __have been watching__ the new workers complete their tasks.

12. Henry (leave / not) __has not left__ early since the new supervisor started working here.

13. Alexandra (work / not) __hasn't worked__ overtime since she got a promotion.

14. Our supervisor (hire) __hasn't hired__ any one new in over two months.

Use the past tense to describe an action that happened at a <u>specific time</u> in the past.

I finished my deliveries <u>an hour ago</u>.
We **had to work** overtime <u>from 5:00 to 8:00</u>.

Use the present perfect to describe an action that happened at an <u>unspecified time</u> in the past.

They**'ve never used** this equipment.
I**'ve applied** to that company twice.

A **Complete the sentences.** Use the correct form of the verbs in the past or the present perfect.

1. Bob (receive) _____received_____ a raise last year.

2. Orlando (receive) _____has received_____ two raises this year, and it's only July.

3. Laura (have) _____has had_____ six job interviews so far this year.

4. Samantha (have) _____had_____ a job interview in Dallas yesterday.

5. We (hear / already) _has already heard_ that presentation many times.

6. I (see / never) _have never seen_ that presentation.

7. Sarah (take) _____took_____ two sick days when she had the flu.

8. Ellen (take) _____has taken_____ two sick days so far.

9. The company (hire) _____has hired_____ three new workers, and we need one more.

10. My company (hire) _____has hired_____ the four new workers that we needed.

B **Ask and answer these questions with a partner.**

1. Have you missed any days of school this year?

2. How many days have you been absent so far?

3. How many different jobs have you had in your life?

4. Where do you work now? How long have you been working there?

5. Where did you work before you started this job?

6. Why did you leave that job?

7. When did you come to this school?

8. How many classes have you taken at this school?

Job Performance · **135**

Active Grammar: Contrast— Simple Past and Present Perfect

A **Complete the sentences. Use the correct form of the verbs in the past or the present perfect.**

• Review the information in the grammar chart at the top of the page.
• Provide additional example sentences. Answer any questions students may have.
• Have students complete the sentences in Exercise A on their own.
• Review the answers with the class. Call on different students to give the reason for their choice of verb. For example:
T: *In Item 8, why did you* use has taken *instead of the simple past of* take?
S: *We don't know when she took the sick days. The time is not specified.*

B **Ask and answer these questions with a partner.**

• Ask students to work in pairs to ask and answer the questions.
• Circulate around the room, helping students to formulate their answers.
• Call on students to report their partners' answers to the class, or call on pairs to ask and answer a few of the questions.

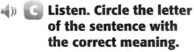 **C** **Listen. Circle the letter of the sentence with the correct meaning.**

(CD2 • TR14)

• Review the instructions and play the audio as students circle their answers.

• Play the audio a second time so students can check their work.

• Review the correct answers with the class.

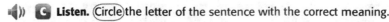

D **Pronunciation: 've and 's Listen and repeat.**

(CD2 • TR15)

• Play the audio once as students follow along in their books. Write 've on the board and say the 've sound in isolation several times. Have students repeat.

• Play the audio again. This time, have students listen and repeat the sentences.

E **Listen again. Circle the letter of the sentence you hear in Exercise D.**

(CD2 • TR16)

• Have students circle the letters of the sentences they hear in Exercise D as you play the audio.

• Play the audio again, so students can check their work.

C **Listen.** (Circle) the letter of the sentence with the correct meaning.

CD2•TR14

1. **a.** The doctor is still seeing patients.

   (b.) The doctor is finished seeing patients for the day.

2. **(a.)** Jamie is still ironing shirts.

   b. Jamie is finished ironing shirts for the day.

3. **(a.)** The men are still planting trees.

   b. The men are finished planting the trees.

4. **(a.)** The teacher has more papers to correct.

   b. The teacher finished all the papers.

5. **a.** Carlos is finished for the day.

   (b.) Carlos is still in his truck, delivering packages.

6. **(a.)** Mary is not going to call any more people today.

   b. Mary will call 100 more people.

7. **(a.)** She retired from the hospital.

   b. She's still working at the hospital.

8. **(a.)** He will drive farther today.

   b. He's going to stop for the day.

D **Pronunciation: 've and 's Listen and repeat.**

CD2•TR15

1. **a.** I sold five cars.   5. **a.** I helped ten customers.

   b. I've sold five cars.   **b.** I've helped ten customers.

2. **a.** She worked five hours.   6. **a.** He planted five trees.

   b. She's worked five hours.   **b.** He's planted five trees.

3. **a.** They made 500 donuts.   7. **a.** She read 20 pages.

   b. They've made 500 donuts.   **b.** She's read 20 pages.

4. **a.** She walked five miles.   8. **a.** I cleaned seven rooms.

   b. She's walked five miles.   **b.** I've cleaned seven rooms.

E **Listen again.** (Circle) the letter of the sentence you hear in Exercise D.

CD2•TR16

Students should circle: 1. b   2. b   3. a   4. b   5. a   6. a   7. b   8. b

136 • Unit 9

More Action!

Put students in pairs. Tell them to look at the sentences in Exercise D and to take turns reading the sets of *a* and *b* sentences. One student should read the *a* sentence and the other student should read the corresponding *b* sentence. It's important for students to read the similar sentences one after the other so they can contrast the verb endings. Have students switch roles so they each get a chance to practice all of the sentences.

136 • Unit 9

Student 1: Turn to page 265. Read **Set A** questions to Student 2.

Student 2: Look at the pictures and listen to Student 1. Write the answer under the correct picture. Use complete sentences.

Then, change roles. Student 2 will read **Set B** and Student 1 will write the answer under the correct picture.

1.

fired one   hired three

2.

ten patients   four doctors

3.

five cars   eight years

4.

one home   four years

5.

at 5:00 A.M.   15

6.

two systems   five years

Job Performance · **137**

👥 F **Working Together Student to Student**

• Read and discuss the instructions, and be sure students understand how to proceed. Before students begin, ask a few volunteers to describe what they see in each picture.

• First, Student 1 reads the Set A statements on page 265 and Student 2 writes each statement next to the correct picture on page 137. Then, they reverse roles, and Student 2 reads the Set B statements on page 265 and Student 1 writes each sentence in the correct place on page 137.

• Check the correct answers with the whole class. Ask students what tense was used in each answer.

Answers for Exercise F.
1. She has fired one employee this year. / She has hired three employees.
2. She talked to four doctors this morning. / She has helped ten patients today.
3. He has repaired five cars today. / He has been working at this garage for eight years.
4. She has been selling homes for four years. / She sold one home this month.
5. He started work at 5:00 A.M. / He has cleared 15 streets so far.
6. He has had his own business for five years. / He has installed two systems today.

The Big Picture: Job Performance

  A **Listen and complete the information about George's job.**

(CD2•TR17)

• Play the audio and have students complete each item.

• Play the audio a second time so students can fill in any answers they missed and check their other answers.

• Go over the answers with the class. Ask students to spell the words to check for correct spelling.

  B **Listen again and answer the questions.**

(CD2•TR17)

• Go over the list of questions and check that students understand the vocabulary.

• Play the audio and have students listen for the answers to the questions.

• Play the audio a second time so students can complete the exercise and check their answers.

138 • Unit 9

 A **Listen and complete the information about George's job.**

CD2•TR17

Job Description for Metro Transit Drivers

1. All applicants must have an in-person __interview__ and a __background__ check.

2. Employee pay starts at $ ___14.80___ an hour.

3. Report to work on time and in ___uniform___.

4. Drive __carefully__ and obey all ___traffic___ and safety laws.

5. __Pick up__ and drop off passengers at designated bus stops.

6. __Collect__ correct fares.

7. Greet and treat __passengers__ with courtesy.

8. All employees with good evaluations receive a $ ___0.75/hour___ pay increase.

9. If the employee has no accidents in five years, pay will increase to $___20___ an hour.

B **Listen again and answer the questions.**

CD2•TR17

1. What year did George begin to work for Metro Transit? ___2005___

2. How much was his starting salary? ___$14.80___

3. Does he know the names of his passengers? ___Yes, he does.___

4. Has his salary increased each year? ___Yes, it has.___

5. How often does he receive an evaluation? ___Every year.___

6. How long has George been working for Metro Transit? ___Answers will vary based on the current year.___

138 • Unit 9

Listen. Write the questions to match the answers. Use the present or present perfect tense.

CD2·TR18

1. How much _overtime does George work_ _____?

   About ten hours a week.

2. How much _is overtime pay_ _____?

   Time and a half.

3. _Has George ever gotten a ticket_ _____?

   Yes, he has.

4. How much _did he pay_ _____?

   $300.

5. _Has anyone gotten a speeding ticket_ _____?

   Yes. George's friend got two.

6. _Does he like the job_ _____?

   Yes, he does.

D **Complete the sentences.** Use the past or present perfect form of the verbs.

1. Before he started at Metro Transit, George (work) ___worked___ as a school bus driver.

2. He (negative-like) ___didn't like___ the noise on the school bus.

3. When George began at Metro Transit, he (earn) ___earned___ $14.80 an hour.

4. He (receive) ___has received___ a pay raise every year since then.

5. His performance evaluations (be / always) ___have___ ___always___ ___been___ very good.

6. He (have / only) ___has___ ___only___ ___had___ two or three passenger complaints, which is less than the company average.

7. Two years ago, he (get) ___got___ a ticket for going through a red light.

8. He (pay) ___paid___ a fine of $100 and the company (charge) ___charged___ him another $200.

9. George (be / always) ___has___ ___always___ ___been___ polite and courteous to the passengers.

Job Performance · **139**

 Listen. Write the questions to match the answers. Use the present or present perfect tense.

(CD2 • TR18)

• Go over the question parts and answers with the class. Answer any questions they may have.

• Play the audio and have students listen to find the answers to the questions.

• Play the audio a second time so students can complete the exercise and check their answers.

• Go over the answers with the class.

D **Complete the sentences. Use the past or present perfect form of the verbs.**

Have students complete the sentences on their own, and then check their answers with a partner. Review the correct answers with the whole class.

Reading: The Changing Workforce

A Discuss.

• Point out the title of the reading section: *The Changing Workforce*. Ask students to explain the meaning of the word *workforce*. (*Workforce is another word for workers, employees, and labor force.*)

• Discuss the questions as a class. On the board, write all the jobs students think of in Item 1.

B Word Builder Match.

• Ask students to match the vocabulary words and definitions.

• Point out that the words the students need to match are in boldface type in the reading so they are easy to find. If students have trouble identifying the definition of the word, tell them to read the sentence that contains the vocabulary word. Reading the sentence may help them put the vocabulary word in context and identify the definition more easily.

• Have students check their answers with a partner.

• Review the correct answers, and ask different students to form original sentences using each word. For example: *In this classroom, the female students outnumber the male students.*

A Discuss.

1. What kinds of jobs do you think will be needed in the future?

2. Do you think your job will be needed in the year 2025? Why or why not?

B Word Builder Match.

_b_ **1.** to outnumber   **a.** to grow larger

_d_ **2.** to age   **b.** to have a greater number than

_a_ **3.** to increase   **c.** to explain

_f_ **4.** to be in demand   **d.** to get older

_c_ **5.** to account for   **e.** to stay

_e_ **6.** to remain   **f.** to be needed or required

C Read.

The workforce of the United States includes everyone who is working now and everyone who is looking for a job. The Bureau of Labor Statistics evaluates the current workforce and employment opportunities. It makes predictions about the future workforce.

Between 2000 and 2010, approximately 17.1 million new workers entered the workforce, bringing the total number of workers in the United States to 149 million. What will the future workforce look like? The number of women **has increased** steadily. Sixty-two percent of all women will be in the workforce by 2016. The workforce is **aging**, too. Baby boomers—people born between 1946 and 1964—make up more than 13 percent of the workforce. Some people in this group are retiring, leaving job openings. However, because of the economy, others are **remaining** on the job longer than expected. One reason why baby boomers are staying in the workforce is because of education. They often have more education than younger workers. In addition, because of a slow economy, older workers continue working because they want to add to their retirement benefits. Health costs are rising, so baby boomers want to work as long as they can.

The workforce will become more ethnically diverse. In 2000, 73.1 percent of the workforce was classified as White, non-Hispanic. In 2010, this number was 69.2 percent, but soon the Hispanic workforce will **outnumber** all other ethnic groups, **accounting for** 16 percent of the total workers by 2016. African Americans will make up 12.3 percent and Asians will make up 5.3 percent.

140 · Unit 9

Teaching Tip

If necessary, spend some time discussing terminology found in the reading, such as *white, Caucasian,* and *African American*.

The labor department divides jobs into two types: goods-producing jobs and service-providing jobs. Goods-producing jobs include manufacturing, agriculture, mining, farming, and fishing. There will be almost no growth in this type of job because most goods are produced in other countries and more machinery is used. For instance, the number of farmers and ranchers is expected to steadily decline. The government expects that service providers will **account for** 20.2 million new jobs for the years from now until 2018. Many of these jobs will require more than a high school degree. Registered nurses, home-care aides, nursing aides, and other health-care professionals will be **in demand**. Why? Because of technological advances in the medical field, preventive care, and the increasing number of older people, more health-care workers will be needed.

Every two years, the United States government publishes the *Occupational Outlook Handbook*, a document that presents specific information about the job market and the job outlook. Some of the information included is salary range, education required, and job responsibilities. This document can be found in the reference section of any local or school library, or online.

Source: Bureau of Labor Statistics; *Occupational Outlook Handbook*

READING NOTE
Interpreting Statistics
It is important to pay attention to and interpret the meaning of statistics in a reading passage. You might want to highlight or underline statistics.

WORD PARTNERSHIPS	
manufacturing	
service-providing	
goods-producing	jobs
health-related	

 Circle *True* **or** *False***.**

1. There are approximately 17.1 million workers in the U.S. True (False)

2. More than half of all U.S. women will be working in the future. (True) False

3. The workforce is getting younger. True (False)

4. Some baby boomers are retiring later than expected. (True) False

5. Baby boomers continue to work because of health-care costs. (True) False

6. By 2016, Hispanics will outnumber both African Americans and Asians in the workforce. (True) False

7. The jobs most in demand in the future will be in goods-producing. True (False)

8. The government expects to see more jobs in medical fields. (True) False

9. The government revises the *Occupational Outlook Handbook* every two years. (True) False

Job Performance · **141**

C Read.

• Ask students to look at the picture and describe the different types of people they see. You may wish to write some cues on the board to help them get started. For example: *male, female, older, younger, Hispanic, Caucasian,* and so on. Students may give responses, such as: *There are fewer females than males. About half of the workers are young.*

• Read the Reading Note aloud. Ask students to highlight or underline statistics they find as they read the text.

• Have students read the text individually. Point out the vocabulary words in bold and the words in the Word Partnerships box on page 141. Have students pay special attention to the sentences where these words appear.

• As students read, move around the room answering questions as necessary.

• After students have read the passage, ask a few students to summarize each paragraph of the reading briefly.

D Circle *True* or *False*.

• Ask students to complete the exercise individually.

• Review the answers with the whole class. After each answer is given, ask a student to locate and read aloud the sentence from the reading that contains the information needed to answer that question correctly.

More Action!

Ask students to read the second paragraph of the reading again and list general characteristics for the labor force in 2010. Discuss the answers with the class. Ask students to identify any information that they found surprising.

Writing Our Stories: Looking at Careers

 Read.

 Read.

- Have students close their books. Write the words *dental hygienist* on the board and ask students to tell what they think this job involves. Confirm correct answers and explain why any incorrect answers are wrong.
- Ask students to read the passage once to themselves without stopping to try to figure out anything they don't understand.
- Ask a few simple questions to check general comprehension. For example: *Do dental hygienists take X-rays?* (Yes.) *Is there a need for a lot of dental hygienists today?* (Yes.)

 B **Check your job skills. Then, discuss your skills with a partner.**

Students check their job skills individually. With a partner, students can compare the list of skills they checked. Tell students to explain to their partners why they have checked a particular skill. For example: *I checked typing. I can type 75 words a minute. I need to type fast at work.*

A **Read.**

My Future Career

Pamela Simmons

October 23

English IV

I am considering a career as a dental hygienist. A dental hygienist usually works in a dentist's office. A dental hygienist removes plaque and deposits from teeth, takes dental X-rays, and tells patients how to clean and floss their teeth. In some offices, dental hygienists administer anesthetics, fill cavities, and assist the dentist.

All dental hygienists receive a license from their state. It is necessary to attend an accredited dental hygiene program. Students must pass a written and clinical examination. Many community colleges offer dental hygienist programs and many dental hygienists who work in dental offices have an associate's degree. Others have bachelor's degrees or even a doctorate.

At school, students study in different settings. They study in classrooms, in laboratories, and in model dental offices. They may take many science courses, such as anatomy and pharmacology. There is a strong job outlook for dental hygienists. In this field, people can work flexible hours or part time. The average salary is $66,570 a year.

I'm interested in this career because I like working with people, and I like the medical field. The working conditions are good. I don't have time to attend a four-year program. A career that only requires a two-year degree and that has a good salary and job outlook appeals to me.

B **Check (✓) your job skills.** Then, discuss your skills with a partner.
(Answers will vary.)

☐ selling	☐ drawing	☐ typing
☐ managing money	☐ designing	☐ repairing
☐ writing	☐ working with numbers	☐ teaching
☐ organizing	☐ supervising people	☐ public speaking
☐ operating equipment	☐ using a computer	☐ helping people

142 · Unit 9

More Action!

Extend the discussion of careers by having students number their five favorite job skills in Exercise B. They can write 1 after the job skill they like best, 2 after their second choice, and so forth. Invite different students to name their favorite skill from the list and tell why they like doing each thing.

C Discuss the meaning of each job characteristic. Then, check (✓) the characteristics that are the most important to you. (Answers will vary.)

- ☐ salary
- ☐ job status
- ☐ possibilities for promotion
- ☐ benefits
- ☐ job security
- ☐ possibilities to travel
- ☐ job training
- ☐ flexibility

> **WRITING NOTE**
>
> **Taking Notes**
> College papers usually require you to do some research. It is important to take notes and to write your paper using your own words. Do not copy word for word. When you take notes, you do not need to write complete sentences.

D Go online. Find information about a job that interests you. Use the *Occupational Outlook Handbook*. You can also find the handbook at your local or school library. Complete the chart. (Answers will vary.)

Career title	
Job description	
Working conditions	
Education or training	
Earnings	
Job outlook	

E Write a paper about the job you chose. Explain why this career is a good choice for you.

F Find and correct the mistakes.
1. I have never ~~take~~ taken a sick day.
2. She has ~~always~~ gotten along with her co-workers ~~always~~.
3. He ~~has spoken~~ spoke to the boss a few minutes ago.
4. She has ~~receive~~ received an award as the top salesperson twice.
5. Have you ~~never~~ ever attended a performance review?
6. They have never ~~went~~ been on a job interview.
7. She has ~~been writing~~ written two reports so far.
8. We ~~have~~ had to work on weekends last month.

More Action!

Take a poll of the answers that students checked in Exercise C. Ask students to rank their choices in order of importance. Create a class chart with the responses. Discuss the results. Which characteristic is the most important to most class members? Which is the least important?

More Action!

When students complete their research in Exercise D, conduct a summary discussion in which students help you compile a list of the ten jobs with the best outlook for the near future. In addition, after students have written their papers for Exercise E, have them orally discuss the career they chose and the reasons why.

C **Discuss the meaning of each job characteristic.**

- Have students work with a partner. Go over the definitions as a class, making sure students understand the correct meaning of each job characteristic.
- Have students check the characteristics that are most important to them.
- Invite students to name the job characteristics that are most important to them. Ask them to explain why they feel this way.

D **Go online.**

- Encourage students to investigate a job in which they are truly interested. You might ask some guiding questions to assist their research.
- Go over the Writing Note. Remind students not to copy long passages, or even whole sentences, but to write just a few words after each heading in the chart.

E **Write a paper about the job you chose.**

Students use the notes they took in Exercise D to write their papers. Suggest that they make use of their responses in Exercise C to explain why this career is a good choice for them.

F **Find and correct the mistakes.**

Have students correct the sentences on their own. Review the correct answers with the whole class.

Practicing on Your Own

A **Rewrite the sentences. Put the adverb or time expression in the correct place in the sentence.**

Ask students to do the activity individually, and then check their answers with a partner.

B **Look at the monthly evaluation reports for two employees at Excel Electronics. Karl is going to receive a promotion. David is going to lose his job. Complete the evaluations. Use the present perfect.**

• Have students complete the evaluation reports on their own. Explain that there can be several different correct answers to each question because students can invent some of their own details. Stress that the important thing is to create sentences using the present perfect. For example, possible correct answers for Item 1 include: *David hasn't been on time one day this month. David has arrived late twice this week.*

• Go over the answers as a class. Ask a few students to write their sentences on the board. Correct any errors with the formation of the present perfect tense.

144 · Unit 9

A **Rewrite the sentences.** Put the adverb or time expression in the correct place in the sentence.

1. Susan has worked overtime. (several times this month)

Susan has worked overtime several times this month.

2. She has followed company policies. (always)

She has always followed company policies.

3. She has spoken to the human resources department about a promotion. (already)

She has already spoken to the human resources department about a promotion.

4. We have received a complaint about her work. (rarely)

We have rarely received a complaint about her work.

5. She has taken an advanced software course. (recently)

She has recently taken an advanced software course.

6. She has been able to solve problems. (usually)

She has usually been able to solve problems.

7. She has completed a sales management course. (just)

She has just completed a sales management course.

B **Look at the monthly evaluation reports for two employees at Excel Electronics.** Karl is going to receive a promotion. David is going to lose his job. Complete the evaluations. Use the present perfect. (Answers will vary.)

Karl	David
1. He has always arrived on time.	**1.** He has been late ten times.
2. He has taken one sick day.	**2.** He has taken five sick days.
3. He has sold 150 televisions.	**3.** He has sold fifteen televisions.
4. He has never made a mistake on bills of sale.	**4.** He has made mistakes on seven bills of sale.
5. He has always written the correct address on delivery notices.	**5.** He has often written the wrong address on delivery notices.
6. He has often worked overtime.	**6.** He has rarely worked overtime.

144 · Unit 9

 **Katie is a sales assistant.** Read her job description.

Davis Jewelry: Sales Assistant

Assist customers
Maintain and restock displays
Perform sales transactions
 accurately
Follow all store procedures and
 polices

  Listen to Katie's performance evaluation. Check (✓) the correct boxes.
CD2·TR19

	Exceeds Expectations	Meets Expectations	Needs Improvement	Unsatisfactory
Reports to work as scheduled			✓	
Appearance is neat	✓			
Shows initiative			✓	
Behaves professionally	✓			
Uses effective sales techniques	✓			
Performs sales accurately				✓

 With a partner, discuss and evaluate Katie's work performance.

1. Has Katie always arrived on time? Has her on-time arrival improved?
 No, she hasn't. Yes, it has.
2. How are Katie's sales? How are her sales techniques?
 Good. She's friendly, respectful, and complimentary.
3. When does Katie make mistakes?
 When it's busy.
4. What has Mr. Davis decided to do?
 Someone will retrain Katie.

Job Performance · 145

English in Action: Performance Evaluations

 Katie is a sales assistant. Read her job description.

Read the job description together. Invite students to comment on and ask questions about the picture. You may also wish to have students answer each other's questions. For example:
S1: *How does Katie look?*
S2: *I think she's scared.*
S3: *I think she's worried about her job evaluation.*

  Listen to Katie's performance evaluation. Check the correct boxes.
(CD2 • TR19)

• Have students study the performance evaluation form first. Answer questions about any expressions students don't understand. For example, expressions such as *initiative, professional manner,* and *transaction* may be unfamiliar.

• Play the audio twice as students mark and check their answers. Review the correct answers with the class.

  With a partner, discuss and evaluate Katie's work performance.

• Have students answer the questions with a partner.
• Call on different students to answer each question orally.

Teaching Tip

Some students may be unfamiliar with performance evaluations. Explain to students that many companies do yearly performance evaluations for all of their employees. These evaluations discuss what tasks an employee did well in the previous year and what tasks an employee may need to improve on in the upcoming year. A performance evaluation may be a written evaluation, a conversation with a supervisor, or both. In some companies, performance evaluations are very important and are used to determine when an employee will receive a promotion.

Job Performance · **145**

Regrets and Possibilities

Unit 10

A Read the thoughts and discuss each picture.

• Ask students to describe what they see in each picture. For example: *In Picture 1, the man is taking a class. In Picture 2, the man is probably at work.*

• Call on different students to read aloud the thought bubbles in the pictures. Discuss how each thought relates to the picture.

• Say: *These people all made decisions that are causing a problem now.* Help students explain the decisions and the resulting situations all the people in the pictures find themselves in. For Item 3, for example: *She doesn't know how to drive. She has to wait in the rain for the bus. She should have learned to drive.*

Unit 10 🏃 Regrets and Possibilities

A Read the thoughts and discuss each picture.

146 · Unit 10

Use *should have* to discuss regret about a past action.

I **should have studied** more.
Meaning: I didn't study enough.

We **should have brought** warm clothes.
Meaning: We didn't bring warm clothes. Now we're cold.

They **shouldn't have left** their umbrellas at home.
Meaning: It rained; they weren't prepared.

A Write the past participle form of each verb.

Base Form	Past Participle		Base Form	Past Participle
buy	have bought		leave	have left
try	have tried		meet	have met
drive	have driven		see	have seen
forget	have forgotten		lose	have lost
fill	have filled		pay	have paid
send	have sent		sleep	have slept
eat	have eaten		take	have taken
break	have broken		tell	have told
feel	have felt		write	have written

B Listen and complete.

CD2·TR20

1. I _____ should have bought _____ a new one.
2. I _____ shouldn't have bought _____ a used one.
3. She _____ should have studied _____ harder.
4. I _____ shouldn't have taken _____ so many courses.
5. I _____ should have left _____ earlier.
6. I _____ should have remembered _____ to bring it.
7. They _____ should have filled _____ the tank.
8. He _____ shouldn't have driven _____ without a license.
9. We _____ should have sent _____ the check on time.
10. She _____ shouldn't have forgotten _____ it.

Regrets and Possibilities · **147**

Active Grammar: Past Modals— *Should have* for Regret

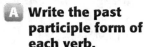

A Write the past participle form of each verb.

- Review the information in the grammar chart at the top of the page. Remind students that they have already studied modals, and in this unit they will learn how to form and use them in the past.
- Provide or elicit additional examples. Answer any questions students may have.
- Ask students to fill in as many of the forms in Exercise A as they can individually, and then check their answers with a partner.
- Review the correct answers with the class.

 B Listen and complete.
(CD2 • TR20)

- Explain that these sentences describe situations in which people made mistakes. Read the instructions and tell students that they will be writing about the mistakes people wish they hadn't made.
- Play the audio and have students write their answers. Play the audio a second time, so students can check their work. Review the correct answers with the whole class.

Teaching Tip

For additional oral practice, ask students to take turns restating each sentence in Exercise B, replacing affirmative statements with negative ones and negative statements with affirmative ones. For example, if the answer was affirmative (*I should have bought a new one*), the student would say: *I shouldn't have bought a used car.* If the answer was negative (*I shouldn't have taken so many courses*), the student would say: *I should have taken fewer courses.*

Regrets and Possibilities · **147**

C **Complete the sentences. Use** *should have* **or** *shouldn't have* **and the correct form of the verb in parentheses.**

• Review the use of *should have* and *shouldn't have* with the class. Then, have students complete the sentences individually.
• Review the correct answers orally.

D **Make a statement about each picture. Use words from the box,** *should have* **or** *shouldn't have,* **and your imagination.**

• Before having students work in pairs, ask them to look at the person in each picture and describe the problem they are having. Review all six pictures in this way. For example, in the first picture a student might say: *The family has too much luggage.*
• Point out the six verbs in the box and remind students to use each one in their sentences. Then, have students work with partners, taking turns making statements about the pictures. Remind students that their sentences may vary. They should use their imagination.
• Review the answers orally with the whole class.

C **Complete the sentences.** Use *should have* or *shouldn't have* and the correct form of the verb in parentheses.

1. I registered for too many courses, and now my grades are falling.

I (take) _____ shouldn't have taken _____ so many courses.

2. Akiko forgot to bring her book, and she needs it for the exam.

She (forget) _____ shouldn't have forgotten _____ her book.

3. Sandra's cell phone rang during the exam.

She (turn off) _____ should have turned off _____ her phone before the exam.

4. Jim stayed up very late. The next morning, he overslept and was late.

He (stay up) _____ shouldn't have stayed up _____ so late.

5. Marie wanted to take a psychology course, but she registered too late.

She (register) _____ should have registered _____ earlier.

6. Paul didn't type his paper and received a low grade.

He (type) _____ should have typed _____ his paper.

D **Make a statement about each picture.** Use words from the box, *should have* or *shouldn't have,* and your imagination. (Answers will vary.)

| bring | put | remember | take | wear | eat |

1. 2. 3.
4. 5. 6.

Active Grammar: *Should have* for Expectation

> Use *should have* to show an expectation.
>
> The bus **should have arrived** by now.
>   Meaning: The bus is late.
>
> I **should have done** better on this exam.
>   Meaning: My grade is lower than expected.

 A **Listen and write the number under the correct picture.**
CD2·TR21

a. __4__   b. __3__   c. __1__

d. __6__   e. __2__   f. __5__

B **Complete the sentences.** Use *should have* or *shouldn't have* and the correct form of the verbs in parentheses.

1. Our professor isn't here. She (arrive) __should have arrived__ at 9:00.

2. Why hasn't the movie started? It (begin) __should have begun__ at 8:20.

3. Paul hasn't gotten his degree yet, but he (graduate) __should have graduated__ last semester.

4. The library (charge / not) __shouldn't have charged__ me a late fee. There was a snowstorm yesterday.

5. The contractors (replace / not) __shouldn't have replaced__ the carpet. It was brand-new!

6. It's 4:00, and Lina (find) __should have found__ out if she has been accepted in the special program.

7. The snow (stop) __should have stopped__ according to the weather forecast.

8. She (gain / not) __shouldn't have gained__ weight if she followed the doctor's diet.

Regrets and Possibilities · **149**

Active Grammar: *Should have* for Expectation

 A **Listen and write the number under the correct picture.**
(CD2 • TR21)

• Go over the information in the grammar box. Check for understanding.
• Look at the pictures together and ask for volunteers to describe them.
• Play the audio once and have students complete the exercise.
• Play it a second time so students can check their answers. Review the answers as a class.

B **Complete the sentences. Use *should have* or *shouldn't have* and the correct form of the verbs in parentheses.**

• Have students complete the sentences individually, reminding them to make sure they use the past participle, not the past form, for the main verb.
• Go over the answers with the class.

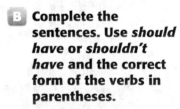

Active Grammar: *May have, Might have, Could have* for Past Possibility

A Match each statement with the correct possibility.

- With the class, discuss the explanation and examples in the grammar box. Then, have students take turns making up possible sentences, using *may have, might have,* or *could have.* Accept any reasonable statements. Model a few examples for students.
I may have forgotten to bring it.
She might have been busy.
They could not have gone to the concert.
They were at a wedding that day.
- Have students complete the exercise on their own.
- Review the correct answers by having one student read a statement from the left column and another student read the correct statement of possibility from the right column.

B Read each sentence. With a partner, write two possibilities in your notebooks. Use *might have, may have,* or *could have* and a verb.

- Have students complete this exercise in pairs.
- Write the numbers 1 through 6 on the board, and have different students fill in the two sentences. Review the answers with the class, making corrections as necessary.

150 · Unit 10

Use *may have, might have,* or *could have* to express past possibility.
I **may (not) have gone** to the movies.
You **might (not) have forgotten** to bring the tickets.
She **could (not) have bought** a new car.
Use *could not have / couldn't have* to express past impossibility.
He **couldn't have been** at work that day. He was in the emergency room with his daughter.

A Match each statement with the correct possibility.

_e_ **1.** Frank didn't come to work yesterday.

_b_ **2.** I wonder where the neighbors went.

_g_ **3.** I saw Tariq with a strange woman. Who was she?

_a_ **4.** Marco was wearing a suit yesterday. He usually wears jeans.

_c_ **5.** Madeline was in a toy store yesterday. What did she buy for her niece?

_f_ **6.** Anna isn't happy with her new job.

_d_ **7.** I can't find my cell phone.

a. He might have had a job interview.

b. They may have gone to Florida.

c. She might have bought her a teddy bear.

d. You could have left it in the restaurant.

e. He may have been sick.

f. She could have taken that other job.

g. That might have been his sister. I hear that she's in town.

B Read each sentence. With a partner, write two possibilities in your notebooks. Use *might have, may have,* or *could have* and a verb.

1. A classmate missed an important exam.

2. A classmate looked sick yesterday. Today, she was absent.

3. A friend was at a travel agency last Saturday.

4. A strange woman was talking to your friend's husband.

5. A friend called you to pick her up at a hospital emergency room.

6. A very large package was delivered to your neighbors' house.

Use *must have* to express a deduction about a past action.

I **must have left** my keys at home.
You **must have left** your cell phone at home.
They **must not have remembered** their notebooks.

  Listen. A man is calling 911 to report a problem in his apartment. Write the letter of the correct deduction under each picture.

CD2•TR22

1. _g_   2. _b_   3. _e_   4. _d_

5. _f_   6. _h_   7. _a_   8. _c_

Deductions

a. The burglar must have used it to hide the other clothes.

b. The burglar must have taken it.

c. The burglar must have dropped the gloves when he left.

d. The burglar must have scared the cat.

e. The burglar must have gotten scared and left through the window.

f. The burglar must have been hungry.

g. Someone must have broken in.

h. The burglar must have put on one of your suits.

Regrets and Possibilities • **151**

More Action!

If appropriate for your class, ask students to role-play phone calls to a 911 line. Have them prepare their scripts in pairs. List the following items on the board as a guide. Be prepared to:

• give your name
• tell your location (address)
• describe the emergency
• say what kind of help you need

Active Grammar: *Must have* for Deduction

 Listen. A man is calling 911 to report a problem in his apartment. Write the letter of the correct deduction under each picture.
(CD2 • TR22)

• Discuss the explanation of *must have* in the grammar box. Explain: *When you are talking about something that probably happened in the past, but you aren't completely sure, you use* must have. Go over the examples, and then provide or elicit additional ones. For example: *You must have been sick. She must have lost her keys. He must have broken his leg.*

• Read the instructions and explain that a home has been robbed. Point to the pictures and ask students to describe what they see in each one. For the first picture they might say: *The lock on the door is broken.* Review all eight pictures in this way.

• Ask students to read deductions *a* through *h*. Review the instructions for the exercise and play the audio. Have students record their answers in the blanks under each picture. Review the answers with the whole class.

Pronunciation: Past Modals
Listen and repeat.
(CD2•TR23)

• Play the audio and ask students to focus on the pronunciation of the affirmative and negative modals with 've. Say just the parts of each sentence with the past modal and have students repeat.
• Replay the audio, pausing after each sentence as students repeat.

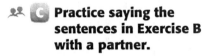

Practice saying the sentences in Exercise B with a partner.

As students practice saying the sentences in pairs, move around the room and offer pronunciation support.

Pronunciation: Word Stress
Listen to the conversation and underline the stressed words.
(CD2•TR24)

• Read aloud the instructions and the first two lines of the dialogue as students follow along in their books. Emphasize the stress on the underlined syllables.
• Play the audio as students follow along. Students underline the stressed words. Play it again so they can check their answers. Review the correct answers with the class.

Practice the conversation in Exercise D with a partner.

Have students complete the activity in pairs.

152 • Unit 10

B Pronunciation: Past Modals Listen and repeat.
CD2•TR23

1. You must've left your book at home.
2. She might've studied French.
3. I should've made an appointment.
4. We could've gone on a vacation.
5. He must've had to work.
6. She couldn't have walked that far.
7. We shouldn't have spoken to her.
8. They shouldn't have arrived late.
9. He may not have had an opportunity.
10. I must not have heard you.

C Practice saying the sentences in Exercise B with a partner.

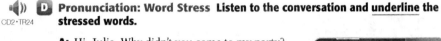

D Pronunciation: Word Stress Listen to the conversation and underline the stressed words.
CD2•TR24

A: Hi, Julia. Why didn't you come to my party? Everyone missed you.

B: What party?

A: I had a party last Saturday.

B: Really? You should've called me.

A: I did. I left a message on your voice mail.

B: I changed my number. You could've sent me an invitation.

A: I did. I e-mailed it two weeks ago.

B: You must've sent it to the wrong address. I've changed my e-mail.

A: You should've told me.

B: Sorry. Anyway, how was the party?

A: It was fun. You should've been there.

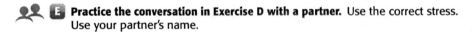

E Practice the conversation in Exercise D with a partner. Use the correct stress. Use your partner's name.

| Use *must have* to express empathy. | My daughter didn't make the soccer team. | She **must have been** disappointed. |

  A Take turns reading the statements. Your partner will respond. Use the subject in parentheses, *must have been*, and an adjective from the box.

(See answers below.)

angry bored embarrassed excited disgusted proud

 You must have been bored.

1. We spent ten very long hours at the museum. (You)
2. My family and I were on vacation when we saw one of our favorite singers. (You)
3. They ordered soup, and there was a cockroach in one of the bowls. (They)
4. I was talking about my boss when she walked in to the room. (You)
5. We were taking a test when my cell phone rang. (Your teacher)
6. My sister was the first person in our family to graduate from college. (Your family)

  B Working Together Student to Student.

Student 1: Turn to page 265.

(The correct verb tense is shown here. Student responses will vary.)

Student 2: Use cues 1–5 to say what happened last weekend. Student 1 will respond.

Example: My homework / be / very difficult

 My homework was very difficult.   You must have been frustrated.

1. I / have to work overtime / all weekend I had to work...
2. I / can't find / keys / for two hours I couldn't find...
3. I / not get / the new job I didn't get...
4. my son / win / football championship My son won...
5. my brother / get / promotion My brother got...

Now change roles. Student 2, turn to page 265. Student 1, use cues 6–10 to tell Student 2 what happened last weekend. Student 2 will respond.

6. my daughter / get engaged My daughter got engaged...
7. I / get lost in a strange neighborhood / for an hour I got lost...
8. at the bank / I / can't express myself in English I couldn't express...
9. I / receive a bonus / at work I received...
10. my friends / have a birthday party / for me My friends had a...

Regrets and Possibilities · **153**

Answers for Exercise A
2. You must have been excited.
3. They must have been disgusted.
4. You must have been embarrassed.
5. Your teacher must have been angry.
6. Your family must have been proud.

More Action!

Have students write out two original situations like those in Exercise A, preferably taken from their own lives. Then, have individuals read their sentences aloud and call on one or two different classmates to give appropriate answers, using *must have been* plus one of the adjectives from the box in Exercise A. For example:

S1: *I was shopping in the convenience store when my bicycle was stolen.*
S2: *You must have been angry.*

Active Grammar: *Must have* for Empathy

A Take turns reading the statements. Your partner will respond. Use the subject in parentheses, *must have been*, and an adjective from the box.

• Go over the definition of *must have* in the box. Ask a pair of students to read the examples in the speech bubbles. Elicit and provide additional examples.
• Go over the directions and model the first item with a volunteer.
• Have students complete the activity in pairs. Review the correct answers by calling on different pairs to role-play each exchange.

B Working Together Student to Student.

• Read and discuss the instructions. Have a pair of students read the sample dialogue in the speech bubbles aloud.
• Have students work in pairs. First, Student 1 turns to page 265 and gives appropriate responses to the cues that Student 2 reads on page 153. Then, students change roles.
• Check the correct answers with the whole class. Ask students what tense was used in each exchange.

The Big Picture: In the Counselor's Office

  A **A high school counselor is talking to Amber, a student. Listen and take notes below.**

(CD2 • TR25)

• Ask students to describe what is happening in the pictures. You might use questions like these to get started: *Who are these people? Where are they? What are they doing?*

• Point out the place where students can take notes. Play the audio and ask students to take notes about what the counselor says to Amber. Pause or replay the audio as needed to give students a chance to finish their notes about Amber.

  B **The counselor is talking to Miguel, another student. Listen and take notes above.**

(CD2 • TR26)

Play the audio and ask students to take notes about what the counselor says to Miguel. Pause or replay the audio as needed to give students a chance to finish their notes about Miguel.

C **Match each student with the correct problems.**

Have students complete the matching exercise on their own. Review the correct answers orally with the class.

 A **A high school counselor is talking to Amber, a student.** Listen and take notes below.

CD2 • TR25

Notes: Amber	Notes: Miguel

 B **The counselor is talking to Miguel, another student.** Listen and take notes above.

CD2 • TR26

C **Match each student with the correct problems.**

Student		Problems	
Amber	_e_	**a.**	relationship
	_a_	**b.**	problems with a class
	_c_	**c.**	college plans
Miguel	_d_	**d.**	poor grades
	_b_	**e.**	lost a job
	_f_	**f.**	needed a job

D Listen again to Amber's conversation. Then, answer the questions.

(CD2•TR25)

1. What job does Amber have at school?
   She's the editor of the paper.
2. What does the counselor think about Amber's work on the school newspaper?
   It's good.
3. Why is Amber upset?
   The vice principal took away her job.
4. Is Amber good at her job?
   Yes, she is.
5. Why is the job important to her?
   She needs it for college applications.
6. What did Amber do? Why? *She wrote a story that wasn't true because she was upset with her boyfriend.*
7. Is she sorry?
   Yes, she is.
8. What is the counselor going to do to help her?
   He's going to talk to the vice principal.

E Complete the sentences. Use *should have* or *shouldn't have* and the verb to express the facts and your opinion.

1. Amber (write) *shouldn't have written* false information.
2. Amber (speak) *should have spoken* to her boyfriend about her feelings.
3. Amber (think) *should have thought* more carefully before she wrote the article.
4. In my opinion, the vice principal (take) *should have taken / shouldn't have taken* away her job.

F Listen to Miguel's conversation again. Then, answer the questions.

(CD2•TR26)

1. Is Miguel a good student? Has he improved?
   He's better. / Yes, he has.
2. Did Miguel do the things that the counselor suggested?
   Yes, he did most of them.
3. What could Miguel have done to improve his math grades?
   He could have gotten a tutor.
4. Which is harder for Miguel—speaking English or writing English?
   Writing
5. Why didn't Miguel get help from a tutor?
   He didn't like the tutor.
6. Where is Miguel working now?
   At the bookstore
7. What is Miguel's work schedule?
   Two nights a week and all day Saturday

G Complete the sentences. Use *must have, could have,* or *couldn't have* and the correct form of the verb in parentheses.

1. Miguel (find) *could have found* a math tutor, but he didn't need to.
2. Miguel's math instructor (be) *must have been* pleased with his progress.
3. Miguel (make) *must have made* a good impression at his job interview.
4. Miguel (find) *could have found* a different writing tutor.
5. Miguel (get) *couldn't have gotten* the job without his counselor's help.

Regrets and Possibilities • **155**

D Listen again to Amber's conversation. Then, answer the questions.

(CD2 • TR25)

Ask students to read through the list of questions. Answer any questions students may have. Then, play the conversation and have students answer the questions.

E Complete the sentences. Use *should have* or *shouldn't have* and the verb to express the facts and your opinion.

Give students two or three minutes to read the sentences and prepare their answers. Then, call on different students to complete each sentence.

F Listen to Miguel's conversation again. Then, answer the questions.

(CD2 • TR26)

Have students read through the list of questions. Answer any questions students may have. Then, play the conversation and have students answer the questions.

G Complete the sentences. Use *must have, could have,* or *couldn't have* and the correct form of the verb in parentheses.

Give students a few minutes to prepare their answers. Then, call on different students to complete each sentence.

Reading: Language and Culture Programs

A Discuss. Then, read.

• Point to the pictures and invite students to comment. Ask: *Who do you think these people are? What are they doing?*
• Invite several different students to answer the discussion questions. Encourage them to add details if they wish. For example: *I have two nieces. They live in Colombia but they're coming here next year.*
• Go over the Reading Note. Ask students to do the task in the reading note before they read the entire passage, or do this step as a class. Go over the words in the Word Partnerships box. Ask students to provide simple definitions of each item in the Word Partnerships box.
• Once students have completed the tasks in the Reading Note, instruct them to read the entire passage. When they finish the reading, invite students to ask about anything they don't understand, and to make any comments about the passage.

A Discuss. Then, read.

1. Do you have children, grandchildren, or nieces and nephews?

2. Can the children speak, read, and write your native language?

3. Do you want the children to learn your native language and culture? Why or why not?

READING NOTE
Preparing to Read Before you read a passage, look at the title. Then, read the first two sentences of each paragraph. Think about the topic. Then, continue to read the passage.

WORD PARTNERSHIPS	
after-school	
cultural	program
intensive	
weekend	

Family 1

I'm from Argentina. My family and I are living in the United States. We've been living here for almost three years now. My children can speak English fluently, and they are in regular classes. I'm disappointed that they don't speak Spanish anymore. They've forgotten our language. I should have done something to help them maintain our language and learn about our Argentinean culture, but it's too late now.

Family 2

My daughter is very excited. This summer, we're going to visit my parents in Korea for the first time. I've been sending her to a Korean school every weekend for the past year. Some friends told me that I should have concentrated on her English, but my husband and I decided that we wanted her to learn Korean, too. She's been writing letters to her grandparents, and the grandparents are thrilled to receive a letter that they can read. We made the right decision.

What can immigrant parents do to help their children learn or **maintain** their native language and culture? Children who grow up speaking one language outside the home and a different language inside the home learn to speak two languages. However, it is hard for these children to learn to read and write their parents' native language at an advanced level. Therefore, many parents send their children to special programs for an average of three to five hours a week. The **mission** of most programs is to help children of immigrant parents and / or grandparents learn their native language and culture. There are Polish schools and Chinese schools, to name a few.

One Korean school in New York City offers six hours of instruction every Saturday. The school teaches reading and conversation, Korean history, and Korean **fine arts**, including art and music. Students include Korean children who were adopted by American couples, Korean-Americans, Koreans, and Americans.

A Greek school in Chicago teaches Greek language to children in their Greek Orthodox Church community. The school day lasts two and a half hours every Saturday. The students can learn to read, write, and speak Greek. One parent explained why she sent her child to the Greek school. She said, "I studied Greek in an after-school program when I was a child, and I wanted my daughter to learn Greek, too. **Besides** learning the culture of my parents, she was also learning another language. The more languages she learns, the better off she'll be in the future." She added, "Sometimes it was a **struggle** to get her to classes, in terms of convenience and other school activities, but I kept her in the classes." When the daughter was older, she even took a trip to Greece with her classmates at the school.

B **Word Builder** **Find the boldfaced words in the reading.** (Circle) the correct definition.

1. What can immigrant parents do to help their children learn or **maintain** their native language and culture? *Maintain* means _____.

   a. to repair   **(b.)** to continue   **c.** to take care of   **d.** to speak

2. The **mission** of most programs is to help children of immigrant parents and / or grandparents to learn the native language and culture. A *mission* is _____.

   (a.) a goal   **b.** a map   **c.** a lesson   **d.** a fight

3. The school teaches reading and conversation, Korean history, and Korean **fine arts**, including art, music, and calligraphy. Which of the following is not a *fine art*?

   a. drawing   **b.** painting   **(c.)** chemistry   **d.** photography

4. **Besides** learning the culture of my parents, she was also learning another language. *Besides* means _____.

   a. but   **(b.)** in addition to   **c.** next to   **d.** if

5. Sometimes it was a **struggle** to get her to classes. *It was a struggle* means

   _____.

   a. it was easy   **b.** it was confusing   **(c.)** it was challenging   **d.** it was exciting

 C **Discuss.**

1. Are you more similar to Family 1 or Family 2? Explain your answer.

2. Is it important to you that your children or future children learn to speak, read, and write your native language? Why or why not?

3. What do you think about weekend language and culture schools for children?

B **Word Builder**
Find the boldfaced words in the reading. Circle the correct definition.

• Remind students to use context to find meaning. This involves reading the whole sentence and figuring out what the key word means based on the rest of the words, or context, in the sentence.
• Read the instructions and do the first item with the whole class. Then, have students complete the exercise individually, and then check their answers with a partner. Review the correct answers.

C **Discuss.**

Have students discuss the questions in pairs or small groups. If possible, ask students to research some local language and cultural schools in your area and share their findings with their partners.

More Action!

If time permits, have a class discussion comparing different viewpoints among various students. Encourage students to give reasons for their opinions. For example:
T: *Why is it important for your children to speak your native language when they grow up?*
S: *I want them to know where they came from. It also could help them in their careers. Knowing more than one language is a big help.*

Writing Our Stories: My Regrets

A. Read the composition.

- Ask students to read the story on their own. What were the writer's three regrets?
- Ask volunteers to share their regrets with the class if they feel comfortable doing so. Ask: *What regrets did you have after you arrived in this country?*

B. You are going to write a composition about your regrets when you moved to this country. Answer the following questions to give you some ideas.

- Read the questions with students and answer any questions they may have. Or, call on volunteers to read each question. You may wish to have a student give a sample answer for each one.
- Write on the board any new vocabulary words that come up and discuss them with the class.

A. Read the composition.

My Regrets

Manny Arias
March 2010
English IV

It's difficult to move to a new city, especially in a new country. Looking back, there are many things that I should have done to prepare.

First of all, there's the language. I studied English in high school, but I didn't take it seriously. I should have studied harder. Also, I could have taken another English class before I came here. Of course, now I'm taking English classes.

Second, good jobs are hard to find. I finished my degree back in my country, but I didn't bring my transcripts. Now, it's difficult to get the transcripts; I should have brought them with me. I've ordered my transcripts from the university, but it's taking a long time for them to arrive. When they arrive, I may be able to find a job in my field.

Finally, I didn't know how to drive when I arrived. In my country, public transportation was very convenient and cheap. But in this state, many jobs are outside of the city and there isn't any public transportation to those locations. One of my friends is teaching me how to drive, but I should have learned earlier. Those are a few of the things that I should have done before I came here.

B. You are going to write a composition about your regrets when you moved to this country. Answer the following questions to give you some ideas.

1. What did you forget to bring with you to this country that you needed?
2. What did you bring with you that you didn't need?
3. What should you have done before you came here?
4. Could you have studied English before you came to this country?
5. Did you contact relatives in this country when you were planning your move to this country?
6. Where did you live when you first came to this country?
7. Did you have information about job opportunities before you came to this country? Were you happy with your first job?

158 · Unit 10

Teaching Tip

If time allows, you may wish to have students write the first drafts of their compositions in class. If possible, review each student's draft and make suggestions for change, including corrections and expansions.

C **Complete the sentences.** Use a verb from the box. Add punctuation.

(Answers may vary.)

asked	shouted	explained	said	complained

1. Sylvia ____*shouted,*____ "Stop slamming the door!"

2. Ivan ____*asked,*____ "When can I take the test?"

3. Marlene ____*said,*____ "We should've called the police."

4. Juliette ____*asked,*____ "Do you have any job openings?"

5. Karen ____*explained,*____ "I must have overslept. I'm sorry I'm late."

6. Al ____*complained,*____ "I've lived here a long time and you've never visited me."

7. José ____*said,*____ "You should have invited her to the party."

D **Write your composition.** Use quotation marks at least once.

 E **Sharing Our Stories** **Read your partner's composition.** <u>Underline</u> the punctuation. What does your partner regret?

F **Find and correct the mistakes.**

1. I could have ~~study~~ *studied* to be a doctor, but I chose computers instead.

2. We should ~~have not~~ *not have* eaten so much. I think I've gained five pounds.

3. You must ~~had~~ *have* enjoyed the party.

4. Peter might ~~has~~ *have* called after 10:00.

5. Edward should ^*have* enjoyed his surprise party, but he didn't.

6. That TV must have ~~be~~ *been* expensive. It's the newest model.

7. The performance must have ~~be~~ *been* exciting.

8. You might ^*have* been upset when I called.

Writing Note

Read and discuss the explanation and examples in the Writing Note. Answer any questions.

C **Complete the sentences.**

• Before students start, tell them that more than one answer is possible in several of the sentences.
• Have students complete the sentences individually. Then, ask different students to write each completed sentence on the board. Review the placement of each set of quotation marks with the class.

D **Write your composition.**

Have students begin or complete their compositions on their own. Remind them to use quotation marks.

E **Sharing Our Stories Read your partner's composition.**

• Have students read a partner's composition. Pair higher-level students with lower-level ones. Students can point out problems with punctuation and grammar.
• If students are comfortable, have volunteers tell the class what their partner regrets.

F **Find and correct the mistakes.**

Have students correct the mistakes, and then check their work with a partner.

More Action!

You might ask groups of students to do a search on the Internet, in local phone books, and other resources to assemble a comprehensive list of language and culture programs available in the area. Suggest that they prepare the information in chart form, listing the national or ethnic group in the first column, the location and hours of the program in the second column, and any other important details in the third column. Post the completed charts in the classroom.

Practicing on Your Own

A **Complete the conversations. Use the verb in parentheses and a modal from the box. Use the present or past modal form.**

Ask students to complete the sentences on their own, and then check their answers with a partner.

 Practicing on Your Own

A **Complete the conversations.** Use the verb in parentheses and a modal from the box. Use the present or past modal form.

have to	doesn't / don't have to	should (not)	may (not)
had to	didn't have to	had better (not)	might (not)
must (not)			could (not)

1. A: Are you free this weekend?

   B: No, I'm not. I (work) ____have to work____ overtime.

2. Driver: What's the problem, Officer?

   Officer: You (not make) _shouldn't have made_ a left turn at that corner.
   Now, (give) I ____have to give / must give____ you a ticket.

3. A: How's the weather?

   B: It's very cloudy. It (rain) ____might rain____ . You (take)
   ____should take____ your umbrella.

4. A: Why are you so late?

   B: It's a nice day, so I decided to walk. I (take) _should have taken_ the bus
   instead.

5. A: Did you hear? Connie's husband was laid off last week.

   B: She (be) ____must be / must have been____ very upset.

6. A: Why does Steven wear blue shirts every day?

   B: I don't know. He (like) ____must like____ the color blue.

7. Teacher: This is your last chance. You (not / miss) ____must not miss____
   another class.

   Student: I promise I won't be absent again.

8. A: Why didn't Peter take his driving test last Friday?

   B: I'm not sure. He (be) ___might / may / must not have been___ ready.

Teaching Tip

For an extended review, have students write ten true sentences about their friends and family, using the modals from the box. For example:
My friend Casey had to leave class early. My sister must have studied hard for the test.
Have students share their sentences with a partner and answer any questions their partner has.

 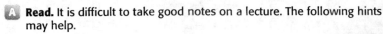

A **Read.** It is difficult to take good notes on a lecture. The following hints may help.

1. Think about the topic. What do you already know about the topic?

2. Listen for cues that will help you understand the lecture. Here are some examples:

   a. *First, second, third, …* – These words introduce steps or stages in a process.

   b. *In addition, moreover,* and *furthermore* – These words introduce more information.

3. Use the Cornell Note-Taking Method. This method was designed in the 1950s by Walter Pauk, a professor at Cornell University.

   a. Use sheets of three-hole notebook paper, 8.5" × 11".

   b. Draw lines on your paper like the example below.

----------- 2.5" ------------	----------------------- 6" ----------------------
Write questions about your lecture notes in this space.	Take notes in this space.
Leave a 2"-deep space here. **Summarize the lecture in this space.**	

4. After the lecture, read your questions and notes aloud. Answer the questions.

5. Think about the topic and your notes.

6. Review your notes every week for ten minutes or more.

B **Go online.** Type "ESL Listening" or "ESL Listening Lectures" to find free lectures. Choose a lecture. Take notes using the Cornell Note-Taking Method.

More Action!

If time permits, give a short sample lecture so students can try out the Cornell Note-Taking Method. For example, review the grammar that they have learned in this unit (You can use this unit's grammar summary on page 255). Or, have them use the method in another class, if possible. After they've taken and reviewed their notes using this method, ask students for their reaction.

English in Action: Taking Notes

A **Read.**

• Read this selection as a class. Have students read Item 1, and ask them to talk about how they take notes.

• Ask students to read Item 2. Ask if anyone listens for cues such as these.

• Have students read Item 3, and then review the Cornell Note-Taking Method. Encourage students to try using this method, and to review their notes every week.

• Have students read Items 4 through 6. Ask if students have ever used any of these note-taking methods. Ask: *In your opinion, what hint or hints are the most effective?*

B **Go online.**

• Have students go online and practice the note-taking method. Alternatively, go online yourself and find a lecture of an appropriate length, level, and topic. Then, give the lecture to the class and have students complete this exercise.

• Afterwards, discuss how the note-taking method worked for an online lecture. Ask: *Was it easier or more difficult to take notes on a lecture online? In what way(s)?*

Business and Industry

A **Look at the map of the western half of the United States. Answer the questions.**

- Before asking students to answer the questions, have them point to any state that they are familiar with and ask them to tell the class what they know. For example:

  S1: *My sister lives in Oklahoma. They have bad winters there.*

  S2: *Hollywood is in California. They make a lot of movies there.*

- Point to the compass in the art. Make sure students understand compass points.

- Point to the state of Washington, and say that it is different from the capital of the United States, Washington, D.C. Point out or ask a student to find Washington, D.C. on the map of the U.S. on page 289. To differentiate between the state of Washington and the U.S. capital, explain that sometimes people refer to the state of Washington as Washington State.

- Ask students to respond to the questions in complete sentences. For example, for Item 1: *Oregon is located north of California.*

A **Look at the map of the western half of the United States.** Answer the questions.

1. Which state is located north of California?
   Oregon
2. Which state is located west of Nevada?
   California
3. Which country is located north of Idaho?
   Canada
4. Which states are located south of Montana?
   Wyoming and Idaho
5. How many states are bordered by Colorado? Name the states.
   Seven: New Mexico, Arizona, Utah, Wyoming, Nebraska, Kansas, Oklahoma
6. How many states are bordered by Arizona? Name the states.
   Five: California, Nevada, Utah, Colorado, New Mexico
7. Which states are located to the north of Texas?
   Oklahoma and New Mexico
8. Which country is located to the southwest of Texas?
   Mexico

162 · Unit 11

More Action!

Invite different students to point out a particular product pictured on the map and say something about it. For example:
Apples are grown in Washington. There are hundreds of varieties of apples.
Guide the discussion so that students talk about many of the products shown on the map. Encourage them to tell about any other products they know of that come from these states.

Active Grammar: The Passive— Present

Subject	Be	Past Participle	
Tuna	is	caught	by fishermen in Oregon.
Apples	are	grown	in Washington State.

Active sentences emphasize the subject that does the action.

Subject	Verb	Object
<u>Fishermen</u>	**catch**	*tuna and salmon* in Oregon.

Passive sentences emphasize the object that receives the action.

Object	Verb	Subject
Tuna and salmon	**are caught**	<u>by fishermen</u> in Oregon.

Note: When the subject is obvious, unknown, or not important, "by" and the subject are **not** necessary.

Tuna and salmon **are caught** in Oregon. (The subject is obvious: We know that fishermen catch the fish, so "by fishermen" isn't necessary.)

A Write each product from the chart next to the correct verb.

A count noun requires either a singular or plural verb.

This apple **is** delicious.
Apples **are** grown in Washington State.

A non-count noun requires a singular verb.

Lettuce **is** grown in Arizona.

Count Nouns		Non-count Nouns	
apples	potatoes	coal	lettuce
cattle (plural)	sheep (plural)	copper	milk
chili peppers	shrimp (plural)	cotton	natural gas
computers	tomatoes	gold	petroleum
grapes	tuna (plural)	hay	
lumber products	Christmas trees		

1. mine — coal, copper, *gold, natural gas, petroleum*

2. catch — shrimp, *tuna, salmon*

3. grow — apples, *chili peppers, grapes, potatoes, tomatoes, Christmas trees, cotton, hay, lettuce*

4. manufacture — computers

5. produce — lumber products, *milk*

6. raise — cattle, *sheep*

B In your notebook, write ten sentences about the map on page 162, five with count nouns and five with non-count nouns. Use the passive. (Answers will vary.)

Apples are grown in Washington State.

Active Grammar: The Passive— Present

A Write each product from the chart next to the correct verb.

• Discuss the passive voice and the sample sentences in the grammar boxes. To demonstrate the points in the grammar box, write this sentence on the board: *Grapes are grown in California.* Ask:

T: *What is the object of this sentence? What receives the action?*

S1: Grapes *receives the action.*

T: *Right. And who performs the action?*

S1: *We don't know. It's probably farm workers.*

T: *That's correct. Farm workers probably grow the grapes. That part is understood.*

• Go over the information on count and non-count nouns in Exercise A.

• Review the meaning of any unfamiliar words.

• Have students complete the exercise and check their answers with a partner.

B In your notebook, write ten sentences about the map on page 162, five with count nouns and five with non-count nouns. Use the passive.

Refer students to the answers in Exercise A to help them select the correct verbs. Provide students with a few examples: *Potatoes are grown in Idaho. Sheep are raised in Nevada.* Elicit sample sentences and correct as needed.

C. Circle the correct form of the verb.

- Review the vocabulary in the Word Partnerships box.
- Have students complete the exercise on their own. Review the correct answers with the whole class.

D. With a partner, ask and answer questions about the product map.

- Review the sample sentences with the class, pointing out the use of the singular and plural forms of the verb *be*.
- Have students ask and answer questions in pairs. Review answers by calling on different pairs to say one question and answer each.
- Write on the board any questions that students have difficulty with. Review how to form the passive if needed.

C Circle the correct form of the verb.

1. Farmers (grow) / are grown corn in Iowa.
2. Sheep raise / (are raised) in Ohio.
3. Milk produces / (is produced) in Wisconsin.
4. Auto companies (manufacture) / are manufactured cars in Michigan.
5. Steel produces / (is produced) in Illinois.
6. Coal mines / (is mined) in Illinois and Kentucky.
7. Many companies (produce) / is produced cereal in Michigan.
8. Owners (raise) / are raised horses in Kentucky.
9. Cattle raise / (are raised) in Tennessee.

WORD PARTNERSHIPS	
grow	vegetables
	flowers
	trees
raise	animals
	children

 D With a partner, ask and answer questions about the product map.

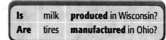

Is	milk	produced in Wisconsin?
Are	tires	manufactured in Ohio?

More Action!

Extend practice with the passive form by displaying pictures of various vegetables, animals, and manufactured products, such as bananas, chickens, and cars. Hold up each picture and ask students to make statements about the picture using the passive voice. Point out that all of the statements don't have to relate to the product map. For example:

Corn is grown in Iowa. Popcorn is sold at the movies. Fresh corn is sold during the summer.

| Where | is | rice | grown? |
| How | are | cars | manufactured? |

A Listen and write the questions. Then, look at the product map and write the answers.

CD3•TR1

Count Nouns	Non-count Nouns
automobiles	clothing
coconuts	coal
electronics	corn
financial services	footwear
soybeans	iron
textiles	rice
	wheat

1. Where are electronics manufactured?

   They are manufactured in South Korea and Singapore.

2. Which grains are grown in China?

   Rice and wheat are grown in China.

3. Where are automobiles manufactured?

   They are manufactured in South Korea.

4. Where is footwear made?

   It is made in Vietnam.

5. What kind of food is grown in Thailand?

   Coconuts and rice are grown in Thailand.

6. Where is coal mined?

   Coal is mined in China.

B In your notebook, write three more questions. Ask and answer the questions with a partner.

Teaching Tip

Invite students to suggest any other products that come from the Asian countries shown on the map. Then, have them make statements about these products using the passive voice. For example: *Silk is made in Thailand.*

Active Grammar: Present Passive— *Wh-* Questions

  A Listen and write the questions. Then, look at the product map and write the answers. (CD3•TR1)

• Go over the information in the grammar box.
• Point out the location of the countries on a world map, so students can see their location within Asia.
• Play the audio once and have students just listen. Then, play it again, pausing after each question to give students time to write them down and answer them. Check their work by asking different students to read one question each to the class.
• Then, have students look at the map to find the answers to the questions they wrote.
• Have them write the answers individually and then check them with a partner.

  B In your notebook, write three more questions. Ask and answer the questions with a partner.

• Pair students of varying language abilities. Have each student write three questions on their own.
• Then, have them take turns asking their partner the questions.

Business and Industry • **165**

Active Grammar: Passive with *By*

A **Rewrite the sentences in the passive. Use *by* when necessary.**

• Go over the information in the grammar box. Provide and elicit additional examples.

• Have students complete the exercise on their own. Then, go over the answers with the whole class. For each item, call on students to say what the subject of the action is and what the action is. For example, in Item 1, the subject of the action is *rice*, and the action is *is grown*.

Use *by* when the **subject** of the action is important and is not obvious.
This candy **is produced** *by* Royal Sweets.
This toy **is made** *by* an American company.

A **Rewrite the sentences in the passive.** Use *by* when necessary.

1. Farmers grow rice in Louisiana.

   Rice is grown by farmers in Louisiana.

2. Construction workers build skyscrapers in New York City.

   Skyscrapers are built by construction workers in New York City.

3. Cardiologists perform heart surgery.

   Heart surgery is performed by cardiologists.

4. A technician usually does my blood test.

   My blood test is usually done by a technician.

5. In Maine, fishermen trap lobsters.

   Lobsters are trapped by fishermen in Maine.

6. All over the world, soccer fans watch the World Cup.

   The World Cup is watched all over the world by soccer fans.

7. Someone cuts and fertilizes his lawn.

   His lawn is cut and fertilized by someone.

8. Specially trained bakers design wedding cakes.

   Wedding cakes are designed by specially trained bakers.

9. Flight attendants serve beverages during flights.

   Beverages are served by flight attendants during flights.

10. Cranberry farmers grow cranberries in New Jersey and Massachusetts.

    Cranberries are grown in New Jersey and Massachusetts.

166 · Unit 11

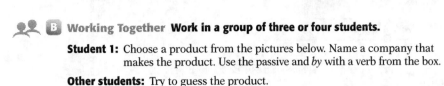

B Working Together Work in a group of three or four students.

Student 1: Choose a product from the pictures below. Name a company that makes the product. Use the passive and *by* with a verb from the box.

Other students: Try to guess the product.

Student 1: If the students are wrong, make a new statement and give the name of another company that makes the product.

> This product is made
> by _____.
>   name of company

> It's a copy machine!

deliver	refine
design	manufacture
make	produce

1.
2.
3.
4.
5.
6.
7.
8.
9.
10.
11.
12.

C Write four products that you and your family use at home. Complete the sentences. Write one of your sentences on the board. (Answers will vary.)

1. I / We use _____.
                    product
It / They _____ by _____.
              passive verb   name of company

2. I / We use _____.
                    product
It / They _____ by _____.
              passive verb   name of company

3. I / We use _____.
                    product
It / They _____ by _____.
              passive verb   name of company

4. I / We use _____.
                    product
It / They _____ by _____.
              passive verb   name of company

Business and Industry • **167**

B Working Together Work in a group of three or four students.

• Go over the directions and the example. Point out the verbs in the box and review how they are used in the passive voice.

• Have students work in groups to complete the exercise. Suggest that they take turns playing the role of Student 1.

• Review the answers with the whole class. Whenever possible, elicit sentences using several different company names associated with a certain product. Write the company names that students come up with on the board.

C Write four products that you and your family use at home. Complete the sentences. Write one of your sentences on the board.

• Have students complete the exercise individually and then read their sentences to a partner.

• Have partners help each other check for correct use of the passive voice. Encourage them to talk about different products they use at home.

• Have students pick their partner's best sentence. Then, call on students to write the sentence that their partner picked on the board.

Describing a Process

  A **Pronunciation: Syllable Stress Listen and repeat.**

(CD3 • TR2)

• Have students follow along in their books as you play the audio.

• Then, play the audio again, pausing after each word and asking students to repeat. Point out that the syllable that receives the stress changes across each set of three words.

  B **Listen again. Underline the stressed syllable of the words in the chart.**

(CD3 • TR3)

• Pause the audio after each set of three words. If necessary, replay each set of words as students mark the stressed syllable in each word.

• Review the correct answers by having a different student write each set of three words on the board, adding an accent mark on the stressed syllable of each word.

 A **Pronunciation: Syllable Stress Listen and repeat.**

CD3•TR2

Verb	Noun	Adjective
1. pasteurize	pasteurization	pasteurized
2. sterilize	sterilization	sterilized
3. immunize	immunization	immunized
4. separate	separation	separated
5. refrigerate	refrigeration	refrigerated
6. evaporate	evaporation	evaporated
7. ferment	fermentation	fermented

  B **Listen again.** Underline the stressed syllable of the words in the chart.

CD3•TR3

pasteurize   pasteurization   pasteurized

C **Write a sentence under each picture on page 169 to describe the process of gathering chocolate beans.** Use the cues below. Two sentences require active verbs, and the others require passive verbs.

1. the ripe pods / gather / every few weeks during the season

2. the workers / cut down / the pods / from the cacao trees

3. the pods / split open / and / the seeds / remove

4. the seeds / put in large wooden boxes for fermentation

5. the seed pulp / drain / for six to eight days

6. the seeds / dry / by machine or the sun

7. the workers / put / the seeds / into large sacks

8. the beans / export / to chocolate makers all over the world

168 · Unit 11

Teaching Tip

Students may feel that there are two stresses in some of the words in Exercise A. Ask them to mark the strongest, or primary stress, with a mark above the stressed syllable, and the lesser, or secondary stress, with a mark below that syllable. Demonstrate if necessary.

1. <u>The ripe pods are gathered every</u> <u>few weeks during the season.</u>

2. <u>The workers cut down the</u> <u>pods from the cacao trees.</u>

3. <u>The pods are split open, and</u> <u>the seeds are removed.</u>

4. <u>The seeds are put in large</u> <u>wooden boxes for fermentation.</u>

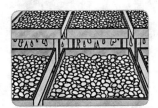

5. <u>The seed pulp is drained for</u> <u>six to eight days.</u>

6. <u>The seeds are dried by machine</u> <u>or the sun.</u>

7. <u>The workers put the seeds</u> <u>into large sacks.</u>

8. <u>The beans are exported to</u> <u>chocolate makers all over the</u> world.

C Write a sentence under each picture on page 169 to describe the process of gathering chocolate beans. Use the cues below. Two sentences require active verbs, and the others require passive verbs.

• Point out the eight pictures. Explain that students will be writing one sentence under each picture using the cues from Exercise C on page 168.

• Because there is quite a bit of specialized vocabulary in this exercise, you may want to do a few sentences or the entire exercise with the whole class. As you go along, pause to explain new terms, such as *ripe, pods,* and *split open.* Refer to the pictures as you elicit or define each term.

More Action!

Provide further practice with the vocabulary and verb forms in Exercise C by having students write sentences using the terms in new contexts. For example:

S1: *I enjoy eating pea pods when I have Chinese food.*

S2: *Bananas are usually cut down before they are completely ripe.*

The Big Picture: T-shirts— From the Field to Your Closet

 A **Talk about the pictures. Then, listen and take notes.**

(CD3•TR4)

• Ask students to comment on the pictures. Ask questions such as: *What are these people doing? What kind of place is this? What is happening to the T-shirts now?*

• Play the audio as students listen. Answer any questions they may have.

• Play the audio again, and have students take notes when they hear information about each picture. You may wish to pause the audio after each section to give students time to take notes. Explain that they will be using the notes to answer questions on the next page. Point out that there is not a lot of room to write, so their notes should be short. (If necessary, students can take notes on another sheet of paper.) Remind students to write just the important ideas, and not complete sentences.

• Ask individual students to explain each step of the process in their own words.

  A **Talk about the pictures.** Then, listen and take notes.

CD3•TR4

1.

2.

3.

4.

5.

6.

7.

8.

9.

170 • Unit 11

🔊 **B** **Listen again and answer the questions.**

CD3·TR4

1. Which countries are the three top cotton producers in the world?
   China, the United States, and India
2. How is cotton picked in China—by hand or by machine?
   By hand
3. What happens at the ginner?
   The cotton is cleaned.
4. Where are the bales of cotton sent?
   They're sent to spinners.
5. What percent of the cotton fabric is dyed different colors?
   20 percent
6. Does one person complete an entire T-shirt? Explain.
   No, one worker sews the sleeves, another sews the neck, and so on.
7. What is the original cost for a T-shirt?
   $3.00
8. Why is the T-shirt price increased in the warehouse?
   Because of shipping costs, warehouse space, and inventory costs
9. How much is the price increased at the department store?
   Over 200 percent
10. How long does it take before a T-shirt is sent to a discount store?
    Six weeks

C **Complete the sentences.** Use an active or passive verb.

clean	knit	send
dye	pick	sew
embroider	sell	ship

1. The cotton _____*is picked*_____ by the workers.
2. The cotton _____*is cleaned*_____ at the ginner.
3. The bales of cotton _____*are sold*_____ to spinners.
4. Knitting machines _____*knit*_____ the cotton yarn into fabric.
5. The dye houses _____*dye*_____ the fabric different colors.
6. The fabric _____*is sent*_____ to a sewing plant.
7. The T-shirts _____*are sewn*_____ together piece by piece.
8. The printers _____*embroider*_____ designs on the T-shirts.
9. The T-shirts _____*are shipped*_____ to warehouses.

D **Complete the sentences.**

1. After the patterns are cut, the workers _____*sew the pieces*_____.
2. When the T-shirts are sold to the department stores, the price _____*is increased*_____ by over 200 percent.
3. Before a T-shirt is discounted, the store _____*sells*_____ it for the full price.
4. The T-shirts are discounted after they _____*are sent to discount stores*_____.
5. The unsold T-shirts _____*are sold*_____ for $14 or less when _____*they are sold in discount stores*_____.

Business and Industry · **171**

🔊 **B** **Listen again and answer the questions.**

(CD3 • TR4)

• Ask students to read through the questions. Explain any vocabulary items that students don't understand. Play the audio and have students listen carefully.

• Call on different students to answer each question. Remind them that they can refer back to the notes they took on page 170 as they formulate their answers.

C **Complete the sentences. Use an active or passive verb.**

• Have students work alone to fill in the verbs, using the ones from the list. Remind them to refer back to their notes on page 170 as necessary.
• Review the correct answers with the class.

D **Complete the sentences.**

• Have students complete the sentences on their own, and then check their answers with a partner.
• Review the correct answers with the whole class.

Reading: An Alternative Energy Source

A Discuss. Then, read.

- Point to the pictures and help students figure out what they show. Ask: *What is the name of this machine? Have you ever seen a windmill? What does a windmill do? How do you think it works?*
- Invite several different students to answer the discussion questions. If students have difficulty naming alternative energy sources, offer an example: *Solar power uses the rays from the sun to heat homes and fuel cars.*
- Read the information in the Reading Note together. Ask students to read the article to themselves, listing pros and cons as suggested in the Reading Note.
- When they are finished, invite them to ask about anything they don't understand and to make comments about the reading. Write any new vocabulary words on the board. Define and discuss each one.

A Discuss. Then, read.

1. Can you list two sources of alternative energy?
2. How can today's cars save energy?

READING NOTE

Listing Pros and Cons
Some readings discuss the pros and cons of an issue. As you read, make a list of the pros and cons. This will help you discuss the reading more easily.

"**Hybrid**" cars—cars that use two sources of power—are becoming more and more popular. These cars use gasoline, but they also have batteries to supply power to an electric motor. Hybrid cars send fewer pollutants into the air. Consumers need clean sources of electricity to run their hybrid cars. They also need clean energy to run other appliances, such as microwaves, TVs, and computers. What new power sources are being used to help protect our environment?

A significant source of **green**, environmentally safe energy is wind. For hundreds of years, windmills have been used by farmers to pump water. Today, millions of windmills and wind turbines are found throughout the world. Cities such as Houston, Texas, and Chicago, Illinois, are using wind energy to generate some of their power. A number of U.S. universities are using wind energy as one of their power sources. About 2.3 percent of California's power is generated by wind turbines. In West Texas, wind turbine engines have become a source of income for people who own groups of wind turbines, or **wind farms**.

Wind has an advantage over other energy sources, such as coal and gas, which cause pollution. It does not generate harmful emissions like coal and gas do. The average household **consumes** approximately 10,000 kilowatt-hours (kWh) of electricity. With green energy, a household can use less energy. A 10-kWh wind turbine generates enough power to serve a typical household for a year. Wind energy is included as one of the options in "green power" plans in some of today's electric companies. The top three energy users of wind energy in 2009 were Germany, Denmark, and the United States.

Although wind is a clean source of energy, not everyone is in favor of wind turbine engines. First of all, **opponents** of wind energy say that large birds may fly into the moving blades and be killed. **Advocates**, or supporters, of wind energy say that more birds are killed by cars than by wind turbines. Second, opponents say that wind turbine generators are noisy and disturb neighborhoods. Advocates say that wind turbines are

172 · Unit 11

Teaching Tip

Have some students research where the electric power they use comes from. Is it water power or does the local utility company burn fuel to make electricity? As they present their findings to the class, discuss the advantages and disadvantages of each type of energy source based on what students learned in the reading.

no louder than refrigerators. Third, residents complain that wind turbines are ugly and reduce the value of their property. However, one wind advocacy group says that one wind farm attracted over 350,000 visitors, and there has been no evidence that housing prices have been affected. There are both positives and negatives of wind energy, but it looks as though it is here to stay.

B **Answer the questions.**

1. What were windmills originally used for?
   to pump water
2. Which cities are using wind as a source of power?
   Houston and Chicago
3. What percent of California's power is wind energy?
   2.3 percent
4. Why have wind turbine farms become popular in West Texas?
   They're a source of income.
5. What type of wind turbine can save energy for a household?
   A 10-kwh wind turbine
6. Which countries were the top three users of wind energy in 2009?
   Germany, Denmark, and the United States

C Word Builder **Complete the definitions.**

1. A **hybrid** car ___*uses two sources*___ of power.

2. **Green** energy is ___*environmentally safe*___ energy.

3. A **wind farm** is ___*a group of*___ wind turbines.

4. Households **consume**, or ___*use*___, a lot of energy.

5. **Opponents** of wind energy are people who ___*are not in favor of*___ wind energy.

6. **Advocates** of wind energy are ___*supporters*___ of the energy choice.

D **Read the sentences.** Write *pro* or *con*.

1. Windmills send no pollutants into the air. ___*pro*___

2. Wind energy does not generate harmful emissions. ___*pro*___

3. Wind energy may harm birds. ___*con*___

4. Wind turbine generators are noisy. ___*con*___

5. A wind turbine is no louder than a refrigerator. ___*pro*___

6. Wind turbine engines may lower housing prices in a neighborhood. ___*con*___

Business and Industry • **173**

B **Answer the questions.**

• Have students complete the exercise individually by going back to the reading and looking for the answers.
• Review answers with the whole class.

C **Word Builder Complete the definitions.**

Do the exercise as a class or have students complete it individually. Go over the correct answers with the whole class.

D **Read the sentences. Write *pro* or *con*.**

• Have students complete the exercise on their own, and then discuss their answers with a partner.
• Go over the correct answers with the whole class. Ask students to point out the word or words that prompted them to answer *pro* or *con*.

Writing Our Stories: Business and Industry in My Country

A Read.

• Ask students to look at the map and take turns describing what they see. They might mention the cities and geographical features such as mountains and bodies of water. Invite them to add any other information they may know about Japan. For example: *Japan has a large population contained in a small amount of space.*

• Go over the Writing Note. Have students read the story on their own and look for the phrases mentioned in the Writing Note.

• Ask simple comprehension questions, such as: *Is rice an important crop in Japan?* (Yes, it is grown in many parts of Japan.) *What are the best known Japanese manufactured products?* (Cars and electronics.)

A Read.

Business and Industry in Japan

Hideo Tokuda

April 2010

English IV

I am from Tokyo, Japan. Tokyo is located in the eastern part of Japan on Honshu, the largest of the four islands in Japan. Tokyo is also the capital city. Japan is an island. It is bordered by the Pacific Ocean to the east, the Sea of Japan to the west, and the China Sea to the southwest. Because much of Japan is mountainous, the Japanese people live in a small area of the country. Japan has a very large population of 127,078,679 (2009), and we need to import many products, such as wood and natural gas, because many natural resources are not found in my country.

Rice is an important product for Japanese people. Rice is grown in many parts of Japan. Many vegetables, including sugar beets and radishes, and fruit, such as apples, are grown on Japanese farms. Fishing is also a large industry. In fact, Japan supplies about 15 percent of the world's fish.

Japan is best known for its automobiles and electronics. Three of the largest automobile companies in the world are Japanese. Japan is also known for its consumer electronics. For example, televisions, game consoles, and DVD players are manufactured by Japanese companies. Look in your home. How many Japanese-made electronics can you find?

WRITING NOTE

For example, such as, including

For example, such as, and **including** introduce examples, but they are used in different ways. Note the punctuation and placement of the transitions in the examples.

Many minerals, **such as** copper and iron ore, can be found in my country.

Many industries are in trouble right now. **For example,** two steel plants have laid off workers.

Tourists can visit a number of famous places in Japan, **including** Kyoto and Mt. Fuji.

B Complete the sentences with examples. (Answers will vary.)

1. Dye houses dye the T-shirts a variety of colors, such as _____ and _____.

2. T-shirts are sold at discounted prices at many stores, including _____, _____, and _____.

3. There are many countries represented in my class. For example, there are students from _____, _____, and _____.

4. My country has natural resources, including _____ and _____.

5. Agricultural products, such as _____ and _____, are grown in my country.

C In your notebook, draw a map of your native country. Show the bordering countries. Then, add products and natural resources.

D Write a composition about your native country's industry and products. Use the questions to guide you.

1. What city and country are you from? Where is it located?

2. What are three major products that are produced in your country?

3. What are the major industries or businesses in your country?

4. What natural resources are found in your country?

 E Sharing Our Stories Exchange papers with a partner. Answer the questions.

1. What city and country is your partner from?

2. What are three products that are produced in your partner's country?

3. What natural resources does your partner's country have?

F Find and correct the mistakes.

1. Coffee is ~~grow~~ *grown* in South and Central America.

2. Italy is ~~bordering~~ *bordered* by Switzerland, France, Austria, and Slovenia.

3. After the cotton ^*is* picked, it is sent to the ginner.

4. France and Italy ~~is~~ *are* known for their fashions.

5. Dairy cows ~~raise~~ *are raised* by farmers.

6. My country ~~locates~~ *is located* near an ocean.

B Complete the sentences with examples.

Point out that answers will vary. Have students complete the sentences. Check the answers by having different students read one sentence each to the class.

C In your notebook, draw a map of your native country.

Discuss the instructions with the class. Have students use the World Map on page 290 to draw their maps. They may need to do research ahead of time on the products and natural resources and where they are found.

D Write a composition about your native country's industry and products.

Discuss the instructions and the guiding questions with the class. Suggest that they model their compositions after Exercise A on page 174.

E Sharing Our Stories Exchange papers with a partner. Answer the questions.

Have students read their partner's papers and answer the questions. If they can't answer a question, they should point that out to their partner.

F Find and correct the mistakes.

Have students correct the mistakes and then check their work with a partner.

Teaching Tip

Students may need more guidance on how to research information for their topic in Exercises C and D. If this is the case, you may consider reviewing page 177 before your students complete Exercises C and D. The activities on page 177 should prepare students to complete the research portion of Exercise C independently. See additional notes on page 177.

More Action!

Have students present the information on their native countries to the class. Hang up the students' maps in the classroom.

Practicing on Your Own

A **Look at the map. Complete the sentences using verbs in the box.**

- Have students complete the sentences on their own, using the verbs in the list and referring to the map.
- Review the answers with the class, pointing out alternate answers whenever possible. For example: *Footwear is designed in Italy. Footwear is manufactured in Italy.*

B **In your notebook, write three more sentences about the map.**

- Have students complete the exercise on their own.
- Then, ask volunteers or call on students to write one of their sentences on the board.

C **Write questions and answers about the product map.**

Have students complete the sentences on their own and then check their answers with a partner.

A **Look at the map.** Complete the sentences using verbs in the box.

> build
> design
> make
> manufacture
> produce
> raise

1. Watches <u>are designed</u> in Switzerland.
2. Automobiles <u>are manufactured</u> in <u>England, Germany, France, and Italy</u>
3. Glass and crystal <u>are designed and manufactured in Ireland</u>
4. Ships <u>are built in England</u>.
5. Footwear <u>is produced / is designed in Spain and Italy</u>
6. Sheep <u>are raised in England</u>.

B **In your notebook, write three more sentences about the map.**

C **Write questions and answers about the product map.** (Answers may vary.)

1. (watches) <u>Where are watches designed and manufactured?</u>
   <u>They're designed and manufactured in Switzerland.</u>

2. (software) <u>Where is software developed?</u>
   <u>It is developed in Ireland.</u>

3. (textiles) <u>Where are textiles produced / made?</u>
   <u>They are made in Spain.</u>

 A Working Together **Work in a group of three or four students.** Choose a state to research.

B **Go online.** Find information about the state you chose. Draw a map of the state in the space below. Mark the places and location of products on your map.

1. Put a star next to the state capital.

2. Label the bordering states.

3. Label three major cities.

4. Label the largest airport in the state.

5. Write three agricultural products that are grown in the state.

6. Write three major industries that are operated in the state.

 C Working Together **Present your research to your classmates.**

English in Action: Doing a Research Assignment

 A **Working Together**

Divide up students of mixed ability into groups of three to four. Have the groups decide on a state to research. Try to have each group choose a different state so there is no overlap.

B **Go online. Find information about the state you chose. Draw a map of the state in the space below.**

• Read the instructions with the class.

• Suggest that students divide up the work. For example, one person could research the geographical information, another could research the products, and so forth.

• Allow class time for students to complete the assignment, or arrange for them to meet outside of class.

 C **Working Together**

• Provide verbs that students can use to describe their state, including *border, grow, locate, manufacture,* and *produce.* Review how these verbs are formed in the passive, for example: *Montana is bordered by Idaho.*

• Have students present their reports to the class, using the passive form of these verbs as often as possible. Encourage the class to ask questions.

Teaching Tip

Another way to form groups for Exercise A would be to have a student come to the front of the room and name a state he or she wants to research. Invite two or three other students interested in the same state to join the student. Form as many groups as necessary to include all students. It would also be interesting if students chose states from various areas of the country.

Technology: Yesterday and Today

  A **Listen. Write the year that each item was invented.**

(CD3 • TR5)

• As a warm-up, invite students to comment on the pictures. Read the information under each picture and explain any unfamiliar vocabulary. Ask: *Are there any items here that you have never seen? Are there any items here that you have never heard of?*

• The first time you play the audio, ask students to just listen. Then, play the audio a second time and have students complete the exercise. You may wish to pause the audio after each statement to give students time to write their answers.

Unit

12 Technology: Yesterday and Today

  A **Listen.** Write the year that each item was invented.
CD3·TR5

1. an insulin pump
Dean Kamen, _1960s_

2. an anti-shoplifting device
Arthur Minasy, _1965_

3. video games
Ralph Baer, _1966_

4. a compact fluorescent bulb
Ed Hammer, _1970s_

5. an artificial heart
Robert Jarvik, _1978_

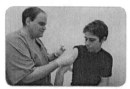

6. the hepatitis B vaccine
Baruch Blumberg, _1980_

7. a space shuttle
NASA, _1981_

8. a laptop computer
Sir Clive Sinclair, _1987_

9. a personal human transporter
Dean Kamen, _2001_

Subject	Be	Past Participle	
The space shuttle	was	completed	in 1981.
		invented	by NASA.
747 jumbo jets	were	developed	in 1970.
		designed	by Boeing.

A **Complete the information.** Use the present or past form of the passive. Use the past or the present tense.

1. The first anti-shoplifting device (invent) _____was invented_____ by a consultant for the New York City Police Department, Arthur Minasy. These tags (attach) _____were attached_____ to store merchandise. When a customer bought the item, the tag (remove) _____was removed_____. The tag set off an alarm if a customer walked through the door without paying. The tags (use) _____are used_____ in many department stores today.

2. The first compact fluorescent bulb (invent) _____was invented_____ by a General Electric engineer named Ed Hammer. Hammer (assign) _____was assigned_____ to develop more energy-efficient bulbs in the mid-70s, when there was an energy crisis in the U.S. Hammer worked for years. Finally in 1976, the compact fluorescent bulb shape (create) _____was created_____. General Electric didn't sell the bulb at first because of production costs. Then, the design (discover) _____was discovered_____ by other designers and it (copy) _____was copied_____ by other companies. Today, the bulbs (sell) _____are sold_____ in all stores.

B **Answer the questions.** Use the past form of the passive.

1. When was the first artificial heart invented?
   It was invented in 1978.
2. Why was it invented?
   It was invented to help heart patients.
3. By whom was the artificial heart invented?
   It was invented by Robert Jarvik.
4. When was the hepatitis B vaccine developed?
   It was developed in 1980.
5. Why was the fluorescent bulb created?
   It was created to save energy.
6. When was the first space shuttle launched?
   It was launched in 1981.
7. Which organization was the shuttle developed by?
   It was developed by NASA.

Technology: Yesterday and Today • 179

Active Grammar: The Passive— Past

A **Complete the information. Use the present or past form of the passive. Use the past or the present tense.**

- Review the grammar chart. Point out that the last column in the chart is used to give additional information about who did something or when something was done.
- Read the instructions and call students' attention to the base forms of the verbs in parentheses. Go over the sample answer.
- Have students complete the exercise individually. Review the answers with the whole class.

B **Answer the questions. Use the past form of the passive.**

- Ask students to complete the activity individually and then check their answers with a partner.
- To check the correct answers with the class, have different students write one sentence each on the board. As you review the answers, make any necessary corrections and answer any questions students may have.

Active Grammar:
Active vs. Passive

A **Read the paragraph. Underline the passive verbs. Circle the active verbs.**

• Ask students to cover up the paragraph. Point to the picture and ask them to tell anything they already know about the Model T car. Ask: *What company made the Model T?* (Ford) *What year do you think it was invented?* (1908) *What is important about the Model T?* (It was an inexpensive car, so many people could afford it.)

• Have students read the paragraph to themselves. Then, have students paraphrase each passive construction in the paragraph in their own words. For example, a paraphrase for *was developed* might be *was invented*.

B **Circle *A* for active or *P* for passive.**

• Remind students that a passive sentence must have the verb *be* plus a past participle.

• Have students complete the activity on their own. Review the answers with the whole class.

A **Read the paragraph. Underline the passive verbs. Circle the active verbs.**

The automobile <u>was developed</u> before 1900, and cars <u>were already used</u> in Europe on a limited basis. In the United States, Henry Ford (developed) a more affordable car in 1908 (called) the Model T. The first moving assembly line <u>was installed</u> in his factory in 1913. This (reduced) the cost and time of producing a car. A Model T <u>was assembled</u> in 93 minutes and (cost) $850. By 1927, more than fifteen million cars (were) on the roads in the United States.

B **(Circle) *A* for active or *P* for passive.**

1. The first cars didn't have windshield wipers.	(A)	P
2. People got out of their cars to clean their windshields.	(A)	P
3. The first windshield wipers were invented by Mary Anderson.	A	(P)
4. They were operated from the inside of the car.	A	(P)
5. The electronic ignition system was invented by Kettering and Coleman.	A	(P)
6. Before this, people turned a crank to start their engines.	(A)	P
7. Before 1929, people could not listen to the radio in their cars.	(A)	P
8. The first car radio was designed by Paul Galvin.	A	(P)
9. The radio was not installed at the automobile factory.	A	(P)
10. Car owners took their cars to a separate company for radio installation.	(A)	P
11. Turn signals were invented by Buick in 1938.	A	(P)
12. Before this, people used their hands to signal a turn.	(A)	P

180 · Unit 12

Teaching Tip

For further review of the passive, have students circle the verb *be* and underline the past participles in each sentence in Exercise B.

Talk about each advance in car and traffic technology. Use the chart below. What did people do before each item was invented?

> The electronic ignition system was invented by Charles Kettering and Clyde Coleman in 1911. Before that, people turned a crank by hand in order to start their cars.

WORD PARTNERSHIPS

parking — lot / meter / place / spot

Invention	Inventor	Year
1. windshield wipers	Mary Anderson	1903
2. automatic traffic signal	Garrett Morgan	1923
3. car radio	Paul Galvin	1929
4. parking meter	Carlton Cole Magee	1932
5. turn signals	Buick	1938
6. air-conditioning	Packard	1939
7. air bags	General Motors	1973

D **Complete the sentences.** Use the passive voice.

1. One of the first automatic traffic signals (develop) ___was developed___ by Garrett Morgan.

2. Before this, many people (kill) ___were killed___ in traffic accidents.

3. Three positions (feature) ___were featured___ on this device: Go, Stop, and All-Direction Stop. The All-Direction Stop allowed pedestrians to cross safely.

4. Morgan's device (use) ___was used___ until today's system of red, yellow, and green lights.

5. The first parking meters (install) ___were installed___ in Oklahoma City.

6. They (meet) ___were met___ with resistance by drivers.

7. Several of the first parking meters (destroy) ___were destroyed___ by angry citizens.

8. The air bag (invent) ___was invented___ by General Motors.

9. Air bags (offer) ___were offered___ as an option in the 1973 Chevys.

10. For more than ten years, air bags (consider – *negative*) ___weren't considered___ important by drivers. Now they are standard equipment.

Technology: Yesterday and Today • 181

 Talk about each advance in car and traffic technology. Use the chart below. What did people do before each item was invented?

• Read through the chart with the class. Answer any questions they may have about what the various inventions do.
• Read the model in the speech balloon and ask students to point out the passive construction.
• Complete the activity with the class. Have students take turns telling who invented each device and when it was invented. Encourage them to imagine what people did before each device was invented.
• Point out that these answers will vary. For example, a possible answer for Item 5 could be: *Before turn signals were invented, people put their hand out the window to signal a turn.*
• Have students pause after each sentence so you can confirm their answer or make a correction if necessary.

D **Complete the sentences. Use the passive voice.**

• Have students complete this activity individually and then check their answers with a partner.
• Review the correct answers with the whole class.

Active Grammar:
Passive with *By*

 Rewrite the sentences. Use the passive voice. Use *by* when necessary.

• Go over the information in the grammar boxes. Answer any questions students may have.

• Review the instructions and the two example sentences before having students complete the activity individually.

• When students are finished, have a different student write each sentence on the board.

• Review the sentences with the whole class, making corrections as necessary.

In early times, the medicine man cured people.
In early times, people were cured **by the medicine man**.
Many years ago, hospitals did not sterilize equipment.
Many years ago, equipment was not sterilized.

Use *by* when the subject of the action is important or is not obvious.

A **Rewrite the sentences.** Use the passive voice. Use *by* when necessary.

1. The Romans began the first hospitals.

   The first hospitals were begun by the Romans.

2. Today, doctors and hospitals sterilize all equipment.

   Today, all equipment is sterilized.

3. Sir Alexander Fleming discovered penicillin in 1928.

   Penicillin was discovered by Sir Alexander Fleming in 1928.

4. Bernard Fantus established the first blood bank in the United States in 1937.
   The first blood bank in the United States was established by
   Bernard Fantus in 1937.

5. Ian McDonald invented ultrasound in 1958.

   Ultrasound was invented by Ian McDonald in 1958.

6. Sound waves create pictures of internal organs.

   Pictures of internal organs are created by sound waves.

7. The Federal Drug Administration (FDA) approved the hepatitis B vaccine in 1981.

   The hepatitis B vaccine was approved by the FDA in 1981.

8. Most colleges require students to have the hepatitis B vaccine.

   The hepatitis B vaccine is required by most colleges.

9. Doctors performed the first laser surgery to correct vision in 1987.

   The first laser surgery to correct vision was performed in 1987.

10. Doctors perform many operations on an outpatient basis.

   Many operations are performed on an outpatient basis.

B Pronunciation: Compound Nouns **Listen and repeat.**

 CD3·TR6

1. **saf**ety razor
2. **air** conditioner
3. **lie** detector
4. **mi**crowave oven
5. **ball**point pen

6. **park**ing meter
7. **con**tact lenses
8. **seat** belt
9. **la**ser printer
10. **cell** phone

> The first word receives more stress than the second word.

 C Working Together **List nine inventions you can see or find in your classroom or in your bag.** Then, answer the questions about each invention. *(Answers will vary.)*

1. _____
2. _____
3. _____

4. _____
5. _____
6. _____

7. _____
8. _____
9. _____

1. What is the name of the invention?
2. How many years ago do you think it was invented?
3. What is it made of?
4. What is it used for?
5. What did people use before we had this invention?

> This is called "liquid paper." I think it was invented about 20 years ago. I don't know what it's made of. It is used for covering up mistakes on paper. Before this was invented, people used special erasers and special paper.

 B Pronunciation: Compound Nouns Listen and repeat.

(CD3 • TR6)

• Read the information in the note box. Play the audio once while students only listen. Then, play it again and have students repeat each phrase.
• Point out that the first word (or first syllable of the first word) always gets the strongest stress.

C Working Together List nine inventions you can see or find in your classroom or in your bag. Then, answer the questions about each invention.

• Begin the exercise by brainstorming a few inventions with the whole class. Read the example about liquid paper.
• Have students complete the exercise individually. Then, put students into pairs and have them ask each other about the inventions on their partner's list.

Teaching Tip

Have students practice the words from Exercise B in pairs. After a few minutes of practice, call on different students to pronounce the words for the class. Correct pronunciation as necessary and have students repeat.

More Action!

Ask students to think of and say other two-word phrases aloud. Write the phrases on the board, using capital letters for the word or syllable that gets the strong stress. For example: *TENnis racket, ENGlish book,* and *SOCcer team.* Then, have different students read aloud the list on the board.

D Listen and answer the questions.

(CD3 • TR7)

Ask students to just listen as you play the audio. Then, play the audio a second time and call on different students to answer the questions.

E Interview a partner from another country (if possible).

• Have students read through the interview questions and ask about anything they don't understand. Then, have pairs interview each other.

• Ask pairs to present their interviews to the class.

F Write two things about your education and your partner's education that were similar. Then, write two things that were different.

• Have students complete the activity on their own.

• Then, have partners compare what they have written about the similarities and differences in their educational backgrounds.

G In a group of three or more students, talk about your partner's education.

Make sure the pairs are split up so partners from Exercises E and F are not in the same group. Have students take turns sharing information about their partner's education.

D Listen and answer the questions.

CD3 • TR7

1. Where was Hui-Fen educated?
   In Taiwan
2. What were some of the rules in her school?
   They were required to wear uniforms.
3. How were students punished if they did not do their homework? They were hit or had to stand with books on their heads.
4. When were students allowed to date?
   In college
5. What language is spoken at home in Taiwan? In what language are students educated?
   Taiwanese / Chinese
6. When is school closed?
   In the summer and in January or February
7. What other information do you remember about Hui-Fen's education?
   Answers will vary.

E Interview a partner from another country (if possible).

1. When were you born? Where were you born?
2. Where were you raised?
3. Were you educated in private school or in public school?
4. Were you involved in any after-school sports or activities?
5. Were you required to wear a uniform?
6. Were you allowed to date?
7. When was school closed for vacations?
8. What languages were taught?
9. Were students expected to stand when they answered a question?
10. How many hours of homework were you assigned?
11. How often were exams given?

F Write two things about your education and your partner's education that were similar. Then, write two things that were different. (Answers will vary.)

Similarities	Differences
1.	1.
2.	2.

G In a group of three or more students, talk about your partner's education.

Your original partner must be in a different group.

184 • Unit 12

More Action!

Make a class chart that shows the answers to the questions in Exercise E. Encourage students to make observations about the data. For example, *Most of us were required to wear a school uniform. Some of us were expected to stand when answering a question,* and so on.

Tense	Passive Form
Simple present	Air bags **are installed** in all cars.
Present continuous	Those cars **are being repaired**.
Simple past	Air bags **were** first **installed** in 1973.
Past continuous	My car **was being repaired** while I was waiting.
Future with *will*	A new model **will be delivered** tomorrow.
Future with *be going to*	That car **is going to be inspected** tomorrow.
Present perfect	Many improvements **have been made** to today's cars.

> All passives have a form of the verb *to be*.

A Complete the sentences. Use the passive with the correct tense.

1. The tallest building in the world (build) ___was built___ in Dubai.

2. A memorial (install) ___will be / is going to be installed___ in downtown Manhattan in the future.

3. I believe that future cars (manufacture) ___will be / are going to be manufactured___ with solar panels.

4. Many diabetics' lives (change) ___have been changed___ since the invention of the insulin pump.

5. When (the book / write) ___was the book written___ ?

6. An AIDS vaccine (research) ___is being researched___ now.

7. 3D movies (already / produce) ___have already been produced / are already being produced___ for theaters.

8. When ___will___ TVs with 3D technology (sell) ___be sold___ at the price of other TVs?

9. Some inventions (discover) ___are / were discovered___ by mistake.

10. The traffic signal (repair) ___wasn't repaired___, so a police officer was directing traffic.

Active Grammar: The Passive— Other Tenses

A Complete the sentences. Use the passive with the correct tense.

• Go over the information and examples in the grammar boxes.

• Have students write their answers individually and then compare them with a partner. Review the correct answers with the whole class.

Teaching Tip

To make sure students know which tenses they are using, ask volunteers to say which tense they used for each item in Exercise A. Remind students to use the chart if they need help identifying tenses. For example, the simple past is used in Item 1.

The Big Picture: Shopping Technology

  Listen as you look at the pictures of shopping technology.

(CD3 • TR8)

• Ask students to describe what they see happening in the pictures. Ask: *What are these people doing? Have you ever done this? When do you think this item was invented?*

• As students listen to the audio, have them point to each picture as they hear it described.

  Listen again. Then, complete the chart.

(CD3 • TR8)

• Tell students to listen, write the dates, and take notes in the right-hand column of the chart. Point out that they might not have time to write complete sentences.

• Ask volunteers to read their notes aloud to the class. Have other students add any information that might have been left out. Play the audio again as necessary.

 Listen as you look at the pictures of shopping technology.

CD3 • TR8

 Listen again. Then, complete the chart.

CD3 • TR8

Invention	Date	How did the invention help people?
1. catalogs	1872	Customers could see more merchandise.
2. a cash register	1884	People received immediate receipts.
3. a shopping cart	1900s	Customers could buy more merchandise.
4. a credit card	1950	People didn't need cash.
5. a bar code (U.P.C.)	1973	Checkout is faster because prices appear automatically.
6. online shopping	1990s	Fast and convenient; people can compare prices.

C Match each statement with an invention from the chart on page 186.

1. Before this invention, all receipts were handwritten. _2_

2. This invention was invented in 1973. _5_

3. With this advance in technology, it's easy to compare prices. _6_

4. This idea was developed by a traveling salesman. _1_

5. This invention was designed by a grocery store owner. _3_

6. This advance was first used by business travelers. _4_

D Read the questions. Then, listen again and answer the questions.

CD3·TR8

1. Why was a traveling salesman necessary?
   Because people lived far from the city.
2. How did Ward travel?
   By horse and wagon.
3. How did his idea help his customers?
   They could see more merchandise.
4. Where did store owners keep their money before 1884?
   In a drawer or cash box.
5. How did the cash register make shopping simpler?
   Receipts were immediate.
6. Why did customers need shopping carts?
   They could buy more items.
7. Who were the first credit card users?
   Business travelers.
8. What invention do supermarket clerks use?
   Bar code scanners.
9. How does the bar code make supermarket clerks' jobs easier?
   Prices appear automatically.
10. How does online shopping save customers money?
    They can compare prices.

E Complete the sentences. Use the active or passive.

1. The first mail-order catalog (print) ___was printed___ in 1872.
   Customers (look) ___looked___ through the catalog and (order)
   ___ordered___ the items they wanted.

2. Before 1950, customers (pay) ___paid___ for their purchases
   with cash or by check. The first credit cards (issue) ___were issued___
   to business travelers. With a credit card, people (*negative* - need)
   ___didn't need___ to carry a lot of cash.

3. The first U.P.C. scanner (install) ___was installed___ in a supermarket
   in Ohio. Today, supermarket clerks simply (scan) ___scan___
   each item. The price (appear) ___appears___ on their cash
   register's screen.

Technology: Yesterday and Today · **187**

C Match each statement with an invention from the chart on page 186.

• Review the example answer with the class.
• Have students complete this exercise individually. Then, review the correct answers with the whole class.

D Read the questions. Then, listen again and answer the questions.

(CD3 • TR8)

• Play the audio for the class, pausing occasionally so students can take notes.
• Play the audio a second time and have students complete their answers. Then, check the answers as a class.

E Complete the sentences. Use the active or passive.

• Have students write their answers individually and then compare them with a partner.
• Review the correct answers with the whole class.

More Action!

Form two teams (or several sets of teams if you have a large class) and have an active/passive competition. The first person on Team A says a sentence that can be formulated in both the active and passive voice. For example: *He gave me the book.* The first person on Team B must say the sentence correctly using the opposite form: *The book was given to me.* If a student cannot rephrase a sentence correctly, they are out of the game, and the next student on the team will have to rephrase the same sentence. The game continues until one student or team is left. Tell students that the first sentence can be either active or passive, but the person on the opposing team must always respond with the opposite form.

Reading: Cell Phone Controversy

A Discuss.

- Point to the pictures in Exercise B and invite students to comment. Ask: *What are the drivers doing in each of these pictures? Are they driving safely?*
- Have students read the questions to themselves. Then, have a class discussion based on their answers.

B Word Builder Match.

- Ask students to complete the matching activity individually and then check their answers with a partner.
- Review the correct answers with the class, answering any questions students may have about the meaning of either a vocabulary word or a word used in the definition.

C Read.

- Read the Reading Note to the class. Then, have students read the first paragraph of the article and compare it to the Summary of Paragraph 1 in the Reading Note. Ask if they feel that the summary is accurate.
- Have students read the article on their own. Then, have them read it a second time, underlining any words or sentences they don't understand. Review the reading, explaining new vocabulary to the class as necessary.

A Discuss.

1. Do you own a cell phone? Is it hand-held or hands-free?

2. Does your state have any laws about the use of cell phones when driving?

B Word Builder Match.

_c_ **1.** controversy	**a.** not permitted by law
_e_ **2.** relationship	**b.** the time it takes to react
_a_ **3.** banned	**c.** disagreement or argument
_f_ **4.** evidence	**d.** to limit; to control
_g_ **5.** distraction	**e.** a connection or association
_b_ **6.** response time	**f.** facts that prove something is true
_d_ **7.** to restrict	**g.** something that causes a person to lose concentration

READING NOTE

Reading Long Passages

As you read a long passage, it is a good idea to summarize each paragraph. This will help you remember what you have read.

Example

Summary of Paragraph 1: More people are using cell phones than ever before, and this has created controversy.

C Read.

Cell phone technology was developed during the 1970s and 1980s. It was not until the 1990s, however, that cell phones came into everyday use. In 1995, 24 percent of adults in the United States reported that they owned a cell phone. By 2009, that number was 89 percent. This little invention has produced a major **controversy**. What is the **relationship** between hand-held phones and car accidents? Some people think that hand-held phones are responsible for car accidents. Do you know the law for cell phone usage in your area?

In June 2001, the governor of the state of New York signed the first law in the United States that **banned** the use of hand-held phones by drivers. Violators are now fined $180 for a violation. New York followed the example set by other countries. The use of cell phones by drivers is banned in Portugal and India. In several other countries, including Germany and Spain, drivers are required to use hands-free sets. Many countries are beginning to add text messaging to this law.

188 · Unit 12

More Action!

For further practice with summarizing paragraphs, have students summarize the other paragraphs in the article. Then, call on volunteers to read their summaries aloud. Ask students for their opinions of the summaries. Revise the summaries as a class as needed.

Some people in the cell phone industry are trying to fight these laws. They say that there is not enough **evidence** to prove that only cell phone usage causes accidents. A study by the American Automobile Association (AAA) said that other distractions, such as eating or applying makeup, are more serious.

Other studies show that cell phone use contributes to accidents. According to the National Highway Traffic Safety Administration (NHTSA), in 2008, almost 6,000 people were killed and half a million were injured due to drivers who were **distracted** by cell phones. Men and women under the age of 20 were the most frequent offenders.

A study at the University of Utah showed that all cell phone use in cars is a distraction. Sixty-four drivers were asked to perform simple tasks, such as changing a radio station, listening to music, talking on a hands-free cell phone, and talking on a hand-held cell phone. Then, researchers measured their **response time** when they were braking or stopping a car. When people were using a cell phone, their responses were much slower. This was true of both hands-free phones and hand-held phones.

What can drivers expect in the future? More laws will be passed to **restrict** the use of hand-held cell phones, especially text messaging. Manufacturers will continue to encourage cell phone safety in their instructions. Some auto companies have already installed voice-activated dialing services in their new models. You can be sure that companies are busy inventing technology for safer ways to use cell phones.

D (Circle) *True* or *False.*

1. The U.S. was the first country to enact cell phone restrictions.   True   (False)

2. The American Automobile Association said that using a hand-held phone is more distracting than eating in a car.   True   (False)

3. The NHTSA reported that young people were most often caught using cell phones while driving.   (True)   False

4. A study at the University of Utah showed that hands-free cell phones are safer than hand-held cell phones.   True   (False)

5. Response time slowed down when drivers used cell phones.   (True)   False

6. According to the reading, auto companies have begun installing voice-activated dialing services.   (True)   False

E **Complete the sentences.** Use words from Exercise B.

1. Television is a ___distraction___ for children when they are doing homework.

2. The museum ___banned___ the use of cell phones. Visitors must go outside to make phone calls.

3. What is the ___relationship___ between drinking and driving?

4. After the accident, the parents decided to ___restrict___ their daughter's driving privileges. She can only drive during the day with an adult in the car.

5. The ___evidence___ shows that the car's brakes failed.

6. There is an ongoing ___controversy___ about how to spend taxes.

Technology: Yesterday and Today • **189**

D **Circle *True* or *False.***

• Have students complete the exercise on their own and then check their answers with a partner.
• Review the answers with the whole class.

E **Complete the sentences. Use words from Exercise B.**

• Have students complete the exercise on their own and then check their answers with a partner.
• Review the answers with the whole class.

Writing Our Stories: An Opinion Letter

 Read the letter from a customer to a restaurant owner.

• Go over the Writing Note at the bottom of the page. Have students read the letter to themselves. Have them check off each point mentioned in the Writing Note as they come across it in the letter. Call on a student to summarize what the letter says.

• Point out the first sentence where the problem is stated, and have a student read it aloud. Then, have students restate in their own words some of the reasons the writer gave for her opinion. Point out the restatement of the opinion at the end of the letter.

Read the letter from a customer to a restaurant owner.

25 Glen Street
Tampa, Florida 33661
March 17

Dear Mr. Lombardi:

Please consider a ban on cell phones at your restaurant. This past Friday evening, my husband and I were enjoying dinner at your restaurant when a woman at the next table received a call. Her loud conversation continued for ten minutes. My husband and I were looking forward to a relaxing evening, a good dinner, and quiet conversation. We didn't pay $47.00 to listen to another customer's personal problems.

Please follow the example of several other restaurants in the city that have posted signs, "Cell phone usage limited to emergencies only."

Sincerely,

Teresa Santiago

Teresa Santiago

WRITING NOTE

A Letter Expressing Your Opinion

1. Put your address at the top on the left side.
2. Begin with *Dear* [name of official / *Sir* or *Madam*]
3. State your problem. Be clear. State your reasons for your complaint.
4. End with *Sincerely*.
5. Sign your name.
6. Print your name clearly underneath your signature.

B **Work with a partner.** Write the reasons under the correct heading. Add one more reason under each heading. *(Answers will vary.)*

> **a.** Drivers need two hands on the wheel.
> **b.** Drivers spend hours in traffic. Talking to friends passes the time.
> **c.** There are not enough studies to prove that drivers using hand-held cell phones cause more accidents.
> **d.** A person who is talking on the phone is not concentrating on the road.

Drivers should be allowed to use hand-held cell phones:

1. *b* _____
2. *c* _____
3. _____

Drivers should not be allowed to use hand-held cell phones:

1. *a* _____
2. *d* _____
3. _____

C **Write a letter to your mayor.** Express *your* opinion.

Your city is considering a ban on using cell phones in cars and in restaurants.

1. Give your opinion in the first sentence, and then give two or three reasons.
2. End your letter according to the Writing Note.

 D **Sharing Our Stories** **Exchange papers with a partner.** Answer the questions.

1. What is your partner's opinion?
2. What are your partner's reasons for his / her opinion?

E **Find and correct the mistakes.**

1. The accident was ~~causing~~ *caused* by a driver talking on a cell phone.
2. The driver *was* ˄distracted when her cell phone rang.
3. Yesterday I ~~was seen~~ *saw* an accident.
4. Olivia's parents ~~were~~ bought her a headset for her cell phone.
5. The man at the next table ˄ *was* talking on his cell phone.
6. She was ~~gave~~ *given* a ticket for driving while using a cell phone.

 B **Work with a partner. Write the reasons under the correct heading. Add one more reason under each heading.**

• Read the instructions. Then, have students copy the reasons on the correct lines and add a reason of their own for each topic.
• Review the reasons students came up with. Discuss them as a class.

C **Write a letter to your mayor. Express *your* opinion.**

• Review the instructions with the class and discuss the format the letters must follow, referring to the Writing Note on page 190. Remind students that they can look back at the letter on page 190 to get ideas for their own letters.
• Have students write their letters in class or for homework. When you go over the letters, avoid discussing spelling or grammar errors and focus on the correct use and placement of opinion statements and reasons in the letter.

 D **Sharing Our Stories Exchange papers with a partner. Answer the questions.**

Have students exchange papers with a partner and answer the questions. If time permits, have students share their partner's opinion and reasons with the class.

E **Find and correct the mistakes.**

Have students complete this activity on their own. Review the correct answers with the whole class.

Teaching Tip

Some students may wish to write their letters on another topic; for example, to the principal or program director of your school about a situation at the school they would like to see changed. Or, they might write about the lack of parking spaces or the need for a water fountain on their floor. Help students correct their letters and encourage them to send their letters to the principal or program director.

Practicing on Your Own

A Complete the article. Use the active or passive and the correct verb tense.

• Have students complete the activity individually.
• Check the answers with the whole class.

B In your notebook, write seven questions about the article.

• Encourage students to write several passive voice questions to practice the structure. For example: *When was the first artificial heart implanted?*
• Call on volunteers to read their questions to the class. Ask other students to answer the questions, using the correct verb tense and voice.

A Complete the article. Use the active or passive and the correct verb tense.

Heart disease is the number one cause of death in the United States. For years, doctors have been developing tests, medications, and procedures to help patients with heart disease. In the most serious cases, a heart transplant (require) _____was required_____ .
1

On December 3, 1967, Dr. Christiaan Barnard (perform) _____performed_____ the first heart transplant in Cape Town, South Africa. The heart of an auto
2
accident victim (transplant) _____was transplanted_____ into the body of Louis
3
Washkansky, a 55-year-old man. He (live) _____lived_____ for 18 days
4
following the operation.

Since that day, over fifteen thousand heart transplants have been performed. The major difficulty in these procedures (be) _____was_____ the
5
rejection of the new heart by the recipient's immune system. In 1969, an anti-rejection drug, cyclosporine, (discover) _____was discovered_____ by Jean-
6
Francois Borel. Today, heart transplants (perform) _____are performed_____
7
throughout the world.

The first artificial heart (implant) _____was implanted_____ in Dr. Barney
8
Clark in 1982. This mechanical heart (attach) _____was attached_____ by
9
tubes and wires to a large machine. The heart (name) _____was named_____
10
the Jarvik-7 after its inventor, Dr. Robert Jarvik. Dr. Clark (live)
_____lived_____ for 112 days. The next patient survived for 620 days,
11
but research with the new heart (discontinue) _____was discontinued_____ .
12
Since then, there (be) _____have been_____ many medical advances.
13
A French professor and leading heart transplant specialist, Alain F. Carpentier,
(test) _____(see below)_____ a new type of artificial heart in the near future.
14
It (develop) _____(see below)_____ by Dr. Carpentier and (manufacture)
15
_____(see below)_____ by him along with two other companies.
16

B In your notebook, write seven questions about the article.

14. will be testing / is going to test
15. will be developed / is being developed
16. will be / is going to be / is being manufactured

A **Working Together** **Work in a group of three or four students.** Match the problem in each picture with a solution below.

1. _b_

2. _c_

3. _d_

She's been in the shower for half an hour.

4. _a_

5. _f_

6. _e_

a. Take short showers of four to five minutes.

b. Install a programmable thermostat.

c. Use compact fluorescent light bulbs.

d. Plug TVs, DVD players, and other electronics into power strips.

e. Buy energy-efficient appliances. Look for the Energy Star label.

f. Wash full loads of clothes.

Compact fluorescent light bulb

 B **Interview a partner about saving energy at home.** Check (✓) *Yes* or *No*. (Answers will vary.)

Questions	Yes	No
1. Do you have a programmable thermostat?		
2. Do you only wash full loads of laundry?		
3. Do you unplug your TV and other electronics when you are not using them?		
4. Do you take short showers?		
5. If you have a computer, is it plugged into a power strip?		
6. Do you have energy-efficient windows?		

Technology: Yesterday and Today • **193**

English in Action: Saving Energy at Home

 A **Working Together Work in a group of three or four students. Match the problem in each picture with a solution below.**

• Arrange students in groups of mixed language ability. Have groups talk about the pictures. Elicit the answer for Item 1.

• Have students complete the exercise as a group.

• Call on a member from each group to provide the answer to one item.

B **Interview a partner about saving energy at home. Check *Yes* or *No*.**

Have students interview each other and check off their partner's answers.

More Action!

If time permits, make a class chart with the total number of *yes* and *no* answers for each question in Exercise B. Then, have students make statements about the data. For example, for Item 3: *Two people unplug their TV when they aren't using it. Ten people do not unplug it.*

Unit 13

Music

A Match the musicians with the kind of music.

- Read aloud the names of the types of music. Ask students to describe in their own words what each type of music is like. For any music types that students don't recognize, give your own simple definition. For example: *Heavy metal music developed in the 1960s and 1970s. It was popular in the United States and the United Kingdom. Heavy metal music is usually very loud.* If possible, bring photographs of people performing each type of music to class.

- Ask students to look at the pictures and tell anything they know about the people they see. Respond by restating what students say in your own words. For example:
S: *Beyoncé sings pop songs. I like her.*
T: *Right. Beyoncé is a famous pop singer.*

- Have students match the music types in the word box to the pictures. (Only six of the listed music types will be used.) Elicit answers from the class.

B Discuss.

Have students discuss the questions with a partner. Circulate around the room and help with vocabulary as needed.

A Match the musicians with the kind of music.

classical	hip-hop	pop	R&B (rhythm and blues)
country	jazz	rap	rock
heavy metal	opera	reggae	salsa

1. Bob Marley
reggae

2. Taylor Swift
country

3. Celia Cruz
salsa

4. Beyoncé
pop

5. The Black Eyed Peas
hip-hop

6. Green Day
rock

B Discuss.

1. What's your favorite kind of music?

2. Who is your favorite singer or band?

More Action!

Bring one or two music recordings that tell a story to class. (Country music and blues songs often tell stories in their lyrics.) Be sure that the songs do not contain inappropriate language. Then, discuss the songs. Ask students to listen and see if they can follow the story in the song. Have students take turns summarizing portions of the story for the class.

An adjective clause describes or gives information about a noun. Adjective clauses begin with relative pronouns, such as **who, whom, which,** and **whose.**

who – replaces a subject (person)
The student **who is sitting next to me** plays in a rock band.
which – replaces a subject or object (thing)
I just saw the movie *Crazy Heart,* **which has good music.**
whom – replaces an object
He's writing a song for his son, **whom he named after his father.**
whose – replaces a possessive form
This is the singer **whose song you just heard.**

A **Underline** the adjective clauses. Circle the relative pronoun and draw an arrow to the noun it modifies.

1. Celine Dion, who was born in Quebec, Canada, grew up in a musical family.

2. Dion performed with her family, who toured Canada, when she was a child.

3. When Dion was twelve, she and her mother sent a demo tape, which was later heard by a producer.

4. Her first English-language album was *Unison,* which she recorded in 1990.

5. In 1992, Dion, whose career was steadily building, recorded the theme to the movie *Beauty and the Beast.*

6. In 1994, Dion married her manager, whose second marriage ended in divorce.

7. In 2001, Dion and her husband had a son, whom they named Rene-Charles.

8. In 2003, Dion began a series of performances at Las Vegas's Caesar's Palace, which negotiated a 36-month contract.

Active Grammar: Adjective Clauses with *Who, Which, Whom,* and *Whose*

A **Underline the adjective clauses. Circle the relative pronoun and draw an arrow to the noun it modifies.**

• Review the grammar box. Discuss the meaning of the terms *adjective clause, relative pronoun,* and *indirect object.* (An adjective clause gives additional information about a noun. Relative pronouns, which include *who, which, whom,* and *whose,* are pronouns that mark the beginning of an adjective clause. An indirect object is something that receives the direct object of a sentence.) Invite students to ask about any aspect of usage they don't understand.
• Point out the picture and ask students to share anything they know about Celine Dion.
• Review the sample answer with the class. Then, have students mark up the rest of the sentences on their own and compare their work with a partner.
• Review the correct answers with the class.

B Look at the picture.
Complete the adjective
clauses.

• Invite students to make
general comments about
the people in the picture.
For example: *Several
people are wearing
cowboy hats. That singer
has a big guitar.*

• Review the sample
answer with the class.
Have a student name the
adjective clause. *(who is
sitting in the front)*

• Have students
complete the sentences
individually and then
check their answers with
a partner. Review the
correct answers with the
whole class.

C In your notebook,
write five sentences
about your classmates.

• Read the instructions
and the sample sentence.
Ask students to make up
as many sentences about
their classmates as they
can in three minutes.

• Call on different
students to read their
sentences aloud. When
there is an error in a
student sentence, restate
it in correct form and
ask the student to repeat.

B Look at the picture. Complete the adjective clauses. (Answers may vary.)

1. The girl who _____ is sitting in the front _____ is saying,
"How many shows have you seen?"

2. The couple who __ is sitting next to her / is wearing yellow shirts __ is saying,
"This is our tenth show."

3. The woman who _____ is sitting in a wheelchair _____ is saying,
"I'm your biggest fan."

4. The woman who ___ is wearing a pink shirt and a cowboy hat ___ is
signing autographs.

5. The woman who _____ is standing in front of the booth _____ is taking
a picture of her friend.

6. The woman who _____ is talking to her husband / is wearing _____ is saying,
"I only bought a few souvenirs."   a purple shirt

C In your notebook, write five sentences about your classmates. (Answers will vary.)

The student _____ who is sitting next to the window _____ is from
_____
name of country

196 · Unit 13

Teaching Tip

To practice adjective clauses further,
ask students to make additional
sentences about the people in the
picture using adjective clauses with
who.

D Answer the questions about you and your classmates. (Answers will vary.)

1. Who do you sit next to in class? _____

2. How long have you been in this country? _____

3. Who has a difficult work schedule? _____

4. Who has long hair? _____

5. Who often listens to music before class begins? _____

E Working Together **Work with a group of three or four students.** Complete the sentences. Use the information from Exercise D. (Answers will vary.)

> Sung Kul, **who is in a band**, is from Korea.
> Beata, **whom I sit next to**, is from Poland.

1. _____, who ___sits next to me___,
   name of student

   is from _____.
   native country

2. _____, whom _____,
   name of student

   is from _____.
   native country

3. _____, who _____,
   name of student

   is from _____.
   native country

4. _____, whose _____,
   name of student

   is from _____.
   native country

5. _____, who _____,
   name of student

   is from _____.
   native country

F In your notebook, write five more sentences about your classmates. Use adjective clauses that begin with *who*, *whom*, *which*, or *whose*. (Answers will vary.)

D Answer the questions about you and your classmates.

• Have students answer the questions individually.
• Ask volunteers to share their answers with the class. Have students with the same answer for a question raise their hands.

E Working Together Work with a group of three or four students. Complete the sentences. Use the information from Exercise D.

• Review the directions and the sample answer with the class. Then, have groups complete the exercise together. Set a time limit for the activity.
• Have one person from each group read aloud a sentence that his or her group wrote. Choose one sentence from each group to write on the board as an example.

F In your notebook, write five more sentences about your classmates. Use adjective clauses that begin with *who, whom, which,* or *whose.*

• Have students use the answers from Exercise E as a model for their sentences for Exercise F. Encourage the class to vary the topics of their sentences.
• Invite volunteers to read their sentences aloud to the class.

Teaching Tip

If some students find Exercise F too challenging, suggest that they work with a partner. First, the pair should choose which students in the class to describe. Then, they should make notes about a few aspects of those people's lives. For example: *John is very tall. John plays basketball on Friday mornings.* Then, have the partners work together to write sentences containing an adjective clause: *John, who is very tall, plays basketball on Friday mornings.*

Active Grammar: Adjective Clauses with *That*

 A **Rewrite the sentences. Use *that* where possible. Write *X* if no change is possible.**

• Go over the grammar chart. Discuss the meaning of the terms *restrictive* and *non-restrictive adjective clause*. (A restrictive adjective clause is necessary to identify the noun it describes. The sentence would not have the same meaning without the restrictive adjective clause. A non-restrictive adjective clause gives additional information about a noun but does not change the reader's understanding of the noun in any significant way. A non-restrictive adjective clause is often marked by commas, but a restrictive clause never is.)

• Invite students to ask about any aspect of usage they don't understand. Elicit or provide additional examples of restrictive and non-restrictive adjective clauses.

• Have students complete Exercise A on their own. Check answers as a class. Explain each answer to ensure that students understand when to use adjective clauses with *that*.

To introduce an adjective clause, the relative pronoun *that* can be used instead of *who, which,* or *whom*. Use *that* only with **restrictive adjective clauses**. A **restrictive clause** identifies the noun it describes.

Restrictive clause:	We paid the man **whom we hired to sing at our wedding**.
	or We paid the man **that we hired to sing at our wedding**.
Meaning:	The adjective clause is necessary to understand who "the man" is.
Note:	No commas are necessary with restrictive clauses.

Don't use *that* with **non-restrictive adjective clauses**. A **non-restrictive clause** gives extra information about the noun it describes.

Non-restrictive clause:	We paid Dave Jones, **whom we hired to sing at our wedding**.
Incorrect:	We paid Dave Jones, **that we hired to sing at our wedding**.
Meaning:	We know who Dave Jones is. The adjective clause gives extra information about Dave Jones.
Note:	Use a comma to separate a non-restrictive adjective clause.

A **Rewrite the sentences.** Use *that* where possible. Write *X* if no change is possible.

1. The Black Eyed Peas is a group which sings hip-hop.

   The Black Eyed Peas is a group that sings hip-hop.

2. *Elephunk* is the 2003 album which sold more than any other hip-hop album.

   Elephunk is the 2003 album that sold more than any other hip-hop album

3. Green Day, whose band sold 15 million copies worldwide, started in Berkeley, California.

   X

4. Taylor Swift, who has already won multiple awards, has a long career ahead of her.

   X

5. Beyoncé used to sing with a group which was named Destiny's Child.

   Beyoncé used to sing with a group that was named Destiny's Child

6. Jay-Z performed in two videos with a singer whom he married in 2008.

   Jay-Z performed in two videos with a singer that he married in 2008

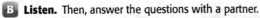 **B** **Listen.** Then, answer the questions with a partner.

CD3•TR9

1. What is the grandson listening to?
An MP3 player
2. What are the grandmother and grandson talking about?
Music
3. What did the grandmother listen to when she was younger?
45s and LPs
4. What was inconvenient about 45s and LPs?
They took up a lot of space and you had to turn them over.
5. What is the grandson glad about?
That technology has improved
6. What did some people think about LPs?
That the sound quality was better
7. What does the grandmother have in the basement?
A turntable
8. What are they going to do next?
Play some dance records from the 70s
9. Have you ever listened to 45s or LPs?
(Answers will vary.)

C **Write each adjective clause in the correct sentence.**

that holds digital audio files	that has a small hole in the middle and plays multiple songs on both sides
~~that holds computer data~~	
that plays 45s and LPs	that has a large hole in the middle and plays one song on each side
that you insert into your ears	

1. A CD is a small disk that holds computer data

2. An MP3 player is a device that holds digital audio files .

3. Earphones are devices that you insert into your ears .

4. An LP is a record that has a small hole in the middle and plays multiple songs on both sides

5. A 45 is a record that has a large hole in the middle and plays one song on each side

6. A turntable or record player is a machine that plays 45s and LPs

Music • **199**

  B **Listen. Then, answer the questions with a partner.**

(CD3•TR9)

• Play the audio and have students listen only.
• Then, play the audio a second time and have students complete the exercise. You may wish to pause the audio after each statement to give students time to write and then check their answers.

C **Write each adjective clause in the correct sentence.**

Have students complete the exercise on their own. Then, check answers as a class.

Teaching Tip

Students may need clarification on some of the vocabulary used in the audio recording for Exercise B. To clarify the meaning of these vocabulary words—*LP, 45, turntable,* and *record player*—go online and print out pictures to show the class.

Music • **199**

Active Grammar:
Adjective Clauses with *When* and *Where*

A Complete the sentences about country singer Tim McGraw.

- Go over the grammar chart. Use the example sentences to clarify the usage of *when* and *where* in an adjective clause. Elicit or provide additional examples as needed.
- Read and discuss the instructions. Then, have students complete the sentences on their own. Review the correct answers with the whole class.

B Complete the sentences.

- Have students complete the sentences on their own and then read them to a partner. Encourage students to correct each other's work.
- Then, invite several different students to read their sentences aloud to the class.

Adjective clauses can also begin with *when* and *where*.
Tim McGraw has appeared in a movie each year since **2004**, *when he appeared in his first movie*.
Faith Hill was born in **Mississippi**, *where she grew up singing in church*.

A Complete the sentences about country singer Tim McGraw.

a. Tim McGraw was born in Delhi, Louisiana.

b. He went to Nashville, Tennessee, in the early '90s to start a recording career.

c. In 1995, McGraw had a hit album.

d. He went on a tour in 1996 and performed with Faith Hill.

e. McGraw and Hill married in October 1996.

f. McGraw and Hill's first child was born in 1997.

g. The couple recorded a duet in 1998.

1. _Delhi, Louisiana_ is the town where _Tim McGraw was born_.

2. He went to _Nashville_, where he _started a recording career_.

3. _1995_ was the year when McGraw _had a hit album_.

4. In _1996_, when _he went on tour_, he met his future wife, country performer Faith Hill.

5. _October_ is the month when McGraw and Hill _married_.

6. _1997_ is the year when their _first child was born_.

7. 1998 is the year when _they recorded a duet_.

B Complete the sentences. (Answers will vary.)

1. _____ is the place where I grew up.

2. I attend _____, where I study _____.

3. _____ is the year when I _____.

More Action!

For further practice identifying adjective clauses with *when* and *where*, have students underline the adjective clause in each sentence in Exercise B. Tell students to circle the word the adjective clause begins with. Ask for volunteers to share their answers.

A **Complete the sentences about your musical preferences.** (Answers will vary.)

1. _____ is my favorite musician.
2. _____ is my favorite type of music.
3. _____ is my favorite musical group.
4. _____ is my favorite American singer.
5. _____ is my favorite radio station.
6. _____ is my favorite place to go dancing.

B **Rewrite your preferences from Exercise A.** Then, discuss your preferences with a partner. (Answers will vary.)

1. _____, who is my favorite musician, is from _____.
   name of musician   name of country

2. _____, which is popular in _____, is my
   type of music   name of country
   favorite type of music.

3. _____, which is my favorite musical group, plays
   name of group
   _____.
   type of music

4. _____, whose music is _____, is my favorite
                                              adjective
   American singer.

5. _____, which is at _____ FM/AM, is my
   letters of radio station   numbers
   favorite radio station.

6. _____, which is located in _____, is my
   name of club   name of city
   favorite place to go dancing.

C **Complete the questions.** Then, ask a partner the questions. (Answers will vary.)

| Do you know a music store where I can buy some country music? | Yes, I do. You should try the CD Den. It's on Broad Street. |

1. Do you know a music store where _____?
2. Do you know a movie theater where _____?
3. Do you know a dance club where _____?
4. Do you know a restaurant where _____?
5. Do you know a supermarket where _____?
6. Do you know an auto repair shop where _____?

Music • **201**

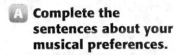

Your Musical Preferences

A **Complete the sentences about your musical preferences.**

- Have students complete the exercise individually.
- Invite volunteers to share their lists with the class, or call on students to ensure that those who don't usually participate in class have a chance to share their answers. If students have a favorite musician or musical group that is not commonly known, ask the student to bring in a picture of the musician or group to share with the class.

B **Rewrite your preferences from Exercise A. Then, discuss your preferences with a partner.**

- Review how to complete the exercise. You may wish to have several different students use their answers from Exercise A to complete the first sentence in different ways.
- Then, have students complete the exercise on their own and discuss their preferences with a partner.

C **Complete the questions. Then, ask a partner the questions.**

- Ask two students to read the text in the speech balloons.
- Have students complete the questions on their own.
- Then, ask pairs to role-play their conversations for the class.

Music • **201**

The Big Picture: The History of Country Music

Discuss.

• Point to the map and help students locate where country music got its start in the United States. Have them name some of the states in that area if they can. (Tennessee, Georgia, and so on.)

• Discuss the answers to the questions. Bring in a map showing where the British Isles are located or ask a volunteer to locate it on a world map.

Listen to the history of country music. Then, circle *True* or *False*.

(CD3 • TR10)

• Play the audio and have students listen only.

• Then, play the audio a second time and have students mark their answers.

• Review the correct answers with the whole class.

Discuss.

1. Look at the picture. Have you ever heard these instruments?

2. What state is labeled on the map? What do you know about this state?

3. What countries make up the British Isles?

B Listen to the history of country music. Then, (circle) *True* or *False*.

CD3 · TR10

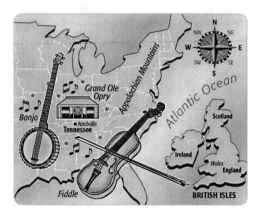

1. Today's country music was originated by immigrants from the British Isles.   (True)   False

2. The people from Appalachia sang all the time.   (True)   False

3. People sang to make their work go more slowly.   True   (False)

4. Country music, which the Appalachians sang, was very complicated.   True   (False)

5. The banjo, which became popular among country musicians, came from South America.   True   (False)

6. The fiddle was the main instrument of country music.   (True)   False

7. The first superstars of country music recorded in 1947.   True   (False)

8. The Carter Family and Jimmy Rodgers, who all sang country music, became the first superstars of country music.   (True)   False

---

More Action!

If possible, play a song from one of the countries of the British Isles, and then play an American country music song. Ask students to note and discuss the similarities.

C **With a partner, ask and answer the questions.**

1. How long ago did the country sound appear in the Appalachian Mountains?
   (Answers will vary.)
2. What countries did the music come from?
   England, Wales, Scotland, and Ireland
3. Why did the immigrants choose the United States?
   Because it was similar to their homes
4. What kind of banjo did country musicians use?
   A five-string banjo
5. When did the fiddle stop being the main instrument in country music?
   In the 1930s
6. Which musician played the melody of the songs?
   The fiddler
7. Besides the banjo and the fiddle, what other instruments are used in country music?
   Electric guitars and keyboards
8. What year did Jimmy Rodgers and the Carter Family first record?
   In 1927

D **Complete the sentences.** Use a relative pronoun from the box.

that	who	which	whom	whose

1. The music, ___which___ is called country music, came from the British Isles.

2. The people ___who / that___ immigrated to this country moved to a land similar to their native land.

3. Today's country music began in the Appalachian Mountains, ___which___ extend from the northeast to the south.

4. The music, ___which___ was very simple, was sung all the time.

5. The immigrants, ___who___ came from the British Isles, brought their music with them.

6. The fiddler, ___whose___ instrument was country music's main instrument until the 1930s, made people dance.

7. The fiddler, ___whom___ the community considered a very important part of the music, was necessary in every band.

8. The banjo ___that___ came from Africa had five strings and was used to play a different kind of music.

9. Jimmy Rodgers and the Carter Family, ___whom___ a Virginia record company first recorded, were the earliest superstars of country music.

C **With a partner, ask and answer the questions.**

• Have students discuss the questions with a partner.
• Review the answers with the class.

D **Complete the sentences. Use a relative pronoun from the box.**

• Review the uses of the relative pronouns in the word box. Answer any questions students may have.
• Have students complete the sentences on their own and then check their answers with a partner. Review the correct answers with the whole class, correcting mistakes as needed.

Reading: Music and New Orleans

Discuss. Then, read.

- Discuss the questions with the class. Have a student find Louisiana on the map of the U.S. on page 289. Make sure students know that it is located in the southern part of the U.S.
- Have a student point out France on the world map on page 290.
- Elicit the answer to Question 2. (New Orleans is famous for its jazz music.)
- Go over the Reading Note. Elicit other words that have a variety of word forms. For example: *society, social / environment, environmental.*
- Have students read the text silently.

Discuss. Then, read.

1. Find New Orleans on the map.
2. What kind of music is New Orleans famous for?
3. Look at the photo. What kind of music do you think they are playing?

READING NOTE
Understanding Word Forms
When you study vocabulary, it is important to learn different word forms so that you can use the words correctly.

Noun	Adjective
culture	cultural
music	musical
popularity	popular

The history of New Orleans is different from many other U.S. cities. The city was founded in 1718 by the French. Then, the city was governed by the Spanish. In 1803, Louisiana territories were again controlled by France, and then France sold the territories to the United States. This transaction was called the Louisiana Purchase.

New Orleans began as a French-speaking **culture** with a love of good food, wine, music, and dancing. Later, Africans, some free and some slaves, came to the city. Many of them came through the Caribbean and brought West Indian culture with them. After that, African Americans and Creoles, who were a mix of French and African cultures, brought another cultural and **musical** mix to the city.

The beginnings of jazz were in the African American communities, but jazz was also influenced by the ethnic variety of New Orleans. Bands led by brass instruments, such as trumpets and trombones, participated in many community events like parades and even funerals. People in the neighborhoods joined the parades and funeral processions and danced along. **Music** was a part of every event.

During the end of the 19th century, some **musicians** began to do something called improvising. As they played, they began to change the music and play what they liked along with the other musicians. This was also a time when the Creoles and black musicians began to combine their styles. Jelly Roll Morton (1890–1941) was one of the musicians that became a well-known composer and piano player. His compositions spread the **popularity** of jazz.

Jazz began to spread to other cities when job opportunities opened in the north. Jazz was especially **popular** in clubs in Chicago and New York City. This also meant that jazz began to change from the original sounds that were in New Orleans.

During the 1920s, Louis Armstrong (1901–1971) developed his style as a solo artist. His recordings with his bands made him an international star.

In 1961, Preservation Hall opened in the French Quarter. It was a place for experienced and new musicians to perform and try to **preserve** traditional jazz, which had to compete with rock and modern jazz.

After Hurricane Katrina hit New Orleans in 2005, many musicians were displaced. Homes were destroyed, and much of the population had to leave the city. Since that time, charitable organizations have donated money, instruments, furniture, homes, and more to aid musicians in rebuilding the musical culture in New Orleans.

B Complete the sentences.

1. _____France_____ was the first country to govern New Orleans.

2. Examples of brass instruments are trumpets and ___trombones___.

3. Music was played at ____funeral____ processions and parades.

4. Creole is a mix of ____French____ and African cultures.

5. ___Improvising___ means that a musician makes original changes to the music while he is playing.

6. Chicago and __New York City__ were popular places for jazz musicians.

7. __Louis Armstrong__ became an international star.

8. At Preservation Hall, the musicians want to ____preserve____ traditional jazz.

9. Musicians have received _(Answers will vary.)_ from charitable organizations since Hurricane Katrina.

C Word Builder (Circle) the correct answers.

1. The (culture) / cultural of New Orleans is different from other U.S. cities.

2. New Orleans has a rich music / (musical) culture.

3. Traditional jazz had to compete with popularity / (popular) rock and modern jazz.

4. One culture / (cultural) tradition in New Orleans is the funeral procession.

5. Jelly Roll Morton helped spread the (popularity) / popular of jazz.

6. The different ethnic groups helped build a different music / (musical) form.

B Complete the sentences.

Have students complete the sentences, referring back to the text as needed to find the correct answers. Point out that answers will vary for Item 9.

C Word Builder Circle the correct answers.

• Have students circle the correct answers.
• Go over the answers as a class, asking students to indicate what part of speech the word is that they circled.

More Action!

Play examples of jazz music from Preservation Hall or Louis Armstrong. Have students listen for the different brass instruments and see if they can differentiate between a trumpet and trombone sound.

Writing Our Stories: My Autobiography

A **Read Armin's time line of his life in the United States.**

- Ask students to read the time line. Point out the abbreviations for the months. Also, point out that a time line of someone's life doesn't necessarily have to start at the beginning of one's life, but instead can start at a specific point, as in this example.
- Ask some simple comprehension questions about the time line. For example:

T: *When did Armin first come to the U.S.?*
S1: *In July of 1993.*
T: *Did he enroll in English class before or after he started selling phone cards?*
S1: *He enrolled in English class before he started selling phone cards.*

B **Read Armin's autobiography.**

Ask students to read the autobiography. Ask: *Is there anything you don't understand about what you read?* Invite students to answer each other's questions if possible.

C **Make a time line.**

- Have students jot down ideas that they may want to include in their time line. Tell them not to worry about writing complete sentences.
- Then, ask students to use these ideas to create their time lines.

A **Read Armin's time line of his life in the United States.**

Time Line

July 1993	——	came to the United States
Aug. 1993	——	began to promote soccer games in local parks
Jan. 1995	——	enrolled in English class
Aug. 1995	——	bought 10,000 phone cards to sell
Sept. 1995	——	started selling phone cards
Oct. 1995	——	quit the promotion business
Nov. 1995	——	became a successful phone-card salesman
July 1996	——	opened a business as a distributor
July 1998	——	entered a partnership with phone-card makers
Now	——	has a very successful business

B **Read Armin's autobiography.**

In July 1993, I immigrated to the United States with my wife and children. I didn't have any business contacts here, but in my country I used to be a promoter. I tried to continue the same business here.

Soccer was popular among the immigrants here, so I began to promote soccer games in the local parks. I arranged for closed-circuit TV broadcasts of the games because people were very interested in soccer games, especially professional games between South American teams.

In 1995, a friend of mine told me about phone cards. I offered to sell them for him even though I didn't know anything about phone cards. I was a good salesman and sold more and more cards because I had confidence in myself. In October, the promotion business, which was not very stable, was finished. Sometimes I had no work for two months, so I decided to quit the promotion business in August. I concentrated on selling phone cards. I bought 10,000 cards, which I sold in a short time. In November 1995, my sales were excellent and business was strong, so I decided to become a phone-card distributor.

In July 1996, I opened an office as a phone-card distributor. Many people wanted to sell phone cards, so business grew quickly. Two years later, I was able to form a partnership with phone-card makers. Today, I have two offices and a very successful distribution business, which sells cards in over 5,000 stores.

C **Make a time line.** Choose six to ten significant events in your life. Write the year and a phrase about the event on a time line.

Teaching Tip

If you feel that students need more input and examples before creating their own time lines, make a brief time line of your own life.

D **In your notebook, write your autobiography.** Use the information in your time line. Try to use a few adjective clauses in your story. Before you turn in your paper, check for run-on sentences.

 E **Sharing Our Stories** **Exchange papers with a partner.** Answer the questions about your partner's paper.

1. When did your partner come to this country?

2. What significant events did your partner describe?

3. What events interested you the most?

F **Find and correct the mistakes.**
1. The singer ~~who his~~ *whose* music I like has written many hit songs.
2. Placido Domingo was a famous tenor ~~whose know~~ *who was known* worldwide.
3. Faith Hill, ~~whom is married~~ *who is married* to another country singer, is one of the most popular female country singers.
4. The Beatles toured all over the United States and they went to New York City, ~~and they were~~ *where they were* very popular.
5. Jeff Bridges performed many of the songs in his movie, ~~who was named~~ *which was named* *Crazy Heart*.
6. Celine Dion spent three years performing in Las ~~Vegas, her performances~~ *Vegas, where her performances* regularly sold out.
7. The person ~~who performing~~ *who is performing* there has always been my favorite singer.

Writing Note
Read the Writing Note and the example sentences. Discuss what constitutes a run-on sentence. Run-on sentences occur when:
a. You use *and* to connect several ideas instead of using commas after each idea.
b. You run two complete sentences together with no punctuation.

D **In your notebook, write your autobiography.**

Have students use the time lines they prepared in Exercise C as an outline for their autobiography. Suggest that they use Armin's life story as a reference as they write their autobiographies.

 E **Sharing Our Stories Exchange papers with a partner.**

Have students exchange their papers with a partner and write down the answers to the questions. If time permits, have students revise their papers based on feedback from their partner and from you.

F **Find and correct the mistakes.**

• Have students complete this exercise on their own.
• Then, write the sentences on the board and have students come up and correct them.

Practicing on Your Own

A **Circle the correct relative pronouns.**

Ask students to complete the exercise on their own and then check their answers with a partner.

B **In your notebook, combine each pair of sentences into one longer sentence with an adjective clause. Use *that, who, whose, which, whom, where,* or *when*.**

• Ask students to read the instructions and look at the example answer.
• Answer any questions students may have. Then, have them complete the exercise individually.
• Review the correct answers with the class.

A **Circle the correct relative pronouns.**

1. Nashville, **who / (which) / where** is located in Tennessee, is known as Music City.

2. For many years, the headquarters of country music has been Nashville, **when / (where) / which** many of the singers live.

3. Two music producers, Owen Bradley and Chet Atkins, created the Nashville Sound, **whom / (which) / where** was a more popular and sophisticated sound.

4. Chet Atkins, **whom / (who) / which** is the most recorded solo artist, built a billion-dollar business and recording center.

5. Hip-hop, **who / that / (which)** originated in New York City, is a combination of music, fashion, and culture.

6. Hip-hop culture became a way of expression for teenagers **where / (that) / whom** were looking for a way out of violence and drugs.

7. Celia Cruz, **whom / which / (who)** was known as the "Queen of Salsa," won three Grammy awards and four Latin Grammys.

B **In your notebook, combine each pair of sentences into one longer sentence with an adjective clause.** Use *that, who, whose, which, whom, where,* or *when*.

1. Johnny Cash was one of the most famous country singers. Johnny Cash almost always wore black. *Johnny Cash, who almost always wore black, was one of the most famous country singers.*

2. John Lennon was successful after leaving the Beatles. His wife, Yoko Ono, sang with him. *John Lennon, whose wife Yoko Ono sang with him, was successful after leaving the Beatles.*

3. Disco music was popularized in the late 1970s. In the late 1970s, the movie *Saturday Night Fever* was a big hit. *Disco music was popularized in the late 1970s, when the movie Saturday Night Fever was a big hit.*

4. Placido Domingo was a famous tenor. Many other artists performed with him. *Placido Domingo was a famous tenor whom many other artists performed with / with whom many other artists performed.*

5. On September 11, 2009, Jay-Z had a concert in New York City. The concert benefited the New York Police and Fire Widows and Children Charity Fund. *On September 11, 2009, Jay-Z had a concert that benefited the New York Police and Fire Widows and Children Charity Fund.*

6. On June 4, 2004, the city of Union City, New Jersey, dedicated a park to the salsa singer Celia Cruz. Many Cuban refugees live in Union City. *On June 4, 2004, the city of Union City, New Jersey, where many Cuban refugees live, dedicated a park to the salsa singer Celia Cruz.*

More Action!

For additional practice with adjective clauses, have students see how many sentences they can write about a famous person or a person they know well. Invite volunteers to read their sentences to the class.

 A Working Together Go online. Work with a partner. Search for a U.S. musical performer. Put the name in quotation marks (" ") and type "bio" in the search area. Find out the following information:

1. What is the performer's original or given name?

2. Where was the performer born?

3. Did this person grow up in a musical family? Describe the family.

4. What kind of music is the performer known for?

5. How did the person get started in a music career?

6. When did the person get a recording contract?

7. What is the name of the performer's first hit song?

8. Find three more interesting facts about the performer.

WORD PARTNERSHIPS	
a hit	song
a popular	

B Read the suggestions for making a presentation.

1. Show a picture of your performer.

2. Go online and find a song or excerpt (piece) of a song that you can play for the class.

3. Before your presentation, check the pronunciation of any new words with your teacher.

4. Practice your presentation. Time yourself.

 C Working Together Prepare a five- to seven-minute presentation about the performer. Present your information to the class.

Student 1: Present the information in 1–4 of Exercise A.

Student 2: Present the information in 5–8 of Exercise A.

Music • **209**

English in Action: Doing Online Research

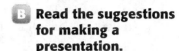

A Working Together

Have students work with a partner to research a performer. Suggest that students look up the questions together or divide the questions up and research them separately.

B Read the suggestions for making a presentation.

Remind students that Items 1 and 2 are suggestions for their presentation. If they can't find a song to play for the class, that is fine. (If students would like to play a song, tell them to make sure it is appropriate for the classroom.) Students can also print out lyrics of a song and read them to the class.

C Working Together

• Encourage students to practice their presentations so they don't stumble over vocabulary and ideas.
• Have pairs present their findings to the class. Bring in a CD player if you know that students are going to be playing music.
• Encourage students in the audience to ask questions about the presentations.

Let's Get Organized

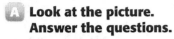

A **Look at the picture. Answer the questions.**

Discuss the picture with the class. Then, ask several different students to answer each question. If students are unfamiliar with the word *infer*, explain that it means to come up with a conclusion based on the facts you already know.

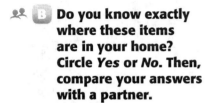

B **Do you know exactly where these items are in your home? Circle *Yes* or *No*. Then, compare your answers with a partner.**

• Have students take the quiz individually.
• Discuss students' answers as a class. Do students consider themselves organized? Why or why not?

Unit 14 Let's Get Organized

A **Look at the picture.** Answer the questions.

1. Does an organized desk indicate an organized person?
2. What can you infer about the person who works at this desk?
3. Is your desk (or room) organized or disorganized?

B **Do you know exactly where these items are in your home?** Circle *Yes* or *No*. Then, compare your answers with a partner. *(Answers will vary.)*

1. postage stamps	Yes	No	7. checkbook	Yes	No
2. scissors	Yes	No	8. car title	Yes	No
3. pencil sharpener	Yes	No	9. address book	Yes	No
4. aspirin	Yes	No	10. Social Security card	Yes	No
5. passport	Yes	No	11. birth certificate	Yes	No
6. rental agreement or deed	Yes	No	12. last test paper	Yes	No

---

More Action!

Create a class chart compiling the results of the answers to Exercise B. Then, analyze the data as a class. Ask students which items they feel are the most and least important to know the whereabouts of. Ask for ideas on where important papers could be kept safely.

| Verb + Infinitive

There are many verbs that require the infinitive form (*to* + base verb). Gradually, you'll learn the list.

I plan *to attend* college in the fall.
He promised *to babysit* for his cousin tonight.

Use an infinitive after the following verbs:

(be) able	forget	manage	remember
afford	hate	need	seem
agree	hope	offer	try
ask	intend	plan	volunteer
choose	know how	prefer	wait
decide	learn (how)	prepare	want
expect	like	promise	wish
fail	love	refuse	would like

A Complete the sentences about yourself. (*Answers will vary.*)

1. I would like to _____ next year.

2. I plan to _____.

3. I need to _____.

4. I want to _____.

5. I have decided to _____.

6. I will try to _____ next year.

7. I know how to _____.

8. I expect to _____.

B Ask your teacher these questions. (*Answers will vary.*)

1. Why did you decide to become a teacher?

2. Do you know how to speak another language?

3. Would you like to learn my first language?

4. Do you want to teach English in another country?

5. Where would you like to travel?

6. In addition to teaching, what else do you like to do?

7. Do you know how to cook any ethnic foods?

8. Would you agree to end class early today?

Let's Get Organized · **211**

Active Grammar: Verb + Infinitive

A Complete the sentences about yourself.

• Review the list of verb + infinitive combinations and the explanation. Provide or elicit sentences using the combinations.

• Have students complete Exercise A on their own. Elicit answers. Be aware that some students may not feel comfortable sharing some of this information about themselves.

B Ask your teacher these questions.

Do this exercise with the whole class. Call on different students to ask you the questions from the list. Answer all questions as truthfully as possible. On the board, write any answers that use new vocabulary items.

Teaching Tip

Provide further practice with the construction of sentences with verb + infinitive. Ask a few students to write one of their sentences from Exercise A on the board. Call on other students to come up to the board and underline the verb + infinitive combination in each sentence.

Distractions and Excuses

  A Listen and read. Then, discuss.

(CD3•TR11)

• Write the word *procrastinator* on the board and discuss what it means. (A procrastinator is someone who always puts off work until later and is therefore behind on or late with assignments.)
• Ask students to read the passage on their own. Answer any vocabulary questions they may have. Then, ask different students to describe various things that they do and don't procrastinate about. For example:

T: *Are you a procrastinator?*
S: *Sometimes. I always do my homework on time, but sometimes I go weeks without cleaning the house.*

  B Listen. Answer the questions about Scott's plans.

(CD3•TR12)

• Play the audio once as students just listen.
• Then, play it a second time as students write the answers to the questions. You may wish to pause the audio periodically to give students a chance to answer the questions and check their answers.
• Remind students to write words and phrases only, not complete sentences.

  A Listen and read. Then, discuss.

CD3•TR11

Are You a Procrastinator?

Everyone has plans and goals. Some plans are short-term and can be accomplished in a few hours or on a weekend: I'm going to wash the car. I plan to organize my closet. I want to gather all my photos from the past five years and put them in a photo album. I need to study for the test next week. I plan to start an exercise program. Some goals are far in the future and will take years to accomplish: I expect to get my nursing degree. I want to start my own business. Do you find yourself making plans but not accomplishing them? Is it difficult to take the first step? Is it impossible to find the time? Could you be a procrastinator? A procrastinator waits for the last minute. A procrastinator believes, "There is always tomorrow."

  B Listen. Answer the questions about Scott's plans.

CD3•TR12

1. When did Scott plan to paint the kitchen?
   Saturday
2. Why didn't he paint the kitchen?
   A game was on TV.
3. When does he plan to paint the kitchen?
   Next weekend
4. Who did he intend to call?
   A classmate
5. Why didn't he make the call?
   He forgot.
6. When is he going to make the call?
   Tonight
7. What did he promise to do with his daughter?
   Help her with a school project
8. Why didn't he help his daughter?
   He had to work overtime.
9. When is he going to help his daughter?
   Tomorrow
10. How much was he supposed to read?
    Four chapters
11. When does he need to finish the assignment?
    Before next Tuesday
12. Why does he need to finish the assignment?
    There's an exam.

212 • Unit 14

C **Listen and read.** Then, discuss.

CD3·TR13

It's hard to get started on your plans. It's easy to make excuses! Once you start on a goal, there are always distractions. You sit down to work at the computer, but first you check your e-mail, and then you start to chat with friends. Or, you are supposed to write a paper for class, but a friend calls and wants to go to the mall with you. Or, you sit down to type your paper, and you realize that it's time for your favorite TV show.

D **Write your top three distractions.** (Answers will vary.)

Example: _____the telephone_____

1. _____ 2. _____ 3. _____

E **Work with a partner.** Write excuses for not doing your homework. Use the verbs in the box. (Answers will vary.)

| had to | forgot to | didn't know how to | needed to | promised to |

1. _I didn't do my homework because I had to . . ._

2. _____

3. _____

4. _____

5. _____

F **Working Together** **Student to Student.** (Answers will vary.)

Student 1: Turn to page 266. Read **Set A** sentences to Student 2.

Student 2: Listen to Student 1 and write the sentences you hear.

Then change roles. Student 2, turn to page 266. Read **Set B** sentences. Student 1, write the sentences you hear.

1. _____

2. _____

3. _____

4. _____

5. _____

Let's Get Organized · 213

C **Listen and read. Then, discuss.**

(CD3 • TR13)

Play the audio. Then, call on one or two students to summarize in their own words what they heard and read.

D **Write your top three distractions.**

• Have students fill in their answers.
• Review the answers with the whole class. Discuss the similarities and differences among the answers.

E **Work with a partner. Write excuses for not doing your homework. Use the verbs in the box.**

• Pair students of mixed language ability. Review the sample answer. Have higher-level students help their partners with vocabulary as needed.
• Ask volunteers to share some of their answers by writing them on the board. If necessary, have other students correct any mistakes.

F **Working Together Student to Student.**

• Read and discuss the instructions.
• Have students check their work on page 266.

More Action!

Have students write three things they would like to accomplish in the next two weeks on a piece of paper. Encourage them to use the verb + infinitive construction. Ask them to sign the paper. Place the slips of paper in an envelope and tell students you will open it and give them back their lists two weeks from today. Suggest that they try to accomplish those three things during the next two weeks.

Active Grammar: Verb + Object + Infinitive

A **Advice for Paul. Restate each comment using an infinitive.**

• Discuss the verb + object + infinitive sample sentences and review the list of verbs.

• Invite students to make up original sentences using each verb. If students are unfamiliar with any of the verbs, elicit sentences using them and write them on the board. Suggest that students copy the sentences into their notebooks for later study.

• Go over the sample answers in Exercise A with the class. Then, call on different students to restate each sentence.

B **Working Together Complete the sentences about Manika and her family. She is starting college, and her parents are about to leave. Use your imagination.**

• Do the first item together. Then, give students five to ten minutes to write their answers with a partner.

• Call on different students to read their sentences aloud. Write any problematic sentences on the board and correct them.

Active Grammar   Verb + Object + Infinitive

Many verbs require an object or an object pronoun.

Use an **object + the infinitive form** after the following verbs:

advise	encourage	hire	remind	urge
allow	expect	invite	require	want
ask	forbid	permit	teach	warn
convince	help	persuade	tell	

My mother **asked _me_ to clean** my room.

The teacher **expected _us_ not to arrive late**.

A **Advice for Paul.** Restate each comment using an infinitive.

> His teacher expected him to turn in his report on time.

1. His teacher said, "Turn in your report on time." (expect)

> His teacher told him not to hand in his report late.

2. His teacher said, "Don't hand in your report late." (tell)

3. His teacher said, "Buy a notebook and organize your papers." (advise)   *His teacher advised him to buy a notebook and organize his papers.*

4. His mother said, "Get up earlier." (urge)   *His mother urged him to get up earlier.*

5. His sister said, "Buy a wall calendar for your bedroom." (tell)   *His sister told him to buy a wall calendar for his bedroom.*

6. His boss said, "Don't be late for work again." (warn)   *His boss warned him not to be late for work again.*

7. His father said, "Don't talk on your cell phone when you study." (remind)   *His father reminded him not to talk on his cell phone when he studied.*

8. His grandmother said, "Let's clean up your room." (help)   *His grandmother helped him to clean up his room.*

B **Working Together Complete the sentences about Manika and her family.** She is starting college, and her parents are about to leave. Use your imagination. *(Answers will vary.)*

1. Manika's family helped her to _____.

2. Manika's father is telling her to _____.

3. Manika's mother advised her to _____.

4. Her mother is reminding her to _____.

5. Her parents allowed her to _____.

6. Manika's sister asked her to _____.

7. Manika's sister doesn't want Manika to _____.

8. Manika's parents expect her to _____.

C
Write your to-do list for today or tomorrow. Number the items in order of importance. Look at a partner's list. Do you think your partner will complete everything?

(Answers will vary.)

D
Work with a partner. Complete the sentences. *(Answers will vary.)*

1. Gloria got a speeding ticket in another state. She doesn't want to pay the fine. She believes that she only needs to pay a ticket for the state she lives in.

    a. Her friend <u>told her not to pay the ticket</u>.

    b. Her brother convinced <u>her to sign the ticket and send in the fine</u>.

2. Your brother lost his credit card.

    a. You advised _____.

    b. The bank expects _____.

3. John has begun to hang around with a group of troublemakers. Two of them have dropped out of school and two have been in trouble with the law.

    a. His parents have forbidden _____.

    b. The baseball coach has invited _____.

4. Ella was accepted to college, but she doesn't have enough money for tuition.

    a. Her parents have persuaded _____.

    b. Her high school counselor advised _____.

C
Write your to-do list for today or tomorrow. Number the items in order of importance. Look at a partner's list. Do you think your partner will complete everything?

• Have students work in pairs or groups. Tell them they can brainstorm their lists in no particular order and then number them after they finish.

• Ask pairs or groups to share their to-do lists with the class. Encourage other students in the class to ask questions about the items on the lists.

D
Work with a partner. Complete the sentences.

• Review the sample answers. Then, give students five to ten minutes to write their answers with a partner.

• Call on different pairs to read each sentence aloud. Write any problematic sentences on the board and correct them.

Active Grammar: *Be* + Adjective + Infinitive

  A **Listen and read.**

(CD3 • TR14)

• Review the meaning of the adjectives in the list. Invite students to make up some original sentences using *be* + adjective + infinitive.
• Play the audio and have students mark their answers.
• Review the answers with the class.

  B **Pronunciation: Stressed Syllables**

(CD3 • TR15)

• Play the audio for the first item and review the answer with the class.
• Play the audio for the rest of the activity and have students mark their answers.
• Review the correct answers with the class.

  C **Work with a partner.**

• Point out the example sentence in the speech bubble.
• Have students use the phrases to make up sentences with their partner. Encourage them to use other adjectives from the chart at the top of the page.
• Call on volunteers to share their sentences with the class.

D **In your notebook, write your sentences from Exercise C.**

• Have students write their sentences in their notebooks.
• Invite a few students to share a favorite sentence or two with the class.

216 • Unit 14

 Active Grammar

Be + Adjective + Infinitive

Use the infinitive form *after* these adjectives:

dangerous	good	important	polite	selfish
difficult	hard	impossible	possible	stressful
easy	healthy	interesting	reasonable	terrible
expensive	helpful	necessary	romantic	wonderful

 A **Listen and read.** Then, discuss. <u>Underline</u> the adjectives. (Circle) the infinitives.

CD3•TR14

It's <u>important</u> (to make) a schedule of your day, and it's <u>necessary</u> (to schedule) your study time. It's <u>easy</u> (to say,) "I'll get it done sometime today." It's more <u>helpful</u> (to make) an appointment with yourself. If <u>possible</u>, find a time that is the most <u>productive</u> for you. What is your most <u>productive</u> time (to do) your schoolwork? Maybe it is immediately after class or as soon as you get home.

 B **Pronunciation: Stressed Syllables** **Listen and mark the stressed syllables.**

CD3•TR15

1. dán · ger · ous
2. i · de · a · lís · tic
3. im · pós · si · ble
4. ín · ter · est · ing
5. po · líte

6. réa · son · a · ble
7. re · a · lís · tic
8. ro · mán · tic
9. stréss · ful
10. thought · ful

  C **Work with a partner.** Make sentences about your daily lives. Then, say the sentences to each other.

It's difficult It's impossible It's stressful	to	work and go to school. find time to exercise. stick to a schedule. get to class on time. keep my school papers in order. get enough sleep. find time for myself.

It's difficult to find time to exercise.

 D **In your notebook, write your sentences from Exercise C.**

216 • Unit 14

Give suggestions for staying organized. Use the adjectives in the box.

| easy | helpful | important | necessary |

1. file your important papers
2. check your appointment calendar daily
3. make a to-do list
4. hang a calendar in your kitchen or bedroom
5. plan your day
6. schedule your study time
7. organize your desk
8. post notes on your desk to help you remember things

> It's helpful to file your important papers.

 Give two more suggestions to a partner for organizing your day.

Working Together **Look at Ali's list of weekend homework assignments.** Ali likes to study in the morning. With a group of classmates, plan his study time. Write the assignments in the chart. Does Ali have enough time to complete all his work?

(Answers will vary.)

Grammar workbook – pages 153–156

Read article about Elvis (two pages)

Go to library and research a musician

Write a composition about a popular musician

Study infinitives for quiz on Monday

Saturday	Sunday
9:00	9:00
10:00	10:00
11:00	11:00

Let's Get Organized • 217

More Action!

For oral practice, use Exercise G as the basis for a group debate. Have groups discuss whether or not Ali has enough time to complete his homework. Divide the class into several debating groups based on the size of the class and the opinions of the groups.

Give suggestions for staying organized. Use the adjectives in the box.

• Read the example in the speech balloon.
• Ask pairs to read their sentences aloud. If any students disagree, discuss the topic as a class.

Give two more suggestions to a partner for organizing your day.

Have students write down their suggestions in their notebook and then share their ideas with a partner.

Working Together Look at Ali's list of weekend homework assignments. Ali likes to study in the morning. With a group of classmates, plan his study time. Write the assignments in the chart. Does Ali have enough time to complete all his work?

• Ask students: *How long do you think each of these assignments will take?* Then, have students work in pairs to complete a study schedule for Ali.
• Discuss the completed schedules as a class.

The Big Picture:
The Procrastinator

A Look at the picture. Then, discuss.

Ask students to answer the questions and comment on the picture. Ask: *What is Diana supposed to be doing? Who do you think these people are? Do you ever end up talking on the phone when you should be studying?*

B Listen to Diana's telephone conversations. In your notebook, take notes about her phone calls. Who called? What did each person want?

(CD3 • TR16)

• Go over the directions. Play the audio once as students just listen. Play it a second time, pausing after Diana speaks with each person.
• Ask individual students to describe the conversation in their own words. Students can use the notes they took. Ask students the questions in the direction line.

C Listen again. Circle *True* or *False*.

(CD3 • TR16)

• Ask students to mark their answers individually.
• Then, play the audio again and ask them to check their answers.
• Review the correct answers with the whole class.

A Look at the picture. Then, discuss.

1. Diana is supposed to be studying. Is her bedroom a good place to study?

2. What do you think her father is going to say?

B Listen to Diana's telephone conversations. In your notebook, take notes about her phone calls. Who called? What did each person want?

CD3·TR16

C Listen again. (Circle) *True* or *False*.

CD3·TR16

		True	False
1.	Susan was able to stop and talk with Diana.	True	**False**
2.	Susan has to study for the math test.	True	**False**
3.	Diana's father expects her to do well in school.	**True**	False
4.	Diana called Jake at his job.	**True**	False
5.	Jake needs to write his lab report.	**True**	False
6.	He plans to see Diana later tonight.	True	**False**
7.	Alex is at school now.	**True**	False
8.	Alex asked her to join his study group.	**True**	False
9.	Katie invited Diana to go to the mall.	**True**	False
10.	Diana decided to stay home and study.	True	**False**

D **Listen again.** Then, complete the sentences. Use the infinitive form.

CD3·TR16

Susan

1. Susan isn't able *to talk on the phone now* .

2. She needs *to write a paper* .

3. She promised *to call tomorrow* .

Dad

4. He expects *Diana to do well* .

5. He reminded *her to clean her room* .

Jake

6. He plans *to finish his homework* .

7. He encouraged *her to go to the math center* .

Alex

8. He asked *her to come and study with him* .

9. He volunteered *to meet her tomorrow before class* .

10. They agreed *to meet in the cafeteria at 9:00* .

Katie

11. She invited *Diana to go to the mall* .

12. Diana decided *to go to the mall* .

 E **Diana failed the math test.** Her mother asked her some questions. With a partner, ask the questions and give Diana's answers. *(Answers may vary.)*

1. Why / agree / go to the mall?

2. When / plan / talk to your teacher?
   When do you plan to talk to your teacher?
3. How many hours / plan / study every night?
   How many hours do you plan to study every night?
4. When / expect / organize your room?
   When do you expect to organize your room?
5. need / quit your job?
   Do you need to quit your job?
6. expect / pass this course?
   Do you expect to pass this course?

> Why did you agree to go to the mall?

 F **Work with a partner.** In your notebook, write a conversation between Diana and her mother. Diana is upset about the test, and her mother is giving her advice.

Let's Get Organized · **219**

D **Listen again. Then, complete the sentences. Use the infinitive form.**

(CD3 • TR16)

• Play the audio one section at a time. Pause after each section so students can complete the statements.
• Review the correct answers with the class. Replay segments of the audio as necessary to clarify any questions students may have.

E **Diana failed the math test. Her mother asked her some questions. With a partner, ask the questions and give Diana's answers.**

• Role-play the text in the speech bubble with a student.
• Then, have students ask and answer the questions with a partner.
• Review the answers with the whole class.

F **Work with a partner. In your notebook, write a conversation between Diana and her mother. Diana is upset about the test, and her mother is giving her advice.**

• Have students write their conversations in pairs. Remind them to use the verb + infinitive form.
• Circulate around the room providing help with vocabulary and the grammar structure as needed.
• Invite volunteer pairs to role-play their conversations for the class.

Reading:
Active Learning

 Circle the techniques you use when you study English. Add one more.

- Ask students to complete the exercise on their own.
- Then, lead a class discussion about which techniques students like and why. Which technique is the most popular?

 Read.

- Read the Reading Note aloud.
- Ask students to read the passage on their own, using the ideas for active reading in the note.
- After they read, have students ask about anything they didn't understand in the text. Ask them if they found the active reading ideas helpful.

 Circle the techniques you use when you study English. Add one more. *(Answers will vary.)*

1. I make lists and charts.
2. I look at the book.
3. I use an English study site on the Internet.
4. I study with a partner.
5. I try to read the newspaper.
6. I listen to a CD.
7. I repeat the sentences in the book aloud.
8. _____

> **READING NOTE**
>
> **Active Reading**
> When you read, try to be active. Take notes in the margins. Use a highlighter to mark new vocabulary. Write questions that you can ask the teacher about the reading.

B **Read.**

It is helpful to become an active student outside of class. These students are all "active learners." How do they approach learning?

. . . .

Because **I'm pressed for time**, I have to plan carefully to find study time. One of the only places I have **downtime** is in my car. After we study a unit, I record ten or fifteen sentences from the book on a CD. I listen to the CD and memorize the sentences as I sit in traffic. I'm sure that other drivers think I'm crazy!

Richard

. . . .

For me, it's important to have a study partner. When I'm taking a new class, I look for a person who is serious about studying. After class, we meet in the library and review the material we studied in class. For example, I ask my partner the questions we practiced in class, and she answers them. Then, we switch roles. When we learned the past participles, we gave each other quizzes. I think this is the best way to study because my grammar has already **improved**.

Marjorie

. . . .

I take work with me wherever I go. I don't have a lot of time, so I study when I can. Reading is my most difficult subject, so I use index cards to make flash cards of new vocabulary. I also use index cards to take notes on the book I'm reading. Then, when I have a break at work, I review the cards. It's a very **convenient** way to study.

Mary Ann

220 · Unit 14

Country music is my ticket to English. Country music is easy to understand because the songs tell a story. I listen to Carrie Underwood and other popular country singers. I often find the **lyrics** online so I can understand the words and sing along. Sometimes I ask an American student to help me **figure out** the words.

Alex

C **Circle** *True* **or** *False.*

1. Richard has sufficient time to study.	True	(False)
2. Richard memorizes songs in his car.	True	(False)
3. Marjorie studies with a classmate.	(True)	False
4. Marjorie likes to work with a serious student.	(True)	False
5. Mary Ann has trouble with reading and vocabulary.	(True)	False
6. Mary Ann thinks index cards are a difficult way to study.	True	(False)
7. Alex thinks country music is challenging to understand.	True	(False)
8. Alex gets help from American students.	(True)	False

D **Word Builder** **Match the boldfaced words with their definitions.**

__d__ **1.** I'm **pressed for time**.   **a.** understand

__e__ **2.** I have **downtime** in my car.   **b.** words

__c__ **3.** My grammar has already **improved**.   **c.** gotten better

__f__ **4.** It's a very **convenient** way to study.   **d.** very busy

__b__ **5.** I sing along with the **lyrics**.   **e.** free time

__a__ **6.** She can help me to **figure out** the words.   **f.** easy

E **Complete the sentences.** Use words from the box.

pressed for time   downtime   lyrics   convenient   improved   figure out

1. I like to read the ____lyrics____ of songs. It helps me to learn vocabulary.

2. It's ____convenient____ to listen to English CDs in my car.

3. I haven't been able to ____figure out____ how to do this math problem.

4. When I'm _pressed for time_, I do at least one homework assignment.

5. During my ____downtime____, I take out my cards and study.

6. My English has ____improved____ since I began studying with a partner.

Let's Get Organized • **221**

C **Circle** *True* **or** *False.*

• Have students complete the exercise on their own. Tell them to refer back to the text to find the answers.
• Review answers with the whole class.

D **Word Builder**
Match the boldfaced words with their definitions.

Have students complete the matching exercise on their own and then check their answers with a partner. Answer any questions they may have.

E **Complete the sentences. Use words from the box.**

• Have students complete the sentences on their own.
• Review the correct answers with the class.

Writing Our Stories: My Study Habits

A Read.

• Invite students to talk about the desk in the picture. Ask: *What do you like about how this desk is organized? How would you set up this desk?*

• Then, have students read the text on their own. Answer any questions they may have.

B Underline the prepositional phrases of location in the paragraphs above. Then, describe the locations in the picture below.

• Review prepositions of location by brainstorming a few examples and writing them on the board. For example: *in front of, behind, next to, under,* and so on.

• Ask students to underline the prepositional phrases in the text on this page. Check the answers with the whole class by having students follow along in their books as you slowly read the passage aloud, one sentence at a time. Have students raise their hands when they hear a prepositional phrase. Call on a student to read the phrase aloud.

• Then, have students look at the picture and complete the exercise by filling in the missing information. Ask them to check their answers with a partner.

A Read.

I think I have good study habits. My study area is a large table in the corner of my bedroom. There's a large desk lamp in the corner. On the left side of my desk is my laptop. The printer is in back of the computer. Above the desk, attached to the wall, is a long, narrow shelf, about six inches wide. It holds envelopes, a pencil sharpener, a small clock, a jar with pens and pencils — everything I need — all in easy reach. To the right of my desk is a small bookcase for my books, notebooks, and papers. I keep a large calendar over my desk for my work schedule and appointments. I'm glad I have such a good place to study!

I like to study in the evening from 7:00 to 9:30. I always do my writing first because it's my least favorite assignment. When I'm finished with my writing, I relax a little and start my reading assignments. I leave my grammar and vocabulary for last because that is the easiest homework for me.

It's difficult to study after 9:30 because I share my bedroom with my older sister. When she gets home from work, she likes to watch TV in the bedroom or talk on the phone with her boyfriend. That's the time that I go online and chat with my friends. Study time is over.

B Underline the prepositional phrases of location in the paragraphs above. Then, describe the locations in the picture below. *(Answers will vary.)*

1. The textbooks are _on the front right corner of the desk_.
2. The cell phone is _on the front left corner of the desk_.
3. There's a cup of coffee _in front of the photo_.
4. _Behind the coffee mug_ is a photo of his girlfriend.
5. The laptop computer is _in the middle / center of the desk_.
6. There is a bottle of water _next to the banana_.
7. The wastebasket _next to the desk_ is overflowing.

Write a composition about your study area and study time.

1. Draw a picture of your study area. It could be your kitchen table, a desk in your bedroom, or the school library.

2. Look at the picture. Does it include everything you use? Where are your books, your pencils, your dictionary, your backpack or bag? What other items are in the picture?

3. Carefully write a description of your study area. Details add interest. Describe the locations.

4. Write about how you organize your study time.

D **Sharing Our Stories** **Exchange papers with a partner.** Answer the questions.

(Answers may vary.)

1. Where does your partner study? _____

2. What subject does your partner like to study first? _____

3. What time does your partner study? _____

E **Find and correct the mistakes.**

1. I like study at the kitchen table. *to*

2. It's difficult find time to study. *to*

3. My mother told ~~he~~ to be home by 12:00. *him*

4. ~~Is~~ impossible to complete all this homework. *It is*

5. She promised to ~~helped~~ me. *help*

6. My father encouraged my sister ~~did~~ her best. *to do*

7. The teacher urged ~~to~~ us to use the computer lab.

8. My grandfather offered to ~~paid~~ my tuition. *pay*

WORD PARTNERSHIPS	
	eat
a place to	relax
	study

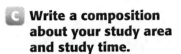 **Write a composition about your study area and study time.**

• Go over the information in the Writing Note. Encourage students to use details in their composition.

• Discuss the assignment with the class and answer any questions. Have students draw their picture and write their composition for homework. Students should be prepared to show and read their descriptions at the next class session.

D **Sharing Our Stories Exchange papers with a partner. Answer the questions.**

• Have students review their partner's paper and answer the questions.

• If time permits, have students share their answers with the class.

E **Find and correct the mistakes.**

• Have students correct the errors and then check their answers with a partner.

• Then, have the first students who finish the exercise write the corrected sentences on the board. Go over the answers with the whole class and check for understanding.

Teaching Tip

Some students may benefit from making a rough outline before they write their composition. Suggest that they think about the order in which they will present facts and how they will divide their composition into paragraphs. Then, they can write their composition using the outline as a guide.

Practicing on Your Own

A Write questions. Give answers about your weekend plans.

• Have students complete the sentences on their own.

• Review the answers with the class, discussing students' answers.

B Rewrite each sentence. Use the verb in parentheses. You will need to change the wording in some of the sentences.

Have students complete the sentences on their own and then check their answers with a partner.

A **Write questions.** Give answers about your weekend plans. (Answers will vary.)

1. How many hours / need to study?

A: How many hours do you need to study this weekend?

B: I need to study for three hours this weekend.

2. Where / plan / go?

A: Where do you plan to go?

B: _____

3. Who / expect / visit?

A: Who do you expect to visit?

B: _____

4. What movie / would like / see?

A: What movie would you like to see?

B: _____

5. What / hope / do?

A: What do you hope to do?

B: _____

B **Rewrite each sentence.** Use the verb in parentheses. You will need to change the wording in some of the sentences.

1. Luis's parents said, "We know you will do well in college." (expect)

Luis's parents expect him to do well in college.

2. Laura's father said, "Take art lessons." (encourage)

Laura's father encouraged her to take art lessons.

3. My brother said, "Become an engineer." (tell)

My brother told me to become an engineer.

4. My high school counselor said, "Apply for a scholarship." (advise)

My high school counselor advised me to apply for a scholarship.

5. My friend said, "Don't turn in your paper late." (warn)

My friend warned me not to turn in my paper late.

A **Working Together** **Work in a group of three or four students.** Complete the chart about your study areas.   (Answers will vary.)

Name	Where do you study?	Is it quiet?	Is it comfortable?	Is it free of distractions?	Is there good lighting?

B **Read.**

> "What is a good place to study?"

1. A good place to study is quiet.

2. A good place to study is comfortable. You should have a comfortable chair. Beds and sofas are not good places to sit while studying.

3. A good place to study has space for your books and computer and a place for you to write.

4. A good place to study is free of distractions. Turn off your cell phone. Do not sit in front of a window. Do not study in front of your computer, where you might want to chat with friends.

5. A good place to study has good lighting. Use a desk lamp or a ceiling light. It is a good idea to study in a room with a window for natural light, but don't study in front of the window.

6. A good place to study has easy access to study materials, such as highlighter markers, pens, pencils, a pencil sharpener, an eraser, and a dictionary.

7. A good place to study is free of unnecessary materials, such as magazines, MP3 players, or bills.

 C **Working Together** **Look at the chart in Exercise A.** How can you improve each person's study area?

More Action!

If time permits, have a member of each group from Exercise A report their answers to the class and discuss the similarities and differences in the responses. Decide as a class the top three ways for improving one's study area.

English in Action: Choosing a Study Area

 A **Working Together Work in a group of three or four students. Complete the chart about your study areas.**

• Go over the categories in the chart and check that students understand the questions. Ask students why these are important questions to ask about study areas.

• Divide the class into groups and have them complete the chart.

• If time permits, have each group compile their group's results and share them with the class. Discuss the data. Find out which part of the chart has the most and fewest answers in common.

B **Read.**

Have students read the text to themselves. Review any unfamiliar vocabulary and check for understanding.

 C **Working Together Look at the chart in Exercise A. How can you improve each person's study area?**

Have students work in the same groups that they were in for Exercise A. Have them complete the exercise, using information in the reading to help them decide on ways to improve each group member's study area.

Becoming a Citizen

Discuss.

Discuss the questions with the class. Make sure students understand what a citizen is. Encourage any students who have completed the process to share their experiences.

Listen to Marco and Luciana's story about becoming United States citizens.

(CD3 • TR17)

• Ask students to look over the pictures and explain what they think is happening in each one. Supply vocabulary as necessary. Correct student statements and refine vague statements in more detail using key vocabulary. For example:

S: *In Picture 4, she's talking with someone.*

T: *Right. She's having an interview.*
An INS worker is interviewing her.

• Play the audio and have students listen.
• Point out the five steps in The Naturalization Process box and ask students to read them to themselves. Explain terms such as *immigration, naturalization,* and *certified mail* as needed.
• Go over the vocabulary in the Word Partnerships box and provide explanations as needed.

Discuss.

1. Are you a United States citizen? Is anyone in your family a citizen?

2. What are the benefits of becoming a citizen?

3. What are the responsibilities of being a citizen?

Listen to Marco and Luciana's story about becoming United States citizens.
CD3 • TR17

1.  **2.** **3.**

4.  **5.**  **6.**

The Naturalization Process
1. Fill out the application.
2. Send the application, three photographs, and copies of requested documents and check(s) to your regional Immigration and Naturalization Service (INS) office. Send your letter via certified mail.
3. Send copies of your fingerprints.
4. Go for your interview and English test.
5. Take the Oath of Allegiance to the United States at your swearing-in ceremony.

WORD PARTNERSHIPS	
file	an application an extension a tax return
fill out	an application a check a form

Teaching Tip

Write the words *Rights* and *Responsibilities* on the board. Then, with students, brainstorm some of the rights and responsibilities that U.S. citizens have. Some rights include: *freedom of religion, freedom of speech,* and *trial by jury.* Some responsibilities include: *obey the laws, vote in elections, pay taxes,* and *jury duty.*

More Action!

Ask students to use the pictures to retell Marco and Luciana's story in their own words.

More Action!

Look up the Oath of Allegiance mentioned in the Naturalization Process box. Distribute copies to the class and read it aloud to students.

Use a *gerund* form (base verb form + *ing*) after the following verbs:

admit	consider	enjoy	miss	regret
anticipate	continue	finish	postpone	resent
appreciate	delay	hate	practice	start
avoid	discuss	imagine	quit	stop
begin	dislike	like	recall	suggest
can't help	doesn't / don't mind	love	recommend	understand
can't stand				

They **missed** *seeing* their family during the holiday season.
She **regretted** not *working* with people who spoke English.

CD3·TR18

A **Listen.** Complete each sentence with the gerund you hear.

1. Marco and Luciana discussed ___becoming___ citizens.

2. They delayed ___starting___ the process because Luciana's English was not strong.

3. Luciana regretted ___not taking___ English classes earlier.

4. She began ___studying___ English at a local adult school.

5. A friend recommended ___enrolling___ in a citizenship class.

6. They didn't mind ___attending___ class one night a week.

7. Marco and Luciana enjoyed ___learning___ about U.S. history.

8. They practiced ___asking___ one another questions.

9. Luciana couldn't help ___being___ nervous before the test.

10. They enjoyed ___celebrating___ with their friends after the ceremony.

B **Say the sentences aloud.** Use the gerund form.

1. People usually discuss (leave) *leaving* their countries for many years before making a final decision.

<speech balloon> People usually discuss *leaving* their countries for many years before making a final decision. </speech balloon>

2. They all anticipate (have) *having* a better life for their children.

3. New immigrants can't help (worry) *worrying* about money and work.

4. Some immigrants begin (study) *studying* English soon after they arrive.

5. Other students postpone (enroll) *enrolling* in English classes.

6. Many new immigrants start (work) *working* in low-paying jobs.

7. Older immigrants recommend (find) *finding* friends and activities in the United States.

Becoming a Citizen · **227**

Active Grammar: Verb + Gerund

 A **Listen. Complete each sentence with the gerund you hear.**
(CD3 • TR18)

• Review the Verb + Gerund chart with the class. Ask different students to make up original sentences using each verb in the chart.

• Discuss the meaning of any verbs that are new to the class and write sample sentences using these verbs in the verb + gerund format on the board.

• Have students listen and complete the sentences with the gerunds they hear.

• Play the audio again and have students finish writing or check their answers.

• Go over the correct answers with the class.

B **Say the sentences aloud. Use the gerund form.**

• Go over the example in the speech balloon with the class.

• Then, have students take turns saying the sentences with the appropriate gerund. Review the correct answers with the class.

More Action!

Extend Exercise B by calling on different students to restate the sentences a second time. This time, students should keep the verb and gerund shown in each sentence but change the sentence so that it makes a true statement about their own lives. For example, for Item 2:
Original: *They all anticipate having a better life for their children.*
Revised: *I anticipate having a good time at the party tonight.*

C **Practice the conversation.** Work with a group of three or four students. Talk about your preparations for coming to the United States. Use the verbs in the box.

A: I began learning English before I came here. How about you?

B: No, I didn't study English. I regret not taking classes before I left.

A: I continued working until a few days before I left.

B: Me, too. I couldn't stop working.

anticipate	discuss	recall	start
begin	finish	regret	stop
continue	quit	remember	

D **What do you like about the United States?** What don't you like? Write two or three items in each column. (Answers will vary.)

like / enjoy	don't mind	dislike / don't like	can't stand

E **Working Together** **Work in a group of three or four students.** Compare your information from Exercise D.

A: I **can't stand** ***wearing*** a heavy winter coat, hat, and gloves.

B: Why?

A: I come from a tropical country. I **don't like** ***wearing*** heavy clothing.

C **Practice the conversation. Work with a group of three or four students. Talk about your preparations for coming to the United States. Use the verbs in the box.**

- Review the meaning of the verbs in the box. Use any verbs that students aren't familiar with in a sentence. Write a sample sentence for each of these new verbs on the board so that students can copy it into their notebooks if they wish.
- Have students work in small groups. Ask one group to role-play the sample dialogue. Then, students should take turns describing their experiences using the verbs in the box.

D **What do you like about the United States? What don't you like? Write two or three items in each column.**

Have pairs of mixed language ability spend a few minutes filling out the chart. Point out or elicit the meaning of *can't stand* (dislike strongly). Have higher-level students help lower-level ones with vocabulary as needed.

E **Working Together Work in a group of three or four students. Compare your information from Exercise D.**

Have students read the sample dialogue and talk about the information they wrote in the chart for Exercise D. If time permits, invite volunteer pairs to present their conversations to the class.

> Use a gerund (base verb + *ing*) after the following prepositions:
>
> after   before   besides   by   in addition to   instead of   while   without
>
> **After *studying*** for the naturalization test, she easily passed the test.

A **Restate the sentences.** Use a gerund.

> Before applying for citizenship, I lived here for ten years.

1. Before I **applied** for citizenship, I lived here for ten years.
2. After I **obtained** the application for naturalization, I had my fingerprints taken.
   After obtaining
3. After I **filled out** the application, I wrote the check.
   After filling out
4. Before I **sent** in the paperwork, I needed to include three photographs.
   Before sending
5. After I **sent** in the papers, I waited a long time.
   After sending
6. While I **waited**, I studied for the naturalization test.
   While waiting
7. Before I **took** the Oath of Allegiance, I had an interview.
   Before taking
8. After I **took** the Oath of Allegiance, I became a citizen.
   After taking

B **Look at Paul's activities from 1998 to 2010.** Complete the sentences.

> 1998 – applied for a visa
> 2001 – received his visa
> 2002 – arrived in the United States
> 2003 – began to study English; worked as a taxi driver
> 2005 – found a job at an auto body repair garage
> 2007 – applied for citizenship
> 2008 – became a citizen
> 2010 – married girlfriend; opened his own garage

1. After ___waiting___ for three years, Paul ___received___ a visa.
2. After ___receiving___ his visa, Paul ___came___ to the United States.
3. Instead of ___studying___ English in Poland, Paul waited until he ___came___ to the United States.
4. While ___working___ as a taxi driver, Paul ___studied___ English.
5. After ___driving___ a taxi for two years, Paul ___found___ a new job.
6. After ___marrying___ his girlfriend, Paul ___opened___ his own garage.

Becoming a Citizen • 229

Active Grammar: Preposition + Gerund

A **Restate the sentences. Use a gerund.**

- Read and discuss the explanation in the grammar box. Have students take turns making up possible sentences. Ask them to use a gerund with a preposition from the chart. For example: *We went straight home after leaving school. I studied a lot before taking the test.*
- Read aloud the instructions and the example sentence.
- Then, call on different students to restate the rest of the sentences. Write just the preposition + gerund forms on the board.

B **Look at Paul's activities from 1998 to 2010. Complete the sentences.**

- Briefly discuss the time line with the class. Ask students to point out the verb in each time line item. Then, have students complete the exercise on their own.
- Call on different students to provide the answers. Ask them to spell the missing words to check for spelling accuracy.

Active Grammar: Verb + Preposition + Gerund / *Be* + Adjective Phrase + Gerund

 A Complete the sentences. Then, read your sentences to a partner.

• Review the contents of the two grammar charts with the class. Point out that the items in the first chart consist of a verb and preposition followed by a gerund. The items in the second chart consist of *be* and an adjective phrase followed by a gerund.

• Have pairs of students complete the sentences.

• Review the exercise with the class by calling on different students to read their sentences. Be sure to call on students who don't usually raise their hand.

Use a gerund (base verb + *ing*) after the following verb and preposition phrases:

adjust to	complain about	give up	succeed in
approve of	count on	insist on	talk about
argue about	depend on	keep on	think about
believe in	dream about	look forward to	warn about
care about	forget about	plan on	worry about

Use a gerund (base verb + *ing*) after the following *be* + adjective and preposition phrases:

be afraid of	be good at	be interested in	be tired of
be capable of	be guilty of	be opposed to	be upset about
be famous for	be in favor of	be proud of	

A Complete the sentences. Then, read your sentences to a partner. *(Answers will vary.)*

Before coming to the United States, …

1. I dreamed about _____

2. I planned on _____

3. I looked forward to _____

4. I worried about _____

5. I was interested in _____

After coming to the United States, …

6. I am proud of _____

7. I have adjusted to _____

8. I often complain about _____

9. I think about _____

10. I'm tired of _____

230 · Unit 15

Teaching Tip

Extend the practice with these two grammar constructions by asking students to make up sentences using the constructions not included in Exercise A. For example:

1. *I don't approve of allowing young children to stay up late.*
2. *I am opposed to allowing young children to stay up late.*

B **Pronunciation: Linking** **Listen to the conversation.** Then, practice the conversation with a partner.

> When a word begins with a vowel, link it with the word before.
> I **plan ‿on** working full time.   He's **good ‿at** fixing things.

A: I thought life here was going to be easy. I just can't ‿adjust to living here. I miss seeing my family.

B: You'll ‿always miss them. I plan ‿on visiting my family once ‿a year.

A: And, I'm afraid ‿of losing my job if ‿I leave.

B: Yesterday you were complaining ‿about working so much ‿overtime!

A: I gave ‿up working ‿at my family's business to come here.

B: You didn't like working there anyway. And you plan ‿on ‿opening your own business some day, don't you?

A: You're right, but I'm tired ‿of listening to English ‿all day! I'm thinking ‿of going back to Korea.

B: You've ‿only been here for nine months. Everybody feels like ‿you at first. Concentrate ‿on learning ‿English and making ‿a few friends.

C **Work with a partner and give your opinion and reasons for your opinion.** Use the phrases in the box.

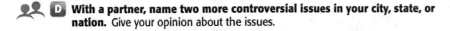

| I agree with | I approve of | | I'm not in favor of |
| I'm in favor of | I disagree with / I don't agree with | I'm against |

1. Limit new immigration
2. Require English only in government offices
3. Issue national identity cards
4. Prohibit the sale of automatic weapons
5. Increase the tax on cigarettes
6. Build fences on the Mexican and Canadian borders
7. Raise the retirement age

D **With a partner, name two more controversial issues in your city, state, or nation.** Give your opinion about the issues.

 B **Pronunciation: Linking**
(CD3 • TR19)

• Read and discuss the explanation in the box. Point out the prepositions beginning with a vowel in the sample sentences.
• Play the audio and ask students to focus only on pronouncing the links between the words that are marked in each sentence. You may wish to say just these parts of each sentence and have students repeat them.
• Have students practice the conversation in pairs. Call on different pairs to say one sentence each for the class, pronouncing the links between the words.

C **Work with a partner and give your opinion and reasons for your opinion.**

• Have pairs pick one or two topics to discuss. Set a time limit for the discussions.
• Then, ask pairs which topics they discussed and their opinions on each topic. If other pairs discussed the same topic, ask them to share their opinions and reasons as well.
• If time permits, discuss the topics as a class.

D **With a partner, name two more controversial issues in your city, state, or nation.**

• Discuss the meaning of *controversial*.
• Have students discuss the issues with a partner or write a composition about their opinions for homework and share it with their partner or the class.

Active Grammar: Contrast— Infinitives and Gerunds

A **Complete the sentences. Use the gerund or the infinitive form of the verb in parentheses.**

• Go over the example sentences in the grammar box. Provide additional examples and check that students understand the difference between infinitives and gerunds. (Point out that both gerunds and infinitives can follow a verb, but only gerunds follow prepositions.)

• Explain that the best way to learn when to use a gerund or an infinitive is to practice using different verbs. Students will learn the correct use of each over time and should not get discouraged.

• Have students complete the exercise on their own and then check their answers with a partner.

• Review the correct answers with the class. Elicit reasons for each correct answer.

B **Ask and answer the questions with a partner or in a small group.**

• Form groups of students with mixed language abilities. Set a time limit for the group discussion.

• Ask a person from each group to give their responses to each question.

Active Grammar
Contrast: Infinitives and Gerunds

> It was **impossible *to find*** a job in my country.
> My friends **didn't encourage** me ***to speak*** English.
> He **enjoyed *working*** at the real estate office.
> **After *working*** for a few years at the factory, I found another job.

A **Complete the sentences.** Use the gerund or the infinitive form of the verb in parentheses.

1. It was impossible (find) ___to find___ a job in my country.
2. I have missed (see) ___seeing___ my family and friends.
3. I intend (visit) ___to visit___ my native country next year.
4. I expect my cousin (arrive) ___to arrive___ soon.
5. Have you ever considered (become) ___becoming___ a citizen?
6. How long do you plan on (stay) ___staying___ in this country?
7. He is capable of (learn) ___learning___ another language.
8. My parents appreciated (receive) ___receiving___ a check from me each month.
9. She's proud of (start) ___starting___ her own business.
10. My sister promised (e-mail) ___to e-mail___ me often.
11. Besides (have) ___having___ difficulty finding a job when I first arrived, I didn't like (live) ___living___ with my uncle.
12. Carlos enjoys (read) ___reading___ books about U.S. history.
13. My uncle refused (change) ___to change___ his long name when he came here.
14. Sometimes I regret (come) ___coming___ to this country.
15. My cousin complains about (wear) ___wearing___ heavy winter clothes.
16. In addition to (sponsor) ___sponsoring___ his sister, Andre is supporting his parents.

B **Ask and answer the questions with a partner or in a small group.**

1. When do you anticipate finishing your English studies?
2. Why did you decide to come to the United States?
3. Have you ever considered becoming a citizen?
4. What have you missed doing since you came here?
5. What do you enjoy doing in this country?
6. What do you advise new immigrants to bring with them?

232 · Unit 15

Listen. An immigrant is talking about citizenship. Write the questions. Then, ask and answer the questions with a partner.

CD3·TR20

1. why / they / decide / come / to the United States?

Why did they decide to come to the United States?

Because of the job opportunities

2. what / be / their families / worried about?

What were their families worried about?

Finding a place to live

3. who / help / them / find an apartment?

Who helped them to find an apartment?

A cousin

4. what / be / Martin / good at?

What is Martin good at?

He's good at fixing things and working with wood.

5. what / he / design?

What did he design?

He designed a kitchen.

6. what / they / can afford / do?

What can they afford to do?

They can afford to pay for their daughter's dance classes and their son's math tutor. They also take a vacation every year.

7. what / they / appreciate / have?

What do they appreciate having?

They appreciate having a nice apartment.

8. what / he / would like / do?

What would he like to do?

He'd like to become a citizen and sponsor his brother.

Becoming a Citizen · **233**

 Listen. An immigrant is talking about citizenship. Write the questions. Then, ask and answer the questions with a partner.

(CD3 ● TR20)

• Read and discuss the instructions. Play the audio once as students just listen.

• Ask students to point out some sentences in the exercise that will be answered with a gerund and some that will be answered with an infinitive.

• Play the audio a second time. Then, have students take turns answering the questions using an infinitive or a gerund. Repeat correct responses and restate incorrect responses using the correct form.

The Big Picture: Running a Campaign

Discuss.

• Ask students to answer the questions and describe what is happening in the pictures. Ask additional questions, for example: *How are these people preparing for the campaign? What issues do you think these people are talking about?*

• Lead students to understand what the people in the pictures are doing in relation to the political campaign. (The people in the third picture in the left column are discussing the signs they will make and the mail they will send out. In the Supermart, the woman is getting people to register to vote. In the last picture in the right column, the candidate is practicing a speech.)

Listen. Then, retell the story about the local political campaign.
(CD3 • TR21)

• Play the audio and have students take notes. Remind them that their task is to retell the story they hear in their own words.

• Play the audio again. Call on different students to retell part of the story on the audio.

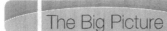
Discuss.

1. Look at the pictures. Who is running for political office?
2. What are the people doing?

Listen. Then, retell the story about the local political campaign.
CD3·TR21

More Action!

If possible, have students research information on a local political campaign. Encourage them to gather newspapers, flyers, and other print materials about the campaign. They can present their findings in the form of a chart, listing the main points made by the candidate or the organizers of the issue, or they can give short presentations about their findings.

🔊 **C** Listen again and (circle) *True* or *False*.

CD3·TR21

1. Manuel is a U.S. citizen.   (True)   False
2. Manuel has always been involved in politics.   True   (False)
3. Manuel votes in every election.   True   (False)
4. Manuel and John are good friends.   (True)   False
5. Manuel's and John's families enjoy spending time together.   (True)   False
6. John owns a bookstore and community computer center.   (True)   False
7. John hires senior citizens for his bookstore.   True   (False)
8. John is running for mayor.   True   (False)

D Complete the sentences.

donate	have	set	spend
give	organize	shake	work

1. John complained about ___shaking___ hands.
2. John is looking forward to ___giving___ interviews.
3. Andrea is good at ___organizing___ people.
4. Their friends have been talking about ___having___ a voter-registration drive.
5. They're thinking about ___setting___ up tables at the supermarkets.
6. They are not worried about ___spending___ too much money.
7. John's friends have insisted on ___donating___ services.
8. Kathy quit ___working___ to help with her husband's campaign.

👥 **E** Ask and answer the questions about the story with a partner.
Use the names in the box. Use different verb tenses.

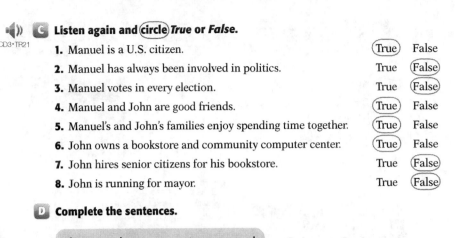

| Manuel |
| Kathy |
| everyone |
| friends |
| the children |
| the families |

Who enjoys spending time together?

The families do.

1. who / enjoy / spend time together
2. who / interested in / work on the campaign
   Who is interested in working on the campaign? / Everyone
3. who / quit / work
   Who quit working? / Kathy
4. who / interested in / make signs
   Who is interested in making signs? / The children
5. who / insist on / donate services
   Who insisted on donating services? / Friends
6. who / like / help John practice for the debate
   Who likes helping John practice for the debate? / Manuel
7. who / enjoy / stuff envelopes
   Who enjoys stuffing envelopes? / The children

Becoming a Citizen · **235**

🔊 **C** Listen again and circle *True* or *False*.
(CD3 • TR21)

• Ask students to read the sentences. Answer any questions they may have.
• Then, play the audio and have students circle their answers. Review the correct answers with the class.

D Complete the sentences.

• Have students complete the sentences on their own.
• Then, review the correct answers with the class. Ask students to spell the gerund forms.
• As needed, review the spelling rules for gerunds. For example, dropping the final -*e* for verbs ending in *e* and doubling the final consonant for words like set: *set* → *setting*.

👥 **E** Ask and answer the questions about the story with a partner. Use the names In the box. Use different verb tenses.

• Review the names of people listed in the box. Then, have pairs of students take turns asking and answering questions based on the cues given. Move around the room helping out as needed.
• Review the correct answers with the class.

Reading:
The Naturalization Test

A Discuss.

• Point to the picture and invite students to comment. Ask: *Who do you think these people are? What are they doing?* (They are being sworn in as citizens.) Introduce the term *to swear in*.

• Discuss the two questions. Invite students who have already taken the test to talk about their experiences.

• Review the information in the Culture Note. Point out that *INS* stands for *Immigration and Naturalization Service* and it is a branch of the U.S. government.

• Review the Reading Note. Encourage students to use the strategies mentioned when they answer the sample questions in Exercise B. Answer any questions students may have.

B Read the Naturalization Test sample questions. Fill in the circle next to the correct answer.

• Go over the first question and talk about the sample answer. Tell students it is important that they practice completely filling in the circle next to the correct answer since on the real test, the results are tabulated by a computer that only records answers for circles that are completely filled in.

• Then, have students take the test individually.

A Discuss.

1. Do you know anyone who has taken the Naturalization Test?

2. What is the best way to prepare for the test?

> **CULTURE NOTE**
>
> **The Naturalization Test** is required for anyone who wants to become a U.S. citizen. An INS examiner asks a citizenship applicant a group of questions from a list of 100 questions. The questions are about U.S. history and government.

> **READING NOTE**
>
> **Multiple-Choice Test Strategies**
> Before taking a multiple-choice test, remember to:
> 1. Read the directions first. Ask the teacher or test examiner questions if you do not understand something.
> 2. Read the question carefully.
> 3. Read all of the answers. Try to eliminate wrong answers.
> 4. Select your answer. Fill in the circle next to your answer.
> 5. Watch the time. If you have limited time, make sure you know how much time is left. You may have to work more quickly.

B Read the Naturalization Test sample questions. Fill in the circle next to the correct answer.

1. What do the stars on the flag mean?
   - ○ **a.** There is one star for each one hundred citizens.
   - ○ **b.** There is one star for each citizen.
   - ● **c.** There is one star for each state of the union.
   - ○ **d.** There is one star for each president.

2. How many states are there in the United States?
   - ○ **a.** 48
   - ○ **b.** 49
   - ○ **c.** 50
   - ○ **d.** 51

3. When is Independence Day?
   - ○ **a.** January 1st
   - ○ **b.** July 4th
   - ○ **c.** September 1st
   - ○ **d.** November 25th

4. What do the thirteen stripes on the flag represent?
   - ○ **a.** The first thirteen presidents
   - ○ **b.** The original thirteen colonies
   - ○ **c.** The first thirteen days of the country
   - ○ **d.** Thirteen laws

5. From which country did the United States fight to win independence?

  ○ **a.** Ireland   ○ **c.** France

  ○ **b.** Germany   ○ **d.** Great Britain

6. Who was the first president of the United States?

  ○ **a.** Abraham Lincoln   ○ **c.** George Washington

  ○ **b.** John Adams   ○ **d.** Benjamin Franklin

7. Who becomes the president of the United States if the president dies?

  ○ **a.** the Secretary of State   ○ **c.** the First Lady

  ○ **b.** the Secretary of Defense   ○ **d.** the Vice President

8. Who makes the laws in the United States?

  ○ **a.** judges   ○ **c.** the president

  ○ **b.** congress   ○ **d.** the governors

9. Who was president during the Civil War?

  ○ **a.** Abraham Lincoln   ○ **c.** Richard Nixon

  ○ **b.** George Washington   ○ **d.** Franklin D. Roosevelt

10. What is the 50th state of the union?

  ○ **a.** Alaska   ○ **c.** Puerto Rico

  ○ **b.** Hawaii   ○ **d.** Florida

11. Who was the president during the Great Depression and World War II?

  ○ **a.** Franklin D. Roosevelt   ○ **c.** John F. Kennedy

  ○ **b.** Thomas Jefferson   ○ **d.** Dwight Eisenhower

12. In what month do we vote for the president?

  ○ **a.** January   ○ **c.** July

  ○ **b.** April   ○ **d.** November

13. Which state borders Canada?

  ○ **a.** Montana   ○ **c.** Tennessee

  ○ **b.** Arizona   ○ **d.** North Carolina

14. What movement tried to end racial discrimination?

  ○ **a.** the Boston Tea Party

  ○ **b.** the Vietnam War protests

  ○ **c.** the Civil Rights Movement

  ○ **d.** the Women's Suffrage Movement

Check your answers below.

1. c   2. c   3. b   4. b   5. d   6. c   7. d   8. b   9. a   10. b   11. a
12. d   13. a   14. c

Check your answers below.

• Have students use the answer key to correct their tests.

• After they have finished, answer any questions they may have about words or ideas they didn't understand or questions they got wrong.

Writing Our Stories:
A Political Platform

 Read the two political platforms. Which person would you vote for? Why?

• Ask students to read the two platforms silently, underlining any words or sentences they don't understand. Discuss each platform with the class, answering questions about the meaning of words and phrases as needed. If time permits, call on one male and one female student and have each student read the political platforms aloud to the class.

• Call on individuals to tell who they would vote for and why. Ask a second student to summarize each person's opinion and then give their own opinion. For example:

S1: *I like Ms. Velez because she's in favor of improving education.*

S2: *Ali would vote for Ms. Velez because she wants to improve the schools in the community. I agree with Ali's choice.*

B **Imagine you're a candidate for the town council.**

• Read and discuss the instructions. Point out the phrases in the box that students should include in their writing.

• Suggest that students make a rough outline of what they are going to argue before they begin writing.

A **Read the two political platforms.** Which person would you vote for? Why?

I believe in improving our community by attracting development to our town. I'm in favor of lowering taxes in order to attract much-needed new businesses, including the new paint factory, to our town. Our town must begin building the factory right away. We need new jobs for our citizens. I'm opposed to building a new library. We already have a library. The new library can wait, but jobs can't. In addition to creating jobs, I'm in favor of increasing parking meter fees to fifty cents per half hour. I manage a successful business, and the downtown areas need income to improve parking and the sidewalks. I have fifteen years of experience on the town council. You can count on me to serve you.

Douglas McMurphy

It's time for a change. The citizens of this town are used to hearing the same promises. They're tired of seeing heavy traffic and breathing factory pollution. They miss having peace and quiet in their community. We don't need more development. Instead of building a paint factory, we should start building a new library. As a former high school teacher and member of the Board of Education, I'm proud of the improvements we've made in educating our children. More students are applying to college than ever before. Imagine having a place where adults and children can enjoy reading, using free computer facilities, and listening to authors read from their books. A vote for me is a vote for education in a livable community.

Angela Luisa Velez

B **Imagine you're a candidate for the town council.** In your notebook, write your opinion of (1) the new factory, (2) the new library, and (3) the increase of parking meter fees to fifty cents per half hour. Choose one other issue to discuss. Use the phrases in the box.

> be opposed to   be in favor of   believe in

More Action!

Before you discuss the platforms in Exercise A, make two columns on the board. Write the names of the candidates at the top of the columns. Using phrases from the two texts, help students compare the platforms of the two candidates.

C (Circle) *Fragment* **or** *Correct.*

1. After the airplane landed.   (Fragment)   Correct

2. He regrets not studying English before.   Fragment   (Correct)

3. When I considered leaving my country.   (Fragment)   Correct

4. Because I needed to learn English.   (Fragment)   Correct

5. I dislike taking the bus instead of driving myself.   Fragment   (Correct)

6. Is easy to learn English.   (Fragment)   Correct

D Before you turn in your paper, check for sentence fragments.

 E **Sharing Our Stories** Exchange your papers from Exercise B with a partner. (Circle) the answers.

1. My partner is **opposed to / in favor of** the new factory.

2. My partner is **opposed to / in favor of** the new library.

3. My partner is **opposed to / in favor of** the parking increases.

F Find and correct the mistakes.

1. The mayor isn't interested in ~~run~~ running for another term.

2. The students have finished ~~to read~~ reading two novels.

3. ~~Because~~ I haven't registered to vote yet. (Answers will vary.)

4. I'm tired of ~~walk~~ walking in the snow.

5. I've missed ~~see~~ seeing my family.

6. The council is opposed to building a new parking garage.

7. When I arrived in this country. (Answers will vary.)

8. My daughter can't stand ~~wears~~ wearing heavy winter clothes.

Becoming a Citizen • **239**

C **Circle** *Fragment* or *Correct.*

• Review the Writing Note. Explain that we often use sentence fragments in speaking, but they must not be used in writing.

• Have students circle their answers. Then, review the correct answers with the class.

D **Before you turn in your paper, check for sentence fragments.**

Remind students to check the paragraphs they wrote in Exercise B on page 238 for sentence fragments. Have them refer to the sample sentences in the Writing Note if they are unsure whether or not their sentences are complete sentences or fragments.

E **Sharing Our Stories Exchange your papers from Exercise B with a partner. Circle the answers.**

Have students exchange their papers or notebooks with a partner. Their partner should be able to find the answers to the three items in their partners' papers. If they cannot, they should ask their partners to add that missing information.

F **Find and correct the mistakes.**

Write the sentences on the board and ask students to come up and correct them. If students make a mistake, ask the class to fix the error.

Practicing on Your Own

 Complete each sentence. Use the gerund form of the verb.

Ask students to complete the sentences on their own and then check their answers with a partner.

B **Complete the sentences with the gerund or infinitive form.**

Have students fill in the correct infinitive or gerund form. You can suggest that they review the example sentences on page 232 before completing this exercise.

Practicing on Your Own

A **Complete each sentence.** Use the gerund form of the verb.

1. Before (register) _registering_ for classes, she has to complete an application.

2. She can't stand (wait) _waiting_ in long lines to register.

3. She has postponed (look) _looking_ for a job until she knows her class schedule.

4. She is going to buy her textbooks after (attend) _attending_ her first class.

5. After she begins (study) _studying_, she will have more confidence.

6. She liked (go) _going_ to class and (meet) _meeting_ new people.

7. She has missed (see) _seeing_ her family, so she started (send) _sending_ them e-mails every other day.

8. In class, she practices (speak) _speaking_, (read) _reading_, and (write) _writing_.

9. She believes in (work) _working_ as hard as possible to achieve her goals.

10. After (study) _studying_ for a year, she will be ready to enroll in an accounting degree program.

B **Complete the sentences with the gerund or infinitive form.**

1. After (arrive) _arriving_ in this country, Pierre lived with his brother.

2. He didn't mind (take) _taking_ care of his nieces and nephews.

3. He didn't know how (speak) _to speak_ much English, but he could read.

4. His brother persuaded him (enroll) _to enroll_ in English classes.

5. Instead of (work) _working_ full time, he decided (take) _to take_ a part-time job at his brother's company.

6. He has enjoyed (study) _studying_ and he is a good student.

7. He has been trying (speak) _to speak_ as much English as possible.

8. He hopes (finish) _to finish_ his English classes in a year.

240 · Unit 15

More Action!

Students may enjoy making up original exercises similar to the ones on this page. If possible, have students prepare their exercises on the computer, print them out, and then give them to you to check. Make any necessary corrections and make class copies. Have students complete a few of the exercises in class or as homework. Go over the answers together.

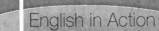
CULTURE NOTE

To become a U.S. citizen, you must show that you understand basic English. During your Naturalization Test:

1. You must read one or more sentences and show that you understand the meaning.
2. You must write one of three sentences, and the testing officer must be able to understand your writing.
3. You must answer questions about your application.
4. You must answer six out of ten questions about the U.S. government correctly. The testing officer will ask the questions.

 A **Listen and write the questions.** Then, match each question with the correct answer.

CD3·TR22

_f_	**1.**	What is the Bill of Rights ?	**a.** The president
_g_	**2.**	What is one of the rights of the Constitution ?	**b.** George Washington
_e_	**3.**	What is the voting age ?	**c.** Congress
_h_	**4.**	How many senators are there ?	**d.** Four years
_b_	**5.**	Who was the first president ?	**e.** Eighteen years of age
_c_	**6.**	Who makes the laws ?	**f.** The first ten amendments of the Constitution
_a_	**7.**	Who is the Commander in Chief of the military ?	**g.** Freedom of speech
_d_	**8.**	How long is a president's term of office ?	**h.** 100

 B **Working Together** **Work with a small group of students.** Answer the questions.

(Answers will vary.)

1. Who is the president of the United States? _____
2. Who is the vice president of the United States? _____
3. Who is your state's governor? _____
4. What is the capital of your state? _____
5. Who is one of your state senators? _____

C **Go online.** Find information on the naturalization process. Try to find a practice test. Enter "naturalization test" or "how to become a citizen" in the search box. Do the practice activities.

Becoming a Citizen · **241**

English in Action: The Naturalization Test

 A **Listen and write the questions.**

(CD3 • TR22)

• Go over the information in the **Culture Note**. You can find examples of information on the test at the U.S. Citizenship and Immigration Services website: www.uscis.gov.
• Play the audio once and have students write as many of the questions as they can.
• Play the audio again and have students finish writing the questions. Then, have them complete the activity.
• Go over the answers as a class. Answer any questions.

B **Working Together**

• Have students answer the questions with a group.
• Check the answers with the class.

C **Go online.**

Review the **Culture Note** at the top of the page. Students can find information about and examples of the Naturalization Test at the U.S. Citizenship and Immigration Services website: www.uscis.gov. If possible, go online and print out practice tests or activities and have students complete them in class. Go over the correct answers and answer any questions.

Teaching Tip

For further writing and listening practice, have students take turns reading the questions on this page to each other. Their partner should write the sentences as dictated by his or her partner. After students have written the sentences their partner has dictated, they should answer the questions. Have students switch roles so each student gets a chance to both speak and write. Have them focus on their spelling and handwriting.

Unit 1

Simple Present Tense

STATEMENTS

Subject	Verb	
I	**study**	
You	**do not study**	
They	**don't study**	English.
He	**studies**	
She	**does not study**	
	doesn't study	

> **Note:**
> Use the present tense to describe everyday activities, habits, and repeated actions.

YES / NO QUESTIONS

Do/Does	Subject	Verb
Do	I	
	you	**work**?
	they	**study** in the library?
Does	she	**walk** to school?
	he	

SHORT ANSWERS

Yes, you **do**.	No, you **don't**.
Yes, I **do**.	No, I **don't**.
Yes, they **do**.	No, they **don't**.
Yes, she **does**.	No, she **doesn't**.
Yes, he **does**.	No, he **doesn't**.

> **Note:**
> Use the auxiliaries *do* and *does* to form present tense questions. Do not change the main verb.

WH- QUESTIONS

Question Word	Do/Does	Subject	Verb
What		I	
Where	**do**	you	
Why		they	**study**?
How	**does**	she	
How often		he	

WHO QUESTIONS

Who	Verb with -s	
	studies	English?
Who	**goes**	to work?
	lives	close to school?

> **Notes:**
> 1. *Who* asks about the subject.
>
> 2. *Who* takes a singular verb. The answer may be singular or plural.
>   **Who** *studies English?*   Joe **does**.
>   **Who** *goes to work?*   Joe and Sara **do**.

Present Continuous Tense

STATEMENTS

Subject	Be	(not)	Verb + -ing
I	**am**		
He She	**is**	(not)	us**ing** a computer. study**ing** for a test. sitt**ing** at a desk.
We You They	**are**		

Notes:
1. Use the present continuous to talk about an action that is happening now.
 I **am using** a computer.
2. Use the present continuous to talk about an action that is temporary.
 He **is not studying** right now.

YES / NO QUESTIONS

Be	Subject	Verb + -ing
Am	I	
Is	he she	speak**ing** English?
Are	we you	

SHORT ANSWERS

Affirmative	Negative
Yes, you **are**.	No, you **aren't**.
Yes, he **is**.	No, he **isn't**.
Yes, she **is**.	No, she **isn't**.
Yes, we **are**.	No, we **aren't**.
Yes, I **am**.	No, I'm **not**.

WHO QUESTIONS

Who	is	speak**ing** English?

ANSWERS

You **are**.
Joe **is**.
Marta **is**.
Marta and I **are**.
Marta and Joe **are**.
I **am**.

WH- QUESTIONS

Wh- Word	Be	Subject	Verb + -ing
What Where Why	am	I	study**ing**? read**ing**? writ**ing**?
	is	he she	
	are	they	

Non-action Verbs

appear	have	miss	smell
believe	hear	need	sound
belong	know	own	taste
feel	like	prefer	understand
hate	look	see	want

Notes:
1. Some verbs in English do not usually take the present continuous tense. They are called non-action verbs. These verbs often show feelings, senses, beliefs, and possession.
 He **knows** my name.
 I **miss** my grandparents.
2. Some verbs can show both action and non-action.
 I **have** a computer.   They are **having** a party.
 I **think** he is a good   She is **having** a baby.
 teacher.   I'm **thinking** about my vacation.

Unit 2

Simple Past Tense

STATEMENTS

I You He They	**moved** **didn't move**	to the United States.

YES / NO QUESTIONS

Did	Subject	Verb
Did	you they he she	**have** any pets? **live** in the country? **play** sports?

WH- QUESTIONS

Wh- Word	Did	Subject	Verb
Where	did	you	**go** to school?
What	did	they	**study** at school?
When	did	she	**come** here?
Why	did	he	**leave** his country?
How	did	it	**happen**?

SHORT ANSWERS

Yes, I **did**.	No, I **didn't**.
Yes, they **did**.	No, they **didn't**.
Yes, he **did**.	No, he **didn't**.
Yes, she **did**.	No, she **didn't**.

Past Tense of Be

STATEMENTS

I He She It	**was** **was not** **wasn't**	fast.
You We They	**were** **were not** **weren't**	young.

Note:
Use the past tense to describe past actions or events.
*I **was** young.*
*It **wasn't** difficult.*
*They **were** young.*

PAST STATEMENTS WITH THERE + BE

There	**was**	a garden.
	was not **wasn't**	a refrigerator.
	were	few schools.
	were not **weren't**	large schools.

YES / NO QUESTIONS

Be	Subject	Place / Adjective
Was	he it	in the city?
Were	you they	busy?

SHORT ANSWERS

Yes, he **was**.	No, he **wasn't**.
Yes, it **was**.	No, it **wasn't**.
Yes, I **was**.	No, I **wasn't**.
Yes, they **were**.	No, they **weren't**.

Used to

Subject	Used to	Verb
I You She They	**used to**	**live** in Peru. **use** candles for light. **grow** all of our vegetables.

Notes:
Use *used to* to talk about a habit or a routine that you did in the past, but that you don't do now.

*I **used to live** in New York.*
Now I live in Sacramento.

· Grammar Summary

Simple Past Tense Questions with *Who* as Object

WHO QUESTIONS			
Who	Did	Subject	Verb
Who	**did**	you	**come** here with?
		she	**call**?
		they	**visit**?

ANSWERS

I came here **with my family**.

She called **her sister**.

They visited **their cousins**.

Note:
In these questions,
Who is the object.

Simple Past Tense Questions with *Who* as Subject

WHO QUESTIONS	
Who	Past verb
Who	**came** here alone?
	brought a pet here?
	left family behind?

ANSWERS

Julia did.

Beata did.

Li did.

Note:
In these questions, *Who* is the subject.

Unit 3

Future with *Be Going To*

STATEMENTS			
Subject	*Be*	*Going to*	Verb
I	**am (not)** **'m not**		
You	**are (not)** **'re not**		**move.**
He She	**is (not)** **isn't**	**going to**	**change** jobs. **get** married.
They	**are (not)** **'re not**		

Notes:

1. Use *be going to* to talk about future plans.

2. Use *be going to* when you already know something will be true.
   It ***is going to rain***.
   Meaning: I heard the weather report.
   We ***are going to have*** *a test*.
   Meaning: The teacher announced the test.

3. *Going to* is often pronounced *gonna* in speaking. Do not write *gonna*. Use the long form.
   It ***is going to be*** *a difficult test*.

YES / NO QUESTIONS			
Be	Subject	*Going to*	Verb
Am	I		
Are	you		**move?**
Is	he she	**going to**	**change** jobs? **go** to college?
Are	they		

SHORT ANSWERS	
Yes, you **are**.	No, you **aren't**.
Yes, I **am**.	No, I **'m not**.
Yes, he **is**.	No, he **isn't**.
Yes, she **is**.	No, she **isn't**.
Yes, they **are**.	No, they **aren't**.

WH- QUESTIONS

Wh- Word	Be	Subject	Going to	Verb
What	**am**	I		**do** tomorrow?
Where	**are**	you		**study** next year?
How	**are**	they	going to	**get** there?
Who	**is**	he		**visit**?
Who	**is**	—		**help** you?
When	**is**	it		**happen**?

ANSWERS

You**'re going to work**.

I**'m going to study** in California.

They**'re going to drive**.

He**'s going to visit** his cousins.

My teacher **is going to help** me.

It**'s going to happen** tomorrow.

Present Continuous with Future Meaning

If a specific time in the future is stated or clear, the present continuous can express future time.

I'm working tomorrow.   *He is leaving* at 4:00.

Future with *Will* for Promises and Offers

STATEMENTS

Subject	Will	Verb
I You He She They	**will** **'ll** **will not** **won't**	do it.

Notes:

1. Use *will* to make a promise or an offer to help.

2. It is common to use the contraction *'ll.*
   I'll help you.

3. The negative contraction of *will not* is *won't.*
   I won't forget.

Future with *Will* for Predictions

Use *will* to make a prediction about the future.

*The United States **will make** new immigration laws.*

*There **will be** more electric cars.*

Future Time Clauses: Statements

<u>If I **study** hard</u>, I**'ll graduate** in two years.
  (time clause)   **(main clause)**

<u>When I **have** time</u>, I**'m going to finish** my degree.
  (time clause)   **(main clause)**

I**'ll graduate** in two years <u>if I **study** hard.</u>
  (main clause)   (time clause)

I**'m going to finish** my degree <u>when I **have** time.</u>
  (main clause)   (time clause)

Notes:

1. *After, before,* and *when* also introduce time clauses.

2. Use a comma when the time clause is at the beginning of a sentence.

3. Do *not* use a comma when the time clause is at the end of a sentence.

4. Use the simple present tense in the time clause. Use the future tense in the main clause.

Modals: *Must / Must not*

STATEMENTS		
Subject	*Must*	Verb
I	**must**	**stop** at a red light.
You		**drive** at the speed limit.
He	**must not**	**drive** without a license.
Drivers		

Notes:
1. *Must* shows rules, obligation, or necessity.
   You **must stop** at a stop sign.

2. *Must not* shows that an action is not permitted.
   Drivers **must not drive** through a red light.

3. *Must* in the question form is very formal and is rarely used.
   Must I pay my ticket?

Modals: *Have to*

AFFIRMATIVE STATEMENTS		
Subject	*Have to*	Verb
I	**have to**	**stop** at a red light.
You		**drive** with a license.
He	**has to**	**wear** a seat belt.
She		
They	**have to**	

Notes:
1. *Have to* shows necessity or obligation.
   I **have to get** car insurance.
   She **has to babysit** her niece.

2. *Have to* can substitute for *must*.
   You **must stop** at a red light.
   You **have to stop** at a red light.

NEGATIVE STATEMENTS		
Subject	*Don't / Doesn't have to*	Verb
I	**do not have to**	**buy** a new car.
You	**don't have to**	**work** today.
She	**does not have to**	**go** to school today.
	doesn't have to	
They	**do not have to**	
	don't have to	

Notes:
1. *Doesn't have to / Don't have to* show that something is not necessary.
   You **don't have to own** a car.

2. Do not confuse *don't have to* with *must not*.
   I **must not buy** a new car.
   (Incorrect: It is not against the law.)
   I **don't have to buy** a new car.
   (Correct: It is not necessary.)

YES / NO QUESTIONS WITH *HAVE TO*			
Do / Does	Subject	*Have to*	Verb
Do	I	**have to**	**do** laundry?
	you		
Does	he		**buy** stamps?
	she		**see** the dentist?
Do	they		

Modals: *Can / Can't*

AFFIRMATIVE STATEMENTS		
Subject	*Can*	Verb
I You She He They	**can** **can't**	**drive**. **park** in this area.

YES / NO QUESTIONS		
Can	Subject	Verb
Can	I you she they	**drive** a truck? **swim**? **speak** French?

Notes:
1. *Can* shows ability. *Can't* shows inability.
   I **can** drive a car.
   I **can't** drive a truck.
2. *Can* also shows that an action is permitted. *Can't/Cannot* shows that an action is *not* permitted.
   I **can drive** at night by myself.
   You **can't drive** through red lights.

Modals: *Could – Past Form*

STATEMENTS		
Subject	*Could*	Verb
I You He They	**could** **couldn't**	**speak** English. **find** a job. **register** for classes.

YES / NO QUESTIONS		
Could	Subject	Verb
Could	I he she	**speak** English? **find** a job? **register** for classes?

Note:
Could shows past ability.
I **could** drive when I came to this country.
My uncle **could** find an apartment for us easily.
I **couldn't** speak English when I came here.

Modals: *Should / Should not*

STATEMENTS		
Subject	*Should*	Verb
I You She He They	**should** **should not** **shouldn't**	**drive** carefully. **buy** a new car. **drive** at night. **park** there.

Note:
Should expresses an opinion or advice.
I **should buy** a smaller car. Small cars get good gas mileage.
Should not / Shouldn't show that something is *not* a good idea.
You **shouldn't park** there. There is not enough space.

Modals: *Had better / Had better not*

STATEMENTS		
Subject	*Had better*	Verb
I You She He They	**had better** **'d better** **had better not** **'d better not**	**wear** a seat belt. **use** a car seat. **drive** without a license. **forget** to fill the gas tank.

Note:
Had better expresses a strong warning.
Had better is stronger than **should**.
   You'd better check your tire.
   (Or you'll get a flat tire.)
   I'd **better not miss** another class.
   (Or I'll fail the class.)

Unit 5

Note: Refer to Units 1 to 4 for questions with present tense, present continuous tense, past tense, and future questions with *be going to* + verb.

CAN; FUTURE WITH *WILL*		
Can **Will**	I you they she he	**play** soccer?

QUESTIONS WITH *WHO* AND *WHOSE*	
Whose umbrella is that?	It's mine.
Who likes sports?	I do.
Who do you play cards with?	With my cousins.

Notes:
1. *Whose* asks questions about possession.
2. *Who* asks questions about the subject or object.

Who Questions

PRESENT			
Subject	**Who** goes	to the gym every day?	Beth <u>does</u>.
Object	**Who** does Beth go	to the gym with?	She goes <u>with her sister</u>.

PAST			
Subject	**Who** went	to the gym?	<u>Jim</u> did.
Object	**Who** did Jim go	to the gym with?	He went <u>with his wife</u>.

Questions with *How*

How do you get to work?	By bus.
How far do you live from school?	About three miles.
How long did you wait?	Thirty minutes.
How much money do you have?	$4.39
How many tickets do you have?	Just two.
How often do you come to school?	Three days a week.

Tag Questions

Present with *be*	You **are** from Thailand,	**aren't** you?
	It **isn't** cold today,	**is** it?
Present continuous	They **are having** a nice time,	**aren't** they?
	They **aren't having** a bad time,	**are** they?
Simple present	He **plays** soccer every day,	**doesn't** he?
	He **doesn't play** tennis,	**does** he?
Past *be*	They **were** at the park,	**weren't** they?
	They **weren't** at home,	**were** they?
Past	You **took** some pictures,	**didn't** you?
	You **didn't take** these pictures,	**did** you?
Future with *will*	She **will plant** more roses,	**won't** she?
	She **won't plant** any vegetables,	**will** she?

Unit 6

Modals: *May* and *Might* for Possibility

STATEMENTS		
Subject	*May / Might*	Verb
I	**may**	
You	**may not**	**go** on vacation.
They	**might**	**need** a visa.
He	**might not**	

Note:
Use *may or might* to express possibility.
I **might go** on vacation. = Maybe I will go on vacation.
He **may not need** a visa. = Maybe he will not need a visa.

Continuous Modals: *May, Might, Could*

STATEMENTS			
Subject	*May / Might*	Be	Verb + *-ing*
I			
You	**might**		**going** away.
They	**may**	**be**	**driving**.
She			

Note:
Use the continuous modal form to discuss possibilities about something that is happening now.
    A: *Where are they going?*
    B: *They **might be going** to Europe.*

Modals: *Must* for Deduction

STATEMENTS		
Subject	*Must*	Verb
I		
You		**have** the flu.
They	**must**	**speak** French.
He		

Notes:
1. Use *must* to make a deduction.
   Situation: Ann is in Paris. She is talking to a store clerk in Paris, and she is having no trouble communicating.
   *Ann **must speak** French.*
   *The clerk **might be speaking** English to her.*

2. Use *must* to express empathy (show that you understand another person's feelings).
   *You **must be** tired.*

Modals: *Could* for Suggestions

> **Note:**
> Use *could* to make a suggestion.
> **A:** *How should I go to the airport?*
> **B:** *You* **could take** *the shuttle.*

Modals: *Would rather* and *Would prefer to*

YES / NO QUESTIONS			
Would	Subject	*Rather*	Verb
Would	you he she they	**prefer to** **rather**	drive or fly?

ANSWERS			
Subject	*Would*	*Prefer to / Rather*	Verb
I You They He	**would** **'d**	**prefer to** **rather**	fly. drive.

> **Notes:**
> 1. Use *would rather* and *would prefer to* to express a preference.
>   *I* **would rather go** *to New York than Miami.*
>   *I* **would prefer to go** *to Chicago than Dallas.*
>
> 2. The contraction is *'d rather* or *'d prefer to.*
>   *He* **'d rather fly**.
>   *They* **'d prefer to drive**.

Unit 7

Present Perfect Continuous

STATEMENTS			
Subject	*Have*	*Been*	Verb + *-ing*
I You	**have**	**been**	play**ing** tennis for an hour.
He	**has**		
They	**have**		

For and *Since*

> **Notes:**
> 1. *For* shows an amount of time.
>   **for** *a few minutes*
>   **for** *three days*
>
> 2. *Since* shows when an action started.
>   **since** *2009*
>   **since** *Monday*
>   **since** *she moved to the city*

> **Notes:**
> 1. The contractions for the present perfect:
>   I have – *I've*   you have – *you've*
>   he has – *he's*   they have – *they've*
>
> 2. The *present continuous* describes an
>   action that is happening now.
>   *I* **am playing** *tennis.*
>
> 3. The *present perfect continuous* describes
>   an action that began <u>in the past</u> and is
>   <u>continuing now</u>.
>   *I* **have been playing** *tennis for an hour.*

Have / Has	Subject	Been	Verb + -ing
Have	you		watch**ing** a game?
Has	she	**been**	play**ing** with a team?
Have	they		work**ing** hard?

ANSWERS

Yes, I **have**.	No, I **haven't**.
Yes, she **has**.	No, she **hasn't**.
Yes, they **have**.	No, they **haven't**.

How long Questions

How long	Have	Subject	Been	Verb + -ing
How long	**have**	I / you	**been**	study**ing** English?
	has	he		liv**ing** here?
	have	they		

Note:
How long asks about a length of time.
He**'s been studying** English <u>for two months</u>.
I**'ve been living** here <u>for three years</u>.

Unit 8

Present Perfect Tense

STATEMENTS WITH *FOR* / *SINCE*			
I / You	**have** / **haven't**	**worked** there	**for** two years.
He	**has** / **hasn't**		**since** January.
They	**have** / **haven't**		**since** the company opened.

Notes:
1. To form the present perfect tense, use *have/has* and the past participle.

2. Use the present perfect tense to describe an action that began in the past and is still <u>true in the present.</u>
   They **have been** in the city **for** many years.   She **hasn't seen** him **since** they broke up.

3. Use the present perfect tense to describe changes.
   He **has lost** over fifty pounds **since** he started exercising.   In the past year, Lily **has grown** three inches.

PAST PARTICIPLES

See page 116 for irregular verb chart.

Present Perfect Tense for the Recent Past

Notes:
1. Use the *present perfect tense* with words such as *just, lately,* and *recently* to describe an action in the recent past.

2. Put *just* between *have / has* and the main verb.
   I **have just quit** my job.

3. Put *lately* at the end of a sentence.
   He **hasn't been** in class **lately**.

4. Put *recently* between *have / has* and the main verb or at the end of the sentence.
   They **have recently become** grandparents.
   They **have become** grandparents **recently**.

Present Perfect with *Already* and *Yet*

Notes:
1. *Already* shows that an action is completed. Use *already* in affirmative sentences. You can use the present perfect tense or the past tense with *already*.
   She has **already bought** the invitations.   She **already bought** the invitations.

2. Put *already* between *have / has* and the main verb or at the end of the sentence.
   She **has already bought** the invitations.   She **has bought** the invitations **already**.

3. *Yet* shows the action has not been completed. Use *yet* in questions and negative sentences. Use the present perfect tense or the past tense with *yet*. Put *yet* at the end of the sentence.
   Has she **sent** the invitations **yet**?   Did she **send** the invitations **yet**?   She **hasn't sent** the invitations **yet**.

Contrast: Present Perfect, Present Perfect Continuous, and Simple Past

Notes:
1. Use the *present perfect tense* to describe actions that began in the past and are true in the present. The present perfect also describes events in the recent past.
   I **have been** in this country for three years.   They **have just won** the lottery.

2. Use the *present perfect continuous tense* to describe actions that began in the past and are continuing now.
   We **have been living** in this country for three years.

3. Use the *past tense* to show an action <u>completed</u> in the past.
   She **graduated** from college <u>in 2009</u>.   They **moved** to New Mexico <u>two years ago</u>.

Unit 9

Present Perfect with *How long* and *How many*

Notes:
1. *How long* asks about an amount of time. Use *how long* with the present perfect continuous.
   How long has she **been repairing** TVs?
   She **has been repairing** TVs <u>for two hours</u>.

2. *How many* asks about a specific number. Use *how many* with the present perfect .
   How many TVs has she **repaired**?
   She **has repaired** <u>three TVs</u>.

Present Perfect for Repeated Actions

Notes:
1. Use the *present perfect tense* for repeated past actions.

2. The following time expressions often signal a repeated action.
   from time to time   I have been late **from time to time**.
   a few times   She has worked overtime **a few times**.

3. *Ever* and *never* are often used with the *present perfect*. *Ever* means "in your lifetime" or "in your experience."
   Have you **ever been** to China? Yes, I have. / No, I've **never been** to China.

Present Perfect: Word Order

1. Place definite and indefinite time expressions **at the end of the sentence**.
   *I began to work here **in 2005**.*
   *I have been working here **for two years**.*
   *I have changed jobs **twice**.*
   *She's taken four breaks today **so far**!* (Meaning: up until now)

2. Place adverbs of frequency **before the main verb**.
   *Laura has **never** received a warning at work.*
   *She has **always** been an excellent employee.*

3. Place *just* and *finally* **before the main verb**.
   *Henry has **just** gotten a raise.*
   *Andrea has **finally** finished her project.*

4. Place *already* before the main verb or at the end of the sentence.
   *They have **already** repaired three computers.*
   *They have repaired three computers **already**.*

5. Place *yet* and *recently* at the end of the sentence.
   *I've spoken to him **recently**.*
   *Bill hasn't finished the project **yet**.*

Contrast: Present Perfect and Present Perfect Continuous

Notes:
1. Some verbs can be used in either the simple present perfect tense or the present perfect continuous tense.
   *I **have lived** in this town for six years.*
   *I **have been living** in this town for six years.*

   *They **have worked** on this project since last month.*
   *They **have been working** on this project since last month.*

2. Other verbs, especially non-action verbs, use the simple present perfect tense.
   Non-action: hear   see   need   think (to express an opinion)
   Action: listen   watch   deliver   think

Contrast: Simple Past and Present Perfect

Notes:
1. Use the past tense to describe an action at a <u>specific time</u> in the past.
   *I **finished** my deliveries <u>an hour ago</u>.*
   *We **had to work** overtime <u>from 5:00 to 8:00</u>.*

2. Use the present perfect to describe an action that happened at an <u>unspecified time</u> in the past.
   *They**'ve never used** this equipment.*
   *I**'ve applied** to that company twice.*

Past Modals: *Should have* for Regret and Expectation

STATEMENTS		
I You We They He She It	**should have** **shouldn't have**	**left** earlier. **studied** harder.

Notes:
1. Use *should have* to discuss regret about a past action.
   *I **should have studied** more.*
   Meaning: I didn't study enough.
   *We **should have brought** warm clothes.*
   Meaning: We didn't bring warm clothes. Now we're cold.
   *They **shouldn't have left** their umbrellas at home.*
   Meaning: It rained; they weren't prepared.
2. Use *should have* to show an expectation.
   *The bus **should have arrived** by now.*
   Meaning: The bus is late.
   *I **should have done** better on this exam.*
   Meaning: My grade is lower than expected.

May have, Might have, and *Could have* for Past Possibility

STATEMENTS		
Subject	*May / Might / Could + Have*	Past Participle
I You She They	**may (not) have** **might (not) have** **could (not) have**	**gone** to the movies. **forgotten** to bring it. **bought** a new car.

Notes:
1. Use *may have, might have,* or *could have* to express past possibility.
   *I **may not have taken** it.* (Meaning: Maybe I didn't take it.)
   *She **might have remembered** it.* (Meaning: Maybe she remembered it.)
2. *Could not have / Couldn't have* express past impossibility.
   *He **couldn't have been** at work that day. He was in the emergency room with his daughter.*

Past Modals: *Must have*

STATEMENTS		
Subject	*Must + Have*	Past Participle
I You She They	**must have** **must not have**	**left** his keys at home. **had** a doctor's appointment.

Notes:
1. Use *must have* to express a deduction about a past action.
   He **must have left** his keys at home.
2. Use *must have* to express empathy.
   A: *I didn't pass my driver's test.*
   B: *You* **must have been** *disappointed.*

Unit 11

The Passive: Present Tense

Active sentences emphasize the subject that does the action.
        Subject   Verb   Object
    Fishermen **catch** *tuna and salmon* in Oregon.

Passive sentences emphasize the object that receives the action.
        Object   Verb   Subject
    Tuna and salmon **are caught** by fishermen in Oregon.

Note:
When the subject is obvious, unknown, or not important, "by" and the subject are **not** necessary.
    Tuna and salmon **are caught** in Oregon. (The subject is obvious: We know that fishermen catch the fish, so "fishermen" isn't necessary.)

YES / NO QUESTIONS		
Is	milk	**produced** in Wisconsin?
Are	tires	**manufactured** in Ohio?

SHORT ANSWERS	
Yes, it **is**.	No, it **isn't**.
Yes, they **are**.	No, they **aren't**.

WH- QUESTIONS			
Where	**is**	rice	**grown?**
How	**are**	cars	**manufactured?**

ANSWERS
Rice **is grown** in many Asian countries.
Cars **are manufactured** in factories on assembly lines.

Passive with *By*

Notes:
1. Use *by* when the **subject** of the action is important and is not obvious.

This candy **is produced** by Royal Sweets. This toy **is made** by an American company.	(This is the name of a particular company.)

2. Don't use *by* if the doer of the action is obvious.

This chocolate **is made** in Switzerland.	(*By* is not necessary. We know that a candy company makes the candy.)
Cows **are raised** on farms.	(The meaning is clear. It is obvious that farmers raise the cows.)

Unit 12

The Passive: Past Tense

Subject	*Be*	Past Participle	
The space shuttle	**was**	**built**	in 1976.
		invented	by NASA.
747 jumbo jets	**were**	**developed**	in 1970.
		designed	by Boeing.

Passive with *By*

In early times, the medicine man **cured** people.
In early times, people were cured **by the medicine man.**

Many years ago, hospitals **did not sterilize** equipment.
Many years ago, equipment **was not sterilized.**

Note:
Use *by* when the subject of the action is important or is not obvious.

The first hospitals were begun **by the Romans.**

The Passive: Other Tenses

Tense	Passive Form
Simple present	Airbags **are installed** in all cars.
Present continuous	Those cars **are being repaired**.
Simple past	Airbags **were** first **installed** in 1973.
Past continuous	My car **was being repaired** while I was waiting.
Future with *will*	A new model **will be delivered** tomorrow.
Future with *be going to*	That car **is going to be inspected** tomorrow.
Present perfect	Many improvements **have been made** to today's cars.

Note:
All passives have a form of the verb *to be*.

Unit 13

Adjective Clauses with *Who, Which, Whom,* and *Whose*

Adjective clauses begin with relative pronouns such as ***who, whom, which,*** and ***whose.***

who – replaces a subject (person)
    <u>The student</u> ***who is sitting next to me*** plays in a rock band.

which – replaces a subject or object (thing)
    I just saw <u>the movie</u> *Crazy Heart,* ***which has good music.***

whom – replaces an indirect object
    He's writing a song for <u>his son</u>, ***whom he named after his father.***

whose – replaces a possessive form
    This is <u>the singer</u> ***whose song you have just heard.***

Adjective Clauses with *That*

Notes:
To introduce an adjective clause, the relative pronoun *that* can be used instead of *who, which,* or *whom.*

1. Use *that* only with **restrictive adjective clauses**. A **restrictive clause** identifies the noun it describes.
   Restrictive clause: *We paid the man **whom we hired to sing at our wedding**.*
   or *We paid the man **that we hired to sing at our wedding**.*
   Meaning: The adjective clause is necessary to understand who "the man" is.

2. No commas are necessary with restrictive clauses.

3. Don't use *that* with **non-restrictive adjective clauses**. A **non-restrictive clause** gives extra information about the noun it describes.
   Non-restrictive clause: *We paid Dave Jones, **whom we hired to sing at our wedding**.*
   Incorrect: *We paid Dave Jones, **that we hired to sing at our wedding**.*
   Meaning: We know who Dave Jones is. The adjective clause gives extra information about Dave Jones.

4. Use commas to separate non-restrictive clauses.
   *Dave Jones, **whom we hired for our wedding**, has a popular wedding band.*

Adjective Clauses with *When* and *Where*

Adjective clauses can also begin with *when* and *where.*

*Tim McGraw has appeared in a movie each year since **2004**, **when** he appeared in his first movie.*

*Faith Hill was born in **Mississippi**, **where** she grew up singing in church.*

Unit 14

Verb + Infinitive

Note:
There are many verbs that require the infinitive form (*to* + main verb). Gradually, you'll learn the list.
   *I **plan to attend** college in the fall.*   *He **promised to babysit** for his cousin tonight.*

Use an infinitive after the following verbs:

(be) able	fail	like	prefer	try
afford	forget	love	prepare	volunteer
agree	hate	manage	promise	wait
ask	hope	need	refuse	want
choose	intend	offer	remember	wish
decide	know how	plan	seem	would like
expect	learn (how)			

Verb + Object + Infinitive

Notes:
1. Many verbs require an object or an object pronoun.

advise	encourage	hire	remind	urge
allow	expect	invite	require	want
ask	forbid	permit	teach	warn
convince	help	persuade	tell	

2. Use an **object + the infinitive form** after the following verbs:

   My mother **asked _me to clean_** my room.
   The teacher **expected _us to prepare_** for the test.

Be + Adjective + Infinitive

Use the infinitive form after the following adjectives:

dangerous	good	important	polite	selfish
difficult	hard	impossible	possible	stressful
easy	healthy	interesting	reasonable	terrible
expensive	helpful	necessary	romantic	wonderful

It**'s important _to make_** a schedule of my activities.
It **was helpful _to have_** a study partner.

Unit 15

Verb + Gerund

Use a gerund form (base verb + *-ing*) after the following verbs:

admit	dislike	practice
anticipate	doesn't / don't mind	quit
appreciate	enjoy	recall
avoid	finish	recommend
begin	hate	regret
can't help	imagine	resent
can't stand	like	start
consider	love	stop
continue	miss	suggest
delay	postpone	understand
discuss		

They **missed _seeing_** their family during the holiday season.
She **regretted not _working_** with people who spoke English.

Preposition + Gerund

> **Use a gerund (base verb + -ing) after the following prepositions:**
>
> | | | | |
> |---|---|---|---|
> | after | besides | in addition to | while |
> | before | by | instead of | without |
>
> *After **studying** for the naturalization test, she easily passed the test.*
> *In addition to **playing** tennis, he also plays soccer.*

Verb + Preposition + Gerund

> **Use a gerund (base verb + -ing) after the following verb and preposition phrases:**
>
> | | | | |
> |---|---|---|---|
> | adjust to | complain about | give up | succeed in |
> | approve of | count on | insist on | talk about |
> | argue about | depend on | keep on | think about |
> | believe in | dream about | look forward to | warn about |
> | care about | forget about | plan on | worry about |

Be + Adjective Phrase + Gerund

> **Use a gerund (base verb + -ing) after the following *be* + adjective and preposition phrases:**
>
> | | | | |
> |---|---|---|---|
> | be afraid of | be good at | be interested in | be tired of |
> | be capable of | be guilty of | be opposed to | be upset about |
> | be famous for | be in favor of | be proud of | |
>
> *I **am good at understanding** spoken English.*
> *She **is not interested in going** to that film.*

Contrast: Infinitives and Gerunds

> *It was **impossible to find** a job in my country.*
> *My friends **didn't encourage** me **to speak** English.*
> *He **enjoyed working** at the real estate office.*
> *After **working** for a few years at the factory, I found another job.*

Present Continuous Verbs

1. For most verbs, add *-ing*.
walk-walking   play-playing   eat-eating

2. If a verb ends in *e*, drop the *e* and add *-ing*.
write-writing   come-coming   drive-driving

3. If a verb ends in a consonant + vowel + consonant, double the final consonant and add *-ing*.
sit-sitting   run-running   put-putting

Present Tense: Third Person

1. For most verbs, add *-s*.
make-makes   call-calls   sleep-sleeps

2. If a verb ends with a consonant and a *y*, change the *y* to *i* and add *-es*.
try-tries   cry-cries   apply-applies

3. If a verb ends with *sh*, *ch*, *x*, or *z*, add *-es*.
wash-washes   watch-watches   fix-fixes

4. These verbs are irregular in the third person.
have-has   do-does

Past Verbs

1. For most verbs, add *-d* or *-ed*.
rent-rented   save-saved

2. If a verb ends in a consonant + *y*, change the *y* to *i* and add *-ed*.
try-tried   study-studied

3. If a verb ends in a consonant + vowel + consonant, double the final consonant and add *-ed*.
stop-stopped   rob-robbed

4. If a verb ends in *w*, *x*, or *y*, do not double the consonant. Add *-ed*.
play-played   relax-relaxed   snow-snowed

Comparative Adjectives: *-er*

1. For most adjectives, add *-r* or *-er*.
   cold-colder   short-shorter   tall-taller

2. If a one-syllable adjective ends in a consonant + vowel + consonant, double the final consonant and add *-er*.
   big-bigger   thin-thinner   sad-sadder

3. If an adjective ends in a consonant + *y*, change the *y* to *i* and add *-er*.
   happy-happier   heavy-heavier   friendly-friendlier

Superlative Adjectives: *-est*

1. For most adjectives, add *-st* or *-est*.
   large-largest   short-shortest   tall-tallest

2. If a one-syllable adjective ends in a consonant + vowel + consonant, double the final consonant and add *-est*.
   big-biggest   thin-thinnest   sad-saddest

3. If an adjective ends in a consonant + *y*, change the *y* to *i* and add *-est*.
   busy-busiest   noisy-noisiest   friendly-friendliest

Dictations

Unit 1

Page 8, Exercise C

1. Are any students eating?
2. Are all the students writing in their notebooks?
3. Does anyone have a pencil sharpener?
4. Do you go to work after class?
5. Who is sitting next to you?
6. How many hours do you study for this class?

Unit 3

Page 39, Exercise C

1. We'll have better jobs after we learn English.
2. She'll help you with the party.
3. He won't need to work next semester.
4. The environment will be cleaner.
5. You'll need to prepare for the final exam.
6. Cars will be more efficient.
7. I'll help you after class.

Student to Student

Unit 5

Page 72, Exercise A

Student 1: Read the questions in Set A to Student 2.

Student 2: Read the questions in Set B to Student 1.

Set A

1. Who cooked when you were growing up?
2. Who taught you how to cook?
3. Do you watch cooking programs on TV?
4. Is your kitchen big enough for you?
5. What kind of cooking classes did you take before now?

Set B

6. Does your husband like to cook?
7. What classes did you take together?
8. What was the first dish that you cooked?
9. How does your husband like the food you cook?
10. Why did you decide to go to cooking school?

Unit 6

Page 89, Exercise C

Student 1: Read Set A sentences to Student 2. Then, turn to page 89. Listen to Student 2 and write each sentence you hear next to the correct picture.

Student 2: Read Set B sentences to Student 1.

Set A

1. They might move to a warmer climate.
2. They may not go to college right away.
3. They could take their honeymoon later.
4. They may get full-time jobs.
5. They would rather rent an apartment first.
6. They would prefer to be closer to their grandchildren.

Set B

1. They may volunteer at the library.
2. They'd prefer to buy a house in a couple of years.
3. They may not work at the same place.
4. They could move in with their children.
5. They would rather study part time.
6. They might wait to have children.

Unit 7

Page 103, Exercise C

Student 1: Read Set A sentences to Student 2. Then, turn to page 103. Listen to Student 2 and write each sentence next to the correct picture.

Student 2: Read Set B sentences to Student 1.

Set A

1. You haven't been coming to work on time.
2. It's been making a strange noise.
3. They've been running for two hours.
4. It's been leaking oil.
5. We've been receiving a lot of complaints.
6. They've been drinking a lot of water.
7. I've been feeling very tired.
8. My stomach has been bothering me.

Set B

1. It's been overheating in traffic.
2. I've been having trouble sleeping.
3. They've been getting lots of support.
4. You've been making mistakes in your work.
5. Roger has been leading for 30 minutes.
6. It hasn't been running smoothly.
7. You've been arguing with your co-workers.
8. I haven't been eating well.

Unit 9

Page 137, Exercise F

Student 1: Read Set A questions to Student 2. Then, turn to page 137 and listen to Student 2. Write the answer under the correct picture. Use complete sentences.

Student 2: Read Set B questions to Student 1.

Set A

1. Has she fired any employees this year?
2. How many doctors did she talk to this morning?
3. How many cars has he repaired today?
4. How long has she been selling homes?
5. What time did he start work this morning?
6. How long has he had his own business?

Set B

1. How many employees did she hire?
2. How many patients has she helped today?
3. How long has he been working at this garage?
4. Did she sell any homes this month?
5. How many streets has he cleared so far?
6. Has he installed more than one system today?

Unit 10

Page 153, Exercise B

Student 1: Listen to Student 2 talk about the weekend. Be a good listener and give an appropriate response. Use *must have been* and an adjective from the box. Then, turn to page 153.

Student 2: Listen to Student 1 talk about the weekend. Be a good listener and give an appropriate response. Use *must have been* and an adjective from the box.

Example: My homework / be / very difficult

My homework was very difficult.

You must have been frustrated.

excited	surprised	proud
scared	thrilled	frustrated
pleased	disappointed	worried
exhausted		

Page 213, Exercise F

Student 1: Read Set A sentences to Student 2. When you are finished, turn to page 213. Write the sentences you hear.

Student 2: Read Set B sentences to Student 1.

Set A

1. Every time I start to study, my kids interrupt me.
2. I wanted to get up early, but I forgot to set the alarm clock.
3. I want to exercise after work, but I'm too tired when I get home.
4. I need to get a cavity filled, but I hate to go to the dentist.
5. I've decided to buy a computer, but I can't decide which one to buy.

Set B

1. I'd like to save some money every month, but I love to shop.
2. I would love to travel, but I can't afford it right now.
3. I need to study more, but I often have to work overtime.
4. I decided to clean the basement, but there was a good movie on TV.
5. We need to write our wills, but we haven't hired a lawyer yet.

Unit 1

CD 1, Track 1, Page 5

A. Listen to the story about Sophie and Lizzy, two college roommates. Complete the questions with *Do* or *Does*. Then, answer the questions.

Sophie: Hi, I'm Sophie, and I'm a morning person. When the sun comes up, I feel great. I get a lot of things done in the morning, so I take courses early in the morning. I'm finished with my classes by noon. I like to keep everything neat and in order. If things are out of place, I go crazy! My favorite subjects are science and math, so I think I'm going to major in chemistry or computer science. I really like computers. I do all of my work on my computer, so I prefer to study in my room at my own desk. I almost never write by hand. Oh, and I always hand in my class work on time. But my roommate, Lizzy, is completely different from me. We get along well, though.

Lizzy: Hi, I'm Lizzy. Sophie and I are complete opposites. She's a morning person, but I'm a night owl. I rarely go to bed before 2 A.M., so I don't get up until noon. I take all afternoon classes. I don't care about keeping my things in order. I can always find my things even if I have to look on the floor or under the bed. Sophie hates that. She's really neat. My favorite subjects are literature, writing, and art. I love to write, and I love to draw. I think I'll major in art history or English literature. I have a computer, but I almost never use it. I prefer to write everything by hand. I only use the computer to type my papers, which are sometimes late. I often have to talk to my professors about my late papers. Sophie is completely different from me, but she's a great roommate.

CD 1, Track 2, Page 6

B. Pronunciation: Linking /do you/. Listen and repeat.

1. What do you do?
2. Where do you work?
3. How do you get home?
4. Where do you live?
5. Why do you study here?
6. What do you do on weekends?

CD 1, Track 3, Page 10

The Big Picture: The University of Texas at San Antonio

The University of Texas is a large university with many campuses all over Texas. This is a description of the University of Texas at San Antonio, which is located in southeastern Texas.

The University of Texas at San Antonio, or U.T.S.A., is a four-year public university with a graduate school. U.T.S.A.'s main campus is located on a suburban campus, 15 miles from downtown San Antonio. The university has a large undergraduate student population of over 24,000. Two percent of the students come from other countries. In addition, over three thousand students are in graduate programs. The university employs 1,224 faculty.

Students who want to attend U.T.S.A. must turn in the following: first, a completed application with a $40 application fee. An online application is available. Second, they must have an official high school transcript and official ACT or SAT scores. There is no minimum score for students in the top 25 percent of their high school classes.

Like most other universities, U.T.S.A. offers many academic majors. Students can major in the liberal arts, sciences, or technical fields. Here are just a few of the possible majors: accounting, criminal justice, engineering, and international business.

U.T.S.A. offers many facilities and student services to help the students be successful in their college studies. For students who need extra help for their college courses, there is academic help. There is also a health clinic and personal counseling for students. When the students aren't studying, they can take advantage of the many extracurricular activities. There are many athletic teams for both men and women. There are also student organizations that cover many different interests including sports teams and drama.

To help prepare new and transfer students for life at U.T.S.A., the university offers an orientation program. Students learn about life on a college campus, get help registering for courses, and find out about the student services available. Family members are welcome, too.

CD 1, Track 4, Page 11

C. Listen and write short answers to the questions about the university.

1. Is the university a two-year university?
2. Does the university have only one campus?
3. Is there a graduate school at the university?

4. Does the university require students to pay an application fee?

5. Is it a private university?

6. Are there opportunities for women to participate in sports?

7. Is there an orientation for new students?

8. Are families welcome to come to the orientation?

Unit 2

CD 1, Track 5, Page 19
B. Look at the pictures and listen to the comparison between life in colonial times and life today. Number the pictures.

The colonial period in the United States lasted from 1607 to 1776. Most early colonists were men and women from England who decided to start a new life in North America. They settled along the eastern coast of what is now the United States. Life at that time was very different from life today.

1. Most people lived on small farms. People grew their own food.

2. They didn't cook on stoves. They cooked their food over open fires.

3. When they needed milk, they milked their own cows. They didn't buy milk at the supermarket.

4. Houses functioned without electricity or modern conveniences. People read and worked by candlelight.

5. They didn't sleep on mattresses with box springs. They used to sleep on feather beds.

6. In the evening, instead of watching TV, they read to each other and played games.

7. When people wanted to communicate with friends or relatives far away, they didn't have phones or e-mail. They used to write letters.

8. For transportation, there were no cars. People used horses and wagons.

CD 1, Track 6, Page 22
A. Pronunciation: *Used to*. Listen and repeat.

1. In colonial times, people used to drive horses and wagons.

2. People used to cook over open fires.

3. People used to grow their own food.

4. They used to write letters.

5. They used to attend very small schools.

CD 1, Track 7, Page 24
A. Complete the questions. Then, listen to Eric talk about his childhood. Take notes in your notebook. Answer the questions.

Oscar: Eric, where were you born?

Eric: I was born in a small town in Peru. On the coast.

Oscar: How many brothers and sisters do you have?

Eric: There are four boys—and I'm the youngest.

Oscar: Did your grandparents live in the same town?

Eric: Yes, my grandparents, my two aunts, my five uncles. We all lived in the same town. And, I had a lot of cousins.

Oscar: Did you live in the city or the country?

Eric: In the country. My family owned a small farm. In the winter, I had to get up early and milk our cow.

Oscar: How about school? Did you walk to school or take the bus?

Eric: In our town, there were no school buses. I used to ride my bike to school.

Oscar: What did you do after school?

Eric: After school, I played soccer with my brothers and cousins.

Oscar: How about the summer? What did you do in the summer?

Eric: In the summer, we used to work in the fields with my father.

Oscar: Did you go on vacation?

Eric: We never went on vacation. My mother said we didn't need a vacation because we lived in the country. A few times each summer, my mom packed a big lunch, and we drove to the ocean.

Oscar: Did you see your relatives a lot?

Eric: All the time. There was always something to celebrate: a birthday, a wedding, or a holiday. We all used to go to grandmother's house. My mother and aunts used to cook inside, and the men barbecued a pig outside. My grandmother always made the desserts. They were wonderful—cakes and rice pudding and *mazamorra morada*.

CD 1, Track 8, Page 26
The Big Picture: Benjamin Franklin

Benjamin Franklin was born in Boston, Massachusetts, on January 17, 1706. At that time, school was not required, and Franklin only attended school for two years. For the rest of his life, he continued to read and study on his own, and he even learned five foreign languages. When he was 12, he began to work at his brother's printing office and learned quickly. By the age of 17, he was an excellent printer. Franklin then moved

to Philadelphia in 1728, and at the young age of 22, he opened his own printing shop in that city. He published a newspaper, the *Pennsylvania Gazette*. He knew that many people could not read well, so his publications had many cartoons and pictures.

Benjamin Franklin was respected in Philadelphia. He helped to improve everyday life for the people in the city. In 1732, he started the first public library in America so that people could borrow and read books. In 1736, he helped to organize the first fire department in Philadelphia because most of the houses were wood, and there were many fires. He was also postmaster in Philadelphia and helped to set up the routes for mail delivery. He also spoke to the officials of the city and encouraged them to pave the city streets.

Franklin was also an inventor. He was always asking questions and trying to improve everyday life. At the time, colonial fireplaces sent black smoke throughout the house. Franklin invented a stove that used less wood and gave off more heat. As postmaster, he invented the odometer. The odometer measured distance, and Franklin used it to set up mail routes in the city. Franklin wore glasses and became tired of taking his glasses off to see far away, so he invented bifocals. Franklin also experimented with electricity and realized that lightning is a form of electricity. He invented the lightning rod to protect homes from lightning.

As the years passed, Franklin became a leader in the city and in the country. He signed the Declaration of Independence, which stated that the 13 colonies were a free and independent nation. He served as a minister to France during the war with England. When he returned, he signed the Constitution, which established the new government.

Benjamin Franklin died on April 17, 1790, and was buried in Philadelphia.

Unit 3

CD 1, Track 9, Page 34
A. Listen. Write the number of each statement under the correct picture.
1. I'm going to pay attention and take careful notes.
2. I'm going to apply for unemployment.
3. I'm going to vote in the next election.
4. The children are going to live with you on the weekends.
5. My mother will help me after the baby comes.
6. I will send e-mails to my family every night.
7. We're going to live in my apartment because it's bigger.
8. I'm going to register for only two courses this semester.
9. I will start working in a law office in two weeks.

CD 1, Track 10, Page 35
A. Listen. Complete the sentences. Some of the sentences are negative.
Ellie: Congratulations, Julie! We're high school graduates!
Julie: Finally! I'm so excited. How do you feel, Ellie?
Ellie: I feel great. So, what are you going to do? Are you going away to college?
Julie: No, I'm not. Things are tough right now, so I'm going to live at home and go to the community college.
Ellie: So am I. Your mother's a teacher. Are you going to study education, too?
Julie: Me? No. I'm going to study engineering and architecture. What about you?
Ellie: I'm not sure. I'm going to talk to a counselor on Monday. Are you going to study full time?

Julie: No. I'm going to keep my job at the department store. I'm going to take classes at night.
Ellie: Too bad. We're not going to have the same schedule. I'm going to take classes during the day and work in my father's restaurant at night.
Julie: OK. Well, good luck. Maybe I'll see you on the weekend.
Ellie: OK. See you around.

CD 1, Track 11, Page 37
B. Listen and circle the meaning.
1. They're watching TV.
2. I'm doing laundry tonight.
3. She's taking her daughter to the doctor on Tuesday.
4. The students are writing essays.
5. I'm taking two classes next semester.
6. I'm listening to the radio.
7. He's not going to class next week.
8. We're not taking a vacation this year.
9. I'm texting a friend.

CD 1, Track 12, Page 38
A. Pronunciation: 'll. Listen and repeat.
1. I'll do it.
2. I'll get it.
3. I'll call you.
4. I'll help him.
5. I'll be there.
6. They'll paint it.
7. She'll do it.
8. He'll answer it.
9. We'll help you.

The Big Picture: After the Baby Comes

Laura: Thanks for arranging the baby shower, Melissa. I had a great time.

Melissa: So did I. It was a lot of fun. So, are you still looking for a house?

Laura: No, we looked at a few houses, but some of them were too expensive, and others needed a lot of work.

Melissa: So, what are you going to do? You need a bigger place.

Laura: I know, but I think we have a solution. We really like our building and our neighborhood, so we're going to look at a few bigger apartments in our building. Besides, it's close to work.

Melissa: Speaking of work, what about your job? Are you still working?

Laura: This is my last week.

Melissa: Then, what are you going to do?

Laura: Well, I have two months maternity leave, but first Brady and I have to finish shopping for the baby.

Melissa: Where are you going to put everything? Your apartment is small!

Laura: We're going to look at apartments tonight. We might get lucky and find one we like. If we do, we're going to move as soon as possible.

Melissa: You're an only child, Laura. Do you even know how to change diapers?

Laura: I used to babysit when I was a teenager, so yes, I know how to change diapers. And Brady and I are taking a parenting class. We're learning a lot.

Melissa: Good. You know, you're going to have to make some big changes. No more late nights out on the town.

Laura: You're right. We used to go out three or four times a week, but we'll be spending a lot of time at home. Besides, I'm too tired to go out, and the baby's not even here yet.

Melissa: What about the cats? Are you going to give them away?

Laura: No! Are you crazy? But we're not going to leave them alone with the baby. That's another reason why we need more space.

Melissa: Is your mother going to help?

Laura: Yes. She's going to be a big help. Brady can only take two weeks off.

Melissa: Are you going to go back to work full time?

Laura: Mm-hmm, but I'm going to work a three-day schedule. My mother will take care of the baby while I'm at work.

Melissa: You're lucky. Call me if you need help.

Laura: Thanks! I will.

Unit 4

D. Listen. Rebecca is talking about her schedule. Check the tasks that she has completed.

Uh, let's see, what do I have to do today? Do I need stamps? Hmm. I don't think so. I bought a few yesterday. Here they are. OK, so I have to mail my gas bill and my phone bill. I can mail them in the mailbox near the Laundromat. I have to do some laundry, or I won't have any clean clothes to wear. While my clothes are in the wash, I can go to the supermarket. I have to get some eggs, milk, and something for dinner. Oh, did I deposit my check? Yes, I did, and here's the deposit slip from last Saturday. And, . . . I have to call to confirm my dentist's appointment. I don't remember if my appointment's at 9:00 or at 10:00. All right. I'm ready to go, but I have to remember to put gas in the car. The tank's almost empty.

A. Pronunciation: *Can* and *can't*. **Listen.** Marcus is talking about his driving experience. Complete the sentences with *can* or *can't*.

I'm a new driver, and I'm a terrible driver. I finally got my driving permit three months ago. It took me three tries to pass the written test. Now, I can only drive with a licensed driver in my car, so my mom or dad has to be in the car with me. I can back up, but I can't parallel park. I'm a terrible parker, so I sometimes drive around the block a few times to find an easy space to park in. I can drive on a busy highway, but I feel nervous. I can't drive at night alone because I'm only 17. I can't drive with the radio playing because I can't concentrate. Maybe I need to take the bus.

A. Pronunciation: *'d better / 'd better not*. Listen and complete the sentences. Then, listen again and repeat.

1. **I'd better stay** home. I don't feel well.
2. **You'd better put** the baby in the car seat.
3. **She'd better call** the police and report the accident.
4. **We'd better take** the party inside. It's beginning to rain.
5. **He'd better not have** another piece of cake. He'll get sick.
6. **You'd better not get** a dog. Your landlord won't allow it.
7. **She'd better slow** down. The roads are icy.
8. **I'd better not buy** that. I can't afford it.

CD 1, Track 17, Page 58
The Big Picture: Getting a Driver's License
I'm so excited. Tomorrow, my mother's taking me to the Division of Motor Vehicles to get my learner's permit. I have to have my parent's signature on my application because I'm only 16. I have to show proof of my age, too. I grew up in Peru, but I was born here in the U.S., so I can show my U.S. passport. People can also use original birth certificates, a permanent resident card, or citizenship papers. I've already taken the D.A.T.A. course, and I'm going to take the written test today. There are 40 questions and signs on the test. I have to get 75 percent correct to pass the test. I speak English well, but my reading is still a little weak. I don't have to take the test in English because the DMV gives the test in 30 languages, including mine—Spanish. I also have to take a hearing test and a vision test to check my eyesight. Then, they're going to take my picture.

After I pay 48 dollars, I can get my learner's permit. My permit is good for two years, but I have to practice for 50 hours and have my permit for a year before I can get an intermediate license. I was hoping that my sister could teach me to drive, but in my state, I must have an adult 21 years or older in the car with me. That's the law for people under 18. My sister's only 19, so my mother's going to teach me.

I'm going to practice as much as I can before the road test. My mother will drive me to the road test because I must have a licensed driver 21 years or older in the car with me. My parents will get the auto insurance card, and we need to show the car's registration. Of course, I also have to show my learner's permit. Then, I can take the road test. Wish me luck!

CD 1, Track 18, Page 65
A. Listen and repeat.
1. accelerator
2. brake
3. bumper
4. clutch
5. hood
6. horn
7. signal
8. steering wheel
9. gear shift
10. tires
11. trunk
12. windshield
13. windshield wipers

Unit 5

CD 1, Track 19, Page 68
A. People are talking about activities they enjoy. Circle the question word. Then, listen and answer the questions.

Gina: How do I spend my free time? I like to go dancing. My friends and I go dancing almost every weekend. Every Friday and Saturday night, we go dancing at clubs in our area. We get together with other friends, and we make new friends. We like all kinds of music, but we usually go to clubs that play Latin music. A couple times a month, I take a dance class. Dancing is a really good way to keep in shape. I don't need to work out at a gym. Dancing keeps me fit.

Roberto: I spend my time taking care of my tropical fish. I have a large aquarium in my living room, and I take good care of my fish. I have many books about tropical fish. I also have a few friends who like keeping fish, too. We get together once a week at a coffee shop nearby and talk about what's new with our fish and what new fish we've bought. I also participate in an online discussion with other people who keep fish. Watching my fish is very relaxing after a hard day at work.

Yelena: After I retired, I was bored and I needed something to do. One day, I saw two men playing chess in the lounge in my building.

It brought back memories for me. My father taught me how to play chess, and I even joined the chess team in high school. When I was in college, I didn't have time for chess. And then, I began to work, and I stopped playing chess. Now, I'm playing again. Chess is a game for people who like to think. I'm getting older, and I want to keep my mind sharp. I play every evening. Tomorrow, I'm going to start teaching my grandson how to play.

CD 1, Track 20, Page 71
A. Pronunciation: Tag Questions Listen and repeat. Pay attention to the arrows.
1. They like to fish, don't they?
2. Fishing isn't expensive, is it?
3. They will cook their fish, won't they?
4. They don't fish every day, do they?
5. They're fishing in a lake, aren't they?
6. It isn't a hot day, is it?
7. Fishing isn't tiring, is it?
8. They hope to catch a lot, don't they?

CD 1, Track 21, Pages 74 and 75
The Big Picture: A Trip to Vancouver, British Columbia
The Yang family is now in Vancouver staying with Victor, William's younger brother. Victor and his family moved to Vancouver three years ago.

Victor decided to move to Vancouver after he visited the city on a business trip. He liked the clean streets, the natural setting, and the economic opportunities. At first, his wife, Lin, didn't want to move there, but after a couple of months, she met a few other immigrants from Hong Kong. They introduced her to more people in the neighborhood. Now, Lin likes Vancouver very much, and she has a job. She works three mornings a week at her daughter's elementary school. There are many other children there who speak Cantonese or Mandarin, so the school needs experienced teachers like Lin, who can speak both languages.

Right now, Victor and Lin are taking William and his family around Vancouver. This morning, they visited Granville Island. They walked around in the Public Market and enjoyed looking at the local and imported fruits, vegetables, and other foods and flowers. They decided to have some tea at an outdoor café and watch the boats come into the harbor.

It's 12:00 now, and they're on their way to Gastown, the oldest part of Vancouver. Later, they're going to take a trolley tour around the city. They're going to stop at Queen Elizabeth Park and visit the Rose Garden. They're also going to visit the zoo. After that, they're going to have dinner in Chinatown with some friends.

William and his family are having a wonderful time. They can't wait until Victor and his family come to San Francisco next year.

Unit 6

CD 1, Track 22, Page 86
A. Listen. Write the number next to the correct response.
1. My husband had a car accident yesterday, but his injuries were minor.
2. We moved last month, and my son has never been away from his friends and grandparents before.
3. I have to get up at 5:00 every day this week.
4. Anna has an important job interview.
5. It doesn't snow in Lilia's native country. She doesn't have any winter clothes yet.
6. My friends are studying for exams, so they can't go out with me this weekend.
7. There was a hurricane in my cousin's area. We're waiting for him to call.
8. My son and his wife are going to have their first child.

CD 1, Track 23, Page 86
C. Listen and complete each suggestion.
1. **A:** My car broke down. I need to get to work.
   B: You could take the bus.
2. **A:** We want to take a vacation, but we can't afford to spend a lot of money.
   B: You could go to the beach.
3. **A:** My sister's going to Rome, but the hotels are expensive.
   B: She could exchange apartments.
4. **A:** My family wants to stay at my house, but I don't have enough beds.
   B: They could bring sleeping bags.
5. **A:** My children are coming home from college, but flights are too expensive.
   B: They could take an overnight train.
6. **A:** My brother wants to study Spanish in another country.
   B: He could go to Mexico.

CD 1, Track 24, Pages 90 and 91
The Big Picture: Planning a Vacation
Gina: Hi, Drew, how are you today?
Drew: I'm doing well, Gina, and you?
Gina: OK, thanks. I guess it's that time of year. I thought you would be coming into the office soon.
Drew: Well, you've been helping to plan our vacations for a long time. This year, I want to do something different.
Gina: Is this going to be a family vacation?
Drew: Yes, our kids are getting older. They like to travel.
Gina: How old is Gabby? She must be ten.
Drew: No, she's 12, and Leo is eight.
Gina: I can't believe it! I remember when Gabby was born.
Drew: Time flies. So, let's talk about our vacation. We're going to be away during Maryann's 40th birthday, so I want to do something special. It's going to be a surprise from me and the kids.
Gina: That's a great idea. So, where do you want to go?
Drew: I want to go somewhere where we haven't been before. A friend told me something about Flathead Lake in Montana.
Gina: Flathead Lake? Good idea. It's a great place for a family. There's a great lodge there, and it's in a beautiful location. The lake is spectacular, and the view of the mountains is beautiful.
Drew: You know, Leo is 8. He'll do anything, and he's very enthusiastic about this trip. He loves the outdoors. Gabby is almost a teenager. She's becoming a little harder to please.
Gina: Don't worry. Lots of families go there with kids of all ages. There are lots of activities that might interest her. The staff at the lodge organizes events for the kids.

Drew: This is near a lake, so there must be a lot of water sports, right?

Gina: Definitely. You can go sailing, swimming, and waterskiing. And, there's a heated pool, too.

Drew: Maryann might like that. I know she would rather spend time by the pool than in a cool lake.

Gina: I think you're right. And, there are plenty of other sports, too. You and your family are pretty active, aren't you?

Drew: Yes, we are.

Gina: So, you'll enjoy the sports that the lodge offers: basketball, soccer, baseball, and tennis. They give lessons, too.

Drew: What happens when the weather's bad?

Gina: No problem. The lodge offers arts and crafts, games, and movies.

Drew: This place sounds perfect. How far is it from a major town?

Gina: Only ten minutes. There are shuttles from the lodge every hour.

Drew: Is there anything else to see in the area?

Gina: Yes, there's a national park nearby. You can tour the park. And, you can see the wild animals in the area.

Drew: Leo will really like that. Do you have any brochures?

Gina: Let's see. Here you are. Take them home and talk to your kids. Then, give me a call.

Drew: OK, because we need to talk about how much this is going to cost me.

Gina: Don't worry. It's very reasonable.

Drew: We'll have to talk about flights, too. I want to make sure I get an aisle seat.

Gina: I'll start checking flights right away. Call me when you've made a decision.

Drew: Thanks, Gina.

CD 1, Track 25, Page 91
E. Pronunciation: 'd rather. Listen. Complete the sentences with *I'd, He'd, She'd, We'd,* or *They'd.*
1. **We'd** rather go camping.
2. **They'd** rather stay in a cabin.
3. **He'd** rather go fishing.
4. **She'd** rather go swimming.
5. **She'd** rather not stay in a tent.
6. **He'd** rather not go to malls.
7. **They'd** rather not eat at home.
8. **I'd** rather not stay at a hotel.

CD 1, Track 26, Page 97
A. Listen and answer the questions.
A: Good morning. I'm going to ask you some questions.
B: OK.
A: May I see your passport, please?
B: Yes, here it is.
A: Where did you visit?
B: I went to Barcelona and Madrid.
A: Where did you stay?
B: I stayed in a hotel in Barcelona. And I stayed at my sister's apartment in Madrid.
A: Was your luggage always with you?
B: Yes, it was in the hotel in Barcelona, and in my sister's apartment in Madrid.
A: Did you pack your luggage?
B: Yes, I did.
A: Did anyone ask you to carry anything in your bag?
B: No, just presents from my sister for Christmas.
A: Please put your bag here. Open your bag, please.
B: Oh, they're just presents for my family.
A: I'm sorry. You can't put wrapped presents in your carry-on bag. You'll have to unwrap them or put them in your checked bag.
B: Right now?
A: Yes, right now.
B: OK.
A: Thank you. Here's your passport.

Unit 7

CD 2, Track 1, Page 100
B. Pronunciation: 've been / 's been. Listen and repeat.
1. **a.** She's taking dancing lessons.　**b.** She's been taking dancing lessons.
2. **a.** She's learning how to drive.　**b.** She's been learning how to drive.
3. **a.** He's playing baseball.　**b.** He's been playing baseball.
4. **a.** I'm looking for a new apartment.　**b.** I've been looking for a new apartment.
5. **a.** She's recovering from her accident.　**b.** She's been recovering from her accident.
6. **a.** He's studying Chinese.　**b.** He's been studying Chinese.
7. **a.** He's working hard.　**b.** He's been working hard.
8. **a.** I'm training for a new job.　**b.** I've been training for a new job.

CD 2, Track 2, Page 100
C. Listen again. Circle the sentence you hear. Then, practice the sentences with a partner.
1. She's been taking dancing lessons.
2. She's been learning how to drive.
3. He's playing baseball.

4. I've been looking for a new apartment.
5. She's recovering from her accident.
6. He's studying Chinese.
7. He's been working hard.
8. I'm training for a new job.

CD 2, Track 3, Page 100
D. Listen to the conversation.
A: Hi, Juan. What've you been up to?
B: I've been painting the house.
A: And how's your family?
B: We're all fine. Maribel is 16 now, so I've been teaching her how to drive.
A: Good luck with that! And your parents? How are they?
B: They've been enjoying their retirement. They've been visiting their grandchildren a lot.
A: Oh, that's nice. Tell them I asked about them.
B: I sure will.

CD 2, Track 4, Page 105
C. Listen. Then, complete the questions.
Reporter: Congratulations! You just won the state championship!
Robert: Thank you.
Reporter: Robert, how old are you?
Robert: Seven.
Reporter: Seven! And how long have you been playing tennis?
Robert: Since I was three.
Reporter: Who taught you how to play?
Robert: My father. And I take private lessons, too.
Reporter: Here at the tennis club?
Robert: Yes. I've been taking lessons for two years.
Reporter: How many days a week do you play?
Robert: About three or four. I want to practice every day, but my parents say three or four days is enough. I like to play video games with my friends, too.
Reporter: Are you going to continue with your tennis?
Robert: Uh-huh. I'm going to be a professional tennis player when I'm older.

CD 2, Track 5, Page 106
The Big Picture: A Soccer Game
Today is the championship match between the Kings and the Stars. The game started at 2:00. It's the second half with only ten minutes left to play. An announcer has been calling the action on the field. The Stars have the lead with the score 2 to 1. The Kings have been fighting back, but the Stars' goalkeeper has been stopping every ball.

The stadium is sold out, with more than 35,000 fans in the stadium. The fans have been cheering, waving their banners, and shouting at the officials. Some fans have been banging drums and dancing in the aisles.

It's hot today, and the concession workers have been working hard. They've been walking up and down the steps selling water, soda, and other drinks. The lines at the refreshment stands are long. People have been waiting for 15 minutes or more to get their food.

The players have been drinking a lot of water and energy drinks because of the high temperatures. The officials have been watching everyone carefully to prevent any illegal moves. One official has been issuing yellow cards, but no red cards yet. A few of the players have been pushing each other and pulling shirts, but so far, no players are out of the game.

The Stars' coach has been shouting at his players and substituting players. He's been putting in his best defensive players. The Kings' coach has been putting in his fastest and best players. Everyone has been watching number 7. He has the ball, and it looks like he's about to score again!

CD 2, Track 6, Page 113
A. Listen and repeat.
1. I have a bruise.
2. She has a sprained ankle.
3. She has tendonitis.
4. He has a concussion.
5. He has a pulled hamstring.
6. He has a torn rotator cuff.

CD 2, Track 7, Page 113
B. Listen. Take notes about each injury and its treatment.

Conversation 1
Patient: Dr. Lopez, my shoulder is very weak. If I try to lift something, it really hurts.
Doctor: I've looked at your X-rays. You have a torn rotator cuff.
Patient: A torn rotator cuff? That's serious.
Doctor: Yes, it is. You're going to need surgery. It'll be two to three months before you can throw a football.

Conversation 2
Patient: My ankle really hurts.
Doctor: Well, fortunately you didn't break it. It's only a sprain.
Patient: Oh, good. So what should I do?
Doctor: First, stay off of it as much as possible. When you go home, you should elevate it. Then, put ice on it for 15 to 20 minutes. After that, take the ice off and wait an hour. Then, you can ice it again. Continue doing that all day today and call me tomorrow.

Conversation 3

Doctor: John, who's the president?
John: The president? George Bush?
Doctor: OK, coach. John has a concussion.
Coach: A concussion? Can he play next week?
Doctor: No! He lost consciousness for about 45 seconds, and he's confused. He's dizzy.
Coach: He's the leader of my team. We need him.
Doctor: I'm sorry, but this is a serious injury. His brain needs time to heal. He needs quiet and rest. He might have headaches, too. I want to take an X-ray. Could you take him into the locker room, please?

Conversation 4

Doctor: How do you feel today, Carl?
Carl: Well, my leg still hurts. I tried to run, but after a minute, the pain in my hamstring came back.
Doctor: Carl, you're going to need surgery on that pulled hamstring. I'll schedule the surgery.
Carl: Surgery. Wow. When will I be able to run again?
Doctor: A physical therapist will work with you. Every person is different. You may need a couple months of therapy.

Conversation 5

Doctor: I've looked at your X-rays. It looks like you have tendonitis in your wrist.

Patient: Tendonitis? What's that?
Doctor: You're doing the same motions over and over when you play tennis. Your tendons need rest.
Patient: Oh, I see. What do I have to do?
Doctor: No tennis or heavy lifting for three weeks. Then, come back and see me.
Patient: What can I take for the pain? I'm having trouble sleeping.
Doctor: I'll write down a few over-the-counter medications that you can take. You don't need a special prescription right now.

Conversation 6

Doctor: Ooh. That's a big bruise you've got there.
Patient: I know. It's really killing me.
Doctor: Have you been putting ice on it?
Patient: No, I put heat on it.
Doctor: Oh, you should ice it instead. Put ice on it for about 15 minutes. Then, let your leg warm up. After that, ice it again. The bruise is going to start to change color. Right now, it's a little swollen and red, but soon it'll turn bluish or greenish. That means it's getting better.
Patient: Oh, I see. I've been taking aspirin. Is that OK?
Doctor: No, I'll give you something else to take for the pain.

Unit 8

CD 2, Track 8, Page 114
B. Listen. Kathy and Gloria are talking about plans for a family reunion. Circle *True* or *False*.
Gloria: Hi, Kathy. This is Gloria.
Kathy: Gloria! How are you? We haven't spoken in ages!
Gloria: I know. We get so busy. Have you heard about the reunion?
Kathy: What reunion?
Gloria: We're going to have a family reunion. Angela's planning it.
Kathy: It's about time. We've been talking about that for years. Has she picked a date yet?
Gloria: It'll be in August. I think she mentioned the weekend of August 15th.
Kathy: August 15th. That's in two months. Where's it going to be?
Gloria: At a resort near Angela's. She was able to get a special family package, so the prices will be very reasonable. She's going to send out invitations soon.
Kathy: She can't do this by herself. What can I do to help?

Gloria: Everybody's going to help with the food. Tom and Will are going to plan the activities. I think they're going to design T-shirts for everyone, too.
Kathy: T-shirts? That'll be fun.
Gloria: How many of us are there?
Kathy: About 75. Plus two more. Jenny just had twins.
Gloria: Twins? That's great news. How's she doing?
Kathy: She hasn't been getting much sleep, but she's fine.
Gloria: Good. Did you hear that Michael has changed jobs?
Kathy: Really? What's he doing now?
Gloria: He's just opened a small business. He installs large-screen TVs and sound systems in homes.
Kathy: Hmm. Maybe he could help my husband.
Gloria: Maybe. OK, I've got some more phone calls to make. I've gotta go.
Kathy: Me, too. It'll be great to see everyone. See you in August.

CD 2, Track 9, Page 116
C. Listen and repeat.

Base form	Simple past	Past participle	Base form	Simple past	Past participle
be	was / were	been	leave	left	left
bear	bore	born	lose	lost	lost
become	became	become	make	made	made
begin	began	begun	meet	met	met
break	broke	broken	pay	paid	paid
bring	brought	brought	put	put	put
buy	bought	bought	quit	quit	quit
catch	caught	caught	read	read	read
come	came	come	ride	rode	ridden
do	did	done	say	said	said
drink	drank	drunk	see	saw	seen
drive	drove	driven	sell	sold	sold
eat	ate	eaten	send	sent	sent
fall	fell	fallen	sit	sat	sat
feel	felt	felt	sleep	slept	slept
find	found	found	speak	spoke	spoken
forget	forgot	forgotten	spend	spent	spent
freeze	froze	frozen	steal	stole	stolen
get	got	got / gotten	take	took	taken
give	gave	given	teach	taught	taught
go	went	gone	tell	told	told
grow	grew	grown	think	thought	thought
have	had	had	throw	threw	thrown
hear	heard	heard	win	won	won
know	knew	known	write	wrote	written

CD 2, Track 10, Page 118
A. Pronunciation: Stress Listen to the stress as each speaker clarifies the information. Underline the stressed word.

1. **A:** I hear that David has bought a sailboat.
   B: Not exactly. He's bought a motorboat.
2. **A:** I hear that Amy has moved to North Carolina.
   B: Close. She's moved to South Carolina.
3. **A:** I hear that Nora has gotten her driver's license.
   B: No, just the opposite. She's lost her driver's license.
4. **A:** I hear that Joe and Tom have just opened an Italian restaurant.
   B: Not Italian. They've opened a Mexican restaurant.

CD 2, Track 11, Page 119
A. Angela is planning a family reunion. Listen and check the things that have already been completed.

Gloria: How are the reunion plans coming?

Angela: Very well. Everyone wants to help. I asked a few people to help out with the plans, so I have a small committee. It's made things much easier.

Gloria: And the date is the fifteenth, right? August 15th?

Angela: Yes. We've already made the invitations. Tony's son made the invitations on the computer. We're going to send them out next week.

Gloria: Were you able to find everyone's address?

Angela: I think we have them all.

Gloria: Have you done anything else yet?

Angela: Well, we haven't planned the games or the activities, but we've already planned the menu. The resort is going to grill chicken for us, and everyone is going to bring a salad or a side dish. And, we're going to order a big cake for dessert.

Gloria: How about decorations?

Angela: We're not going to get too crazy with the decorations. But, we have bought some colorful tablecloths. The resort is providing the silverware, of course.

Gloria: Angela, you're not going to try to do everything yourself, are you? You need time to talk to people and have fun yourself.

Angela: That won't be a problem. The resort staff is going to help. We've reserved a large room, and the resort will provide staff to help with the setup, serve the food, and clean up.

Gloria: Well, it was a great idea to have the reunion at a resort. Let me know if there's anything I can do. I've already gathered photos to show at the party.

Angela: Thanks, Gloria. It's going to be a lot of fun. If I think of anything else, I'll give you a call.

CD 2, Track 12, Page 122
The Big Picture: Gossip

Conversation 1

A: Have you heard about Diana?

B: No. What happened?

A: Well, remember her engagement party?

B: Sure.

A: She's not engaged anymore.

B: No! I really liked Chris.

A: She's broken off the engagement. She met this new guy who moved into the apartment building, and she's fallen in love with him.

B: And what about Chris?

A: She's given him back his ring.

B: Really?

Conversation 2

A: Have you seen Rosa lately?

B: Hmm-mm. I spoke to her yesterday.

A: She looks great, doesn't she?

B: Yes, she said her vacation was really relaxing.

A: She didn't take a vacation. She went to a clinic.

B: A clinic?

A: Yes, she had a face-lift. That's why she looks so good.

B: Let me know the name of that clinic! I'm going to make an appointment myself.

Conversation 3

A: Have you heard about Amy? She's in big trouble.

B: What happened this time?

A: She took her mom's car without her permission. And she had an accident on the way to the mall.

B: Oh, no! Was she hurt?

A: No, she hit a mailbox. But she's been grounded for a month. I've tried to call her three times, but her parents won't let me talk to her. They've taken away her cell phone.

Conversation 4

A: You've heard about Paul, haven't you?

B: No. What about Paul?

A: He's just been promoted.

B: Promoted?

A: Yup. To assistant sales manager.

B: You've got to be kidding. He's got the worst sales record in the company. He hasn't made a sale this month.

A: I know. But it helps when your cousin is the head of the sales department.

B: That explains it.

Conversation 5

A: You know Mary Johnson, don't you?

B: Yeah. We used to take the bus together.

A: Well, guess what?

B: What?

A: She's going out with a man twice her age!

B: Twice her age? Let's see. I guess Mary's about 35.

A: That's what I guess. And this guy, he must be about 70.

B: What's the attraction?

A: Money. I've heard that he has lots of it!

B: Well, I hope she's happy.

Conversation 6

A: Have you heard about Grandpa Joe?

B: No. Is he OK?

A: OK? Well, first, he's bought a new convertible.

B: A new convertible? He's 70!

A: He's 72. And he's dyed his hair red.

B: Red? No more gray for Grandpa!

A: And he left yesterday.

B: He left?

A: Yes, he's left on a cross-country trip!

B: Good for him!

CD 2, Track 13, Page 123

E. Pronunciation: Surprise Intonation. Listen and repeat.

1. **A:** He bought a new convertible. **B:** A new convertible?
2. **A:** He left yesterday. **B:** He left?
3. **A:** He's just been promoted. **B:** Promoted?
4. **A:** She's run off with a man twice her age. **B:** Twice her age?

Unit 9

CD 2, Track 14, Page 136

C. Listen. Circle the letter of the sentence with the correct meaning.

1. The doctor saw all his patients for the day.
2. Jamie has been ironing shirts for five hours.
3. The men have planted five trees so far.
4. The teacher has checked 30 papers.
5. Carlos has delivered 40 packages.
6. Mary called 100 people today.
7. Jenna worked at the hospital for 50 years.
8. Tim drives a truck between New York and Florida. He's driven 300 miles today so far.

CD 2, Track 15, Page 136

D. Pronunciation: 've and 's Listen and repeat.

1. **a.** I sold five cars.
   b. I've sold five cars.
2. **a.** She worked five hours.
   b. She's worked five hours.

3. **a.** They made 500 donuts.
   b. They've made 500 donuts.
4. **a.** She walked five miles.
   b. She's walked five miles.
5. **a.** I helped ten customers.
   b. I've helped ten customers.
6. **a.** He planted five trees.
   b. He's planted five trees.
7. **a.** She read 20 pages.
   b. She's read 20 pages.
8. **a.** I cleaned seven rooms.
   b. I've cleaned seven rooms.

CD 2, Track 16, Page 136

E. Listen again. Circle the letter of the sentence you hear in Exercise D.

1. I've sold five cars.
2. She's worked five hours.
3. They made 500 donuts.

4. She's walked five miles.
5. I helped ten customers.
6. He planted five trees.
7. She's read 20 pages.
8. I've cleaned seven rooms.

CD 2, Track 17, Page 138
The Big Picture: Job Performance

My name is George Pappas, and I'm a bus driver for Metro Transit. I started here in 2005. Before that, I drove a school bus. In the morning, the kids were quiet, but on the way home, they were really noisy and excited. It was too noisy for me.

One day, I saw an ad in the newspaper for a city bus driver, so I decided to apply. I was lucky—my interview went well, and I had a clear background check. I got the job offer the next week. The starting salary was $14.80 an hour, a dollar more than my job as a school bus driver.

There are some rules that everyone has to follow. I have to be at work on time and in uniform. I have to drive carefully and obey all of the traffic and safety laws. I have to pick up and drop off my passengers only at designated bus stops, and I can't make any exceptions. Of course, I have to collect the correct bus fares and greet and treat the passengers with courtesy. I always say "Good morning" to my passengers, and I know the names of many of the regular passengers.

There is a very clear salary policy in our contract. We receive a written evaluation every year. If the evaluation is good, we receive a 75-cent an hour pay raise. I've been here for five years, and I've always received my raise. If a driver doesn't have any accidents in five years, the pay increases to $20.00 an hour.

CD 2, Track 18, Page 139
C. Listen. Write the questions to match the answers. Use the present or present perfect tense.

A: Thanks for telling me about the job opening, George. What other things should I know about this job?

B: Well, there's lots of opportunity for overtime.

A: Really? How much overtime do you work?

B: Oh, I usually work about ten hours a week overtime. Overtime pay is time and a half.

A: That's nice! What about traffic tickets? Have you ever gotten any tickets?

B: Yes, unfortunately. The company is very strict about tickets. If you get a ticket, you have to pay for it. Also, the company fines you $200.

A: $200! How many tickets have you gotten?

B: Only one. I received a ticket for going through a red light. The light had just turned red when I went through it, but I got a ticket anyway. I had to pay the company $200 plus $100 to the city for the ticket.

A: Wow! Do you know any drivers who have gotten a speeding ticket?

B: Yeah, one of my friends got two. He's not working here anymore. You get fired if you get two or more speeding tickets in the same year.

A: Wow, that's tough.

B: It is, but I guess it's necessary. I don't plan on getting any more tickets. I like this job.

CD 2, Track 19, Page 145
B. Listen to Katie's performance evaluation. Check the correct boxes.

Mr. Davis: Katie, let's go over your evaluation.

Katie: OK.

Mr. Davis: Let's go over some of these areas. You're always available to work, and you dress very professionally, but you've arrived late several times. Since I spoke to you about this, you have improved.

Katie: Well, yes, I've been trying. I was only late once last month.

Mr. Davis: Yes, that is an improvement. OK . . . I see that you also require improvement on showing initiative. Katie, when you don't have a customer, you stand and daydream. If I ask you to do something, you're always willing. But when you don't have customers, you should polish the jewelry and the mirrors, put new paper in the cash register, restock the boxes, and do other things without being asked.

Katie: I understand.

Mr. Davis: You're great with customers—friendly, respectful, complimentary. You seem to enjoy sales, and you're a good salesperson. This is your number one strength.

Katie: Thank you. Customer service is my favorite part of the job.

Mr. Davis: Good, good. . . . Unfortunately, you have made several mistakes. You've entered the wrong price on the register and forgotten to enter in the sales price. You've overcharged some customers and undercharged others. I've received complaints, and the store has lost money. You had several problems during our sale last week.

Katie: I know. When we're busy, I sometimes make mistakes.

Mr. Davis: I've decided to have Ms. Miller retrain you on our sales transactions procedures. Are you available next Saturday? She can work with you then.

Katie: Yes, I am.

Mr. Davis: OK, great. So, Katie, do you have any comments?

Katie: No. I like working here, and I'll try to be more careful. I won't make any more mistakes. You'll see.

CD 2, Track 20, Page 147
B. Listen and complete.
1. I bought a used car, and it's already broken down twice. I should have bought a new one.
2. I didn't buy a new car. I shouldn't have bought a used one.
3. She didn't study very hard for the test, and she got a D. She should have studied harder.
4. I registered for six courses, and now I'm too busy. I shouldn't have taken so many courses.
5. I left too late for the airport and missed my flight. I should have left earlier.
6. I didn't have a photo ID. I should have remembered to bring it.
7. Their car ran out of gas. They should have filled the tank.
8. He got a ticket for driving without a license. He shouldn't have driven without a license.
9. The electric company charged us a late fee. We should have sent the check on time.
10. She forgot to bring her homework. She shouldn't have forgotten it.

CD 2, Track 21, Page 149
A. Listen and write the number under the correct picture.
1. You should've typed this paper.
2. There should've been three hamburgers in here. There are only two.
3. You should've finished by now. What have you been doing?
4. The flight should've arrived at 4:00, but it's not here yet.
5. You should've gotten an A. What happened?
6. They should've won. They made too many errors.

CD 2, Track 22, Page 151
A. Listen. A man is calling 911 to report a problem in his apartment. Write the letter of the correct deduction under each picture.
1. I came home and found my lock broken and my door open.
2. My stereo is missing.
3. The window's open, but I'm sure I locked it when I left.
4. My cat has been hiding under the bed, and he won't come out.
5. A steak is missing, and there are dirty dishes in the sink.
6. My favorite suit is missing.
7. My large suitcase is missing and so are some of my shirts.
8. I found a pair of gloves on the floor.

CD 2, Track 23, Page 152
B. Pronunciation: Past Modals. Listen and repeat.
1. You must've left your book at home.
2. She might've studied French.
3. I should've made an appointment.
4. We could've gone on a vacation.
5. He must've had to work.
6. She couldn't have walked that far.
7. We shouldn't have spoken to her.
8. They shouldn't have arrived late.
9. He may not have had an opportunity.
10. I must not have heard you.

CD 2, Track 24, Page 152
D. Pronunciation: Word Stress. Listen to the conversation and underline the stressed words.
A: Hi, Julia. Why didn't you come to my party? Everyone missed you.
B: What party?
A: I had a party last Saturday.
B: Really? You should've called me.
A: I did. I left a message on your voice mail.
B: I changed my number. You could've sent me an invitation.
A: I did. I e-mailed it two weeks ago.
B: You must've sent it to the wrong address. I've changed my e-mail.
A: You should've told me.
B: Sorry. Anyway, how was the party?
A: It was fun. You should've been there.

CD 2, Track 25, Pages 154 and 155
The Big Picture: In the Counselor's Office
A. The high school counselor is talking to Amber, a high school student. Listen and take notes.
Counselor: Come in, Amber. Have a seat. You look upset.
Amber: Well, you know, I'm the editor of the school newspaper.
Counselor: I know. The paper's been very good this year.
Amber: Thank you. I work very hard on it.
Counselor: Why did you come see me today?
Amber: The vice principal took away my job! I'm not the editor anymore! I need that job for my college applications! How am I going to get into college now?
Counselor: Hold on, hold on. Do you know why he did that?
Amber: I don't know. I'm the best writer on the staff!
Counselor: You must have some idea why he did that.
Amber: Well, I guess maybe he's punishing me.
Counselor: Punishing you? Why would he do that?
Amber: I think he's upset because I wrote a story that wasn't true about the football team.
Counselor: Now, Amber, why did you do that?

Amber: I was upset at my boyfriend. He's the captain of the football team. He had just broken up with me.

Counselor: You must have been very upset.

Amber: Yes, I was.

Counselor: So, do you think the vice principal shouldn't have punished you for printing incorrect information? The team must've been very upset, too.

Amber: I know. Yeah, I guess I shouldn't have done that. I shouldn't have used my job to get back at him. I could print an apology in the newspaper. Do you think the vice principal will give me my job back?

Counselor: It sounds like you're sorry. I'll talk to the vice principal. Maybe he'll suspend you for only one issue, especially if you agree to print an apology.

Amber: Thank you.

CD 2, Track 26, Pages 154 and 155
B. The counselor is talking to Miguel, another student.
Listen and take notes.

Counselor: The last time we talked, Miguel, your classes were not going well.

Miguel: You can say that again. I was failing everything.

Counselor: We talked about the people you could've asked for help and the things you should've done to improve. Do you want to talk about that today?

Miguel: Yeah. I'm doing a little better. I got a C+ in math last quarter.

Counselor: Your teacher must've been pleased.

Miguel: She was.

Counselor: Did you see a tutor?

Miguel: No, I didn't. I could've, but when I talked to my math teacher, she volunteered to give me some extra help. She also showed me a computer program in the learning center that could help me.

Counselor: Great. Now, how about your English class? Have your grades improved?

Miguel: Well, you know, I can speak English easily, but writing's really hard for me.

Counselor: Do you go to the writing center for tutoring?

Miguel: I've been once.

Counselor: That's not enough, Miguel.

Miguel: I know, but I didn't like the tutor.

Counselor: Now, Miguel, there must've been another tutor who could've helped you.

Miguel: Yeah, I guess I'll go back and try again. By the way, I got the part-time job at the bookstore. Thanks for telling me about it. My parents are really happy about it, too.

Counselor: Oh, congratulations! How's the job?

Miguel: Great! I work two nights a week and all day on Saturday. I get discounts on everything. It's an easy job.

Counselor: That's wonderful, Miguel.

Miguel: Thanks, Mr. D. I couldn't have gotten the job without your recommendation.

Counselor: That's my job, Miguel. Now, go to the writing center during your study period.

Unit 11

CD 3, Track 1, Page 165
A. Listen and write the questions. Then, look at the product map and write the answers.
1. Where are electronics manufactured?
2. Which grains are grown in China?
3. Where are automobiles manufactured?
4. Where is footwear made?
5. What kind of food is grown in Thailand?
6. Where is coal mined?

CD 3, Track 2, Page 168
A. Pronunciation: Syllable Stress Listen and repeat.
1. pasteurize   pasteurization   pasteurized
2. sterilize   sterilization   sterilized
3. immunize   immunization   immunized
4. separate   separation   separated
5. refrigerate   refrigeration   refrigerated
6. evaporate   evaporation   evaporated
7. ferment   fermentation   fermented

CD 3, Track 3, Page 168
B. Listen again. Underline the stressed syllable of the words in the chart.

CD 3, Track 4, Page 170
The Big Picture: T-shirts—From the Field to Your Closet
1. The top three cotton producers in the world are China, the United States, and India. China is the top cotton producer of the three.
2. In China, the cotton is picked by hand. Then, it is sent to a ginner where it is cleaned. The cleaned cotton is put into bales, and the quality is determined.
3. The bales are sold to large plants or factories called spinners. At the spinners, the cotton is put on spools. The spools are put on knitting machines, and the cotton is made into cotton fabric.
4. The cotton fabric is sent to a dye house. At the dye house, only 20 percent of the fabric is dyed different colors. The remaining 80 percent is processed white.

5. The fabric is sent to a sewing plant. At the plant, patterns are cut. Then, the pieces are sewn by workers on a line. One worker sews the sleeves, another sews the neck, another does the shoulders, and the last one hems the bottom.
6. The T-shirts are folded and packaged. The T-shirts are sent to printers, where a logo is transferred or embroidered onto the T-shirt. At this stage, the T-shirt only costs about $3.00.
7. The finished T-shirts are shipped to warehouses. Because of many costs, including shipping, warehouse space, and inventory, the T-shirt price is increased.

8. The T-shirts are sold to a department store at an over 200-percent increase to $14. The store immediately doubles the price to $28. The store also has many costs, such as paying for sales help, insurance, and advertising. The T-shirt is marked and offered for sale for $28.
9. After two or three weeks, store customers have bought many of the shirts. Now, not all colors and sizes are available. The store advertises a 15- to 25-percent sale. After two more weeks, the price will be decreased again. Finally, after six weeks, any leftover T-shirts will be sent to discount stores. The price may be reduced to $14 or less.

Unit 12

CD 3, Track 5, Page 178
A. Listen. Write the year that each item was invented.
1. The insulin pump was invented by Dean Kamen in the 1960s. It was invented to give diabetics a better way to control their blood sugar. It was not approved for general use by the Federal Drug Administration until 1983.
2. The first anti-shoplifting tag was invented in 1965 by Arthur Minasy. These tags make it difficult for people to steal items from a store.
3. The first video games were invented by Ralph Baer in 1966. These first games were very simple, not like the colorful realistic games of today. Baer is called the "Godfather of Video Games."
4. The compact fluorescent bulb was first invented in the 1970s by an engineer named Ed Hammer. The bulb was created to save energy.
5. The artificial heart was first designed by Robert Jarvik in 1978. It was developed to keep a patient alive while waiting for a heart transplant.
6. In 1980, a hepatitis B vaccine was developed by Baruch Blumberg. Hepatitis B is a disease that attacks the liver and is often fatal. Today, hepatitis B vaccines are required by most public schools and colleges.
7. NASA is the National Aeronautics and Space Administration. The first space shuttle was launched by NASA in 1981. It orbited the world in less than two hours.
8. The laptop computer was invented by Sir Clive Sinclair in 1987. Today, laptop computers are more popular than desktop computers.
9. The personal human transport vehicle was created by Dean Kamen in 2001. It was designed to be a new type of everyday transportation.

CD 3, Track 6, Page 183
B. Pronunciation: Compound Nouns. Listen and repeat.
1. SAFEty razor
2. AIR conditioner
3. LIE detector
4. MIcrowave oven
5. BALLpoint pen
6. PARKing meter
7. CONtact lenses
8. SEAT belt
9. LAser printer
10. CELL phone

CD 3, Track 7, Page 184
D. Listen and answer the questions.
I'm from Taiwan. I was born there in 1963 and raised in Taipei. I went to public school like most students. School in Taiwan is very strict, and there are a lot of rules. First, we were required to wear a uniform. The girls wore blue skirts and white blouses. The boys wore blue pants and white shirts. I couldn't have long hair. All the girls had to keep their hair above their shoulders. The boys could only have hair one inch long! Very short!

We studied very hard. We went to school from 9:00 to 4:30, and we were assigned about three hours of homework. If we didn't do our homework, we were punished. Maybe the teacher hit our hands with a stick, or we had to stand with a book on our heads. We were given exams in the middle of the year and at the end of the year.

Boys and girls studied in separate classes. The only time we were together was for after-school clubs and activities. We couldn't date in high school. We couldn't call each other on the phone, either. But in college, we were allowed to date.

People in Taiwan speak Taiwanese, but it's a spoken language—not a written language. When we begin school, we are expected to use Chinese for everything. This is very hard for students, especially when we first begin school. Also, when we are in middle school, English is taught as a foreign language. By the time we finish high school, we know Taiwanese, Chinese, and English.

Vacations are similar to the United States. School is closed for two months in the summer, and we have one month off in January or February, around the time of the Chinese New Year.

CD 3, Track 8, Pages 186 and 187
The Big Picture: Shopping Technology
For many years, shopping was a simple process. A person went into a small local store, bought an item, and paid for it with cash. Another popular way of shopping was to buy merchandise from a traveling salesman. Many people lived far from the city, so salesmen traveled around the country by horse and wagon, showing the customers their merchandise.

In 1872, a traveling salesman named Aaron Montgomery Ward had an idea to help his customers see more of his merchandise. Ward decided to print a catalog with pictures of the items that his company sold. The customers could look through the catalog and order the items they wanted. The first mail-order catalog was printed in 1872 and became an immediate success. Catalogs are still a very popular way to shop.

Before 1884, clerks kept money in the store in a drawer or cash box. When a customer bought a product, the clerk wrote a receipt by hand. In 1884, the first cash register was invented by James Ritty. People could receive an immediate printed receipt.

In the 1900s, stores were becoming larger, especially grocery stores. Customers were buying more items at a time. The owner of one of these grocery stores, Sylvan Goldman, had an idea. He put two baskets and wheels on a folding chair and the first shopping cart was invented. Goldman formed a company to design larger and better shopping carts.

Up until this time, people paid by cash or check. In 1950, the first credit cards were issued. At first, credit cards were only used by business travelers for restaurant and hotel bills. In the 1960s, many companies were offering these cards. People did not need to carry so much cash. They could pay later.

Another idea that was developing at this time was the idea of the bar code. At the time, stock clerks had to put a price on every item. The clerk rang up each item on the cash register, punching in the price of each item by hand. Store owners, especially the owners of large supermarkets, needed a way to automatically read information about products during checkout. Several inventors worked on this idea, but there was not a standard way to identify each item. The Uniform Pricing Code, or UPC, was invented in 1973. In 1974, the first UPC scanner was installed in a supermarket in Ohio. It was no longer necessary to put the price on every item. Now supermarket clerks simply scan each item and the price appears on the register.

In the 1990s, another form of shopping became popular—online shopping. The Internet offers an inexpensive way for companies to advertise their products to a worldwide audience. Customers can look at pictures of products, check prices, and place their orders over the Internet. This has made shopping fast and convenient. Customers can also save money by comparing prices from several companies.

Unit 13

CD 3, Track 9, Page 199
B. Listen. Then, answer the questions with a partner.

Grandmother:	What's that thing that you're listening to?
Grandson:	It's called an MP3 player.
Grandmother:	An MP3 player?
Grandson:	It's like a computer. It plays music files that you download from a computer.
Grandmother:	That sounds difficult. I used to play 45s and LPs.
Grandson:	What's a 45?
Grandmother:	It's a small disk like a CD that's made of vinyl. They're usually black. There's one song on one side, and one song on the other. An LP is a bigger disk that can hold an entire album of songs. I used to have lots of 45s and LPs, but they take up a lot of space.
Grandson:	Did you have to turn a 45 over to hear the other song?
Grandmother:	Yes. If I played a 45, I had to turn it over when the song finished.
Grandson:	You're kidding! I'm glad that technology has improved.
Grandmother:	Maybe, but some people still think the sound quality that LPs had was better.
Grandson:	Really? Do you still have any 45s or LPs?
Grandmother:	We have some in the den. I think we have a turntable in the basement.
Grandson:	A turntable? Do you have the kind that I see in the dance clubs?
Grandmother:	I don't think so. My turntable is like a piece of furniture.
Grandson:	Let's go get it. I want to see this old technology.
Grandmother:	OK. We'll play one of my dance records from the '70s.
Grandson:	Can I call my friends? They'd love to see this.
Grandmother:	Sure.

CD 3, Track 10, Page 202
The Big Picture: The History of Country Music
The people who first sang the country sound in the United States lived over a hundred years ago in the

Appalachian Mountains. These people sang all the time—while they were working, while they were doing laundry, while they were worshipping at church, or while they were taking care of their babies. People used to sing to make the work go faster. The music that they sang was very simple.

The music, which is now called country music, came from the British Isles: Scotland, Ireland, England, and Wales. The people who immigrated to the United States moved to a land that was similar to their homeland. These people brought their music with them.

Two instruments were common in country music bands. The five-string banjo, which came from Africa, became popular in country music in the 1920s. The fiddle, which had early roots in Nashville, was the main instrument in country music until the 1930s. The fiddler, who carried the melody of the songs, was usually the main performer in country music bands. Banjos and fiddles are still popular in country music today, but other instruments, such as electric guitars and keyboards, are also used. Jimmy Rodgers and The Carter Family, who first recorded in 1927, became the first superstars of country music.

Unit 14

CD 3, Track 11, Page 212
A. Listen and read. Then, discuss.
Are You a Procrastinator?

Everyone has plans and goals. Some plans are short-term and can be accomplished in a few hours or on a weekend: I'm going to wash the car. I plan to organize my closet. I want to gather all my photos from the past five years and put them in a photo album. I need to study for the test next week. I plan to start an exercise program. Some goals are far in the future and will take years to accomplish: I expect to get my nursing degree. I want to start my own business. Do you find yourself making plans but not accomplishing them? Is it difficult to take the first step? Is it impossible to find the time? Could you be a procrastinator? A procrastinator waits for the last minute. A procrastinator believes, "There is always tomorrow."

CD 3, Track 12, Page 212
B. Listen. Answer the questions about Scott's plans.
I always make a list of the things that I'm supposed to do around the house. I planned to paint the kitchen Saturday, but a big game was on TV. I plan to do it next weekend. A classmate called me, and I intended to call him back, but I forgot. I'll do it tonight. I promised to help my daughter with a school project, but I had to work overtime, so I will try to help her tomorrow. I was supposed to read four chapters in my history textbook, but I haven't done it yet. I need to do it before next Tuesday. The exam will be hard. I really need to be better organized.

CD 3, Track 13, Page 213
C. Listen and read. Then, discuss.
It's hard to get started on your plans. It's easy to make excuses! Once you start on a goal, there are always distractions. You sit down to work at the computer, but first you check your e-mail and then start to chat with friends. Or, you are supposed to write a paper for class, but a friend calls and wants to go to the mall with you.

Or, you sit down to type your paper, and you realize that it's time for your favorite TV show.

CD 3, Track 14, Page 216
A. Listen and read. Then, discuss. Underline the adjectives. Circle the infinitives.
It's important to make a schedule of your day, and it's necessary to schedule your study time. It's easy to say, "I'll get it done sometime today." It's more helpful to make an appointment with yourself. If possible, find a time that is the most productive for you. What is your most productive time to do your schoolwork? Maybe it is immediately after class or as soon as you get home.

CD 3, Track 15, Page 216
B. Pronunciation: Stressed Syllables. Listen and mark the stressed syllables.
1. dan · ger · ous
2. i · de · a ·lis · tic
3. im · pos · si · ble
4. in · ter · est · ing
5. po · lite
6. rea · son · a · ble
7. re · a · lis · tic
8. ro · man · tic
9. stress · ful
10. thought · ful

CD 3, Track 16, Pages 218 and 219
The Big Picture: The Procrastinator

Conversation 1
Diana: Hi, Susan.
Susan: Hi, Diana. What are you doing?
Diana: I'm supposed to be studying for my math test.
Susan: That's tomorrow, right?
Diana: Right. I'm not really worried. I understood everything in class.
Susan: Well, good luck. I can't talk now. I'm writing this English paper.

Diana: The one about cities and pollution?

Susan: Yeah. I'm in the middle of it. I'll call you tomorrow.

Diana: OK.

Conversation 2

Diana: Hi, Dad.

Dad: Hi, Diana. Studying for that math test?

Diana: I'm going to start in a few minutes.

Dad: You're great at math. You'll do well.

Diana: I hope so.

Dad: Remember to clean this room. How can you find anything in here?

Diana: Don't worry, Dad.

Conversation 3

Diana: Jake? You at work?

Jake: Uh-huh. I'm getting off in an hour. I can't come over tonight.

Diana: I won't see you?

Jake: No, I've got science homework to finish. You know, that lab report. How's it going with your math homework?

Diana: I haven't started yet. I'm going to start in a few minutes.

Jake: Why don't you go over to the math center at school? It's quiet there.

Diana: Maybe.

Jake: Well, I'll see you tomorrow night. How about 8:00? After I get out of work?

Diana: That's good. Ciao.

Jake: Bye.

Conversation 4

Diana: Hi.

Alex: Diana, it's Alex.

Diana: Hi, Alex. Are you still at school?

Alex: Uh-huh. I'm here with Carlos and Mia. We're at the library now, and we're studying for the math test tomorrow. Why don't you come over here and study with us? This math is really difficult, and it's helpful to work together.

Diana: I don't know. I think I'll study alone this time.

Alex: If you want to meet before class, we could go over a few of the problems.

Diana: OK. The test is at 10:00. Can we meet in the cafeteria at 9:00?

Alex: Sure. See you then.

Conversation 5

Diana: Hello.

Katie: Hi, Diana. It's me, Katie. I'm going to the mall. They're having a big sale at Gabby's. Want to come?

Diana: A shoe sale? You know, I do need a pair of black boots.

Katie: I'm getting in my car now. I'll pick you up in ten minutes.

Diana: I really should be studying for my math test tomorrow.

Katie: Don't worry. We won't stay long. I'll see you in a few minutes.

Diana: Well . . . OK.

Unit 15

CD 3, Track 17, Page 226

B. Listen to Marco and Luciana's story about becoming United States citizens.

1. Marco came to the United States from Brazil in 2000 when he was 24. Many years have passed, and Marco has learned to speak, read, and write English very well. He changed jobs four times, met Luciana—another immigrant from Brazil—and they got married. Over the years, they've had a very busy life here in the United States. They have had two children, a boy named Alonzo and a girl named Zandra. Their children were born in the United States, so they are already U.S. citizens.

2. Marco and Luciana decided that they wanted to become citizens. They obtained their application papers from the Immigration and Naturalization Service, or the INS. They carefully completed all of the paperwork and mailed in their documents. They expected to wait six months to a year for a response.

3. While waiting for their appointments, Marco and Luciana studied for their naturalization tests. Luciana was nervous because her English was not as strong as Marco's. Marco and Alonzo helped her practice the English sample questions and the questions about U.S. history.

4. Finally, after ten months of waiting, they received an appointment for their naturalization interview and test. The immigration officer spoke to each of them separately. Marco had to answer questions in English, write a sentence in English, and read a sentence in English. Luciana was lucky. The interviewer spoke slowly and Luciana could answer all of the questions about U.S. history.

5. Three months later, Marco and Luciana received their letters of approval. They were going to be U.S. citizens!

6. At the swearing-in ceremony, one hundred other people from many countries recited the Oath of Allegiance to the United States. Then, they signed a paper. They each received a letter from the president of the United States, congratulating them.

A. Listen. Complete each sentence with the gerund you hear.

1. Marco and Luciana discussed becoming citizens.
2. They delayed starting the process because Luciana's English was not strong.
3. Luciana regretted not taking English classes earlier.
4. She began studying English at a local adult school.
5. A friend recommended enrolling in a citizenship class.
6. They didn't mind attending class one night a week.
7. Marco and Luciana enjoyed learning about U.S. history.
8. They practiced asking one another questions.
9. Luciana couldn't help being nervous before the test.
10. They enjoyed celebrating with their friends after the ceremony.

B. Pronunciation: Linking. Listen to the conversation. Then, practice the conversation with a partner.

A: I thought life here was going to be easy. I just can't adjust to living here. I miss seeing my family.

B: You'll always miss them. I plan on visiting my family once a year.

A: And, I'm afraid of losing my job if I leave.

B: Yesterday you were complaining about working so much overtime!

A: I gave up working at my family's business to come here.

B: You didn't like working there anyway. And you plan on opening your own business someday, don't you?

A: You're right, but I'm tired of listening to English all day! I'm thinking of going back to Korea.

B: You've only been here for nine months. Everybody feels like you at first. Concentrate on learning English and making a few friends.

C. Listen. An immigrant is talking about citizenship. Write the questions. Then, ask and answer the questions with a partner.

My wife and I decided to come to the United States because of the job opportunities. In our country, there were very few job opportunities. Our families were worried about us finding a place to live, but fortunately, we had a cousin who was living in Chicago. He helped us to find an apartment.

I was lucky. I'm good at fixing things and working with wood, and I found a job with a contractor. I built kitchen cabinets and tables. The contractor liked my work and my work habits. I was always on time, I worked hard, and I rarely missed a day of work. One day, one of the customers asked me to design a kitchen for a relative.

The next thing I knew, I had my own business. Now, we can afford to pay for our daughter's dance classes and my son's math tutor. We're able to take a vacation every summer. We really appreciate having a nice apartment, and I'm thinking about becoming a citizen. My family is here, our children were born here, and my business is doing well. As a matter of fact, I'd like to sponsor my brother. I'm encouraging him to take English classes to prepare for life here.

The Big Picture: Running a Campaign

Hi, my name is Manuel. I've been a citizen for a few years now, but I never thought that I would get involved in politics. In fact, I've always avoided getting involved. I vote in the major elections, but sometimes I forget to vote in the city elections. Let me tell you what happened. A few years ago, a new neighbor moved in. His name is John. He's a nice guy and a great neighbor. He's married, and he has three children—a boy and two girls—and so do I. Our families have become very friendly. We barbecue together in the summer. Our children play together, and our wives enjoy spending time together. We've even taken a vacation together.

John is an entrepreneur. He has a very successful bookstore and community computer center. He hires high school and college students for the computer center. He also has senior citizen volunteers read to young children three times a week at the bookstore. He has a good business, and he provides a wonderful service for our community.

Well, there's an empty seat on the city council, and John has decided to run for the seat. At first, he complained about shaking hands, but now he's looking forward to giving interviews and meeting people in town. My wife, Andrea, is good at organizing people, so she has a group of neighbors and other volunteers at our house almost every night. They've been talking about having a voter registration drive. It's important to get the vote of everyone that we can. So, they're thinking about setting up registration tables in front of the library, the high school, the mall, and the supermarkets. We're not worried about spending too much money because John knows many people who have insisted on donating their services. They've donated envelopes, printing services, and vans to get people to the polls on election day.

John's wife, Kathy, is anticipating doing a lot of work for the campaign. She quit working temporarily to support John's campaign. Kathy's in charge of getting volunteers to make phone calls. I'm enjoying helping John practice for this month's debate. I'm pretending to be one of his opponents or one of the reporters who will be asking John the tough questions.

A campaign is a lot of work, but it's worth it.

CD 3, Track 22, Page 241
A. Listen and write the questions. Then, match each question with the correct answer.
1. What is the Bill of Rights?
2. What is one of the rights of the Constitution?
3. What is the voting age?
4. How many senators are there?
5. Who was the first president?
6. Who makes the laws?
7. Who is the Commander in Chief of the military?
8. How long is a president's term of office?

Skills Index

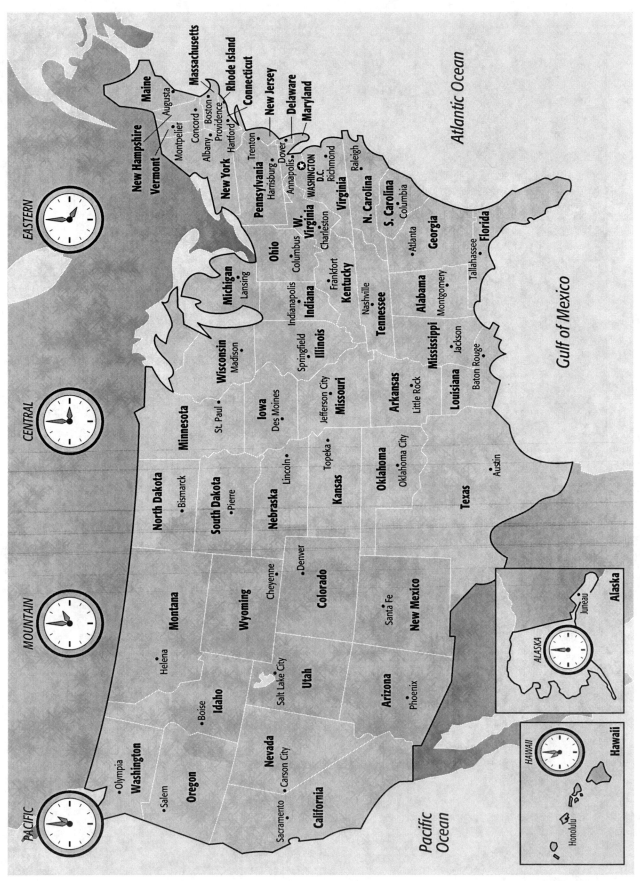

EASTERN

CENTRAL

MOUNTAIN

PACIFIC

Atlantic Ocean

Gulf of Mexico

Pacific
Ocean

Maine
Augusta

Massachusetts
Boston

Rhode Island
Providence

Connecticut
Hartford

New Jersey
Trenton

Delaware
Dover

Maryland
Annapolis

New Hampshire
Concord

Vermont
Montpelier

New York
Albany

Pennsylvania
Harrisburg

WASHINGTON
D.C.

Richmond

Virginia

Raleigh

N. Carolina

S. Carolina
Columbia

W. Virginia
Charleston

Ohio
Columbus

Kentucky
Frankfort

Tennessee
Nashville

Alabama
Montgomery

Georgia
Atlanta

Florida
Tallahassee

Michigan
Lansing

Indiana
Indianapolis

Illinois
Springfield

Wisconsin
Madison

Minnesota
St. Paul

Iowa
Des Moines

Missouri
Jefferson City

Arkansas
Little Rock

Mississippi
Jackson

Louisiana
Baton Rouge

North Dakota
Bismarck

South Dakota
Pierre

Nebraska
Lincoln

Kansas
Topeka

Oklahoma
Oklahoma City

Texas
Austin

Montana
Helena

Wyoming
Cheyenne

Colorado
Denver

New Mexico
Santa Fe

Idaho
Boise

Utah
Salt Lake City

Arizona
Phoenix

Washington
Olympia

Oregon
Salem

Nevada
Carson City

California
Sacramento

ALASKA

Alaska
Juneau

HAWAII

Hawaii
Honolulu

U.S. Map

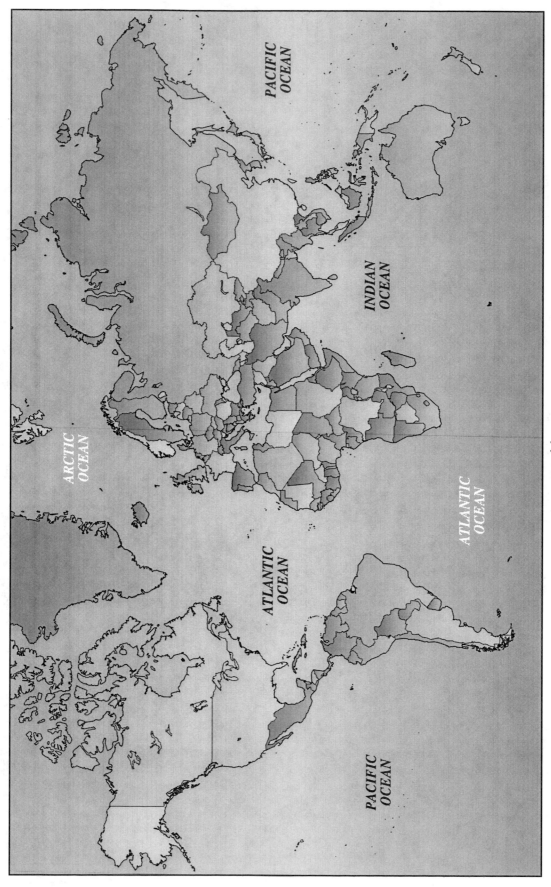

World Map

Learner's dictionaries—essential tools for all stages
of English language learning!

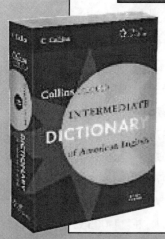

The Heinle Picture Dictionary

Low-beginning to low-intermediate

Unlike other dictionaries, *The Heinle Picture Dictionary* presents new vocabulary in contextualized, thematic readings and offers immediate practice and reinforcement to solidify the acquisition of new vocabulary.

Bilingual editions available

- Words in Context
- Word Partnerships
- Words in Action
- Workbooks, Audio, CD-ROM

Text   978-0-8384-4400-9

Collins COBUILD Illustrated Basic Dictionary of American English

Beginning to low-intermediate

The *Collins COBUILD Illustrated Basic Dictionary of American English* makes vocabulary acquisition efficient and effective by offering beginning-level students extra support through clear, level-appropriate definitions, unparalleled vocabulary support, and a controlled vocabulary list necessary for beginning-level learners.

- Word Worlds
- Spelling Partners
- Sound Partners
- Word Builders

Softcover
with CD-ROM   978-1-4240-0081-4

Collins COBUILD Intermediate Dictionary

Low- to high-intermediate

With full-sentence definitions and vocabulary builders, the *Collins COBUILD Intermediate Dictionary* transforms the learner's dictionary from an occasional reference to the ultimate resource for English language learners.

English/Spanish edition available

- Word Webs
- Word Links
- Word Partnerships
- Picture Dictionary boxes
- Thesaurus entries
- Interactive CD-ROM

Softcover
with CD-ROM   978-1-4240-0776-9

English in Action Series

Level 1

Student Book	978-1-4240-4990-5
Workbook with Audio CD	978-1-111-00565-8
Interactive CD-ROM	978-1-4266-3415-4
Teacher's Guide	978-1-4240-8497-5
Audio CD	978-1-4240-8501-9
Assessment CD-ROM with Exam*View*®	978-1-111-00164-3
Presentation Tool	978-1-111-00561-0

Level 2

Student Book	978-1-4240-4991-2
Workbook with Audio CD	978-1-111-00564-1
Interactive CD-ROM	978-1-4266-3416-1
Teacher's Guide	978-1-4240-8498-2
Audio CD	978-1-4240-8502-6
Assessment CD-ROM with Exam*View*®	978-1-111-00166-7
Presentation Tool	978-1-111-05779-4

Level 3

Student Book	978-1-4240-4992-9
Workbook with Audio CD	978-1-111-00563-4
Interactive CD-ROM	978-1-4266-3417-8
Teacher's Guide	978-1-4240-8499-9
Audio CD	978-1-4240-8503-3
Assessment CD-ROM with Exam*View*®	978-1-111-00167-4
Presentation Tool	978-1-111-00560-3

Level 4

Student Book	978-1-4240-4993-6
Workbook with Audio CD	978-1-111-00562-7
Interactive CD-ROM	978-1-4266-3418-5
Teacher's Guide	978-1-4240-8500-2
Audio CD	978-1-4240-8504-0
Assessment CD-ROM with Exam*View*®	978-1-111-00165-0
Presentation Tool	978-1-111-00559-7

CPSIA information can be obtained
at www.ICGtesting.com
Printed in the USA
FFOW02n1610200913
1852FF

9 781424 085002